U.S. FEDERAL LEGAL RESPONSES TO TERRORISM

YONAH ALEXANDER
AND
EDGAR H. BRENNER
EDITORS

AN INTERNATIONAL LAW INSTITUTE BOOK

 Transnational Publishers

Published and distributed by Transnational Publishers, Inc.
410 Saw Mill River Road
Ardsley, NY 10502, USA

Phone: 914-693-5100
Fax: 914-693-4430
E-mail: info@transnationalpubs.com
Web: www.transnationalpubs.com

Library of Congress Cataloging-in-Publication Data

United States.
  U.S. federal legal responses to terrorism / edited by Yonah Alexander and Edgar
H. Brenner.
  p.cm.
  Excerpts from U.S. Code and other statutory law and legislation.
  ISBN 1–57105–252–6
  1. Terrorism—United States. 2. Terrorists—United States. 3. Alien criminals— .
United States. 4 Criminal law—United States. 5. National security—Law and legis-
lation—United States. I. Title: US federal legal responses to terrorism. II. Alexander,
Yonah. III. Brenner, Edgar H. IV. Title

KF9430 .A3 2002
345.73'02—dc21   2001050817

Manufactured in the United States of America

Contents

TITLE II—ENHANCED SURVEILLANCE PROCEDURES 320

Preface

For the past four decades, the United States has been victimized by both domestic and international terrorism. This pattern of violence began in 1961 with the first U.S. aircraft hijacking—a Puerto Rican individual forced at gunpoint a National Airlines plane to fly to Havana, Cuba, where he was given asylum. Since that incident, an American Ambassador to Guatemala was assassinated in 1968; Iranian radicals seized the U.S. embassy in Tehran and took 66 American diplomats hostage in 1979; a suicide car bomb attack by radical Muslims in 1983 killed 243 U.S. servicemen in Lebanon; a Pan American Airways Boeing 747 crashed in 1988 over Lockerbie, Scotland, killing all 259 people aboard when the plane was blown up by a bomb; in 1993 six people were killed and more than 1,000 were injured when a bomb inside a van exploded underneath the twin 110-story towers of the World Trade Center in New York City; a bomb exploded during the Atlantic Olympic Games in 1996, killing one person and wounding more than 100 others; in 1998, two truck bombings outside the U.S. embassies in Kenya and Tanzania killed 234 people, (12 of them Americans) and wounded over 5,000 others; in 2000 a suicide bombing of the USS Cole killed 17 and wounded 39 American sailors in Aden, Yemen; and finally, the September 11 brutal attacks in New York and Washington, DC and Pennsylvania, killed over 3,000 people, and injured thousands more, the most devastating terrorist act ever recorded in modern history.

Against this background, it is not surprising that in the aftermath of the takeover of the U.S. Embassy in Tehran in 1979 and the bombing of the U.S. Marine barracks in Beirut in 1983, American policy makers have considered terrorism to be a major threat to national security. A case in point is the U.S. congressional action to pass a "long arm" statute, which makes it a federal crime for a terrorist to threaten, detain, seize, injure, or kill an American citizen abroad. This statute enabled the FBI, in a sting operation in international waters off the coast of Cyprus, to arrest Fawaz Younis, a Lebanese operative implicated in the 1985 hijacking of a Jordanian airliner that included Americans who were held hostage. Younis was subsequently convicted and sentenced to life in prison.

Additional statutory action against terrorism was undertaken after the Oklahoma City bombing when President William Clinton signed into law the "Antiterrorism and Effective Death Penalty of 1996". This legislation provided law enforcement agencies with important new tools to intensify its fight against terrorism. More specifically, this legislation authorizes $1 billion in funding for federal anti-terrorism law enforcement efforts; makes it easier for police to trace bombs to the criminals who made them, by requiring chemical taggants in some explosive material; makes it harder for terrorists to raise the money they need to fund their crimes; streamlines exclusion and expulsion procedures for terrorist aliens; allows the president to withhold foreign aid to countries that provide assistance to any county designated as a supporter of terrorism; increases the penalties for conspiracy to commit explosives violations and for specified terrorism-related crimes; allows victims of terrorist acts to sue foreign state sponsors of terrorism; and expands the use of the Victims of Crime Act (VOCA) funds to include terrorism victims.

As a result of this and other legislation a number of judicial actions were undertaken. Consider, for example, the following:

- On June 11, 2001, Oklahoma City bomber Timothy McVeigh, an American terrorist who had wrought destruction on his fellow citizens on April 19, 1999 in what was then the most spectacular terrorist attack in U.S. history was executed. He expressed no remorse for his act of violence that claimed 168 lives. During the same month, a U.S. federal jury indicted fourteen individuals in connection with the 1996 Khobar Towers bombing that killed nineteen American servicemen in Saudi Arabia. Elements of the Iranian government were accused of inspiring and supporting this attack.

- On October 18, 2001, four members of Usama bin Laden's al-Qaida involved in the 1998 East African bombings of the U.S. embassies were sentenced in a New York Federal Court to life in prison without parole.

- On November 7, 2001, Federal authorities raided the offices of al-Barakaat and al- Taqwa, two financial networks run by expatriate Somalis in Columbus, Ohio; Seattle; Boston; Minneapolis, and Northern Virginia. Al- Barakaat and Al-Taqwa are believed to be part of a financial network that is assumed to have raised millions of dollars a year for terrorist networks, including al-Qaida. The treasurer of the Boston office, Mohamed M. Hussein, was arrested on a charge of operating a money transfer business without a state license. A warrant was issued for the president of the

Boston office, Liban Hussein. At this date, the United States has frozen $24 million in assets believed linked to al-Qaida and Usama bin Laden. In addition, the international community (100+ countries) has frozen another $19 million.

• And in December 2001, a grand jury in the United States District Court for the Eastern District of Virginia indicted Zacarias Moussaoui, a member of al-Qaida involved in the September 11 attacks on six criminal counts: conspiracy to commit acts of terrorism transcending national boundaries; conspiracy to commit aircraft piracy; conspiracy to destroy aircraft; conspiracy to use weapons of mass destruction; conspiracy to murder United States employees; and conspiracy to destroy property.

In sum, the United States Federal legal responses to the challenge of terrorism constitute a substantial and far ranging body of statutory law. Because of our governmental system, every prohibition, penalty and governmental program is reflected in legislation passed by the Congress and signed by the President. Most of these laws are codified in the various titles of the United States Code. However, some laws only appear in the United States Statutes at Large. In addition to the laws, there are court rules and sentencing guidelines applicable to terrorism.

In this volume we have selected what we regard as the most important of the federal laws and materials that concern terrorism. Many of these laws are part of the general criminal and civil laws of the United States and apply to various forms of criminal and civil activity, including, but not limited, to terrorism.

We have followed the codification system of the United States Code, including each Title that deals with, or relates to terrorism, in numerical order. Within each Title we have included the applicable Chapters, or parts of a Chapter, also in numerical order so that the Sections within each Chapter, or part, can be read in context. We have, except where noted, included the full text of most Chapters or Parts.

One such exception is Title 8 of the United States Code, which concerns "Aliens and Nationality." Section 1182 of Title 8 lists a variety of grounds that render an alien "inadmissible." We have included only the "Security and Related Grounds" which cover "terrorist activity." Similarly, Section 1227 lists various categories of deportable aliens. We have included only Section 1227(a) (4), "Security and Related Grounds" which cover "terrorist" activity.

The United States Code is a continuing project of the Law Revision Council of the House of Representatives. One of its objectives is to enact every Title of the Code into positive law making the Code "legal evidence of the general and permanent laws and making recourse to the numerous volumes of the United States Statutes at large for this purpose no longer necessary." (Preface to the 1982 edition of the Code).

As of January 23, 2000, 23 Titles of the United States Code are positive law. Since 1926, when the first edition of the Code was published, the entire Code, even those Titles which are not positive law, has governed how both lawyers and the public attempt to understand the complex and extensive body of "general and permanent" laws of the United States.

Many of the Titles relate to the functions of particular federal agencies and departments. For example, Title 8, "Aliens and Nationality," governs the functions of the Immigration and Naturalization Service. Title 10, "Armed Forces" governs the Department of Defense. Title 22 concerns foreign relations and the Department of State. Chapter 65 of Title 22 deals with the elimination of chemical and biological weapons through the process of international agreements.

By contrast Title 18 includes the basic criminal laws of the United States; prohibiting the use of biological weapons (Chapter 10), and chemical weapons, (Chapter 113B).

The sophistication of the Code organization is apparent. As in the case of chemical and biological weapons, the criminal prohibitions are separated from the international relations efforts to control biological and chemical weapons, clearly a different subject.

Also included in this volume is a bill drafted in the wake of the September 11 attacks and dubbed the U.S.A. Patriot Act of 2001. It was passed overwhelmingly by Congress and signed into law by President George W. Bush on October 26, 2001. This legislation provides "new tools" to fight terrorism. For example, it grants federal authorities expanded surveillance and intelligence-gathering powers.

Finally, this book draws on information and analysis generated over the past several years from dozens of international seminars and conferences, as well as fieldwork around the world. A previous work in this area is our four-volume set *Legal Aspects of Terrorism in the United States* (Oceana Publications, 2000) and *Terrorism and the Law* (Transnational Publishers, 2001). Other research studies are being planned for the future, including legislation and court cases in the United Kingdom, India, and elsewhere.

We wish to thank the Stella and Charles Guttman Foundation, the Inter-University Center for Legal Studies (International Law Institute), the Inter-University Center for Terrorism Studies (Potomac Institute for Policy Studies), for their support of our academic research on this important topic of public concern. None of the aforementioned foundations or institutes bears any responsibility for material contained in this publication. We also wish to thank the research assistance of Jim Kirkhope, Kerrie Martin and research interns Alon Lanir, Meredith Gilchrist, Vivek Narayanan, Tyler Richardson, and Chris Wallace at the International Center for Terrorism Studies (Potomac Institute for Policy Studies) and Inter-University Center for Legal Studies (International Law Institute).

Yonah Alexander
and
Edgar H. Brenner
Washington D.C.
December 18, 2001

PART I

United States Code

Title 8—Aliens and Nationality

Chapter 12—Immigration and Nationality

Subchapter II—Immigration

Sec. 1182. Inadmissible aliens

(a) Classes of aliens ineligible for visas or admission

Except as otherwise provided in this chapter, aliens who are inadmissible under the following paragraphs are ineligible to receive visas and ineligible to be admitted to the United States:

(3) Security and related grounds

(A) In general

Any alien who a consular officer or the Attorney General knows, or has reasonable ground to believe, seeks to enter the United States to engage solely, principally, or incidentally in—

(i) any activity (I) to violate any law of the United States relating to espionage or sabotage or (II) to violate or evade any law prohibiting the export from the United States of goods, technology, or sensitive information,

(ii) any other unlawful activity, or

(iii) any activity a purpose of which is the opposition to, or the control or overthrow of, the Government of the United States by force, violence, or other unlawful means, is inadmissible.

(B) Terrorist activities

(i) In general

Any alien who—

(I)   has engaged in a terrorist activity,

(II)   a consular officer or the Attorney General knows, or has reasonable ground to believe, is engaged in or is likely to engage after entry in any terrorist activity (as defined in clause (iii)),

(III) has, under circumstances indicating an intention to cause death or serious bodily harm, incited terrorist activity,

(IV) is a representative (as defined in clause (iv)) of a foreign terrorist organization, as designated by the Secretary under section 1189 of this title, or

(V) is a member of a foreign terrorist organization, as designated by the Secretary under section 1189 of this title, which the alien knows or should have known is a terrorist organization

(ii) "Terrorist activity" defined

As used in this chapter, the term "terrorist activity" means any activity which is unlawful under the laws of the place where it is committed (or which, if committed in the United States, would be unlawful under the laws of the United States or any State) and which involves any of the following:

(I) The highjacking or sabotage of any conveyance (including an aircraft, vessel, or vehicle).

(II) The seizing or detaining, and threatening to kill, injure, or continue to detain, another individual in order to compel a third person (including a governmental organization) to do or abstain from doing any act as an explicit or implicit condition for the release of the individual seized or detained.

(III) A violent attack upon an internationally protected person (as defined in section 1116(b)(4) of title 18) or upon the liberty of such a person.

(IV) An assassination.

(V) The use of any—

(a) biological agent, chemical agent, or nuclear weapon or device, or

(b) explosive or firearm (other than for mere personal monetary gain), with intent to endanger, directly or indirectly, the safety of one or more individuals or to cause substantial damage to property.

(VI) A threat, attempt, or conspiracy to do any of the foregoing.

(iii) "Engage in terrorist activity" defined As used in this chapter, the term "engage in terrorist activity" means to commit, in an individual capacity or as a member of an organization, an act of terrorist activity or an act which the actor knows, or reasonably should know, affords material support to any individual, organization, or government in conducting a terrorist activity at any time, including any of the following acts:

(I)   The preparation or planning of a terrorist activity.

(II)   The gathering of information on potential targets for terrorist activity.

(III)   The providing of any type of material support, including a safe house, transportation, communications, funds, false documentation or identification, weapons, explosives, or training, to any individual the actor knows or has reason to believe has committed or plans to commit a terrorist activity.

(IV)   The soliciting of funds or other things of value for terrorist activity or for any terrorist organization.

(V)   The solicitation of any individual for membership in a terrorist organization, terrorist government, or to engage in a terrorist activity.

(iv) "Representative" defined
As used in this paragraph, the term "representative" includes an officer, official, or spokesman of an organization, and any person who directs, counsels, commands, or induces an organization or its members to engage in terrorist activity.

Sec. 1189. Designation of foreign terrorist organizations

(a) Designation

(1) In general
The Secretary is authorized to designate an organization as a foreign terrorist organization in accordance with this subsection if the Secretary finds that—

(A)   the organization is a foreign organization;

(B) the organization engages in terrorist activity (as defined in section 1182(a)(3)(B) of this title); and

(C) the terrorist activity of the organization threatens the security of United States nationals or the national security of the United States.

(2) Procedure

(A) Notice

Seven days before making a designation under this subsection, the Secretary shall, by classified communication—

(i) notify the Speaker and Minority Leader of the House of Representatives, the President pro tempore, Majority Leader, and Minority Leader of the Senate, and the members of the relevant committees, in writing, of the intent to designate a foreign organization under this subsection, together with the findings made under paragraph (1) with respect to that organization, and the factual basis therefor; and

(ii) seven days after such notification, publish the designation in the Federal Register.

(B) Effect of designation

(i) For purposes of section 2339B of title 18, a designation under this subsection shall take effect upon publication under subparagraph (A).

(ii) Any designation under this subsection shall cease to have effect upon an Act of Congress disapproving such designation.

(C) Freezing of assets

Upon notification under paragraph (2), the Secretary of the Treasury may require United States financial institutions possessing or controlling any assets of any foreign organization included in the notification to block all financial transactions involving those assets until further directive from either the Secretary of the Treasury, Act of Congress, or order of court.

(3) Record

(A) In general

In making a designation under this subsection, the Secretary shall create an administrative record.

(B) Classified information

The Secretary may consider classified information in making a designation under this subsection. Classified information shall not be subject to disclosure for such time as it remains classified, except that such information may be disclosed to a court ex parte and in camera for purposes of judicial review under subsection (c) of this section.

(4) Period of designation

(A) In general

Subject to paragraphs (5) and (6), a designation under this subsection shall be effective for all purposes for a period of 2 years beginning on the effective date of the designation under paragraph (2)(B).

(B) Redesignation

The Secretary may redesignate a foreign organization as a foreign terrorist organization for an additional 2-year period at the end of the 2-year period referred to in subparagraph (A) (but not sooner than 60 days prior to the termination of such period) upon a finding that the relevant circumstances described in paragraph (1) still exist. The procedural requirements of paragraphs (2) and (3) shall apply to a redesignation under this subparagraph.

(5) Revocation by Act of Congress

The Congress, by an Act of Congress, may block or revoke a designation made under paragraph (1).

(6) Revocation based on change in circumstances

(A) In general

The Secretary may revoke a designation made under paragraph (1) if the Secretary finds that—

(i) the circumstances that were the basis for the designation have changed in such a manner as to warrant revocation of the designation; or

(ii) the national security of the United States warrants a revocation of the designation.

(B) Procedure

The procedural requirements of paragraphs (2) through (4) shall apply to a revocation under this paragraph.

(7) Effect of revocation

The revocation of a designation under paragraph (5) or (6) shall not affect any action or proceeding based on conduct committed prior to the effective date of such revocation.

(8) Use of designation in trial or hearing

If a designation under this subsection has become effective under paragraph (1)(B), a defendant in a criminal action shall not be permitted to raise any question concerning the validity of the issuance of such designation as a defense or an objection at any trial or hearing.

(b) Judicial review of designation

(1) In general

Not later than 30 days after publication of the designation in the Federal Register, an organization designated as a foreign terrorist organization may seek judicial review of the designation in the United States Court of Appeals for the District of Columbia Circuit.

(2) Basis of review

Review under this subsection shall be based solely upon the administrative record, except that the Government may submit, for ex parte and in camera review, classified information used in making the designation.

(3) Scope of review

The Court shall hold unlawful and set aside a designation the court finds to be—

(A) arbitrary, capricious, an abuse of discretion, or otherwise not in accordance with law;

(B) contrary to constitutional right, power, privilege, or immunity;

(C) in excess of statutory jurisdiction, authority, or limitation, or short of statutory right;

(D) lacking substantial support in the administrative record taken as a whole or in classified information submitted to the court under paragraph (2), or

(E) not in accord with the procedures required by law.

(4) Judicial review invoked

The pendency of an action for judicial review of a designation shall not affect the application of this section, unless the court issues a final order setting aside the designation.

(c) Definitions

As used in this section—

(1) the term "classified information" has the meaning given that term in section 1(a) of the Classified Information Procedures Act (18 U.S.C. App.);

(2) the term "national security" means the national defense, foreign relations, or economic interests of the United States;

(3) the term "relevant committees" means the Committees on the Judiciary, Intelligence, and Foreign Relations of the Senate and the Committees on the Judiciary, Intelligence, and International Relations of the House of Representatives; and

(4) the term "Secretary" means the Secretary of State, in consultation with the Secretary of the Treasury and the Attorney General.

Sec. 1227. Deportable aliens

(a) Classes of deportable aliens
Any alien (including an alien crewman) in and admitted to the United States shall, upon the order of the Attorney General, be removed if the alien is within one or more of the following classes of deportable aliens:

(4) Security and related grounds

(A) In general
Any alien who has engaged, is engaged, or at any time after admission engages in—

(i) any activity to violate any law of the United States relating to espionage or sabotage or to violate or evade any law prohibiting the export from the United States of goods, technology, or sensitive information,

(ii) any other criminal activity which endangers public safety or national security, or

(iii) any activity a purpose of which is the opposition to, or the control or overthrow of, the Government of the United States by force, violence, or other unlawful means, is deportable.

(B) Terrorist activities
Any alien who has engaged, is engaged, or at any time after admission engages in any terrorist activity (as defined in section 1182(a)(3)(B)(iii) of this title) is deportable.

(C) Foreign policy

(i)   In general
An alien whose presence or activities in the United States the Secretary of State has reasonable ground to believe would have potentially serious adverse foreign policy consequences for the United States is deportable.

(ii)   Exceptions
The exceptions described in clauses (ii) and (iii) of section 1182(a)(3)(C) of this title shall apply to deportability under clause (i) in the same manner as they apply to inadmissibility under section 1182(a)(3)(C)(i) of this title.

(D)   Assisted in Nazi persecution or engaged in genocide Any alien described in clause (i) or (ii) of section 1182(a)(3)(E) of this title is deportable.

Subchapter V—Alien Terrorist Removal Procedures

Sec. 1531. Definitions

As used in this subchapter—

(1)   the term "alien terrorist" means any alien described in section 1227(a)(4)(B) of this title;

(2)   the term "classified information" has the same meaning as in section 1(a) of the Classified Information Procedures Act (18 U.S.C. App.);

(3)   the term "national security" has the same meaning as in section 1(b) of the Classified Information Procedures Act (18 U.S.C. App.);

(4)   the term "removal court" means the court described in section 1532 of this title;

(5)   the term "removal hearing" means the hearing described in section 1534 of this title;

(6)   the term "removal proceeding" means a proceeding under this subchapter; and

(7)   the term "special attorney" means an attorney who is on the panel established under section 1532(e) of this title.

Sec. 1532. Establishment of removal court

(a)   Designation of judges
The Chief Justice of the United States shall publicly designate 5 district

court judges from 5 of the United States judicial circuits who shall constitute a court that shall have jurisdiction to conduct all removal proceedings. The Chief Justice may, in the Chief Justice's discretion, designate the same judges under this section as are designated pursuant to section 103(a) of the Foreign Intelligence Surveillance Act of 1978 (50 U.S.C. 1803(a)).

(b) Terms

Each judge designated under subsection (a) of this section shall serve for a term of 5 years and shall be eligible for redesignation, except that of the members first designated—

(1) 1 member shall serve for a term of 1 year;

(2) 1 member shall serve for a term of 2 years;

(3) 1 member shall serve for a term of 3 years; and

(4) 1 member shall serve for a term of 4 years.

(c) Chief judge

(1) Designation

The Chief Justice shall publicly designate one of the judges of the removal court to be the chief judge of the removal court.

(2) Responsibilities

The chief judge shall—

(A) promulgate rules to facilitate the functioning of the removal court; and

(B) assign the consideration of cases to the various judges on the removal court.

(d) Expeditious and confidential nature of proceedings

The provisions of section 103(c) of the Foreign Intelligence Surveillance Act of 1978 (50 U.S.C. 1803(c)) shall apply to removal proceedings in the same manner as they apply to proceedings under that Act (50 U.S.C. 1801 et seq.).

(e) Establishment of panel of special attorneys

The removal court shall provide for the designation of a panel of attorneys each of whom—

(1) has a security clearance which affords the attorney access to classified information, and

(2) has agreed to represent permanent resident aliens with respect to classified information under section 1534(e)(3) of this title in accordance with (and subject to the penalties under) this subchapter.

Sec. 1533. Removal court procedure

(a) Application

(1) In general
In any case in which the Attorney General has classified information that an alien is an alien terrorist, the Attorney General may seek removal of the alien under this subchapter by filing an application with the removal court that contains—

(A) the identity of the attorney in the Department of Justice making the application;

(B) a certification by the Attorney General or the Deputy Attorney General that the application satisfies the criteria and requirements of this section;

(C) the identity of the alien for whom authorization for the removal proceeding is sought; and

(D) a statement of the facts and circumstances relied on by the Department of Justice to establish probable cause that—

(i) the alien is an alien terrorist;

(ii) the alien is physically present in the United States; and

(iii) with respect to such alien, removal under subchapter II of this chapter would pose a risk to the national security of the United States.

(2) Filing
An application under this section shall be submitted ex parte and in camera, and shall be filed under seal with the removal court.

(b) Right to dismiss
The Attorney General may dismiss a removal action under this subchapter at any stage of the proceeding.

(c) Consideration of application

(1) Basis for decision
In determining whether to grant an application under this section, a single judge of the removal court may consider, ex parte and in camera, in addition to the information contained in the application—

(A) other information, including classified information, presented under oath or affirmation; and

(B) testimony received in any hearing on the application, of which a verbatim record shall be kept.

(2) Approval of order

The judge shall issue an order granting the application, if the judge finds that there is probable cause to believe that—

(A) the alien who is the subject of the application has been correctly identified and is an alien terrorist present in the United States; and

(B) removal under subchapter II of this chapter would pose a risk to the national security of the United States.

(3) Denial of order

If the judge denies the order requested in the application, the judge shall prepare a written statement of the reasons for the denial, taking all necessary precautions not to disclose any classified information contained in the Government's application.

(d) Exclusive provisions

If an order is issued under this section granting an application, the rights of the alien regarding removal and expulsion shall be governed solely by this subchapter, and except as they are specifically referenced in this subchapter, no other provisions of this chapter shall be applicable.

Sec. 1534. Removal hearing

(a) In general

(1) Expeditious hearing

In any case in which an application for an order is approved under section 1533(c)(2) of this title, a removal hearing shall be conducted under this section as expeditiously as practicable for the purpose of determining whether the alien to whom the order pertains should be removed from the United States on the grounds that the alien is an alien terrorist.

(2) Public hearing

The removal hearing shall be open to the public.

(b) Notice

An alien who is the subject of a removal hearing under this subchapter shall be given reasonable notice of—

(1) the nature of the charges against the alien, including a general account of the basis for the charges; and

(2) the time and place at which the hearing will be held.

(c) Rights in hearing

(1) Right of counsel

The alien shall have a right to be present at such hearing and to be represented by counsel. Any alien financially unable to obtain counsel shall be entitled to have counsel assigned to represent the alien. Such counsel shall be appointed by the judge pursuant to the plan for furnishing representation for any person financially unable to obtain adequate representation for the district in which the hearing is conducted, as provided for in section 3006A of title 18. All provisions of that section shall apply and, for purposes of determining the maximum amount of compensation, the matter shall be treated as if a felony was charged.

(2) Introduction of evidence

Subject to the limitations in subsection (e) of this section, the alien shall have a reasonable opportunity to introduce evidence on the alien's own behalf.

(3) Examination of witnesses

Subject to the limitations in subsection (e) of this section, the alien shall have a reasonable opportunity to examine the evidence against the alien and to cross-examine any witness.

(4) Record

A verbatim record of the proceedings and of all testimony and evidence offered or produced at such a hearing shall be kept.

(5) Removal decision based on evidence at hearing

The decision of the judge regarding removal shall be based only on that evidence introduced at the removal hearing.

(d) Subpoenas

(1) Request

At any time prior to the conclusion of the removal hearing, either the alien or the Department of Justice may request the judge to issue a subpoena for the presence of a named witness (which subpoena may also command the person to whom it is directed to produce books, papers, documents, or other objects designated therein) upon a satisfactory showing that the presence of the witness is necessary for the determination of any material matter. Such a request may be made ex parte except that the judge shall inform the Department of Justice of any request for a subpoena by the alien for a witness or material if compliance with such a subpoena would reveal classified evidence or the source of that evidence. The Department of Justice shall be given a reasonable opportunity to oppose the issuance of such a subpoena.

(2) Payment for attendance

If an application for a subpoena by the alien also makes a showing that the alien is financially unable to pay for the attendance of a witness so requested, the court may order the costs incurred by the process and the fees of the witness so subpoenaed to be paid from funds appropriated for the enforcement of subchapter II of this chapter.

(3) Nationwide service

A subpoena under this subsection may be served anywhere in the United States.

(4) Witness fees

A witness subpoenaed under this subsection shall receive the same fees and expenses as a witness subpoenaed in connection with a civil proceeding in a court of the United States.

(5) No access to classified information

Nothing in this subsection is intended to allow an alien to have access to classified information.

(e) Discovery

(1) In general

For purposes of this subchapter—

(A) the Government is authorized to use in a removal proceedings the fruits of electronic surveillance and unconsented physical searches authorized under the Foreign Intelligence Surveillance Act of 1978 (50 U.S.C. 1801 et seq.) without regard to subsections (c), (e), (f), (g), and (h) of section 106 of that Act (50 U.S.C. 1806(c), (e), (f), (g), (h)) and discovery of information derived pursuant to such Act, or otherwise collected for national security purposes, shall not be authorized if disclosure would present a risk to the national security of the United States;

(B) an alien subject to removal under this subchapter shall not be entitled to suppress evidence that the alien alleges was unlawfully obtained; and

(C) section 3504 of title 18 and section 1806(c) of title 50 shall not apply if the Attorney General determines that public disclosure would pose a risk to the national security of the United States because it would disclose classified information or otherwise threaten the integrity of a pending investigation.

(2) Protective orders

Nothing in this subchapter shall prevent the United States from seeking protective orders and from asserting privileges ordinarily available to the United States to protect against the disclosure of classified information, including the invocation of the military and State secrets privileges.

(3) Treatment of classified information

(A) Use

The judge shall examine, ex parte and in camera, any evidence for which the Attorney General determines that public disclosure would pose a risk to the national security of the United States or to the security of any individual because it would disclose classified information and neither the alien nor the public shall be informed of such evidence or its sources other than through reference to the summary provided pursuant to this paragraph. Notwithstanding the previous sentence, the Department of Justice may, in its discretion and, in the case of classified information, after coordination with the originating agency, elect to introduce such evidence in open session.

(B) Submission

With respect to such information, the Government shall submit to the removal court an unclassified summary of the specific evidence that does not pose that risk.

(C) Approval

Not later than 15 days after submission, the judge shall approve the summary if the judge finds that it is sufficient to enable the alien to prepare a defense. The Government shall deliver to the alien a copy of the unclassified summary approved under this subparagraph.

(D) Disapproval

(i) In general

If an unclassified summary is not approved by the removal court under subparagraph (C), the Government shall be afforded 15 days to correct the deficiencies identified by the court and submit a revised unclassified summary.

(ii) Revised summary

If the revised unclassified summary is not approved by the court within 15 days of its submission pursuant to subparagraph (C), the removal hearing shall be terminated unless the judge makes the findings under clause (iii).

(iii) Findings

The findings described in this clause are, with respect to an alien, that—

(I) the continued presence of the alien in the United States would likely cause serious and irreparable harm to the national security or death or serious bodily injury to any person, and

(II) the provision of the summary would likely cause serious and irreparable harm to the national security or death or serious bodily injury to any person.

(E) Continuation of hearing without summary

If a judge makes the findings described in subparagraph (D)(iii)—

(i) if the alien involved is an alien lawfully admitted for permanent residence, the procedures described in subparagraph (F) shall apply; and

(ii) in all cases the special removal hearing shall continue, the Department of Justice shall cause to be delivered to the alien a statement that no summary is possible, and the classified information submitted in camera and ex parte may be used pursuant to this paragraph.

(F) Special procedures for access and challenges to classified information by special attorneys in case of lawful permanent aliens

(i) In general

The procedures described in this subparagraph are that the judge (under rules of the removal court) shall designate a special attorney to assist the alien—

(I) by reviewing in camera the classified information on behalf of the alien, and

(II) by challenging through an in camera proceeding the veracity of the evidence contained in the classified information.

(ii) Restrictions on disclosure

A special attorney receiving classified information under clause (i)—

(I)   shall not disclose the information to the alien or to any other attorney representing the alien, and

(II)   who discloses such information in violation of subclause (I) shall be subject to a fine under title 18, imprisoned for not less than 10 years nor more than 25 years, or both.

(f)   Arguments

Following the receipt of evidence, the Government and the alien shall be given fair opportunity to present argument as to whether the evidence is sufficient to justify the removal of the alien. The Government shall open the argument. The alien shall be permitted to reply. The Government shall then be permitted to reply in rebuttal. The judge may allow any part of the argument that refers to evidence received in camera and ex parte to be heard in camera and ex parte.

(g)   Burden of proof

In the hearing, it is the Government's burden to prove, by the preponderance of the evidence, that the alien is subject to removal because the alien is an alien terrorist.

(h)   Rules of evidence

The Federal Rules of Evidence shall not apply in a removal hearing.

(i)   Determination of deportation

If the judge, after considering the evidence on the record as a whole, finds that the Government has met its burden, the judge shall order the alien removed and detained pending removal from the United States. If the alien was released pending the removal hearing, the judge shall order the Attorney General to take the alien into custody.

(j)   Written order

At the time of issuing a decision as to whether the alien shall be removed, the judge shall prepare a written order containing a statement of facts found and conclusions of law. Any portion of the order that would reveal the substance or source of information received in camera and ex parte pursuant to subsection (e) of this section shall not be made available to the alien or the public.

(k)   No right to ancillary relief

At no time shall the judge consider or provide for relief from removal based on—

(1)   asylum under section 1158 of this title;

(2) by withholding of removal under section 1231(b)(3) of this title;

(3) cancellation of removal under section 1229b of this title;

(4) voluntary departure under section 1254a(e) of this title;

(5) adjustment of status under section 1255 of this title; or

(6) registry under section 1259 of this title.

Sec. 1535. Appeals

(a) Appeal of denial of application for removal proceedings

(1) In general

The Attorney General may seek a review of the denial of an order sought in an application filed pursuant to section 1533 of this title. The appeal shall be filed in the United States Court of Appeals for the District of Columbia Circuit by notice of appeal filed not later than 20 days after the date of such denial.

(2) Record on appeal

The entire record of the proceeding shall be transmitted to the Court of Appeals under seal, and the Court of Appeals shall hear the matter ex parte.

(3) Standard of review

The Court of Appeals shall—

(A) review questions of law de novo; and

(B) set aside a finding of fact only if such finding was clearly erroneous.

(b) Appeal of determination regarding summary of classified information

(1) In general

The United States may take an interlocutory appeal to the United States Court of Appeals for the District of Columbia Circuit of—

(A) any determination by the judge pursuant to section 1534(e)(3) of this title; or

(B) the refusal of the court to make the findings permitted by section 1534(e)(3) of this title.

(2) Record

In any interlocutory appeal taken pursuant to this subsection, the entire record, including any proposed order of the judge, any classified information and the summary of evidence, shall be transmitted to the Court of Appeals. The classified information shall be transmitted under seal. A verbatim record of such appeal shall be kept under seal in the event of any other judicial review.

(c) Appeal of decision in hearing

(1) In general
Subject to paragraph (2), the decision of the judge after a removal hearing may be appealed by either the alien or the Attorney General to the United States Court of Appeals for the District of Columbia Circuit by notice of appeal filed not later than 20 days after the date on which the order is issued. The order shall not be enforced during the pendency of an appeal under this subsection.

(2) Automatic appeals in cases of permanent resident aliens in which no summary provided

(A) In general
Unless the alien waives the right to a review under this paragraph, in any case involving an alien lawfully admitted for permanent residence who is denied a written summary of classified information under section 1534(e)(3) of this title and with respect to which the procedures described in section 1534(e)(3)(F) of this title apply, any order issued by the judge shall be reviewed by the Court of Appeals for the District of Columbia Circuit.

(B) Use of special attorney
With respect to any issue relating to classified information that arises in such review, the alien shall be represented only by the special attorney designated under section 1534(e)(3)(F)(i) of this title on behalf of the alien.

(3) Transmittal of record
In an appeal or review to the Court of Appeals pursuant to this subsection—

(A) the entire record shall be transmitted to the Court of Appeals; and

(B) information received in camera and ex parte, and any portion of the order that would reveal the substance or source of such information, shall be transmitted under seal.

(4) Expedited appellate proceeding
In an appeal or review to the Court of Appeals under this subsection—

(A) the appeal or review shall be heard as expeditiously as practicable and the court may dispense with full briefing and hear the matter solely on the record of the judge of the removal court and on such briefs or motions as the court may require to be filed by the parties;

(B) the Court of Appeals shall issue an opinion not later than 60 days after the date of the issuance of the final order of the district court;

(C) the court shall review all questions of law de novo; and

(D) a finding of fact shall be accorded deference by the reviewing court and shall not be set aside unless such finding was clearly erroneous, except that in the case of a review under paragraph (2) in which an alien lawfully admitted for permanent residence was denied a written summary of classified information under section 1534(c)(3) of this title, the Court of Appeals shall review questions of fact de novo.

(d) Certiorari

Following a decision by the Court of Appeals pursuant to subsection (c) of this section, the alien or the Attorney General may petition the Supreme Court for a writ of certiorari. In any such case, any information transmitted to the Court of Appeals under seal shall, if such information is also submitted to the Supreme Court, be transmitted under seal. Any order of removal shall not be stayed pending disposition of a writ of certiorari, except as provided by the Court of Appeals or a Justice of the Supreme Court.

(e) Appeal of detention order

(1) In general

Sections 3145 through 3148 of title 18 pertaining to review and appeal of a release or detention order, penalties for failure to appear, penalties for an offense committed while on release, and sanctions for violation of a release condition shall apply to an alien to whom section 1537(b)(1) of this title applies. In applying the previous sentence—

(A) for purposes of section 3145 of such title an appeal shall be taken to the United States Court of Appeals for the District of Columbia Circuit; and

(B) for purposes of section 3146 of such title the alien shall be considered released in connection with a charge of an offense punishable by life imprisonment.

(2) No review of continued detention
The determinations and actions of the Attorney General pursuant to section 1537(b)(2)(C) of this title shall not be subject to judicial review, including application for a writ of habeas corpus, except for a claim by the alien that continued detention violates the alien's rights under the Constitution. Jurisdiction over any such challenge shall lie exclusively in the United States Court of Appeals for the District of Columbia Circuit.

Sec. 1536. Custody and release pending removal hearing

(a) Upon filing application

(1) In general
Subject to paragraphs (2) and (3), the Attorney General may—

(A) take into custody any alien with respect to whom an application under section 1533 of this title has been filed; and

(B) retain such an alien in custody in accordance with the procedures authorized by this subchapter.

(2) Special rules for permanent resident aliens

(A) Release hearing
An alien lawfully admitted for permanent residence shall be entitled to a release hearing before the judge assigned to hear the removal hearing. Such an alien shall be detained pending the removal hearing, unless the alien demonstrates to the court that the alien—

(i) is a person lawfully admitted for permanent residence in the United States;

(ii) if released upon such terms and conditions as the court may prescribe (including the posting of any monetary amount), is not likely to flee; and

(iii) will not endanger national security, or the safety of any person or the community, if released.

(B) Information considered
The judge may consider classified information submitted in camera and ex parte in making a determination whether to release an alien pending the removal hearing.

(3) Release if order denied and no review sought

(A) In general
Subject to subparagraph (B), if a judge of the removal court denies the order sought in an application filed pursuant to section 1533 of this title, and the Attorney General does not seek review of such denial, the alien shall be released from custody.

(B) Application of regular procedures
Subparagraph (A) shall not prevent the arrest and detention of the alien pursuant to subchapter II of this chapter.

(b) Conditional release if order denied and review sought

(1) In general
If a judge of the removal court denies the order sought in an application filed pursuant to section 1533 of this title and the Attorney General seeks review of such denial, the judge shall release the alien from custody subject to the least restrictive condition, or combination of conditions, of release described in section 3142(b) and clauses (i) through (xiv) of section 3142(c)(1)(B) of title 18 that—

(A) will reasonably assure the appearance of the alien at any future proceeding pursuant to this subchapter; and

(B) will not endanger the safety of any other person or the community.

(2) No release for certain aliens
If the judge finds no such condition or combination of conditions, as described in paragraph (1), the alien shall remain in custody until the completion of any appeal authorized by this subchapter.

Sec. 1537. Custody and release after removal hearing

(a) Release

(1) In general
Subject to paragraph (2), if the judge decides that an alien should not be removed, the alien shall be released from custody.

(2) Custody pending appeal
If the Attorney General takes an appeal from such decision, the alien shall remain in custody, subject to the provisions of section 3142 of title 18.

(b) Custody and removal

(1) Custody

If the judge decides that an alien shall be removed, the alien shall be detained pending the outcome of any appeal. After the conclusion of any judicial review thereof which affirms the removal order, the Attorney General shall retain the alien in custody and remove the alien to a country specified under paragraph (2).

(2) Removal

(A) In general
The removal of an alien shall be to any country which the alien shall designate if such designation does not, in the judgment of the Attorney General, in consultation with the Secretary of State, impair the obligation of the United States under any treaty (including a treaty pertaining to extradition) or otherwise adversely affect the foreign policy of the United States.

(B) Alternate countries
If the alien refuses to designate a country to which the alien wishes to be removed or if the Attorney General, in consultation with the Secretary of State, determines that removal of the alien to the country so designated would impair a treaty obligation or adversely affect United States foreign policy, the Attorney General shall cause the alien to be removed to any country willing to receive such alien.

(C) Continued detention
If no country is willing to receive such an alien, the Attorney General may, notwithstanding any other provision of law, retain the alien in custody. The Attorney General, in coordination with the Secretary of State, shall make periodic efforts to reach agreement with other countries to accept such an alien and at least every 6 months shall provide to the attorney representing the alien at the removal hearing a written report on the Attorney General's efforts. Any alien in custody pursuant to this subparagraph shall be released from custody solely at the discretion of the Attorney General and subject to such conditions as the Attorney General shall deem appropriate.

(D) Fingerprinting
Before an alien is removed from the United States pursuant to this subsection, or pursuant to an order of removal because such alien is inadmissible under section 1182(a)(3)(B) of this title, the alien shall be photographed and finger-

printed, and shall be advised of the provisions of section 1326(b) of this title.

(c) Continued detention pending trial

(1) Delay in removal

The Attorney General may hold in abeyance the removal of an alien who has been ordered removed, pursuant to this subchapter, to allow the trial of such alien on any Federal or State criminal charge and the service of any sentence of confinement resulting from such a trial.

(2) Maintenance of custody

Pending the commencement of any service of a sentence of confinement by an alien described in paragraph (1), such an alien shall remain in the custody of the Attorney General, unless the Attorney General determines that temporary release of the alien to the custody of State authorities for confinement in a State facility is appropriate and would not endanger national security or public safety.

(3) Subsequent removal

Following the completion of a sentence of confinement by an alien described in paragraph (1), or following the completion of State criminal proceedings which do not result in a sentence of confinement of an alien released to the custody of State authorities pursuant to paragraph (2), such an alien shall be returned to the custody of the Attorney General who shall proceed to the removal of the alien under this subchapter.

(d) Application of certain provisions relating to escape of prisoners

For purposes of sections 751 and 752 of title 18, an alien in the custody of the Attorney General pursuant to this subchapter shall be subject to the penalties provided by those sections in relation to a person committed to the custody of the Attorney General by virtue of an arrest on a charge of a felony.

(e) Rights of aliens in custody

(1) Family and attorney visits

An alien in the custody of the Attorney General pursuant to this subchapter shall be given reasonable opportunity, as determined by the Attorney General, to communicate with and receive visits from members of the alien's family, and to contact, retain, and communicate with an attorney.

(2) Diplomatic contact

An alien in the custody of the Attorney General pursuant to this subchapter shall have the right to contact an appropriate diplomatic or consular official of the alien's country of citizenship or nationality or of any country providing representation services therefore. The Attorney General shall notify the appropriate embassy, mission, or consular office of the alien's detention.

Title 10—Armed Forces

Part IV—Service, Supply, and Procurement

Chapter 137—Procurement Generally

Sec. 2327. Contracts: consideration of national security objectives

(a) Disclosure of Ownership or Control by a Foreign Government.— The head of an agency shall require a firm or a subsidiary of a firm that submits a bid or proposal in response to a solicitation issued by the Department of Defense to disclose in that bid or proposal any significant interest in such firm or subsidiary (or, in the case of a subsidiary, in the firm that owns the subsidiary) that is owned or controlled (whether directly or indirectly) by a foreign government or an agent or instrumentality of a foreign government, if such foreign government is the government of a country that the Secretary of State determines under section 6(j)(1)(A) of the Export Administration Act of 1979 (50 U.S.C. App. 2405(j)(1)(A)) has repeatedly provided support for acts of international terrorism.

(b) Prohibition on Entering Into Contracts Against the Interests of the United States.—Except as provided in subsection (c), the head of an agency may not enter into a contract with a firm or a subsidiary of a firm if—

(1) a foreign government owns or controls (whether directly or indirectly) a significant interest in such firm or subsidiary (or, in the case of a subsidiary, in the firm that owns the subsidiary); and

(2) such foreign government is the government of a country that the Secretary of State determines under section 6(j)(1)(A) of the Export Administration Act of 1979 (50 U.S.C. App. 2405(j)(1)(A)) has repeatedly provided support for acts of international terrorism.

(c) Waiver.—(1)(A) If the Secretary of Defense determines under paragraph (2) that entering into a contract with a firm or a subsidiary of a firm described in subsection (b) is not inconsistent with the national security objectives of the United States, the head of an agency may enter into a contract with such firm or subsidiary after the date on which such head of an agency submits to Congress a report on the contract.

(B)   A report under subparagraph (A) shall include the following:

(i)   The identity of the foreign government concerned.

(ii)   The nature of the contract.

(iii)   The extent of ownership or control of the firm or subsidiary concerned (or, if appropriate in the case of a subsidiary, of the firm that owns the subsidiary) by the foreign government concerned or the agency or instrumentality of such foreign government.

(iv)   The reasons for entering into the contract.

(C)   After the head of an agency submits a report to Congress under subparagraph (A) with respect to a firm or a subsidiary, such head of an agency is not required to submit a report before entering into any subsequent contract with such firm or subsidiary unless the information required to be included in such report under subparagraph (B) has materially changed since the submission of the previous report.

(2)   Upon the request of the head of an agency, the Secretary of Defense shall determine whether entering into a contract with a firm or subsidiary described in subsection (b) is inconsistent with the national security objectives of the United States. In making such a determination, the Secretary of Defense shall consider the following:

(A)   The relationship of the United States with the foreign government concerned.

(B)   The obligations of the United States under international agreements.

(C)   The extent of the ownership or control of the firm or subsidiary (or, if appropriate in the case of a subsidiary, of the firm that owns the subsidiary) by the foreign government or an agent or instrumentality of the foreign government.

(D)   Whether payments made, or information made available, to the firm or subsidiary under the contract could be used for purposes hostile to the interests of the United States.

(d)   List of Firms Subject to Prohibition.—(1) The Secretary of Defense shall develop and maintain a list of all firms and subsidiaries of firms that the Secretary has identified as being subject to the prohibition in subsection (b).

(2)

(A)   A person may request the Secretary to include on the list maintained under paragraph (1) any firm or subsidiary of a firm that the person believes to be owned or controlled by a foreign government described in subsection (b)(2). Upon receipt of such a request, the Secretary shall determine whether the conditions in paragraphs (1) and (2) of subsection (b) exist in the case of that firm or subsidiary. If the Secretary determines that such conditions do exist, the Secretary shall include the firm or subsidiary on the list.

(B)   A firm or subsidiary of a firm included on the list may request the Secretary to remove such firm or subsidiary from the list on the basis that it has been erroneously included on the list or its ownership circumstances have significantly changed. Upon receipt of such a request, the Secretary shall determine whether the conditions in paragraphs (1) and (2) of subsection (b) exist in the case of that firm or subsidiary. If the Secretary determines that such conditions do not exist, the Secretary shall remove the firm or subsidiary from the list.

(C)   The Secretary shall establish procedures to carry out this paragraph.

(3)   The head of an agency shall prohibit each firm or subsidiary of a firm awarded a contract by the agency from entering into a subcontract under that contract in an amount in excess of $25,000 with a firm or subsidiary included on the list maintained under paragraph (1) unless there is a compelling reason to do so. In the case of any subcontract requiring consent by the head of an agency, the head of the agency shall not consent to the award of the subcontract to a firm or subsidiary included on such list unless there is a compelling reason for such approval.

(e)   Distribution of List.—The Administrator of General Services shall ensure that the list developed and maintained under subsection (d) is made available to Federal agencies and the public in the same manner and to the same extent as the list of suspended and debarred contractors compiled pursuant to subpart 9.4 of the Federal Acquisition Regulation.

(f)   Applicability.—

(1) This section does not apply to a contract for an amount less than $100,000.

(2) This section does not apply to the Coast Guard or the National Aeronautics and Space Administration.

(g) Regulations.—The Secretary of Defense, after consultation with the Secretary of State, shall prescribe regulations to carry out this section. Such regulations shall include a definition of the term "significant interest."

Title 18—Crimes and Criminal Procedure

Part I—Crimes

Chapter 1—General Provisions

Sec. 2. Principals

(a) Whoever commits an offense against the United States or aids, abets, counsels, commands, induces or procures its commission, is punishable as a principal.

(b) Whoever willfully causes an act to be done which if directly performed by him or another would be an offense against the United States, is punishable as a principal.

Sec. 3. Accessory after the fact

Whoever, knowing that an offense against the United States has been committed, receives, relieves, comforts or assists the offender in order to hinder or prevent his apprehension, trial or punishment, is an accessory after the fact.

Except as otherwise expressly provided by any Act of Congress, an accessory after the fact shall be imprisoned not more than one-half the maximum term of imprisonment or (notwithstanding section *3571*) fined not more than one-half the maximum fine prescribed for the punishment of the principal, or both; or if the principal is punishable by life imprisonment or death, the accessory shall be imprisoned not more than 15 years.

Sec. 4. Misprision of felony

Whoever, having knowledge of the actual commission of a felony cognizable by a court of the United States, conceals and does not as soon as possible make known the same to some judge or other person in civil or military authority under the United States, shall be fined under this title or imprisoned not more than three years, or both.

Sec. 5. United States defined

The term "United States," as used in this title in a territorial sense, includes all places and waters, continental or insular, subject to the jurisdiction of the United States, except the Canal Zone.

Sec. 6. Department and agency defined

As used in this title:

The term "department" means one of the executive departments enumerated in section *1* of Title 5, unless the context shows that such term was intended to describe the executive, legislative, or judicial branches of the government.

The term "agency" includes any department, independent establishment, commission, administration, authority, board or bureau of the United States or any corporation in which the United States has a proprietary interest, unless the context shows that such term was intended to be used in a more limited sense.

Sec. 7. Special maritime and territorial jurisdiction of the United States defined

The term "special maritime and territorial jurisdiction of the United States," as used in this title, includes:

(1) The high seas, any other waters within the admiralty and maritime jurisdiction of the United States and out of the jurisdiction of any particular State, and any vessel belonging in whole or in part to the United States or any citizen thereof, or to any corporation created by or under the laws of the United States, or of any State, Territory, District, or possession thereof, when such vessel is within the admiralty and maritime jurisdiction of the United States and out of the jurisdiction of any particular State.

(2) Any vessel registered, licensed, or enrolled under the laws of the United States, and being on a voyage upon the waters of any of the Great Lakes, or any of the waters connecting them, or upon the Saint Lawrence River where the same constitutes the International Boundary Line.

(3) Any lands reserved or acquired for the use of the United States, and under the exclusive or concurrent jurisdiction thereof, or any place purchased or otherwise acquired by the United States by con-

sent of the legislature of the State in which the same shall be, for the erection of a fort, magazine, arsenal, dockyard, or other needful building.

(4) Any island, rock, or key containing deposits of guano, which may, at the discretion of the President, be considered as appertaining to the United States.

(5) Any aircraft belonging in whole or in part to the United States, or any citizen thereof, or to any corporation created by or under the laws of the United States, or any State, Territory, district, or possession thereof, while such aircraft is in flight over the high seas, or over any other waters within the admiralty and maritime jurisdiction of the United States and out of the jurisdiction of any particular State.

(6) Any vehicle used or designed for flight or navigation in space and on the registry of the United States pursuant to the Treaty on Principles Governing the Activities of States in the Exploration and Use of Outer Space, Including the Moon and Other Celestial Bodies and the Convention on Registration of Objects Launched into Outer Space, while that vehicle is in flight, which is from the moment when all external doors are closed on Earth following embarkation until the moment when one such door is opened on Earth for disembarkation or in the case of a forced landing, until the competent authorities take over the responsibility for the vehicle and for persons and property aboard.

(7) Any place outside the jurisdiction of any nation with respect to an offense by or against a national of the United States.

(8) To the extent permitted by international law, any foreign vessel during a voyage having a scheduled departure from or arrival in the United States with respect to an offense committed by or against a national of the United States.

Sec. 8. Obligation or other security of the United States defined

The term "obligation or other security of the United States" includes all bonds, certificates of indebtedness, national bank currency, Federal Reserve notes, Federal Reserve bank notes, coupons, United States notes, Treasury notes, gold certificates, silver certificates, fractional notes, certificates of deposit, bills, checks, or drafts for money, drawn by or upon authorized officers of the United States, stamps and other representatives of value, of whatever denomination, issued under any Act of Congress, and canceled United States stamps.

Sec. 9. Vessel of the United States defined

The term "vessel of the United States," as used in this title, means a vessel belonging in whole or in part to the United States, or any citizen thereof, or any corporation created by or under the laws of the United States, or of any State, Territory, District, or possession thereof.

Sec. 10. Interstate commerce and foreign commerce defined

The term "interstate commerce," as used in this title, includes commerce between one State, Territory, Possession, or the District of Columbia and another State, Territory, Possession, or the District of Columbia.

The term "foreign commerce," as used in this title, includes commerce with a foreign country.

Sec. 11. Foreign government defined

The term "foreign government," as used in this title except in sections *112*, *878*, 970, 1116, and 1201, includes any government, faction, or body of insurgents within a country with which the United States is at peace, irrespective of recognition by the United States.

Sec. 16. Crime of violence defined

The term "crime of violence" means—

- (a) an offense that has as an element the use, attempted use, or threatened use of physical force against the person or property of another, or
- (b) any other offense that is a felony and that, by its nature, involves a substantial risk that physical force against the person or property of another may be used in the course of committing the offense.

Sec. 17. Insanity defense

- (a) Affirmative Defense.—It is an affirmative defense to a prosecution under any Federal statute that, at the time of the commission of the acts constituting the offense, the defendant, as a

result of a severe mental disease or defect, was unable to appreciate the nature and quality or the wrongfulness of his acts. Mental disease or defect does not otherwise constitute a defense.
- (b) Burden of Proof.—The defendant has the burden of proving the defense of insanity by clear and convincing evidence.

Sec. 18. Organization defined

As used in this title, the term "organization" means a person other than an individual.

Sec. 21. Stolen or counterfeit nature of property for certain crimes defined

(a) Wherever in this title it is an element of an offense that—

(1) any property was embezzled, robbed, stolen, converted, taken, altered, counterfeited, falsely made, forged, or obliterated; and

(2) the defendant knew that the property was of such character; such element may be established by proof that the defendant, after or as a result of an official representation as to the nature of the property, believed the property to be embezzled, robbed, stolen, converted, taken, altered, counterfeited, falsely made, forged, or obliterated.

(b) For purposes of this section, the term "official representation" means any representation made by a Federal law enforcement officer (as defined in section *115*) or by another person at the direction or with the approval of such an officer.

Chapter 2—Aircraft and Motor Vehicles

Sec. 31. Definitions

When used in this chapter the term—

"Aircraft engine," "air navigation facility," "appliance," "civil aircraft," "foreign air commerce," "interstate air commerce," "landing area," "overseas air commerce," "propeller," "spare part" and "special aircraft jurisdiction of the United States" shall have the meaning ascribed to those terms in sections *40102*(a) and *46501* of title 49.

"Motor vehicle" means every description of carriage or other contrivance propelled or drawn by mechanical power and used for commercial purposes on the highways in the transportation of passengers, passengers and property, or property or cargo;

"Destructive substance" means any explosive substance, flammable material, infernal machine, or other chemical, mechanical, or radioactive device or matter of a combustible, contaminative, corrosive, or explosive nature;

"Used for commercial purposes" means the carriage of persons or property for any fare, fee, rate, charge or other consideration, or directly or indirectly in connection with any business, or other undertaking intended for profit;

"In flight" means any time from the moment all the external doors of an aircraft are closed following embarkation until the moment when any such door is opened for disembarkation. In the case of a forced landing the flight shall be deemed to continue until competent authorities take over the responsibility for the aircraft and the persons and property on board; and

"In service" means any time from the beginning of preflight preparation of the aircraft by ground personnel or by the crew for a specific flight until twenty-four hours after any landing; the period of service shall, in any event, extend for the entire period during which the aircraft is in flight.

Sec. 32. Destruction of aircraft or aircraft facilities

(a) Whoever willfully—

(1) sets fire to, damages, destroys, disables, or wrecks any aircraft in the special aircraft jurisdiction of the United States or any civil aircraft used, operated, or employed in interstate, overseas, or foreign air commerce;

(2) places or causes to be placed a destructive device or substance in, upon, or in proximity to, or otherwise makes or causes to be made unworkable or unusable or hazardous to work or use, any such aircraft, or any part or other materials used or intended to be used in connection with the operation of such aircraft, if such placing or causing to be placed or such making or causing to be made is likely to endanger the safety of any such aircraft;

(3) sets fire to, damages, destroys, or disables any air navigation facility, or interferes by force or violence with the operation of such facility, if such fire, damaging, destroying, disabling, or interfering is likely to endanger the safety of any such aircraft in flight;

(4) with the intent to damage, destroy, or disable any such aircraft, sets fire to, damages, destroys, or disables or places a destructive device or substance in, upon, or in proximity to, any appliance or structure, ramp, landing area, property, machine, or apparatus, or any facility or other material used, or intended to be used, in connection with the operation, maintenance, loading, unloading or storage of any such aircraft or any cargo carried or intended to be carried on any such aircraft;

(5) performs an act of violence against or incapacitates any individual on any such aircraft, if such act of violence or incapacitation is likely to endanger the safety of such aircraft;

(6) communicates information, knowing the information to be false and under circumstances in which such information may reasonably be believed, thereby endangering the safety of any such aircraft in flight; or

(7) attempts or conspires to do anything prohibited under paragraphs (1) through (6) of this subsection; shall be fined under this title or imprisoned not more than twenty years or both.

(b) Whoever willfully—

(1) performs an act of violence against any individual on board any civil aircraft registered in a country other than the United States while such aircraft is in flight, if such act is likely to endanger the safety of that aircraft;

(2) destroys a civil aircraft registered in a country other than the United States while such aircraft is in service or causes damage to such an aircraft which renders that aircraft incapable of flight or which is likely to endanger that aircraft's safety in flight;

(3) places or causes to be placed on a civil aircraft registered in a country other than the United States while such aircraft is in service, a device or substance which is likely to destroy that aircraft, or to cause damage to that aircraft which renders that aircraft incapable of flight or which is likely to endanger that aircraft's safety in flight; or

(4) attempts or conspires to commit an offense described in paragraphs (1) through (3) of this subsection; shall be fined under this title or imprisoned not more than twenty years, or both. There is jurisdiction over an offense under this subsection if a national of the United States was on board, or would have been on board, the aircraft; an offender is a national of the United States; or an offender is afterwards found in the United States. For purposes of this subsection, the term "national of the United States" has the meaning prescribed in section 101(a)(22) of the Immigration and Nationality Act.

(c) Whoever willfully imparts or conveys any threat to do an act which would violate any of paragraphs (1) through (5) of subsection (a) or any of paragraphs (1) through (3) of subsection (b) of this section, with an apparent determination and will to carry the threat into execution shall be fined under this title or imprisoned not more than five years, or both.

Sec. 33. Destruction of motor vehicles or motor vehicle facilities

(a) Whoever willfully, with intent to endanger the safety of any person on board or anyone who he believes will board the same, or with a reckless disregard for the safety of human life, damages, disables, destroys, tampers with, or places or causes to be placed any explosive or other destructive substance in, upon, or in proximity to, any motor vehicle which is used, operated, or employed in interstate or foreign commerce, or its cargo or material used or intended to be used in connection with its operation; or

Whoever willfully, with like intent, damages, disables, destroys, sets fire to, tampers with, or places or causes to be placed any explosive or other destructive substance in, upon, or in proximity to any garage, terminal, structure, supply, or facility used in the operation of, or in support of the operation of, motor vehicles engaged in interstate or foreign commerce or otherwise makes or causes such property to be made unworkable, unusable, or hazardous to work or use; or

Whoever, with like intent, willfully disables or incapacitates any driver or person employed in connection with the operation or maintenance of the motor vehicle, or in any way lessens the ability of such person to perform his duties as such; or

Whoever willfully attempts to do any of the aforesaid acts—shall be fined under this title or imprisoned not more than twenty years, or both.

(b) Whoever is convicted of a violation of subsection (a) involving a motor vehicle that, at the time the violation occurred, carried high-level radioactive waste (as that term is defined in section 2(12) of the Nuclear Waste Policy Act of 1982 (42 U.S.C. 10101(12))) or spent nuclear fuel (as that term is defined in section 2(23) of the Nuclear Waste Policy Act of 1982 (42 U.S.C. 10101(23))), shall be fined under this title and imprisoned for any term of years not less than 30, or for life.

Sec. 34. Penalty when death results

Whoever is convicted of any crime prohibited by this chapter, which has resulted in the death of any person, shall be subject also to the death penalty or to imprisonment for life.

Sec. 35. Imparting or conveying false information

(a) Whoever imparts or conveys or causes to be imparted or conveyed false information, knowing the information to be false, concerning an attempt or alleged attempt being made or to be made, to do any act which would be a crime prohibited by this chapter or chapter 97 or chapter 111 of this title shall be subject to a civil penalty of not more than $1,000 which shall be recoverable in a civil action brought in the name of the United States.

(b) Whoever willfully and maliciously, or with reckless disregard for the safety of human life, imparts or conveys or causes to be imparted or conveyed false information, knowing the information to be false, concerning an attempt or alleged attempt being made or to be made, to do any act which would be a crime prohibited by this chapter or chapter 97 or chapter 111 of this title—shall be fined under this title, or imprisoned not more than five years, or both.

Sec. 36. Drive-by shooting

(a) Definition.—In this section, "major drug offense" means—

(1) a continuing criminal enterprise punishable under section 408(c) of the Controlled Substances Act (21 U.S.C. 848(c));

(2) a conspiracy to distribute controlled substances punishable under section 406 of the Controlled Substances Act (21 U.S.C. 846) section 1013 of the Controlled Substances Import and Export Act (21 U.S.C. 963); or

(3) an offense involving major quantities of drugs and punishable under section 401(b)(1)(A) of the Controlled Substances Act (21 U.S.C. 841(b)(1)(A)) or section 1010(b)(1) of the Controlled Substances Import and Export Act (21 U.S.C. 960(b)(1)).

(b) Offense and Penalties.—(1) A person who, in furtherance or to escape detection of a major drug offense and with the intent to intimidate, harass, injure, or maim, fires a weapon into a group of two or more persons and who, in the course of such conduct, causes grave risk to any human life shall be punished by a term of no more than 25 years, by fine under this title, or both.

(2) A person who, in furtherance or to escape detection of a major drug offense and with the intent to intimidate, harass, injure, or maim, fires a weapon into a group of 2 or more persons and who, in the course of such conduct, kills any person shall, if the killing—

(A) is a first degree murder (as defined in section 1111(a)), be punished by death or imprisonment for any term of years or for life, fined under this title, or both; or

(B) is a murder other than a first degree murder (as defined in section 1111(a)), be fined under this title, imprisoned for any term of years or for life, or both.

Sec. 37. Violence at international airports

(a) Offense.—A person who unlawfully and intentionally, using any device, substance, or weapon—

(1) performs an act of violence against a person at an airport serving international civil aviation that causes or is likely to cause serious bodily injury (as defined in section 1365 of this title) or death; or

(2) destroys or seriously damages the facilities of an airport serving international civil aviation or a civil aircraft not in service located thereon or disrupts the services of the airport, if such an act endangers or is likely to endanger safety at that airport, or attempts or conspires to do such an act, shall be fined under this title, imprisoned not more than 20 years, or both; and if the death of any person results from conduct prohibited by this subsection, shall be punished by death or imprisoned for any term of years or for life.

(b) Jurisdiction.—There is jurisdiction over the prohibited activity in subsection (a) if—

(1) the prohibited activity takes place in the United States; or

(2) the prohibited activity takes place outside the United States and (A) the offender is later found in the United States; or (B) an offender or a victim is a national of the United States (as defined in section 101(a)(22) of the Immigration and Nationality Act (8 U.S.C. 1101(a)(22))).

(c) Bar to Prosecution.—It is a bar to Federal prosecution under subsection (a) for conduct that occurred within the United States that the conduct involved was during or in relation to a labor dispute, and such conduct is prohibited as a felony under the law of the State in which it was committed. For purposes of this section, the term "labor dispute" has the meaning set forth in section 2(c) of the Norris-LaGuardia Act, as amended (29 U.S.C. 113(c)), and the term "State" means a State of the United States, the District of Columbia, and any commonwealth, territory, or possession of the United States.

Chapter 10—Biological Weapons

Sec. 175. Prohibitions with respect to biological weapons

(a) In General.—Whoever knowingly develops, produces, stockpiles, transfers, acquires, retains, or possesses any biological agent, toxin, or delivery system for use as a weapon, or knowingly assists a foreign state or any organization to do so, or attempts, threatens, or conspires to do the same, shall be fined under this title or imprisoned for life or any term of years, or both. There is extraterritorial Federal jurisdiction over an offense under this section committed by or against a national of the United States.

(b) Definition.—For purposes of this section, the term "for use as a weapon" does not include the development, production, transfer, acquisition, retention, or possession of any biological agent, toxin, or delivery system for prophylactic, protective, or other peaceful purposes.

Sec. 175a. Requests for military assistance to enforce prohibition in certain emergencies

The Attorney General may request the Secretary of Defense to provide assistance under section 382 of title 10 in support of Department of Justice activities relating to the enforcement of section 175 of this title in an emergency situation involving a biological weapon of mass destruction. The authority to make such a request may be exercised by another official of the Department of Justice in accordance with section 382(f)(2) of title 10.

Sec. 176. Seizure, forfeiture, and destruction

(a) In General.—(1) Except as provided in paragraph (2), the Attorney General may request the issuance, in the same manner as provided for a search warrant, of a warrant authorizing the seizure of any biological agent, toxin, or delivery system that—

> (A) exists by reason of conduct prohibited under section 175 of this title; or

> (B) is of a type or in a quantity that under the circumstances has no apparent justification for prophylactic, protective, or other peaceful purposes.

(2) In exigent circumstances, seizure and destruction of any biological agent, toxin, or delivery system described in subparagraphs (A) and (B) of paragraph (1) may be made upon probable cause without the necessity for a warrant.

(b) Procedure.—Property seized pursuant to subsection (a) shall be forfeited to the United States after notice to potential claimants and an opportunity for a hearing. At such hearing, the Government shall bear the burden of persuasion by a preponderance of the evidence. Except as inconsistent herewith, the same procedures and provisions of law relating to a forfeiture under the customs laws shall extend to a seizure or forfeiture under this section. The Attorney General may provide for the destruction or other appropriate disposition of any biological agent, toxin, or delivery system seized and forfeited pursuant to this section.

(c) Affirmative Defense.—It is an affirmative defense against a forfeiture under subsection (a)(1)(B) of this section that—

> (1) such biological agent, toxin, or delivery system is for a prophylactic, protective, or other peaceful purpose; and

> (2) such biological agent, toxin, or delivery system, is of a type and quantity reasonable for that purpose.

Sec. 177. Injunctions

(a) In General.—The United States may obtain in a civil action an injunction against—

(1) the conduct prohibited under section 175 of this title;

(2) the preparation, solicitation, attempt, threat, or conspiracy to engage in conduct prohibited under section 175 of this title; or

(3) the development, production, stockpiling, transferring, acquisition, retention, or possession, or the attempted development, production, stockpiling, transferring, acquisition, retention, or possession of any biological agent, toxin, or delivery system of a type or in a quantity that under the circumstances has no apparent justification for prophylactic, protective, or other peaceful purposes.

(b) Affirmative Defense.—It is an affirmative defense against an injunction under subsection (a)(3) of this section that—

(1) the conduct sought to be enjoined is for a prophylactic, protective, or other peaceful purpose; and

(2) such biological agent, toxin, or delivery system is of a type and quantity reasonable for that purpose.

Sec. 178. Definitions

As used in this chapter—

(1) the term "biological agent" means any micro-organism, virus, infectious substance, or biological product that may be engineered as a result of biotechnology, or any naturally occurring or bioengineered component of any such microorganism, virus, infectious substance, or biological product, capable of causing—

(A) death, disease, or other biological malfunction in a human, an animal, a plant, or another living organism;

(B) deterioration of food, water, equipment, supplies, or material of any kind; or

(C) deleterious alteration of the environment;

(2) the term "toxin" means the toxic material of plants, animals, microorganisms, viruses, fungi, or infectious substances, or a recombinant molecule, whatever its origin or method of production, including—

(A) any poisonous substance or biological product that may be engineered as a result of biotechnology produced by a living organism; or

(B) any poisonous isomer or biological product, homolog, or derivative of such a substance;

(3) the term "delivery system" means—

(A) any apparatus, equipment, device, or means of delivery specifically designed to deliver or disseminate a biological agent, toxin, or vector; or

(B) any vector;

(4) the term "vector" means a living organism, or molecule, including a recombinant molecule, or biological product that may be engineered as a result of biotechnology, capable of carrying a biological agent or toxin to a host; and

(5) the term "national of the United States" has the meaning prescribed in section 101(a)(22) of the Immigration and Nationality Act (8 U.S.C. 1101(a)(22)).

Chapter 11B—Chemical Weapons

Sec. 229. Prohibited activities

(a) Unlawful Conduct.—Except as provided in subsection (b), it shall be unlawful for any person knowingly—

(1) to develop, produce, otherwise acquire, transfer directly or indirectly, receive, stockpile, retain, own, possess, or use, or threaten to use, any chemical weapon; or

(2) to assist or induce, in any way, any person to violate paragraph (1), or to attempt or conspire to violate paragraph (1).

(b) Exempted Agencies and Persons.—

(1) In general.—Subsection (a) does not apply to the retention, ownership, possession, transfer, or receipt of a chemical weapon by a department, agency, or other entity of the United States, or by a person described in paragraph (2), pending destruction of the weapon.

(2) Exempted persons.—A person referred to in paragraph (1) is—

(A) any person, including a member of the Armed Forces of the United States, who is authorized by law or by an appropriate officer of the United States to retain, own, possess, transfer, or receive the chemical weapon; or

(B) in an emergency situation, any otherwise nonculpable person if the person is attempting to destroy or seize the weapon.

(c) Jurisdiction.—Conduct prohibited by subsection (a) is within the jurisdiction of the United States if the prohibited conduct—

(1) takes place in the United States;

(2) takes place outside of the United States and is committed by a national of the United States;

(3) is committed against a national of the United States while the national is outside the United States; or

(4) is committed against any property that is owned, leased, or used by the United States or by any department or agency of the United States, whether the property is within or outside the United States.

Sec. 229A. Penalties

(a) Criminal Penalties.—

(1) In general.—Any person who violates section 229 of this title shall be fined under this title, or imprisoned for any term of years, or both.

(2) Death penalty.—Any person who violates section 229 of this title and by whose action the death of another person is the result shall be punished by death or imprisoned for life.

(b) Civil Penalties.—

(1) In general.—The Attorney General may bring a civil action in the appropriate United States district court against any person who violates section 229 of this title and, upon proof of such violation by a preponderance of the evidence, such person shall be subject to pay a civil penalty in an amount not to exceed $100,000 for each such violation.

(2) Relation to other proceedings.—The imposition of a civil penalty under this subsection does not preclude any other criminal or civil statutory, common law, or administrative remedy, which is available by law to the United States or any other person.

(c) Reimbursement of Costs.—The court shall order any person convicted of an offense under subsection (a) to reimburse the United States for any expenses incurred by the United States incident to the seizure, storage, handling, transportation, and destruction or other disposition of any property that was seized in connection with an investigation of the commission of the offense by that person. A person ordered to reimburse the United States for expenses under this subsection shall be jointly and severally liable for such expenses with each other person, if any, who is ordered under this subsection to reimburse the United States for the same expenses.

Sec. 229B. Criminal forfeitures; destruction of weapons

(a) Property Subject to Criminal Forfeiture.—Any person convicted under section 229A(a) shall forfeit to the United States irrespective of any provision of State law—

(1) any property, real or personal, owned, possessed, or used by a person involved in the offense;

(2) any property constituting, or derived from, and proceeds the person obtained, directly or indirectly, as the result of such violation; and

(3) any of the property used in any manner or part, to commit, or to facilitate the commission of, such violation. The court, in imposing sentence on such person, shall order, in addition to any other sentence imposed pursuant to section 229A(a), that the person forfeit to the United States all property described in this subsection. In lieu of a fine otherwise authorized by section 229A(a), a defendant who derived profits or other proceeds from an offense may be fined not more than twice the gross profits or other proceeds.

(b) Procedures.—

(1) General.—Property subject to forfeiture under this section, any seizure and disposition thereof, and any administrative or judicial proceeding in relation thereto, shall be governed by subsections (b) through (p) of section 413 of the Comprehensive Drug Abuse Prevention and Control Act of 1970 (21 U.S.C. 853), except that any reference under those subsections to—

(A) "this subchapter or subchapter II" shall be deemed to be a reference to section 229A(a); and

(B) "subsection (a)" shall be deemed to be a reference to subsection (a) of this section.

(2) Temporary restraining orders.—

(A) In general.—For the purposes of forfeiture proceedings under this section, a temporary restraining order may be entered upon application of the United States without notice or opportunity for a hearing when an information or indictment has not yet been filed with respect to the property, if, in addition to the circumstances described in section 413(e)(2) of the Comprehensive Drug Abuse Prevention and Control Act of 1970 (21 U.S.C. 853(e)(2)), the United States demonstrates that there is probable cause to believe that the property with respect to which the order is sought would, in the event of conviction, be subject to forfeiture under this section and exigent circumstances exist that place the life or health of any person in danger.

(B) Warrant of seizure.—If the court enters a temporary restraining order under this paragraph, it shall also issue a warrant authorizing the seizure of such property.

(C) Applicable procedures.—The procedures and time limits applicable to temporary restraining orders under section 413(e)(2) and (3) of the Comprehensive Drug Abuse Prevention and Control Act of 1970 (21 U.S.C. 853(e)(2) and (3)) shall apply to temporary restraining orders under this paragraph.

(c) Affirmative Defense.—It is an affirmative defense against a forfeiture under subsection (b) that the property—

(1) is for a purpose not prohibited under the Chemical Weapons Convention; and

(2) is of a type and quantity that under the circumstances is consistent with that purpose.

(d) Destruction or Other Disposition.—The Attorney General shall provide for the destruction or other appropriate disposition of any chemical weapon seized and forfeited pursuant to this section.

(e) Assistance.—The Attorney General may request the head of any agency of the United States to assist in the handling, storage, transportation, or destruction of property seized under this section.

(f) Owner Liability.—The owner or possessor of any property seized under this section shall be liable to the United States for any expenses incurred incident to the seizure, including any expenses relating to the handling, storage, transportation, and destruction or other disposition of the seized property.

Sec. 229C. Individual self-defense devices

Nothing in this chapter shall be construed to prohibit any individual self-defense device, including those using a pepper spray or chemical mace.

Sec. 229D. Injunctions

The United States may obtain in a civil action an injunction against—

(1) the conduct prohibited under section 229 or 229C of this title; or

(2) the preparation or solicitation to engage in conduct prohibited under section 229 or 229D of this title.

Sec. 229E. Requests for military assistance to enforce prohibition in certain emergencies

The Attorney General may request the Secretary of Defense to provide assistance under section 382 of title 10 in support of Department of Justice activities relating to the enforcement of section 229 of this title in an emergency situation involving a chemical weapon. The authority to make such a request may be exercised by another official of the Department of Justice in accordance with section 382(f)(2) of title 10.

Sec. 229F. Definitions

In this chapter:

(1) Chemical weapon.—The term "chemical weapon" means the following, together or separately:

(A) A toxic chemical and its precursors, except where intended for a purpose not prohibited under this chapter as long as the type and quantity is consistent with such a purpose.

(B) A munition or device, specifically designed to cause death or other harm through toxic properties of those toxic chemicals specified in subparagraph (A), which would be released as a result of the employment of such munition or device.

(C) Any equipment specifically designed for use directly in connection with the employment of munitions or devices specified in subparagraph (B).

(2) Chemical weapons convention; convention.—The terms "Chemical Weapons Convention" and "Convention" mean the

Convention on the Prohibition of the Development, Production, Stockpiling and Use of Chemical Weapons and on Their Destruction, opened for signature on January 13, 1993.

(3) Key component of a binary or multicomponent chemical system.—The term "key component of a binary or multicomponent chemical system" means the precursor which plays the most important role in determining the toxic properties of the final product and reacts rapidly with other chemicals in the binary or multicomponent system.

(4) National of the united states.—The term "national of the United States" has the same meaning given such term in section 101(a)(22) of the Immigration and Nationality Act (8 U.S.C. 1101(a)(22)).

(5) Person.—The term "person," except as otherwise provided, means any individual, corporation, partnership, firm, association, trust, estate, public or private institution, any State or any political subdivision thereof, or any political entity within a State, any foreign government or nation or any agency, instrumentality or political subdivision of any such government or nation, or other entity located in the United States.

(6) Precursor.—

(A) In general.—The term "precursor" means any chemical reactant which takes part at any stage in the production by whatever method of a toxic chemical. The term includes any key component of a binary or multicomponent chemical system.

(B) List of precursors.—Precursors which have been identified for the application of verification measures under Article VI of the Convention are listed in schedules contained in the Annex on Chemicals of the Chemical Weapons Convention.

(7) Purposes not prohibited by this chapter.—The term "purposes not prohibited by this chapter" means the following:

(A) Peaceful purposes.—Any peaceful purpose related to an industrial, agricultural, research, medical, or pharmaceutical activity or other activity.

(B) Protective purposes.—Any purpose directly related to protection against toxic chemicals and to protection against chemical weapons.

(C) Unrelated military purposes.—Any military purpose of the United States that is not connected with the use of a chemical weapon or that is not dependent on the use of the toxic or poisonous properties of the chemical weapon to cause death or other harm.

(D) Law enforcement purposes.—Any law enforcement purpose, including any domestic riot control purpose and including imposition of capital punishment.

(8) Toxic chemical.—

(A) In general.—The term "toxic chemical" means any chemical which through its chemical action on life processes can cause death, temporary incapacitation or permanent harm to humans or animals. The term includes all such chemicals, regardless of their origin or of their method of production, and regardless of whether they are produced in facilities, in munitions or elsewhere.

(B) List of toxic chemicals.—Toxic chemicals which have been identified for the application of verification measures under Article VI of the Convention are listed in schedules contained in the Annex on Chemicals of the Chemical Weapons Convention.

(9) United states.—The term "United States" means the several States of the United States, the District of Columbia, and the commonwealths, territories, and possessions of the United States and includes all places under the jurisdiction or control of the United States, including—

(A) any of the places within the provisions of paragraph (41) of section 40102 of title 49, United States Code;

(B) any civil aircraft of the United States or public aircraft, as such terms are defined in paragraphs (17) and (37), respectively, of section 40102 of title 49, United States Code; and

(C) any vessel of the United States, as such term is defined in section 3(b) of the Maritime Drug Enforcement Act, as amended (46 U.S.C., App. sec. 1903(b)).

Chapter 18—Congressional, Cabinet, and Supreme Court Assassination, Kidnapping, and Assault

Sec. 351. Congressional, Cabinet, and Supreme Court assassination, kidnapping, and assault; penalties

(a) Whoever kills any individual who is a Member of Congress or a Member-of-Congress-elect, a member of the executive branch of the Government who is the head, or a person nominated to be head during the pendency of such nomination, of a department listed in section 101 of title 5 or the second ranking official in such department, the Director (or a person nominated to be Director during the pendency of such nomination) or Deputy Director of Central Intelligence, a major Presidential or Vice Presidential candidate (as defined in section 3056 of this title), or a Justice of the United States, as defined in section 451 of title 28, or a person nominated to be a Justice of the United States, during the pendency of such nomination, shall be punished as provided by sections 1111 and 1112 of this title.

(b) Whoever kidnaps any individual designated in subsection (a) of this section shall be punished (1) by imprisonment for any term of years or for life, or (2) by death or imprisonment for any term of years or for life, if death results to such individual.

(c) Whoever attempts to kill or kidnap any individual designated in subsection (a) of this section shall be punished by imprisonment for any term of years or for life.

(d) If two or more persons conspire to kill or kidnap any individual designated in subsection (a) of this section and one or more of such persons do any act to effect the object of the conspiracy, each shall be punished (1) by imprisonment for any term of years or for life, or (2) by death or imprisonment for any term of years or for life, if death results to such individual.

(e) Whoever assaults any person designated in subsection (a) of this section shall be fined under this title, or imprisoned not more than one year, or both; and if the assault involved the use of a dangerous weapon, or personal injury results, shall be fined under this title, or imprisoned not more than ten years, or both.

(f) If Federal investigative or prosecutive jurisdiction is asserted for a violation of this section, such assertion shall suspend the exercise of jurisdiction by a State or local authority, under any applicable State or local law, until Federal action is terminated.

(g) Violations of this section shall be investigated by the Federal Bureau of Investigation. Assistance may be requested from any Federal, State, or local agency, including the Army, Navy, and Air Force, any statute, rule, or regulation to the contrary notwithstanding.

(h) In a prosecution for an offense under this section the Government need not prove that the defendant knew that the victim of the offense was an individual protected by this section.

(i) There is extraterritorial jurisdiction over the conduct prohibited by this section.

Chapter 39—Explosives and Other Dangerous Articles

Sec. 831. Prohibited transactions involving nuclear materials

(a) Whoever, if one of the circumstances described in subsection (c) of this section occurs—

(1) without lawful authority, intentionally receives, possesses, uses, transfers, alters, disposes of, or disperses any nuclear material or nuclear byproduct material and—

(A) thereby knowingly causes the death of or serious bodily injury to any person or substantial damage to property or to the environment; or

(B) circumstances exist, or have been represented to the defendant to exist, that are likely to cause the death or serious bodily injury to any person, or substantial damage to property or to the environment;

(2) with intent to deprive another of nuclear material or nuclear byproduct material, knowingly—

(A) takes and carries away nuclear material or nuclear byproduct material of another without authority;

(B) makes an unauthorized use, disposition, or transfer, of nuclear material or nuclear byproduct material belonging to another; or

(C) uses fraud and thereby obtains nuclear material or nuclear byproduct material belonging to another;

(3) knowingly—

(A) uses force; or

(B) threatens or places another in fear that any person other than the actor will imminently be subject to bodily injury; and thereby takes nuclear material or nuclear byproduct material belonging to another from the person or presence of any other;

(4) intentionally intimidates any person and thereby obtains nuclear material or nuclear byproduct material belonging to another;

(5) with intent to compel any person, international organization, or governmental entity to do or refrain from doing any act, knowingly threatens to engage in conduct described in paragraph (2)(A) or (3) of this subsection;

(6) knowingly threatens to use nuclear material or nuclear byproduct material to cause death or serious bodily injury to any person or substantial damage to property or to the environment under circumstances in which the threat may reasonably be understood as an expression of serious purposes;

(7) attempts to commit an offense under paragraph (1), (2), (3), (4) of this section or,

(8) is a party to a conspiracy of two or more persons to commit an offense under paragraph (1), (2), (3), or (4) of this subsection, if any of the parties intentionally engages in any conduct in furtherance of such offense; shall be punished as provided in subsection (b) of this section.

(b) The punishment for an offense under—

(1) paragraphs (1) through (7) of subsection (a) of this section is—

(A) a fine under this title; and

(B) imprisonment—

(i) for any term of years or for life (I) if, while committing the offense, the offender knowingly causes the death of any person; or (II) if, while committing an offense under paragraph (1) or (3) of subsection (a) of this section, the offender, under circumstances manifesting extreme indifference to the life of an individual, knowingly engages in any conduct and thereby recklessly causes the death of or serious bodily injury to any person; and

(ii) for not more than 20 years in any other case; and

(2) paragraph (8) of subsection (a) of this section is—

(A) a fine under this title; and

(B) imprisonment—

(i) for not more than 20 years if the offense which is the object of the conspiracy is punishable under paragraph (1)(B)(i); and

(ii) for not more than 10 years in any other case.

(c) The circumstances referred to in subsection (a) of this section are that—

(1) the offense is committed in the United States or the special maritime and territorial jurisdiction of the United States, or the special aircraft jurisdiction of the United States (as defined in section 46501 of title 49);

(2) an offender or a victim is—

(A) a national of the United States; or

(B) a United States corporation or other legal entity;

(3) after the conduct required for the offense occurs the defendant is found in the United States, even if the conduct required for the offense occurs outside the United States;

(4) the conduct required for the offense occurs with respect to the carriage of a consignment of nuclear material or nuclear byproduct material by any means of transportation intended to go beyond the territory of the state where the shipment originates beginning with the departure from a facility of the shipper in that state and ending with the arrival at a facility of the receiver within the state of ultimate destination and either of such states is the United States; or

(5) either—

(A) the governmental entity under subsection (a)(5) is the United States; or

(B) the threat under subsection (a)(6) is directed at the United States.

(d) The Attorney General may request assistance from the Secretary of Defense under chapter 18 of title 10 in the enforcement of this section and the Secretary of Defense may provide such assistance in accordance with chapter 18 of title 10, except that the Secretary of Defense may provide such assistance through any Department of Defense personnel.

(e)

(1) The Attorney General may also request assistance from the Secretary of Defense under this subsection in the enforcement of this section. Notwithstanding section 1385 of this title, the Secretary of Defense may, in accordance with other applicable law, provide such assistance to the Attorney General if—

(A) an emergency situation exists (as jointly determined by the Attorney General and the Secretary of Defense in their discretion); and

(B) the provision of such assistance will not adversely affect the military preparedness of the United States (as determined by the Secretary of Defense in such Secretary's discretion).

(2) As used in this subsection, the term "emergency situation" means a circumstance—

(A) that poses a serious threat to the interests of the United States; and

(B) in which—

(i) enforcement of the law would be seriously impaired if the assistance were not provided; and

(ii) civilian law enforcement personnel are not capable of enforcing the law.

(3) Assistance under this section may include—

(A) use of personnel of the Department of Defense to arrest persons and conduct searches and seizures with respect to violations of this section; and

(B) such other activity as is incidental to the enforcement of this section, or to the protection of persons or property from conduct that violates this section.

(4) The Secretary of Defense may require reimbursement as a condition of assistance under this section.

(5) The Attorney General may delegate the Attorney General's function under this subsection only to a Deputy, Associate, or Assistant Attorney General.

(f) As used in this section—

(1) the term "nuclear material" means material containing any—

(A) plutonium;

(B) uranium not in the form of ore or ore residue that contains the mixture of isotopes as occurring in nature;

(C) enriched uranium, defined as uranium that contains the isotope 233 or 235 or both in such amount that the abundance ratio of the sum of those isotopes to the isotope 238 is greater than the ratio of the isotope 235 to the isotope 238 occurring in nature; or

(D) uranium 233;

(2) the term "nuclear byproduct material" means any material containing any radioactive isotope created through an irradiation process in the operation of a nuclear reactor or accelerator;

(3) the term "international organization" means a public international organization designated as such pursuant to section 1 of the International Organizations Immunities Act (22 U.S.C. 288) or a public organization created pursuant to treaty or other agreement under international law as an instrument through or by which two or more foreign governments engage in some aspect of their conduct of international affairs;

(4) the term "serious bodily injury" means bodily injury which involves—

(A) a substantial risk of death;

(B) extreme physical pain;

(C) protracted and obvious disfigurement; or

(D) protracted loss or impairment of the function of a bodily member, organ, or mental faculty;

(5) the term "bodily injury" means—

(A) a cut, abrasion, bruise, burn, or disfigurement;

(B) physical pain;

(C) illness;

(D) impairment of a function of a bodily member, organ, or mental faculty; or

(E) any other injury to the body, no matter how temporary;

(6) the term "national of the United States" has the same meaning as in section 101(a)(22) of the Immigration and Nationality Act (8 U.S.C. 1101(a)(22)); and

(7) the term "United States corporation or other legal entity" means any corporation or other entity organized under the laws of the United States or any State, Commonwealth, territory, possession, or district of the United States.

Chapter 40—Importation, Manufacture, Distribution and Storage of Explosive Materials

Sec. 841. Definitions

As used in this chapter—

(a) "Person" means any individual, corporation, company, association, firm, partnership, society, or joint stock company.

(b) "Interstate" or foreign commerce means commerce between any place in a State and any place outside of that State, or within any possession of the United States (not including the Canal Zone) or the District of Columbia, and commerce between places within the same State but through any place outside of that State. "State" includes the District of Columbia, the Commonwealth of Puerto Rico, and the possessions of the United States (not including the Canal Zone).

(c) "Explosive materials" means explosives, blasting agents, and detonators.

(d) Except for the purposes of subsections (d), (e), (f), (g), (h), (i), and (j) of this title, "explosive" means any chemical compound mixture, or device, the primary or common purpose of which is to function by explosion; the term includes, but is not limited to, dynamite and other high explosives, black powder, pellet powder, initiating explosives, detonators, safety fuses, squibs, detonating cord, igniter cord, and igniters. The Secretary shall publish and revise at least annually in the Federal Register a list of these and any additional explosives which he determines to be within the coverage of this chapter. For the purposes of subsections (d), (e), (f), (g), term "explosive" is defined in subsection (j) of such section 844.

(e) "Blasting agent" means any material or mixture, consisting of fuel and oxidizer, intended for blasting, not otherwise defined as an explosive: Provided, That the finished product, as mixed for use or shipment, cannot be detonated by means of a numbered 8 test blasting cap when unconfined.

(f) "Detonator" means any device containing a detonating charge that is used for initiating detonation in an explosive; the term includes, but is not limited to, electric blasting caps of instantaneous and delay types, blasting caps for use with safety fuses and detonating-cord delay connectors.

(g) "Importer" means any person engaged in the business of importing or bringing explosive materials into the United States for purposes of sale or distribution.

(h) "Manufacturer" means any person engaged in the business of manufacturing explosive materials for purposes of sale or distribution or for his own use.

(i) "Dealer" means any person engaged in the business of distributing explosive materials at wholesale or retail.

(j) "Permittee" means any user of explosives for a lawful purpose, who has obtained a user permit under the provisions of this chapter.

(k) "Secretary" means the Secretary of the Treasury or his delegate.

(l) "Crime punishable by imprisonment for a term exceeding one year" shall not mean (1) any Federal or State offenses pertaining to antitrust violations, unfair trade practices, restraints of trade, or other similar offenses relating to the regulation of business practices as the Secretary may by regulation designate, or (2) any State offense (other than one involving a firearm or explosive) classified by the laws of the State as a misdemeanor and punishable by a term of imprisonment of two years or less.

(m) "Licensee" means any importer, manufacturer, or dealer licensed under the provisions of this chapter.

(n) "Distribute" means sell, issue, give, transfer, or otherwise dispose of.

(o) "Convention on the Marking of Plastic Explosives" means the Convention on the Marking of Plastic Explosives for the Purpose of Detection, Done at Montreal on 1 March 1991.

(p) "Detection agent" means any one of the substances specified in this subsection when introduced into a plastic explosive or formulated in such explosive as a part of the manufacturing process in such a manner as to achieve homogeneous distribution in the finished explosive, including—

(1) Ethylene glycol dinitrate (EGDN), C (INFERIOR 2)H (INFE-RIOR 4)(NO (INFERIOR 3)) (INFERIOR 2), molecular weight 152, when the minimum concentration in the finished explosive is 0.2 percent by mass;

(2) 2,3-Dimethyl-2,3-dinitrobutane (DMNB), C (INFERIOR 6)H (INFERIOR 12)(NO (INFERIOR 2)) (INFERIOR 2), molecular weight 176, when the minimum concentration in the finished explosive is 0.1 percent by mass;

(3) Para-Mononitrotoluene (p-MNT), C (INFERIOR 7)H (INFE-RIOR 7)NO (INFERIOR 2), molecular weight 137, when the minimum concentration in the finished explosive is 0.5 percent by mass;

(4) Ortho-Mononitrotoluene (o-MNT), C (INFERIOR 7)H (INFERIOR 7)NO (INFERIOR 2), molecular weight 137, when the minimum concentration in the finished explosive is 0.5 percent by mass; and

(5) any other substance in the concentration specified by the Secretary, after consultation with the Secretary of State and the Secretary of Defense, that has been added to the table in part 2 of the Technical Annex to the Convention on the Marking of Plastic Explosives.

(q) "Plastic explosive" means an explosive material in flexible or elastic sheet form formulated with one or more high explosives which in their pure form has a vapor pressure less than 10- Pa at a temperature of 25 (degrees) C., is formulated with a binder material, and is as a mixture malleable or flexible at normal room temperature.

Sec. 842. Unlawful acts

(a) It shall be unlawful for any person—

(1) to engage in the business of importing, manufacturing, or dealing in explosive materials without a license issued under this chapter;

(2) knowingly to withhold information or to make any false or fictitious oral or written statement or to furnish or exhibit any false, fictitious, or misrepresented identification, intended or likely to deceive for the purpose of obtaining explosive materials, or a license, permit, exemption, or relief from disability under the provisions of this chapter; and

(3) other than a licensee or permittee knowingly—

(A) to transport, ship, cause to be transported, or receive in interstate or foreign commerce any explosive materials, except that a person who lawfully purchases explosive materials from a licensee in a State contiguous to the State in which the purchaser resides may ship, transport, or cause to be transported such explosive materials to the State in which he resides and may receive such explosive materials in the State in which he resides, if such transportation, shipment, or receipt is permitted by the law of the State in which he resides; or

(B) to distribute explosive materials to any person (other than a licensee or permittee) who the distributor knows or has reasonable cause to believe does not reside in the State in which the distributor resides.

(b) It shall be unlawful for any licensee knowingly to distribute any explosive materials to any person except—

(1) a licensee;

(2) a permittee; or

(3) a resident of the State where distribution is made and in which the licensee is licensed to do business or a State contiguous thereto if permitted by the law of the State of the purchaser's residence.

(c) It shall be unlawful for any licensee to distribute explosive materials to any person who the licensee has reason to believe intends to transport such explosive materials into a State where the purchase, possession, or use of explosive materials is prohibited or which does not permit its residents to transport or ship explosive materials into it or to receive explosive materials in it.

(d) It shall be unlawful for any person knowingly to distribute explosive materials to any individual who:

(1) is under twenty-one years of age;

(2) has been convicted in any court of a crime punishable by imprisonment for a term exceeding one year;

(3) is under indictment for a crime punishable by imprisonment for a term exceeding one year;

(4) is a fugitive from justice;

(5) is an unlawful user of or addicted to any controlled substance

(as defined in section 102 of the Controlled Substances Act (21 U.S.C. 802)); or

(6) has been adjudicated a mental defective.

(e) It shall be unlawful for any licensee knowingly to distribute any explosive materials to any person in any State where the purchase, possession, or use by such person of such explosive materials would be in violation of any State law or any published ordinance applicable at the place of distribution.

(f) It shall be unlawful for any licensee or permittee willfully to manufacture, import, purchase, distribute, or receive explosive materials without making such records as the Secretary may by regulation require, including, but not limited to, a statement of intended use, the name, date, place of birth, social security number or taxpayer identification number, and place of residence of any natural person to whom explosive materials are distributed. If explosive materials are distributed to a corporation or other business entity, such records shall include the identity and principal and local places of business and the name, date, place of birth, and place of residence of the natural person acting as agent of the corporation or other business entity in arranging the distribution.

(g) It shall be unlawful for any licensee or permittee knowingly to make any false entry in any record which he is required to keep pursuant to this section or regulations promulgated under section 847 of this title.

(h) It shall be unlawful for any person to receive, possess, transport, ship, conceal, store, barter, sell, dispose of, or pledge or accept as security for a loan, any stolen explosive materials which are moving as, which are part of, which constitute, or which have been shipped or transported in, interstate or foreign commerce, either before or after such materials were stolen, knowing or having reasonable cause to believe that the explosive materials were stolen.

(i) It shall be unlawful for any person—

(1) who is under indictment for, or who has been convicted in any court of, a crime punishable by imprisonment for a term exceeding one year;

(2) who is a fugitive from justice;

(3) who is an unlawful user of or addicted to any controlled substance (as defined in section 102 of the Controlled Substances Act (21 U.S.C. 802)); or

(4) who has been adjudicated as a mental defective or who has been committed to a mental institution; to ship or transport any explosive in interstate or foreign commerce or to receive or possess any explosive which has been shipped or transported in interstate or foreign commerce.

(j) It shall be unlawful for any person to store any explosive material in a manner not in conformity with regulations promulgated by the Secretary. In promulgating such regulations, the Secretary shall take into consideration the class, type, and quantity of explosive materials to be stored, as well as the standards of safety and security recognized in the explosives industry.

(k) It shall be unlawful for any person who has knowledge of the theft or loss of any explosive materials from his stock, to fail to report such theft or loss within twenty-four hours of discovery thereof, to the Secretary and to appropriate local authorities.

(l) It shall be unlawful for any person to manufacture any plastic explosive that does not contain a detection agent.

(m)

(1) It shall be unlawful for any person to import or bring into the United States, or export from the United States, any plastic explosive that does not contain a detection agent.

(2) This subsection does not apply to the importation or bringing into the United States, or the exportation from the United States, of any plastic explosive that was imported or brought into, or manufactured in the United States prior to the date of enactment of this subsection by or on behalf of any agency of the United States performing military or police functions (including any military reserve component) or by or on behalf of the National Guard of any State, not later than 15 years after the date of entry into force of the Convention on the Marking of Plastic Explosives, with respect to the United States.

(n)

(1) It shall be unlawful for any person to ship, transport, transfer, receive, or possess any plastic explosive that does not contain a detection agent.

(2) This subsection does not apply to—

(A) the shipment, transportation, transfer, receipt, or possession of any plastic explosive that was imported or brought into, or manufactured in the United States prior to the date of enactment of this subsection by any person during the period beginning on that date and ending 3 years after that date of enactment; or

(B) the shipment, transportation, transfer, receipt, or possession of any plastic explosive that was imported or brought into, or manufactured in the United States prior to the date of enactment of this subsection by or on behalf of any agency of the United States performing a military or police function (including any military reserve component) or by or on behalf of the National Guard of any State, not later than 15 years after the date of entry into force of the Convention on the Marking of Plastic Explosives, with respect to the United States.

(o) It shall be unlawful for any person, other than an agency of the United States (including any military reserve component) or the National Guard of any State, possessing any plastic explosive on the date of enactment of this subsection, to fail to report to the Secretary within 120 days after such date of enactment the quantity of such explosives possessed, the manufacturer or importer, any marks of identification on such explosives, and such other information as the Secretary may prescribe by regulation.

(p) Distribution of Information Relating to Explosives, Destructive Devices, and Weapons of Mass Destruction.—

(1) Definitions.—In this subsection—

(A) the term "destructive device" has the same meaning as in section 921(a)(4);

(B) the term "explosive" has the same meaning as in section 844(j); and

(C) the term "weapon of mass destruction" has the same meaning as in section 2332a(c)(2).

(2) Prohibition.—It shall be unlawful for any person—

(A) to teach or demonstrate the making or use of an explosive, a destructive device, or a weapon of mass destruction, or to distribute by any means information pertaining to, in whole or in part, the manufacture or use of an explosive, destructive device, or weapon of mass destruction, with the intent that the teaching, demonstration, or information be used for, or in furtherance of, an activity that constitutes a Federal crime of violence; or

(B) to teach or demonstrate to any person the making or use of an explosive, a destructive device, or a weapon of mass destruction, or to distribute to any person, by any means, information pertaining to, in whole or in part, the manufacture or use of an explosive, destructive device, or weapon of mass destruction, knowing that such person intends to use the teaching, demonstration, or information for, or in furtherance of, an activity that constitutes a Federal crime of violence.

Sec. 843. Licenses and user permits

(a) An application for a user permit or a license to import, manufacture, or deal in explosive materials shall be in such form and contain such information as the Secretary shall by regulation prescribe. Each applicant for a license or permit shall pay a fee to be charged as set by the Secretary, said fee not to exceed $200 for each license or permit. Each license or permit shall be valid for no longer than three years from date of issuance and shall be renewable upon the same conditions and subject to the same restrictions as the original license or permit and upon payment of a renewal fee not to exceed one-half of the original fee.

(b) Upon the filing of a proper application and payment of the prescribed fee, and subject to the provisions of this chapter and other applicable laws, the Secretary shall issue to such applicant the appropriate license or permit if—

(1) the applicant (including in the case of a corporation, partnership, or association, any individual possessing, directly or indirectly, the power to direct or cause the direction of the management and policies of the corporation, partnership, or association) is not a person to whom the distribution of explosive materials would be unlawful under section 842(d) of this chapter;

(2) the applicant has not willfully violated any of the provisions of this chapter or regulations issued hereunder;

(3) the applicant has in a State premises from which he conducts or intends to conduct business;

(4) the applicant has a place of storage for explosive materials which meets such standards of public safety and security against theft as the Secretary by regulations shall prescribe; and

(5) the applicant has demonstrated and certified in writing that he is familiar with all published State laws and local ordinances relat-

ing to explosive materials for the location in which he intends to do business.

(c)   The Secretary shall approve or deny an application within a period of forty-five days beginning on the date such application is received by the Secretary.

(d)   The Secretary may revoke any license or permit issued under this section if in the opinion of the Secretary the holder thereof has violated any provision of this chapter or any rule or regulation prescribed by the Secretary under this chapter, or has become ineligible to acquire explosive materials under section 842(d). The Secretary's action under this subsection may be reviewed only as provided in subsection (e)(2) of this section.

(e)

(1)   Any person whose application is denied or whose license or permit is revoked shall receive a written notice from the Secretary stating the specific grounds upon which such denial or revocation is based. Any notice of a revocation of a license or permit shall be given to the holder of such license or permit prior to or concurrently with the effective date of the revocation.

(2)   If the Secretary denies an application for, or revokes a license, or permit, he shall, upon request by the aggrieved party, promptly hold a hearing to review his denial or revocation. In the case of a revocation, the Secretary may upon a request of the holder stay the effective date of the revocation. A hearing under this section shall be at a location convenient to the aggrieved party. The Secretary shall give written notice of his decision to the aggrieved party within a reasonable time after the hearing. The aggrieved party may, within sixty days after receipt of the Secretary's written decision, file a petition with the United States court of appeals for the district in which he resides or has his principal place of business for a judicial review of such denial or revocation, pursuant to sections *701-706* of title 5, United States Code.

(f)   Licensees and permittees shall make available for inspection at all reasonable times their records kept pursuant to this chapter or the regulations issued hereunder, and shall submit to the Secretary such reports and information with respect to such records and the contents thereof as he shall by regulations prescribe. The Secretary may enter during business hours the premises (including places of storage) of any licensee or permittee, for the purpose of inspecting or examining (1) any records or documents required to be kept by such licensee or permittee, under the provisions of this chapter or regulations issued hereunder, and (2) any explosive materials kept or stored by such licensee or permittee at such premises. Upon the request of any State or any political subdivision thereof, the Secretary may make available to such State or any political subdivision thereof, any information which he may obtain by reason of the provisions of this chapter with respect to the identification of persons within such State or political subdivision thereof, who have purchased or received explosive materials, together with a description of such explosive materials.

(g) Licenses and permits issued under the provisions of subsection (b) of this section shall be kept posted and kept available for inspection on the premises covered by the license and permit.

Sec. 844. Penalties

(a) Any person who—

(1) violates any of subsections (a) through (i) or (l) through (o) of section 842 shall be fined under this title, imprisoned for not more than 10 years, or both; and

(2) violates subsection (p)(2) of section 842, shall be fined under this title, imprisoned not more than 20 years, or both.

(b) Any person who violates any other provision of section 842 of this chapter shall be fined under this title or imprisoned not more than one year, or both.

(c)

(1) Any explosive materials involved or used or intended to be used in any violation of the provisions of this chapter or any other rule or regulation promulgated thereunder or any violation of any criminal law of the United States shall be subject to seizure and forfeiture, and all provisions of the Internal Revenue Code of 1986 relating to the seizure, forfeiture, and disposition of firearms, as defined in section 5845(a) of that Code, shall, so far as applicable, extend to seizures and forfeitures under the provisions of this chapter.

(2) Notwithstanding paragraph (1), in the case of the seizure of any explosive materials for any offense for which the materials would be subject to forfeiture in which it would be impracticable or unsafe to remove the materials to a place of storage or would be unsafe to

store them, the seizing officer may destroy the explosive materials forthwith. Any destruction under this paragraph shall be in the presence of at least 1 credible witness. The seizing officer shall make a report of the seizure and take samples as the Secretary may by regulation prescribe.

(3) Within 60 days after any destruction made pursuant to paragraph (2), the owner of (including any person having an interest in) the property so destroyed may make application to the Secretary for reimbursement of the value of the property. If the claimant establishes to the satisfaction of the Secretary that—

(A) the property has not been used or involved in a violation of law; or

(B) any unlawful involvement or use of the property was without the claimant's knowledge, consent, or willful blindness, the Secretary shall make an allowance to the claimant not exceeding the value of the property destroyed.

(d) Whoever transports or receives, or attempts to transport or receive, in interstate or foreign commerce any explosive with the knowledge or intent that it will be used to kill, injure, or intimidate any individual or unlawfully to damage or destroy any building, vehicle, or other real or personal property, shall be imprisoned for not more than ten years, or fined under this title, or both; and if personal injury results to any person, including any public safety officer performing duties as a direct or proximate result of conduct prohibited by this subsection, shall be imprisoned for not more than twenty years or fined under this title, or both; and if death results to any person, including any public safety officer performing duties as a direct or proximate result of conduct prohibited by this subsection, shall be subject to imprisonment for any term of years, or to the death penalty or to life imprisonment.

(e) Whoever, through the use of the mail, telephone, telegraph, or other instrument of interstate or foreign commerce, or in or affecting interstate or foreign commerce, willfully makes any threat, or maliciously conveys false information knowing the same to be false, concerning an attempt or alleged attempt being made, or to be made, to kill, injure, or intimidate any individual or unlawfully to damage or destroy any building, vehicle, or other real or personal property by means of fire or an explosive shall be imprisoned for not more than 10 years or fined under this title, or both.

(f)

(1) Whoever maliciously damages or destroys, or attempts to damage or destroy, by means of fire or an explosive, any building, vehicle, or other personal or real property in whole or in part owned or possessed by, or leased to, the United States, or any department or agency thereof, shall be imprisoned for not less than 5 years and not more than 20 years, fined under this title, or both.

(2) Whoever engages in conduct prohibited by this subsection, and as a result of such conduct, directly or proximately causes personal injury or creates a substantial risk of injury to any person, including any public safety officer performing duties, shall be imprisoned for not less than 7 years and not more than 40 years, fined under this title, or both.

(3) Whoever engages in conduct prohibited by this subsection, and as a result of such conduct directly or proximately causes the death of any person, including any public safety officer performing duties, shall be subject to the death penalty, or imprisoned for not less than 20 years or for life, fined under this title, or both.

(g)

(1) Except as provided in paragraph (2), whoever possesses an explosive in an airport that is subject to the regulatory authority of the Federal Aviation Administration, or in any building in whole or in part owned, possessed, or used by, or leased to, the United States or any department or agency thereof, except with the written consent of the agency, department, or other person responsible for the management of such building or airport, shall be imprisoned for not more than five years, or fined under this title, or both.

(2) The provisions of this subsection shall not be applicable to—

(A) the possession of ammunition (as that term is defined in regulations issued pursuant to this chapter) in an airport that is subject to the regulatory authority of the Federal Aviation Administration if such ammunition is either in checked baggage or in a closed container; or

(B) the possession of an explosive in an airport if the packaging and transportation of such explosive is exempt from, or subject to and in accordance with, regulations of the Research and Special Projects Administration for the handling of hazardous materials pursuant to chapter 51 of title 49.

(h) Whoever—

(1) uses fire or an explosive to commit any felony which may be prosecuted in a court of the United States, or

(2) carries an explosive during the commission of any felony which may be prosecuted in a court of the United States, including a felony which provides for an enhanced punishment if committed by the use of a deadly or dangerous weapon or device shall, in addition to the punishment provided for such felony, be sentenced to imprisonment for 10 years. In the case of a second or subsequent conviction under this subsection, such person shall be sentenced to imprisonment for 20 years. Notwithstanding any other provision of law, the court shall not place on probation or suspend the sentence of any person convicted of a violation of this subsection, nor shall the term of imprisonment imposed under this subsection run concurrently with any other term of imprisonment including that imposed for the felony in which the explosive was used or carried.

(i) Whoever maliciously damages or destroys, or attempts to damage or destroy, by means of fire or an explosive, any building, vehicle, or other real or personal property used in interstate or foreign commerce or in any activity affecting interstate or foreign commerce shall be imprisoned for not less than 5 years and not more than 20 years, fined under this title, or both; and if personal injury results to any person, including any public safety officer performing duties as a direct or proximate result of conduct prohibited by this subsection, shall be imprisoned for not less than 7 years and not more than 40 years, fined under this title, or both; and if death results to any person, including any public safety officer performing duties as a direct or proximate result of conduct prohibited by this subsection, shall also be subject to imprisonment for any term of years, or to the death penalty or to life imprisonment.

(j) For the purposes of subsections (d), (e), (f), (g), (h), and (i) of this section and section 842(p), the term "explosive" means gunpowders, powders used for blasting, all forms of high explosives, blasting materials, fuzes (other than electric circuit breakers), detonators, and other detonating agents, smokeless powders, other explosive or incendiary devices within the meaning of paragraph (5) of section 232 of this title, and any chemical compounds, mechanical mixture, or device that contains any oxidizing and combustible units, or other ingredients, in such proportions, quantities, or packing that ignition by fire, by friction, by concussion, by percussion, or by detonation of the compound, mixture, or device or any part thereof may cause an explosion.

(k) A person who steals any explosives materials which are moving as, or are a part of, or which have moved in, interstate or foreign commerce shall be imprisoned for not more than 10 years, fined under this title, or both.

(l) A person who steals any explosive material from a licensed importer, licensed manufacturer, or licensed dealer, or from any permittee shall be fined under this title, imprisoned not more than 10 years, or both.

(m) A person who conspires to commit an offense under subsection (h) shall be imprisoned for any term of years not exceeding 20, fined under this title, or both.

(n) Except as otherwise provided in this section, a person who conspires to commit any offense defined in this chapter shall be subject to the same penalties (other than the penalty of death) as the penalties prescribed for the offense the commission of which was the object of the conspiracy.

(o) Whoever knowingly transfers any explosive materials, knowing or having reasonable cause to believe that such explosive materials will be used to commit a crime of violence (as defined in section 924(c)(3)) or drug trafficking crime (as defined in section 924(c)(2)) shall be subject to the same penalties as may be imposed under subsection (h) for a first conviction for the use or carrying of an explosive material.

Sec. 845. Exceptions; relief from disabilities

(a) Except in the case of subsections (l), (m), (n), or (o) of section 842 and subsections (d), (e), (f), (g), (h), and (i) of section 844 of this title, this chapter shall not apply to:

> (1) any aspect of the transportation of explosive materials via railroad, water, highway, or air which are regulated by the United States Department of Transportation and agencies thereof, and which pertain to safety;

> (2) the use of explosive materials in medicines and medicinal agents in the forms prescribed by the official United States Pharmacopeia, or the National Formulary;

> (3) the transportation, shipment, receipt, or importation of explosive materials for delivery to any agency of the United States or to any State or political subdivision thereof;

(4) small arms ammunition and components thereof;

(5) commercially manufactured black powder in quantities not to exceed fifty pounds, percussion caps, safety and pyrotechnic fuses, quills, quick and slow matches, and friction primers, intended to be used solely for sporting, recreational, or cultural purposes in antique firearms as defined in section 921(a)(16) of title 18 of the United States Code, or in antique devices as exempted from the term "destructive device" in section 921(a)(4) of title 18 of the United States Code; and

(6) the manufacture under the regulation of the military department of the United States of explosive materials for, or their distribution to or storage or possession by the military or naval services or other agencies of the United States; or to arsenals, navy yards, depots, or other establishments owned by, or operated by or on behalf of, the United States.

(b) A person who had been indicted for or convicted of a crime punishable by imprisonment for a term exceeding one year may make application to the Secretary for relief from the disabilities imposed by this chapter with respect to engaging in the business of importing, manufacturing, or dealing in explosive materials, or the purchase of explosive materials, and incurred by reason of such indictment or conviction, and the Secretary may grant such relief if it is established to his satisfaction that the circumstances regarding the indictment or conviction, and the applicant's record and reputation, are such that the applicant will not be likely to act in a manner dangerous to public safety and that the granting of the relief will not be contrary to the public interest. A licensee or permittee who makes application for relief from the disabilities incurred under this chapter by reason of indictment or conviction, shall not be barred by such indictment or conviction from further operations under his license or permit pending final action on an application for relief filed pursuant to this section.

(c) It is an affirmative defense against any proceeding involving subsections (l) through (o) of section 842 if the proponent proves by a preponderance of the evidence that the plastic explosive—

(1) consisted of a small amount of plastic explosive intended for and utilized solely in lawful—

(A) research, development, or testing of new or modified explosive materials;

(B)   training in explosives detection or development or testing of explosives detection equipment; or

(C)   forensic science purposes; or

(2)   was plastic explosive that, within 3 years after the date of enactment of the Antiterrorism and Effective Death Penalty Act of 1996, will be or is incorporated in a military device within the territory of the United States and remains an integral part of such military device, or is intended to be, or is incorporated in, and remains an integral part of a military device that is intended to become, or has become, the property of any agency of the United States performing military or police functions (including any military reserve component) or the National Guard of any State, wherever such device is located.

(3)   For purposes of this subsection, the term "military device" includes, but is not restricted to, shells, bombs, projectiles, mines, missiles, rockets, shaped charges, grenades, perforators, and similar devices lawfully manufactured exclusively for military or police purposes.

Sec. 846. Additional powers of the Secretary

(a)   The Secretary is authorized to inspect the site of any accident, or fire, in which there is reason to believe that explosive materials were involved, in order that if any such incident has been brought about by accidental means, precautions may be taken to prevent similar accidents from occurring. In order to carry out the purpose of this subsection, the Secretary is authorized to enter into or upon any property where explosive materials have been used, are suspected of having been used, or have been found in an otherwise unauthorized location. Nothing in this chapter shall be construed as modifying or otherwise affecting in any way the investigative authority of any other Federal agency. In addition to any other investigatory authority they have with respect to violations of provisions of this chapter, the Attorney General and the Federal Bureau of Investigation, together with the Secretary, shall have authority to conduct investigations with respect to violations of subsection (d), (e), (f), (g), (h), or (i) of section 844 of this title.

(b)   The Secretary is authorized to establish a national repository of information on incidents involving arson and the suspected criminal misuse of explosives. All Federal agencies having information concerning such incidents shall report the information to the Secretary pursuant to such regulations as deemed necessary to carry out the provisions of this subsection. The repository shall also contain information on incidents voluntarily reported to the Secretary by State and local authorities.

Sec. 847. Rules and regulations

The administration of this chapter shall be vested in the Secretary. The Secretary may prescribe such rules and regulations as he deems reasonably necessary to carry out the provisions of this chapter. The Secretary shall give reasonable public notice, and afford to interested parties opportunity for hearing, prior to prescribing such rules and regulations.

Sec. 848. Effect on State law

No provision of this chapter shall be construed as indicating an intent on the part of the Congress to occupy the field in which such provision operates to the exclusion of the law of any State on the same subject matter, unless there is a direct and positive conflict between such provision and the law of the State so that the two cannot be reconciled or consistently stand together.

Chapter 113B—Terrorism

Sec. 2331. Definitions

As used in this chapter—

(1) the term "international terrorism" means activities that—

(A) involve violent acts or acts dangerous to human life that are a violation of the criminal laws of the United States or of any State, or that would be a criminal violation if committed within the jurisdiction of the United States or of any State;

(B) appear to be intended—

(i) to intimidate or coerce a civilian population;

(ii) to influence the policy of a government by intimidation or coercion; or

(iii) to affect the conduct of a government by assassination or kidnapping; and

(C) occur primarily outside the territorial jurisdiction of the United States, or transcend national boundaries in terms of the means by which they are accomplished, the persons they appear intended to intimidate or coerce, or the locale in which their perpetrators operate or seek asylum;

(2) the term "national of the United States" has the meaning given such term in section 101(a)(22) of the Immigration and Nationality Act;

(3) the term "person" means any individual or entity capable of holding a legal or beneficial interest in property; and

(4) the term "act of war" means any act occurring in the course of—

(A) declared war;

(B) armed conflict, whether or not war has been declared, between two or more nations; or

(C) armed conflict between military forces of any origin.

Sec. 2332. Criminal penalties

(a) Homicide.—Whoever kills a national of the United States, while such national is outside the United States, shall—

(1) if the killing is murder (as defined in section 1111(a)), be fined under this title, punished by death or imprisonment for any term of years or for life, or both;

(2) if the killing is a voluntary manslaughter as defined in section 1112(a) of this title, be fined under this title or imprisoned not more than ten years, or both; and

(3) if the killing is an involuntary manslaughter as defined in section 1112(a) of this title, be fined under this title or imprisoned not more than three years, or both.

(b) Attempt or Conspiracy With Respect to Homicide.—Whoever outside the United States attempts to kill, or engages in a conspiracy to kill, a national of the United States shall—

(1) in the case of an attempt to commit a killing that is a murder as defined in this chapter, be fined under this title or imprisoned not more than 20 years, or both; and

(2) in the case of a conspiracy by two or more persons to commit

a killing that is a murder as defined in section 1111(a) of this title, if one or more of such persons do any overt act to effect the object of the conspiracy, be fined under this title or imprisoned for any term of years or for life, or both so fined and so imprisoned.

(c) Other Conduct.—Whoever outside the United States engages in physical violence—

(1) with intent to cause serious bodily injury to a national of the United States; or

(2) with the result that serious bodily injury is caused to a national of the United States; shall be fined under this title or imprisoned not more than ten years, or both.

(d) Limitation on Prosecution.—No prosecution for any offense described in this section shall be undertaken by the United States except on written certification of the Attorney General or the highest ranking subordinate of the Attorney General with responsibility for criminal prosecutions that, in the judgment of the certifying official, such offense was intended to coerce, intimidate, or retaliate against a government or a civilian population.

Sec. 2332a. Use of certain weapons of mass destruction

(a) Offense Against a National of the United States or Within the United States.—A person who, without lawful authority, uses, threatens, or attempts or conspires to use, a weapon of mass destruction (other than a chemical weapon as that term is defined in section 229F), including any biological agent, toxin, or vector (as those terms are defined in section 178)—

(1) against a national of the United States while such national is outside of the United States;

(2) against any person within the United States, and the results of such use affect interstate or foreign commerce or, in the case of a threat, attempt, or conspiracy, would have affected interstate or foreign commerce; or

(3) against any property that is owned, leased or used by the United States or by any department or agency of the United States, whether the property is within or outside of the United States, shall be imprisoned for any term of years or for life, and if death results, shall be punished by death or imprisoned for any term of years or for life.

(b) Offense by National of the United States Outside of the United States.—Any national of the United States who, without lawful authority, uses, or threatens, attempts, or conspires to use, a weapon of mass destruction (other than a chemical weapon (as that term is defined in section 229F)) outside of the United States shall be imprisoned for any term of years or for life, and if death results, shall be punished by death, or by imprisonment for any term of years or for life.

(c) Definitions.—For purposes of this section—

(1) the term "national of the United States" has the meaning given in section 101(a)(22) of the Immigration and Nationality Act (8 U.S.C. 1101(a)(22)); and

(2) the term "weapon of mass destruction" means—

(A) any destructive device as defined in section 921 of this title;

(B) any weapon that is designed or intended to cause death or serious bodily injury through the release, dissemination, or impact of toxic or poisonous chemicals, or their precursors;

(C) any weapon involving a disease organism; or

(D) any weapon that is designed to release radiation or radioactivity at a level dangerous to human life.

Sec. 2332b. Acts of terrorism transcending national boundaries

(a) Prohibited Acts.—

(1) Offenses.—Whoever, involving conduct transcending national boundaries and in a circumstance described in subsection

(b) —

(A) kills, kidnaps, maims, commits an assault resulting in serious bodily injury, or assaults with a dangerous weapon any person within the United States; or

(B) creates a substantial risk of serious bodily injury to any other person by destroying or damaging any structure, conveyance, or other real or personal property within the United States or by attempting or conspiring to destroy or damage any structure, conveyance, or other real or personal property within the United States; in violation of the laws of any State, or the United States, shall be punished as prescribed in subsection (c).

(2) Treatment of threats, attempts and conspiracies.—Whoever

threatens to commit an offense under paragraph (1), or attempts or conspires to do so, shall be punished under subsection (c).

(b) Jurisdictional Bases.—

(1) Circumstances.—The circumstances referred to in subsection (a) are—

(A) the mail or any facility of interstate or foreign commerce is used in furtherance of the offense;

(B) the offense obstructs, delays, or affects interstate or foreign commerce, or would have so obstructed, delayed, or affected interstate or foreign commerce if the offense had been consummated;

(C) the victim, or intended victim, is the United States Government, a member of the uniformed services, or any official, officer, employee, or agent of the legislative, executive, or judicial branches, or of any department or agency, of the United States;

(D) the structure, conveyance, or other real or personal property is, in whole or in part, owned, possessed, or leased to the United States, or any department or agency of the United States;

(E) the offense is committed in the territorial sea (including the airspace above and the seabed and subsoil below, and artificial islands and fixed structures erected thereon) of the United States; or

(F) the offense is committed within the special maritime and territorial jurisdiction of the United States.

(2) Co-conspirators and accessories after the fact.—Jurisdiction shall exist over all principals and co-conspirators of an offense under this section, and accessories after the fact to any offense under this section, if at least one of the circumstances described in subparagraphs (A) through (F) of paragraph (1) is applicable to at least one offender.

(c) Penalties.—

(1) Penalties.—Whoever violates this section shall be punished—

(A) for a killing, or if death results to any person from any other conduct prohibited by this section, by death, or by imprisonment for any term of years or for life;

(B) for kidnapping, by imprisonment for any term of years or for life;

(C) for maiming, by imprisonment for not more than 35 years;

(D) for assault with a dangerous weapon or assault resulting in serious bodily injury, by imprisonment for not more than 30 years;

(E) for destroying or damaging any structure, conveyance, or other real or personal property, by imprisonment for not more than 25 years;

(F) for attempting or conspiring to commit an offense, for any term of years up to the maximum punishment that would have applied had the offense been completed; and

(G) for threatening to commit an offense under this section, by imprisonment for not more than 10 years.

(2) Consecutive sentence.—Notwithstanding any other provision of law, the court shall not place on probation any person convicted of a violation of this section; nor shall the term of imprisonment imposed under this section run concurrently with any other term of imprisonment.

(d) Proof Requirements.—The following shall apply to prosecutions under this section:

(1) Knowledge.—The prosecution is not required to prove knowledge by any defendant of a jurisdictional base alleged in the indictment.

(2) State law.—In a prosecution under this section that is based upon the adoption of State law, only the elements of the offense under State law, and not any provisions pertaining to criminal procedure or evidence, are adopted.

(e) Extraterritorial Jurisdiction.—There is extraterritorial Federal jurisdiction—

(1) over any offense under subsection (a), including any threat, attempt, or conspiracy to commit such offense; and

(2) over conduct which, under section 3, renders any person an accessory after the fact to an offense under subsection (a).

(f) Investigative Authority.—In addition to any other investigative authority with respect to violations of this title, the Attorney General shall have primary investigative responsibility for all Federal crimes of terrorism, and the Secretary of the Treasury shall assist the Attorney General at the request of the Attorney General. Nothing in this section shall be construed to interfere with the authority of the United States Secret Service under section 3056.

(g) Definitions.—As used in this section—

(1) the term "conduct transcending national boundaries" means conduct occurring outside of the United States in addition to the conduct occurring in the United States;

(2) the term "facility of interstate or foreign commerce" has the meaning given that term in section 1958(b)(2);

(3) the term "serious bodily injury" has the meaning given that term in section 1365(g)(3);

(4) the term "territorial sea of the United States" means all waters extending seaward to 12 nautical miles from the baselines of the United States, determined in accordance with international law; and

(5) the term "Federal crime of terrorism" means an offense that—

(A) is calculated to influence or affect the conduct of government by intimidation or coercion, or to retaliate against government conduct; and

(B) is a violation of—

(i) section 32 (relating to destruction of aircraft or aircraft facilities), 37 (relating to violence at international airports), 81 (relating to arson within special maritime and territorial jurisdiction), 175 (relating to biological weapons), 351 (relating to congressional, cabinet, and Supreme Court assassination, kidnapping, and assault), 831 (relating to nuclear materials), 842(m) or (n) (relating to plastic explosives), 844(e) (relating to certain bombings), 844(f) or (i) (relating to arson and bombing of certain property), 930(c), 956 (relating to conspiracy to injure property of a foreign government), 1114 (relating to protection of officers and employees of the United States), 1116 (relating to murder or manslaughter of foreign officials, official guests, or internationally protected persons), 1203 (relating to hostage taking), 1361 (relating to injury of Government property or contracts), 1362 (relating to destruction of communication lines, stations, or systems), 1363 (relating to injury to buildings or property within special maritime and territorial jurisdiction of the United States), 1366 (relating to destruction of an energy facility), 1751 (relating to Presidential and Presidential staff assassination, kidnapping, and assault), 1992, 2152 (relating to injury of fortifications, harbor defenses, or defensive sea areas), 2155 (relating to destruction of national defense materials, premises, or utilities), 2156 (relating to production of defective national defense materials, premises, or utilities), 2280 (relating to violence against maritime navigation), 2281 (relating to violence against maritime fixed platforms), 2332 (relating to certain homicides and other violence against United States nationals occurring outside of the United States), 2332a (relating to use of weapons of mass destruction), 2332b (relating to acts of terrorism transcending national boundaries), 2332c, 2339A (relating to providing material support to terrorists), 2339B (relating to providing material support to terrorist organizations), or 2340A (relating to torture);

(ii) section 236 (relating to sabotage of nuclear facilities or fuel) of the Atomic Energy Act of 1954 (42 U.S.C. 2284); or

(iii) section 46502 (relating to aircraft piracy) or section 60123(b) (relating to destruction of interstate gas or hazardous liquid pipeline facility) of title 49.

Sec. 2332d. Financial transactions

(a) Offense.—Except as provided in regulations issued by the Secretary of the Treasury, in consultation with the Secretary of State, whoever, being a United States person, knowing or having reasonable cause to know that a country is designated under section 6(j) of the Export Administration Act (50 U.S.C. App. 2405) as a country supporting international terrorism, engages in a financial transaction with the government of that country, shall be fined under this title, imprisoned for not more than 10 years, or both.

(b) Definitions.—As used in this section—

(1) the term "financial transaction" has the same meaning as in section 1956(c)(4); and

(2) the term "United States person" means any—

(A) United States citizen or national;

(B) permanent resident alien;

(C) juridical person organized under the laws of the United States; or

(D) any person in the United States.

Sec. 2332e. Requests for military assistance to enforce prohibition in certain emergencies

The Attorney General may request the Secretary of Defense to provide assistance under section 382 of title 10 in support of Department of Justice activities relating to the enforcement of section 2332c of this title during an emergency situation involving a chemical weapon of mass destruction. The authority to make such a request may be exercised by another official of the Department of Justice in accordance with section 382(f)(2) of title 10.

Sec. 2333. Civil remedies

(a) Action and Jurisdiction.—Any national of the United States injured in his or her person, property, or business by reason of an act of international terrorism, or his or her estate, survivors, or heirs, may sue therefor in any appropriate district court of the United States and shall recover threefold the damages he or she sustains and the cost of the suit, including attorney's fees.

(b) Estoppel Under United States Law.—A final judgment or decree rendered in favor of the United States in any criminal proceeding under section 1116, 1201, 1203, or 2332 of this title or section 46314, 46502, 46505, or 46506 of title 49 shall estop the defendant from denying the essential allegations of the criminal offense in any subsequent civil proceeding under this section.

(c) Estoppel Under Foreign Law.—A final judgment or decree rendered in favor of any foreign state in any criminal proceeding shall, to the extent that such judgment or decree may be accorded full faith and credit under the law of the United States, estop the defendant from denying the essential allegations of the criminal offense in any subsequent civil proceeding under this section.

Sec. 2334. Jurisdiction and venue

(a) General Venue.—Any civil action under section 2333 of this title against any person may be instituted in the district court of the United States for any district where any plaintiff resides or where any defendant resides or is served, or has an agent. Process in such a civil action may be served in any district where the defendant resides, is found, or has an agent.

(b) Special Maritime or Territorial Jurisdiction.—If the actions giving rise to the claim occurred within the special maritime and territorial jurisdiction of the United States, as defined in section 7 of this title, then any civil action under section 2333 of this title against any person may be instituted in the district court of the United States for any district in which any plaintiff resides or the defendant resides, is served, or has an agent.

(c) Service on Witnesses.—A witness in a civil action brought under section 2333 of this title may be served in any other district where the defendant resides, is found, or has an agent.

(d) Convenience of the Forum.—The district court shall not dismiss any action brought under section 2333 of this title on the grounds of the inconvenience or inappropriateness of the forum chosen, unless—

(1) the action may be maintained in a foreign court that has jurisdiction over the subject matter and over all the defendants;

(2) that foreign court is significantly more convenient and appropriate; and

(3) that foreign court offers a remedy which is substantially the same as the one available in the courts of the United States.

Sec. 2335. Limitation of actions

(a) In General.—Subject to subsection (b), a suit for recovery of damages under section 2333 of this title shall not be maintained unless commenced within 4 years after the date the cause of action accrued.

(b) Calculation of Period.—The time of the absence of the defendant from the United States or from any jurisdiction in which the same or a similar action arising from the same facts may be maintained by the plaintiff, or of any concealment of the defendant's whereabouts, shall not be included in the 4-year period set forth in subsection (a).

Sec. 2336. Other limitations

(a) Acts of War.—No action shall be maintained under section 2333 of this title for injury or loss by reason of an act of war.

(b) Limitation on Discovery.—If a party to an action under section 2333 seeks to discover the investigative files of the Department of Justice, the Assistant Attorney General, Deputy Attorney General, or Attorney General may object on the ground that compliance will interfere with a criminal investigation or prosecution of the incident, or a national security operation related to the incident, which is the subject of the civil litigation. The court shall evaluate any such objections in camera and shall stay the discovery if the court finds that granting the discovery request will substantially interfere with a criminal investigation or prosecution of the incident or a national security operation related to the incident. The court shall consider the likelihood of criminal prosecution by the Government and other factors it deems to be appropriate. A stay of discovery under this subsection shall constitute a bar to the granting of a motion to dismiss under rules 12(b)(6) and 56 of the Federal Rules of Civil Procedure. If the court grants a stay of discovery under this subsection, it may stay the action in the interests of justice.

(c) Stay of Action for Civil Remedies.—(1) The Attorney General may intervene in any civil action brought under section 2333 for the purpose of seeking a stay of the civil action. A stay shall be granted if the court finds that the continuation of the civil action will substantially interfere with a criminal prosecution which involves the same subject matter and in which an indictment has been returned, or interfere with national security operations related to the terrorist incident that is the subject of the civil action. A stay may be granted for up to 6 months. The Attorney General may petition the court for an extension of the stay for additional 6-month periods until the criminal prosecution is completed or dismissed.

(2) In a proceeding under this subsection, the Attorney General may request that any order issued by the court for release to the parties and the public omit any reference to the basis on which the stay was sought.

Sec. 2337. Suits against Government officials

No action shall be maintained under section 2333 of this title against—

(1) the United States, an agency of the United States, or an officer or employee of the United States or any agency thereof acting

within his or her official capacity or under color of legal authority; or (2) a foreign state, an agency of a foreign state, or an officer or employee of a foreign state or an agency thereof acting within his or her official capacity or under color of legal authority.

Sec. 2338. Exclusive Federal jurisdiction

The district courts of the United States shall have exclusive jurisdiction over an action brought under this chapter.

Sec. 2339A. Providing material support to terrorists

(a) Offense.—Whoever, within the United States, provides material support or resources or conceals or disguises the nature, location, source, or ownership of material support or resources, knowing or intending that they are to be used in preparation for, or in carrying out, a violation of section 32, 37, 81, 175, 351, 831, 842(m) or (n), 844(f) or (i), 930(c), 956, 1114, 1116, 1203, 1361, 1362, 1363, 1366, 1751, 1992, 2155, 2156, 2280, 2281, 2332, 2332a, 2332b, 2332c, or 2340A of this title or section 46502 of title 49, or in preparation for, or in carrying out, the concealment or an escape from the commission of any such violation, shall be fined under this title, imprisoned not more than 10 years, or both.

(b) Definition.—In this section, the term "material support or resources" means currency or other financial securities, financial services, lodging, training, safehouses, false documentation or identification, communications equipment, facilities, weapons, lethal substances, explosives, personnel, transportation, and other physical assets, except medicine or religious materials.

Sec. 2339B. Providing material support or resources to designated foreign terrorist organizations

(a) Prohibited Activities.—

   (1) Unlawful conduct.—Whoever, within the United States or subject to the jurisdiction of the United States, knowingly provides material support or resources to a foreign terrorist organization, or attempts or conspires to do so, shall be fined under this title or imprisoned not more than 10 years, or both.

(2) Financial institutions.—Except as authorized by the Secretary, any financial institution that becomes aware that it has possession of, or control over, any funds in which a foreign terrorist organization, or its agent, has an interest, shall—

(A) retain possession of, or maintain control over, such funds; and

(B) report to the Secretary the existence of such funds in accordance with regulations issued by the Secretary.

(b) Civil Penalty.—Any financial institution that knowingly fails to comply with subsection (a)(2) shall be subject to a civil penalty in an amount that is the greater of—

(A) $50,000 per violation; or

(B) twice the amount of which the financial institution was required under subsection (a)(2) to retain possession or control.

(c) Injunction.—Whenever it appears to the Secretary or the Attorney General that any person is engaged in, or is about to engage in, any act that constitutes, or would constitute, a violation of this section, the Attorney General may initiate civil action in a district court of the United States to enjoin such violation.

(d) Extraterritorial Jurisdiction.—There is extraterritorial Federal jurisdiction over an offense under this section.

(e) Investigations.—

(1) In general.—The Attorney General shall conduct any investigation of a possible violation of this section, or of any license, order, or regulation issued pursuant to this section.

(2) Coordination with the department of the treasury.—The Attorney General shall work in coordination with the Secretary in investigations relating to—

(A) the compliance or noncompliance by a financial institution with the requirements of subsection (a)(2); and

(B) civil penalty proceedings authorized under subsection (b).

(3) Referral.—Any evidence of a criminal violation of this section arising in the course of an investigation by the Secretary or any other Federal agency shall be referred immediately to the Attorney General for further investigation. The Attorney General shall timely notify

the Secretary of any action taken on referrals from the Secretary, and may refer investigations to the Secretary for remedial licensing or civil penalty action.

(f) Classified Information in Civil Proceedings Brought by the United States.—

(1) Discovery of classified information by defendants.—

(A) Request by united states.—In any civil proceeding under this section, upon request made ex parte and in writing by the United States, a court, upon a sufficient showing, may authorize the United States to—

(i) redact specified items of classified information from documents to be introduced into evidence or made available to the defendant through discovery under the Federal Rules of Civil Procedure;

(ii) substitute a summary of the information for such classified documents; or

(iii) substitute a statement admitting relevant facts that the classified information would tend to prove.

(B) Order granting request.—If the court enters an order granting a request under this paragraph, the entire text of the documents to which the request relates shall be sealed and preserved in the records of the court to be made available to the appellate court in the event of an appeal.

(C) Denial of request.—If the court enters an order denying a request of the United States under this paragraph, the United States may take an immediate, interlocutory appeal in accordance with paragraph (5). For purposes of such an appeal, the entire text of the documents to which the request relates, together with any transcripts of arguments made ex parte to the court in connection therewith, shall be maintained under seal and delivered to the appellate court.

(2) Introduction of classified information; precautions by court.—

(A) Exhibits.—To prevent unnecessary or inadvertent disclosure of classified information in a civil proceeding brought by the United States under this section, the United States may petition the court ex parte to admit, in lieu of classified writings, recordings, or photographs, one or more of the following:

(i)   Copies of items from which classified information has been redacted.

(ii)   Stipulations admitting relevant facts that specific classified information would tend to prove.

(iii)   A declassified summary of the specific classified information.

(B)   Determination by court.—The court shall grant a request under this paragraph if the court finds that the redacted item, stipulation, or summary is sufficient to allow the defendant to prepare a defense.

(3)   Taking of trial testimony.—

(A)   Objection.—During the examination of a witness in any civil proceeding brought by the United States under this subsection, the United States may object to any question or line of inquiry that may require the witness to disclose classified information not previously found to be admissible.

(B)   Action by court.—In determining whether a response is admissible, the court shall take precautions to guard against the compromise of any classified information, including—

(i)   permitting the United States to provide the court, ex parte, with a proffer of the witness's response to the question or line of inquiry; and

(ii)   requiring the defendant to provide the court with a proffer of the nature of the information that the defendant seeks to elicit.

(C)   Obligation of defendant.—In any civil proceeding under this section, it shall be the defendant's obligation to establish the relevance and materiality of any classified information sought to be introduced.

(4)   Appeal.—If the court enters an order denying a request of the United States under this subsection, the United States may take an immediate interlocutory appeal in accordance with paragraph (5).

(5)   Interlocutory appeal.—

(A)   Subject of appeal.—An interlocutory appeal by the United States shall lie to a court of appeals from a decision or order of a district court—

(i)   authorizing the disclosure of classified information;

(ii)   imposing sanctions for nondisclosure of classified information; or

(iii) refusing a protective order sought by the United States to prevent the disclosure of classified information.

(B)   Expedited consideration.—

(i)   In general.—An appeal taken pursuant to this paragraph, either before or during trial, shall be expedited by the court of appeals.

(ii)   Appeals prior to trial.—If an appeal is of an order made prior to trial, an appeal shall be taken not later than 10 days after the decision or order appealed from, and the trial shall not commence until the appeal is resolved.

(iii) Appeals during trial.—If an appeal is taken during trial, the trial court shall adjourn the trial until the appeal is resolved, and the court of appeals—

(I)   shall hear argument on such appeal not later than 4 days after the adjournment of the trial;

(II)   may dispense with written briefs other than the supporting materials previously submitted to the trial court;

(III) shall render its decision not later than 4 days after argument on appeal; and

(IV)   may dispense with the issuance of a written opinion in rendering its decision.

(C)   Effect of ruling.—An interlocutory appeal and decision shall not affect the right of the defendant, in a subsequent appeal from a final judgment, to claim as error reversal by the trial court on remand of a ruling appealed from during trial.

(6)   Construction.—Nothing in this subsection shall prevent the United States from seeking protective orders or asserting privileges ordinarily available to the United States to protect against the disclosure of classified information, including the invocation of the military and State secrets privilege.

(g)   Definitions.—As used in this section—

(1)   the term "classified information" has the meaning given that

term in section 1(a) of the Classified Information Procedures Act (18 U.S.C. App.);

(2) the term "financial institution" has the same meaning as in section 5312(a)(2) of title 31, United States Code;

(3) the term "funds" includes coin or currency of the United States or any other country, traveler's checks, personal checks, bank checks, money orders, stocks, bonds, debentures, drafts, letters of credit, any other negotiable instrument, and any electronic representation of any of the foregoing;

(4) the term "material support or resources" has the same meaning as in section 2339A;

(5) the term "Secretary" means the Secretary of the Treasury; and

(6) the term "terrorist organization" means an organization designated as a terrorist organization under section 219 of the Immigration and Nationality Act.

Chapter 204—Rewards For Information Concerning Terrorist Acts and Espionage

Sec. 3071. Information for which rewards authorized

(a) With respect to acts of terrorism primarily within the territorial jurisdiction of the United States, the Attorney General may reward any individual who furnishes information—

(1) leading to the arrest or conviction, in any country, of any individual or individuals for the commission of an act of terrorism against a United States person or United States property; or

(2) leading to the arrest or conviction, in any country, of any individual or individuals for conspiring or attempting to commit an act of terrorism against a United States person or property; or

(3) leading to the prevention, frustration, or favorable resolution of an act of terrorism against a United States person or property.

(b) With respect to acts of espionage involving or directed at the United States, the Attorney General may reward any individual who furnishes information—

(1) leading to the arrest or conviction, in any country, of any individual or individuals for commission of an act of espionage against the United States;

(2) leading to the arrest or conviction, in any country, of any individual or individuals for conspiring or attempting to commit an act of espionage against the United States; or

(3) leading to the prevention or frustration of an act of espionage against the United States.

Sec. 3072. Determination of entitlement; maximum amount; Presidential approval; conclusiveness

The Attorney General shall determine whether an individual furnishing information described in section 3071 is entitled to a reward and the amount to be paid. A reward under this section may be in an amount not to exceed $500,000. A reward of $100,000 or more may not be made without the approval of the President or the Attorney General personally. A determination made by the Attorney General or the President under this chapter shall be final and conclusive, and no court shall have power or jurisdiction to review it.

Sec. 3073. Protection of identity

Any reward granted under this chapter shall be certified for payment by the Attorney General. If it is determined that the identity of the recipient of a reward or of the members of the recipient's immediate family must be protected, the Attorney General may take such measures in connection with the payment of the reward as deemed necessary to effect such protection.

Sec. 3074. Exception of governmental officials

No officer or employee of any governmental entity who, while in the performance of his or her official duties, furnishes the information described in section 3071 shall be eligible for any monetary reward under this chapter.

Sec. 3075. Authorization for appropriations

There are authorized to be appropriated, without fiscal year limitation, $5,000,000 for the purpose of this chapter.

Sec. 3076. Eligibility for witness security program

Any individual (and the immediate family of such individual) who furnishes information which would justify a reward by the Attorney General under this chapter or by the Secretary of State under section 36 of the State Department Basic Authorities Act of 1956 may, in the discretion of the Attorney General, participate in the Attorney General's witness security program authorized under chapter 224 of this title.

Sec. 3077. Definitions

As used in this chapter, the term—

(1) "act of terrorism" means an activity that—

(A) involves a violent act or an act dangerous to human life that is a violation of the criminal laws of the United States or of any State, or that would be a criminal violation if committed within the jurisdiction of the United States or of any State; and

(B) appears to be intended—

(i) to intimidate or coerce a civilian population;

(ii) to influence the policy of a government by intimidation or coercion; or

(iii) to affect the conduct of a government by assassination or kidnapping;

(2) "United States person" means—

(A) a national of the United States as defined in section 101(a)(22) of the Immigration and Nationality Act (8 U.S.C. 1101(a)(22));

(B) an alien lawfully admitted for permanent residence in the United States as defined in section 101(a)(20) of the Immigration and Nationality Act (8 U.S.C. 1101(a)(20));

(C) any person within the United States;

(D) any employee or contractor of the United States Government, regardless of nationality, who is the victim or intended victim of an act of terrorism by virtue of that employment;

(E) a sole proprietorship, partnership, company, or association composed principally of nationals or permanent resident aliens of the United States; and

(F) a corporation organized under the laws of the United States, any State, the District of Columbia, or any territory or possession of the United States, and a foreign subsidiary of such corporation;

(3) "United States property" means any real or personal property which is within the United States or, if outside the United States, the actual or beneficial ownership of which rests in a United States person or any Federal or State governmental entity of the United States;

(4) "United States," when used in a geographical sense, includes Puerto Rico and all territories and possessions of the United States;

(5) "State" includes any State of the United States, the District of Columbia, the Commonwealth of Puerto Rico, and any other possession or territory of the United States;

(6) "government entity" includes the Government of the United States, any State or political subdivision thereof, any foreign country, and any state, provincial, municipal, or other political subdivision of a foreign country;

(7) "Attorney General" means the Attorney General of the United States or that official designated by the Attorney General to perform the Attorney General's responsibilities under this chapter; and

(8) "act of espionage" means an activity that is a violation of—

(A) section 793, 794, or 798 of this title; or

(B) section 4 of the Subversive Activities Control Act of 1950.

Chapter 213—Limitations

Sec. 3286. Extension of statute of limitation for certain terrorism offenses

Notwithstanding section 3282, no person shall be prosecuted, tried, or punished for any non-capital offense involving a violation of section 32 (aircraft destruction), section 37 (airport violence), section 112 (assaults upon diplomats), section 351 (crimes against Congressmen or Cabinet officers), section 1116 (crimes against diplomats), section 1203 (hostage taking), section 1361 (willful injury to government property), section 1751 (crimes against the President), section 2280 (maritime violence), section 2281 (maritime platform violence), section 2332 (terrorist acts abroad against United States nationals), section 2332a (use of weapons of mass destruction), 2332b (acts of terrorism transcending national boundaries), or section 2340A (torture) of this title or section 46502, 46504, 46505, or 46506 of title 49, unless the indictment is found or the information is instituted within 8 years after the offense was committed.

Title 22—Foreign Relations and Intercourse

Chapter 32—Antiterrorism Assistance

Sec. 2349aa. General authority

Notwithstanding any other provision of law that restricts assistance to foreign countries (other than sections 2304 and 2371 of this title), the President is authorized to furnish, on such terms and conditions as the President may determine, assistance to foreign countries in order to enhance the ability of their law enforcement personnel to deter terrorists and terrorist groups from engaging in international terrorist acts such as bombing, kidnapping, assassination, hostage taking, and hijacking. Such assistance may include training services and the provision of equipment and other commodities related to bomb detection and disposal, management of hostage situations, physical security, and other matters relating to the detection, deterrence, and prevention of acts of terrorism, the resolution of terrorist incidents, and the apprehension of those involved in such acts.

Sec. 2349aa-1. Purposes

Activities conducted under this part shall be designed—

(1) to enhance the antiterrorism skills of friendly countries by providing training and equipment to deter and counter terrorism;

(2) to strengthen the bilateral ties of the United States with friendly governments by offering concrete assistance in this area of great mutual concern; and

(3) to increase respect for human rights by sharing with foreign civil authorities modern, humane, and effective antiterrorism techniques.

Sec. 2349aa-2. Limitations

(a) Services and commodities furnished by agency of United States Government; advance payment

Whenever the President determines it to be consistent with and in furtherance of the purposes of this part, and on such terms and conditions consistent with this chapter as he may determine, any agency of the United States Government is authorized to furnish services and commodities, without charge to funds available to carry out this part, to an eligible foreign country, subject to payment in advance of the value thereof (within the meaning of section 2403(m) of this title) in United States dollars by the foreign country. Credits and the proceeds of guaranteed loans made available to such countries pursuant to the Arms Export Control Act (22 U.S.C. 2751 et seq.) shall not be used for such payments. Collections under this part shall be credited to the currently applicable appropriation, account, or fund of the agency providing such services and commodities and shall be available for the purposes for which such appropriation, account, or fund is authorized to be used.

(b) Consultation in development and implementation of assistance
The Assistant Secretary of State for Democracy, Human Rights, and Labor shall be consulted in the determinations of the foreign countries that will be furnished assistance under this part and determinations of the nature of assistance to be furnished to each such country.

(c) Arms and ammunition; value of equipment and commodities

(1) Arms and ammunition may be provided under this part only if they are directly related to antiterrorism assistance.

(2) The value (in terms of original acquisition cost) of all equipment and commodities provided under this part in any fiscal year shall not exceed 30 percent of the funds made available to carry out this part for that fiscal year.

(d) Information exchange activities
This part does not apply to information exchange activities conducted by agencies of the United States Government under other authority for such purposes.

Sec. 2349aa-4. Authorization of appropriations

(a) There are authorized to be appropriated to the President to carry out this part $9,840,000 for fiscal year 1986 and $14,680,000 for fiscal year 1987.

(b) Amounts appropriated under this section are authorized to remain available until expended.

Sec. 2349aa-5. Administrative authorities

Except where expressly provided to the contrary, any reference in any law to subchapter I of this chapter shall be deemed to include reference to this part and any reference in any law to subchapter II of this chapter shall be deemed to exclude reference to this part.

Sec. 2349aa-7. Coordination of all United States terrorism-related assistance to foreign countries

(a) Responsibility
The Secretary of State shall be responsible for coordinating all assistance related to international terrorism which is provided by the United States Government to foreign countries.

(b) Reports
Not later than February 1 each year, the Secretary of State, in consultation with appropriate United States Government agencies, shall report to the appropriate committees of the Congress on the assistance related to international terrorism which was provided by the United States Government during the preceding fiscal year. Such reports may be provided on a classified basis to the extent necessary, and shall specify the amount and nature of the assistance provided.

(c) Rule of construction
Nothing contained in this section shall be construed to limit or impair the authority or responsibility of any other Federal agency with respect to law enforcement, domestic security operations, or intelligence activities as defined in Executive Order 12333.

Sec. 2349aa-8. Prohibition on imports from and exports to Libya

(a) Prohibition on imports
Notwithstanding any other provision of law, the President may prohibit any article grown, produced, extracted, or manufactured in Libya from being imported into the United States.

(b) Prohibition on exports
Notwithstanding any other provision of law, the President may prohibit any goods or technology, including technical data or other information, subject to the jurisdiction of the United States or exported by any person subject to the jurisdiction of the United States, from being exported to Libya.

(c) "United States" defined

For purposes of this section, the term "United States," when used in a geographical sense, includes territories and possessions of the United States.

Sec. 2349aa-9. Ban on importing goods and services from countries supporting terrorism

(a) Authority

The President may ban the importation into the United States of any good or service from any country which supports terrorism or terrorist organizations or harbors terrorists or terrorist organizations.

(b) Consultation

The President, in every possible instance, shall consult with the Congress before exercising the authority granted by this section and shall consult regularly with the Congress so long as that authority is being exercised.

(c) Reports

Whenever the President exercises the authority granted by this section, he shall immediately transmit to the Congress a report specifying—

(1) the country with respect to which the authority is to be exercised and the imports to be prohibited;

(2) the circumstances which necessitate the exercise of such authority;

(3) why the President believes those circumstances justify the exercise of such authority; and

(4) why the President believes the prohibitions are necessary to deal with those circumstances. At least once during each succeeding 6-month period after transmitting a report pursuant to this subsection, the President shall report to the Congress with respect to the actions taken, since the last such report, pursuant to this section and with respect to any changes which have occurred concerning any information previously furnished pursuant to this subsection.

(d) "United States" defined

For purposes of this section, the term "United States" includes territories and possessions of the United States.

Sec. 2349aa-10. Antiterrorism assistance

(a) Omitted

(b) Assistance to foreign countries to procure explosives detection devices and other counterterrorism technology

(1) Subject to section 2349aa-4(b) of this title, up to $3,000,000 in any fiscal year may be made available—

(A) to procure explosives detection devices and other counterterrorism technology; and

(B) for joint counterterrorism research and development projects on such technology conducted with NATO and major non-NATO allies under the auspices of the Technical Support Working Group of the Department of State.

(2) As used in this subsection, the term "major non-NATO allies" means those countries designated as major non-NATO allies for purposes of section 2350a(i)(3) of title 10.

(c) Assistance to foreign countries

Notwithstanding any other provision of law (except section 2371 of this title) up to $1,000,000 in assistance may be provided to a foreign country for counterterrorism efforts in any fiscal year if—

(1) such assistance is provided for the purpose of protecting the property of the United States Government or the life and property of any United States citizen, or furthering the apprehension of any individual involved in any act of terrorism against such property or persons; and

(2) the appropriate committees of Congress are notified not later than 15 days prior to the provision of such assistance.

Subchapter III—General and Administrative Provisions
Part I—General Provisions

Sec. 2377. Prohibition on assistance to countries that aid terrorist states

(a) Withholding of assistance

The President shall withhold assistance under this chapter to the government of any country that provides assistance to the government of any other country for which the Secretary of State has made a determination under section 2371 of this title.

(b) Waiver

Assistance prohibited by this section may be furnished to a foreign government described in subsection (a) of this section if the President deter-

mines that furnishing such assistance is important to the national interests of the United States and, not later than 15 days before obligating
such assistance, furnishes a report to the appropriate committees of
Congress including—

(1) a statement of the determination;

(2) a detailed explanation of the assistance to be provided;

(3) the estimated dollar amount of the assistance; and

(4) an explanation of how the assistance furthers United States
national interests.

Sec. 2378. Prohibition on assistance to countries that provide military equipment to terrorist states

(a) Prohibition

(1) In general
The President shall withhold assistance under this chapter to the
government of any country that provides lethal military equipment
to a country the government of which the Secretary of State has
determined is a terrorist government for the purposes of section
2405(j) of title 50, Appendix, or 2371 of this title.

(2) Applicability
The prohibition under this section with respect to a foreign government shall terminate 1 year after that government ceases to provide lethal military equipment. This section applies with respect to
lethal military equipment provided under a contract entered into
after April 24, 1996.

(b) Waiver
Notwithstanding any other provision of law, assistance may be furnished
to a foreign government described in subsection (a) of this section if the
President determines that furnishing such assistance is important to the
national interests of the United States and, not later than 15 days before
obligating such assistance, furnishes a report to the appropriate committees of Congress including—

(1) a statement of the determination;

(2) a detailed explanation of the assistance to be provided;

(3) the estimated dollar amount of the assistance; and

(4) an explanation of how the assistance furthers United States
national interests.

Chapter 38—Department of State

Sec. 2711. Counterterrorism Protection Fund

(a) Authority

The Secretary of State may reimburse domestic and foreign persons, agencies, or governments for the protection of judges or other persons who provide assistance or information relating to terrorist incidents primarily outside the territorial jurisdiction of the United States. Before making a payment under this section in a matter over which there is Federal criminal jurisdiction, the Secretary shall advise and consult with the Attorney General.

(b) Authorization of appropriations

There are authorized to be appropriated to the Secretary of State for "Administration of Foreign Affairs" $1,000,000 for fiscal year 1986 and $1,000,000 for fiscal year 1987 for use in reimbursing persons, agencies, or governments under this section.

(c) Designation of Fund

Amounts made available under this section may be referred to as the "Counterterrorism Protection Fund."

Sec. 2712. Authority to control certain terrorism-related services

(a) Authority

The Secretary of State may, by regulation, impose controls on the provision of the services described in subsection (b) of this section if the Secretary determines that provision of such services would aid and abet international terrorism.

(b) Services subject to control

The services subject to control under subsection (a) of this section are the following:

(1) Serving in or with the security forces of a designated foreign government.

(2) Providing training or other technical services having a direct military, law enforcement, or intelligence application, to or for the security forces of a designated foreign government. Any regulations issued to impose controls on services described in paragraph (2) shall list the specific types of training and other services subject to the controls.

(c) Persons subject of controls

These services may be controlled under subsection (a) of this section when they are provided within the United States by any individual or entity and when they are provided anywhere in the world by a United States person.

(d) Licenses

In carrying out subsection (a) of this section, the Secretary of State may require licenses, which may be revoked, suspended, or amended, without prior notice, whenever such action is deemed to be advisable.

(e) Definitions

(1) Designated foreign government

As used in this section, the term "designated foreign government" means a foreign government that the Secretary of State has determined, for purposes of section 2405(j)(1) of title 50, Appendix, has repeatedly provided support for acts of international terrorism.

(2) Security forces

As used in this section, the term "security forces" means any military or paramilitary forces, any police or other law enforcement agency (including any police or other law enforcement agency at the regional or local level), and any intelligence agency of a foreign government.

(3) United States

As used in this section, the term "United States" includes any State, the District of Columbia, the Commonwealth of Puerto Rico, the Commonwealth of the Northern Mariana Islands, and any territory or possession of the United States.

(4) United States person

As used in this section, the term "United States person" means any United States national, any permanent resident alien, and any sole proprietorship, partnership, company, association, or corporation organized under the laws of or having its principal place of business within the United States.

(f) Violations

(1) Penalties

Whoever willfully violates any regulation issued under this section shall be fined not more than $100,000 or five times the total compensation received for the conduct which constitutes the violation, whichever is greater, or imprisoned for not more than ten years, or both, for each such offense.

(2) Investigations
The Attorney General and the Secretary of the Treasury shall have authority to investigate violations of regulations issued under this section.

(g) Congressional oversight

(1) Review of regulations
Not less than 30 days before issuing any regulations under this section (including any amendments thereto), the Secretary of State shall transmit the proposed regulations to the Congress.

(2) Reports
Not less than once every six months, the Secretary of State shall report to the Congress concerning the number and character of licenses granted and denied during the previous reporting period, and such other information as the Secretary may find to be relevant to the accomplishment of the objectives of this section.

(h) Relationship to other laws
The authority granted by this section is in addition to the authorities granted by any other provision of law.

Chapter 47—Nuclear Non-Proliferation

Subchapter II—United States Initiatives to Strengthen the International Safeguards System

Sec. 3244. Actions to combat international nuclear terrorism

(a) Actions to be taken by President
The Congress hereby directs the President—

(1) to seek universal adherence to the Convention on the Physical Protection of Nuclear Material;

(2) to—

(A) conduct a review, enlisting the participation of all relevant departments and agencies of the Government, to determine whether the recommendations on Physical Protection of Nuclear Material published by the International Atomic Energy

Agency are adequate to deter theft, sabotage, and the use of nuclear facilities and materials in acts of international terrorism, and

(B) transmit the results of this review to the Director-General of the International Atomic Energy Agency;

(3) to take, in concert with United States allies and other countries, such steps as may be necessary—

(A) to keep to a minimum the amount of weapons-grade nuclear material in international transit, and

(B) to ensure that when any such material is transported internationally, it is under the most effective means for adequately protecting it from acts or attempted acts of sabotage or theft by terrorist groups or nations; and

(4) to seek agreement in the United Nations Security Council to establish—

(A) an effective regime of international sanctions against any nation or subnational group which conducts or sponsors acts of international nuclear terrorism, and

(B) measures for coordinating responses to all acts of international nuclear terrorism, including measures for the recovery of stolen nuclear material and the clean-up of nuclear releases.

(b) Reports to Congress

The President shall report to the Congress annually, in the reports required by section 3281 o this title, on the progress made during the preceding year in achieving the objectives described in this section.

Chapter 58—Diplomatic Security

Sec. 4801. Findings and purposes

(a) Findings

The Congress finds and declares that—

(1) the United States has a crucial stake in the presence of United States Government personnel representing United States interests abroad;

(2) conditions confronting United States Government personnel and missions abroad are fraught with security concerns which will continue for the foreseeable future; and

(3) the resources now available to counter acts of terrorism and protect and secure United States Government personnel and missions abroad, as well as foreign officials and missions in the United States, are inadequate to meet the mounting threat to such personnel and facilities.

(b) Purposes

The purposes of this chapter are—

(1) to set forth the responsibility of the Secretary of State with respect to the security of diplomatic operations in the United States and abroad;

(2) to maximize coordination by the Department of State with Federal, State, and local agencies and agencies of foreign governments in order to enhance security programs;

(3) to promote strengthened security measures and to provide for the accountability of United States Government personnel with security-related responsibilities;

(4) to set forth the responsibility of the Secretary of State with respect to the safe and efficient evacuation of United States Government personnel, their dependents, and private United States citizens when their lives are endangered by war, civil unrest, or natural disaster; and

(5) to provide authorization of appropriations for the Department of State to carry out its responsibilities in the area of security and counterterrorism, and in particular to finance the acquisition and improvements of United States Government missions abroad, including real property, buildings, facilities, and communications, information, and security systems.

Sec. 4802. Responsibility of Secretary of State

(a) Security functions

(1) The Secretary of State shall develop and implement (in consultation with the heads of other Federal agencies having personnel or missions abroad where appropriate and within the scope of the resources made available) policies and programs, including funding levels and standards, to provide for the security of United States Government operations of a diplomatic nature and foreign government operations of a diplomatic nature in the United States. Such policies and programs shall include—

(A) protection of all United States Government personnel on official duty abroad (other than those personnel under the command of a United States area military commander) and their accompanying dependents;

(B) establishment and operation of security functions at all United States Government missions abroad (other than facilities or installations subject to the control of a United States area military commander);

(C) establishment and operation of security functions at all Department of State facilities in the United States; and

(D) protection of foreign missions, international organizations, and foreign officials and other foreign persons in the United States, as authorized by law.

(2) Security responsibilities shall include the following:

(A) Former Office of Security functions
Functions and responsibilities exercised by the Office of Security, Department of State, before November 11, 1985.

(B) Security and protective operations

(i) Establishment and operation of post security and protective functions abroad.

(ii) Development and implementation of communications, computer, and information security.

(iii) Emergency planning.

(iv) Establishment and operation of local guard services abroad.

(v) Supervision of the United States Marine Corps security guard program.

(vi) Liaison with American overseas private sector security interests.

(vii) Protection of foreign missions and international organizations, foreign officials, and diplomatic personnel in the United States, as authorized by law.

(viii) Protection of the Secretary of State and other persons designated by the Secretary of State, as authorized by law.

(ix) Physical protection of Department of State facilities, communications, and computer and information systems in the United States.

(x) Conduct of investigations relating to protection of foreign officials and diplomatic personnel and foreign missions in the United States, suitability for employment, employee security, illegal passport and visa issuance or use, and other investigations, as authorized by law.

(xi) Carrying out the rewards program for information concerning international terrorism authorized by section 2708(a) of this title.

(xii) Performance of other security, investigative, and protective matters as authorized by law.

(C) Counterterrorism planning and coordination
Development and coordination of counterterrorism planning, emergency action planning, threat analysis programs, and liaison with other Federal agencies to carry out this paragraph.

(D) Security technology
Development and implementation of technical and physical security programs, including security-related construction, radio and personnel security communications, armored vehicles, computer and communications security, and research programs necessary to develop such measures.

(E) Diplomatic courier service
Management of the diplomatic courier service.

(F) Personnel training
Development of facilities, methods, and materials to develop and upgrade necessary skills in order to carry out this section.

(G) Foreign government training
Management and development of antiterrorism assistance programs to assist foreign government security training which are administered by the Department of State under chapter 8 of part II of the Foreign Assistance Act of 1961 (22 U.S.C. 2349aa et seq.).

(b) Overseas evacuations
The Secretary of State shall develop and implement policies and programs to provide for the safe and efficient evacuation of United States

Government personnel, dependents, and private United States citizens when their lives are endangered. Such policies shall include measures to identify high risk areas where evacuation may be necessary and, where appropriate, providing staff to United States Government missions abroad to assist in those evacuations. In carrying out these responsibilities, the Secretary shall—

(1) develop a model contingency plan for evacuation of personnel, dependents, and United States citizens from foreign countries;

(2) develop a mechanism whereby United States citizens can voluntarily request to be placed on a list in order to be contacted in the event of an evacuation, or which, in the event of an evacuation, can maintain information on the location of United States citizens in high risk areas submitted by their relatives;

(3) assess the transportation and communications resources in the area being evacuated and determine the logistic support needed for the evacuation; and

(4) develop a plan for coordinating communications between embassy staff, Department of State personnel, and families of United States citizens abroad regarding the whereabouts of those citizens.

(c) Oversight of posts abroad
The Secretary of State shall—

(1) have full responsibility for the coordination of all United States Government personnel assigned to diplomatic or consular posts or other United States missions abroad pursuant to United States Government authorization (except for facilities, installations, or personnel under the command of a United States area military commander)

(2) establish appropriate overseas staffing levels for all such posts or missions for all Federal agencies with activities abroad (except for personnel and activities under the command of a United States area military commander or regional inspector general offices under the jurisdiction of the inspector (FOOTNOTE 3) General, Agency for International Development).

(d) Federal agency
As used in this subchapter and subchapter III of this chapter, the term "Federal agency" includes any department or agency of the United States Government.

Sec. 4805. Cooperation of other Federal agencies

(a) Assistance

In order to facilitate fulfillment of the responsibilities described in section 4802(a) of this title, other Federal agencies shall cooperate (through agreements) to the maximum extent possible with the Secretary of State. Such agencies may, with or without reimbursement, provide assistance to the Secretary, perform security inspections, provide logistical support relating to the differing missions and facilities of other Federal agencies, and perform other overseas security functions as may be authorized by the Secretary. Specifically, the Secretary may agree to delegate operational control of overseas security functions of other Federal agencies to the heads of such agencies, subject to the Secretary's authority as set forth in section 4802(a) of this title. The agency head receiving such delegated authority shall be responsible to the Secretary in the exercise of the delegated operational control.

(b) Other agencies

Nothing contained in this chapter shall be construed to limit or impair the authority or responsibility of any other Federal, State, or local agency with respect to law enforcement, domestic security operations, or intelligence activities as defined in Executive Order 12333.

(c) Certain lease arrangements

The Administrator of General Services is authorized to lease (to such extent or in such amounts as are provided in appropriation Acts) such amount of space in the United States as may be necessary for the Department of State to accommodate the personnel required to carry out this subchapter. The Department of State shall pay for such space at the rate established by the Administrator of General Services for space and related services.

Sec. 4806. Protection of foreign consulates

The Secretary of State shall take into account security considerations in making determinations with respect to accreditation of all foreign consular personnel in the United States.

Subchapter II—Personnel

Sec. 4821. Diplomatic Security Service

The Secretary of State may establish a Diplomatic Security Service, which shall perform such functions as the Secretary may determine.

Sec. 4822. Director of Diplomatic Security Service

Any such Diplomatic Security Service should be headed by a Director designated by the Secretary of State. The Director should be a career member of the Senior Foreign Service or the Senior Executive Service and should be qualified for the position by virtue of demonstrated ability in the areas of security, law enforcement, management, and public administration. Experience in management or operations abroad should be considered an affirmative factor in the selection of the Director.

Sec. 4823. Special agents

Special agent positions shall be filled in accordance with the provisions of the Foreign Service Act of 1980 (22 U.S.C. 3901 et seq.) and title 5. In filling such positions, the Secretary of State shall actively recruit women and members of minority groups. The Secretary of State shall prescribe the qualifications required for assignment or appointment to such positions. The qualifications may include minimum and maximum entry age restrictions and other physical standards and shall incorporate such standards as may be required by law in order to perform security functions, to bear arms, and to exercise investigatory, warrant, arrest, and such other authorities as are available by law to special agents of the Department of State and the Foreign Service.

Sec. 4824. Contracting authority

The Secretary of State is authorized to employ individuals or organizations by contract to carry out the purposes of this Act, and individuals employed by contract to perform such services shall not by virtue of such employment be considered to be employees of the United States Government for purposes of any law administered by the Office of Personnel Management (except that the Secretary may determine the applicability to such individuals of any law administered by the Secretary concerning the employment of such individuals); and such contracts are authorized to be negotiated, the terms of the contracts to be prescribed, and the work to be performed, where necessary, without regard to such statutory provisions as relate to the negotiation, making and performance of contracts and performance of work in the United States.

Subchapter III—Performance and Accountability

Sec. 4831. Accountability Review Boards

(a) In general

(1) Convening a Board

Except as provided in paragraph (2), in any case of serious injury, loss of life, or significant destruction of property at, or related to, a United States Government mission abroad, and in any case of a serious breach of security involving intelligence activities of a foreign government directed at a United States Government mission abroad, which is covered by the provisions of this chapter (other than a facility or installation subject to the control of a United States area military commander), the Secretary of State shall convene an Accountability Review Board (in this subchapter referred to as the "Board"). The Secretary shall not convene a Board where the Secretary determines that a case clearly involves only causes unrelated to security.

(2) Department of Defense facilities and personnel The Secretary of State is not required to convene a Board in the case of an incident described in paragraph (1) that involves any facility, installation, or personnel of the Department of Defense with respect to which the Secretary has delegated operational control of overseas security functions to the Secretary of Defense pursuant to section 4805 f this title. In any such case, the Secretary of Defense shall conduct an appropriate inquiry. The Secretary of Defense shall report the findings and recommendations of such inquiry, and the action taken with respect to such recommendations, to the Secretary of State and Congress.

(b) Deadlines for convening Boards

(1) In general

Except as provided in paragraph (2), the Secretary of State shall convene a Board not later than 60 days after the occurrence of an incident described in subsection (a)(1) of this section, except that such 60-day period may be extended for one additional 60-day period if the Secretary determines that the additional period is necessary for the convening of the Board.

(2) Delay in cases involving intelligence activities

With respect to breaches of security involving intelligence activities, the Secretary of State may delay the establishment of a Board if, after consultation with the chairman of the Select Committee on Intelligence of the Senate and the chairman of the Permanent Select Committee on Intelligence of the House of Representatives, the Secretary determines that the establishment of a Board would compromise intelligence sources or methods. The Secretary shall promptly advise the chairmen of such committees of each determination pursuant to this paragraph to delay the establishment of a Board.

(c) Notification to Congress

Whenever the Secretary of State convenes a Board, the Secretary shall promptly inform the chairman of the Committee on Foreign Relations of the Senate and the Speaker of the House of Representatives—

(1) that a Board has been convened;

(2) of the membership of the Board; and

(3) of other appropriate information about the Board.

Sec. 4832. Accountability Review Board

(a) Membership

A Board shall consist of five members, 4 appointed by the Secretary of State, and 1 appointed by the Director of Central Intelligence. The Secretary of State shall designate the Chairperson of the Board. Members of the Board who are not Federal officers or employees shall each be paid at a rate not to exceed the maximum rate of basic pay payable for level GS-18 of the General Schedule for each day (including travel time) during which they are engaged in the actual performance of duties vested in the Board. Members of the Board who are Federal officers or employees shall receive no additional pay by reason of such membership.

(b) Facilities, services, supplies, and staff

(1) Supplied by Department of State

A Board shall obtain facilities, services, and supplies through the Department of State. All expenses of the Board, including necessary costs of travel, shall be paid by the Department of State. Travel expenses authorized under this paragraph shall be paid in accordance with subchapter I of chapter 57 of title 5 or other applicable law.

(2) Detail

At the request of a Board, employees of the Department of State or other Federal agencies, members of the Foreign Service, or members of the uniformed services may be temporarily assigned, with or without reimbursement, to assist the Board.

(3) Experts and consultants

A Board may employ and compensate (in accordance with section 3109 of title 5) such experts and consultants as the Board considers necessary to carry out its functions. Experts and consultants so employed shall be responsible solely to the Board.

Sec. 4833. Procedures

(a) Evidence

(1) United States Government personnel and contractors

(A) With respect to any individual described in subparagraph (B), a Board may—

(i) administer oaths and affirmations;

(ii) require that depositions be given and interrogatories answered; and

(iii) require the attendance and presentation of testimony and evidence by such individual.

Failure of any such individual to comply with a request of the Board shall be grounds for disciplinary action by the head of the Federal agency in which such individual is employed or serves, or in the case of a contractor, debarment.

(B) The individuals referred to in subparagraph (A) are—

(i) employees as defined by section 2105 o title 5 (including members of the Foreign Service);

(ii) members of the uniformed services as defined by section 101(3) of title 37;

(iii) employees of instrumentalities of the United States; and

(iv) individuals employed by any person or entity under contract with agencies or instrumentalities of the United States Government to provide services, equipment, or personnel.

(2) Other persons

With respect to a person who is not described in paragraph (1)(B), a Board may administer oaths and affirmations and require that depositions be given and interrogatories answered.

(3) Subpoenas

(A) The Board may issue a subpoena for the attendance and testimony of any person (other than a person described in clause documentary or other evidence from any such person if the Board finds that such a subpoena is necessary in the interests of justice for the development of relevant evidence.

(B) In the case of contumacy or refusal to obey a subpoena issued under this paragraph, a court of the United States within the jurisdiction of which a person is directed to appear or produce information, or within the jurisdiction of which the person is found, resides, or transacts business, may upon application of the Attorney General, issue to such person an order requiring such person to appear before the Board to give testimony or produce information as required by the subpoena.

(C) Subpoenaed witnesses shall be paid the same fee and mileage allowances which are paid subpoenaed witnesses in the courts of the United States.

(b) Confidentiality

A Board shall adopt for administrative proceedings under this subchapter such procedures with respect to confidentiality as may be deemed necessary, including procedures relating to the conduct of closed proceedings or the submission and use of evidence in camera, to ensure in particular the protection of classified information relating to national defense, foreign policy, or intelligence matters. The Director of Central Intelligence shall establish the level of protection required for intelligence information and for information relating to intelligence personnel, including standards for secure storage.

(c) Records

Records pertaining to administrative proceedings under this subchapter shall be separated from all other records of the Department of State and shall be maintained under appropriate safeguards to preserve confidentiality and classification of information. Such records shall be prohibited from disclosure to the public until such time as a Board completes its work and is dismissed. The Department of State shall turn over to the

Director of Central Intelligence intelligence information and information relating to intelligence personnel which shall then become records of the Central Intelligence Agency. After that time, only such exemptions from disclosure under section 552(b) of title 5 (relating to freedom of information), as apply to other records of the Department of State, and to any information transmitted under section 4834(c) of this title to the head of a Federal agency or instrumentality, shall be available for the remaining records of the Board.

(d) Status of Boards

The provisions of the Federal Advisory Committee Act (5 U.S.C. App. 1 et seq.) and section 552b of title 5 (relating to open meetings) shall not apply to any Board.

Sec. 4834. Findings and recommendations by a Board

(a) Findings

A Board convened in any case shall examine the facts and circumstances surrounding the serious injury, loss of life, or significant destruction of property at or related to a United States Government mission abroad or surrounding the serious breach of security involving intelligence activities of a foreign government directed at a United States Government mission abroad (as the case may be) and shall make written findings determining—

(1) the extent to which the incident or incidents with respect to which the Board was convened was security related;

(2) whether the security systems and security procedures at that mission were adequate;

(3) whether the security systems and security procedures were properly implemented;

(4) the impact of intelligence and information availability; and

(5) such other facts and circumstances which may be relevant to the appropriate security management of United States missions abroad.

(b) Program recommendations

A Board shall submit its findings (which may be classified to the extent deemed necessary by the Board) to the Secretary of State, together with recommendations as appropriate to improve the security and efficiency of any program or operation which the Board has reviewed.

(c) Personnel recommendations

Whenever a Board finds reasonable cause to believe that an individual described in section 4833(a)(1)(B) of this title has breached the duty of that individual, the Board shall—

(1) notify the individual concerned,

(2) transmit the finding of reasonable cause, together with all information relevant to such finding, to the head of the appropriate Federal agency or instrumentality, and

(3) recommend that such agency or instrumentality initiate an appropriate investigatory or disciplinary action. In determining whether an individual has breached a duty of that individual, the Board shall take into account any standard of conduct, law, rule, regulation, contract, or order which is pertinent to the performance of the duties of that individual.

(d) Reports

(1) Program recommendations

In any case in which a Board transmits recommendations to the Secretary of State under subsection (b) of this section, the Secretary shall, not later than 90 days after the receipt of such recommendations, submit a report to the Congress on each such recommendation and the action taken with respect to that recommendation.

(2) Personnel recommendations

In any case in which a Board transmits a finding of reasonable cause under subsection (c) of this section, the head of the Federal agency or instrumentality receiving the information shall review the evidence and recommendations and shall, not later than 30 days after the receipt of that finding, transmit to the Congress a report specifying—

(A) the nature of the case and a summary of the evidence transmitted by the Board; and

(B) the decision by the Federal agency or instrumentality to take disciplinary or other appropriate action against that individual or the reasons for deciding not to take disciplinary or other action with respect to that individual.

Sec. 4835. Relation to other proceedings

Nothing in this subchapter shall be construed to create administrative or judicial review remedies or rights of action not otherwise available by law, nor shall any provision of this subchapter be construed to deprive any person of any right or legal defense which would otherwise be available to that person under any law, rule, or regulation.

Subchapter IV—Diplomatic Security Program

Sec. 4851. Authorization

(a) Diplomatic security program

(1) In general
In addition to amounts otherwise available for such purposes, the following amounts are authorized to be appropriated for fiscal years 1986 and 1987, for the Department of State to carry out diplomatic security construction, acquisition, and operations pursuant to the Department of State's Supplemental Diplomatic Security Program, as justified to the Congress for the respective fiscal year for "Administration of Foreign Affairs," as follows:

(A) For "Salaries and Expenses," $308,104,000.

(B) For "Acquisition and Maintenance of Buildings Abroad," $857,806,000.

(C) For "Counterterrorism Research and Development," $15,000,000.

(4) Allocation of amounts authorized to be appropriated
Amounts authorized to be appropriated by this subsection, and by the amendment made by paragraph (2), shall be allocated as provided in the table entitled "Diplomatic Security Program" relating to this section which appears in the Joint Explanatory Statement of the Committee of Conference to accompany H.R. 4151 of the 99th Congress (the Omnibus Diplomatic Security and Antiterrorism Act of 1986).

(b) Notification to authorizing Committees of requests for appropriations
In any fiscal year, whenever the Secretary of State submits to the Congress a request for appropriations to carry out the program described in subsection (a) of this section, the Secretary shall notify the Committee on Foreign Affairs of the House of Representatives and the Committee on Foreign Relations of the Senate of such request, together with a justification of each item listed in such request.

(d) Prohibition on reallocations of authorizations

Section 2696(d) of this title shall not apply with respect to any amounts authorized to be appropriated under this section.

(e) Security requirements of other foreign affairs agencies

Based solely on security requirements and within the total amount of funds available for security, the Secretary of State shall ensure that an equitable level of funding is provided for the security requirements of other foreign affairs agencies.

(f) Insufficiency of funds

In the event that sufficient funds are not available in any fiscal year for all of the diplomatic security construction, acquisition, and operations pursuant to the Department of State's Supplemental Diplomatic Security Program, as justified to the Congress for such fiscal year, the Secretary of State shall report to the Congress the effect that the insufficiency of funds will have with respect to the Department of State and each of the other foreign affairs agencies.

(g) Allocation of funds for certain security programs

Of the amount of funds authorized to be appropriated by subsection (a)(1)(A) of this section, $34,537,000 shall be available to the Secretary of State only for the protection of classified office equipment, the expansion of information systems security, and the hiring of American systems managers and operators for computers at high threat locations.

(h) Furniture, furnishings, and equipment

(1) Use of existing furniture, furnishings, and equipment

If physically possible, facilities constructed or acquired pursuant to subsection (a) of this section shall be furnished and equipped with the furniture, furnishings, and equipment that were being used in the facilities being replaced, rather than with newly acquired furniture, furnishings, and equipment.

Sec. 4852. Diplomatic construction program

(a) Preference for United States contractors

Notwithstanding section 302 of this title, and where adequate competition exists, only United States persons and qualified United States joint venture persons may—

(1) bid on a diplomatic construction or design project which has an estimated total project value exceeding $10,000,000; and

(2) bid on a diplomatic construction or design project which involves technical security, unless the project involves low-level technology, as determined by the Secretary of State.

(b) Exception

Subsection (a) of this section shall not apply with respect to any diplomatic construction or design project in a foreign country whose statutes prohibit the use of United States contractors on such projects. The exception contained in this subsection shall only become effective with respect to a foreign country 30 days after the Secretary of State certifies to the Committee on Foreign Affairs and the Committee on Appropriations of the House of Representatives and the Committee on Foreign Relations and the Committee on Appropriations of the Senate what specific actions he has taken to urge such foreign country to permit the use of United States contractors on such projects, and what actions he shall take with respect to that country as authorized by title II of the State Department Basic Authorities Act of 1956 (22 U.S.C. 4301 et seq.; commonly referred to as the "Foreign Missions Act").

(c) Definitions

For the purposes of this section—

(1) the term "adequate competition" means with respect to a construction or design project, the presence of two or more qualified bidders submitting responsive bids for that project;

(2) the term "United States person" means a person which—

(A) is incorporated or legally organized under the laws of the United States, including State, the District of Columbia, and local laws;

(B) has its principal place of business in the United States;

(C) has been incorporated or legally organized in the United States—

(i) for more than 5 years before the issuance date of the invitation for bids or request for proposals with respect to a construction project under subsection (a)(1) of this section; and

(ii) for more than 2 years before the issuance date of the invitation for bids or request for proposals with respect to a construction or design project which involves physical or technical security under subsection (a)(2) of this section;

(D) has performed within the United States administrative and technical, professional, or construction services similar in complexity, type of construction, and value to the project being bid;

(E) with respect to a construction project under subsection (a)(1) of this section, has achieved total business volume equal to or greater than the value of the project being bid in 3 years of the 5-year period before the date specified in subparagraph (C)(i);

(F)

(i) employs United States citizens in at least 80 percent of its principal management positions in the United States,

(ii) employs United States citizens in more than half of its permanent, full-time positions in the United States, and

(iii) will employ United States citizens in at least 80 percent of the supervisory positions on the foreign buildings office project site; and

(G) has the existing technical and financial resources in the United States to perform the contract; and

(3) the term "qualified United States joint venture person" means a joint venture in which a United States person or persons owns at least 51 percent of the assets of the joint venture.

(d) American minority contractors

Not less than 10 percent of the amount appropriated pursuant to section 4851(a) of this title for diplomatic construction or design projects each fiscal year shall be allocated to the extent practicable for contracts with American minority contractors.

(e) American small business contractors

Not less than 10 percent of the amount appropriated pursuant to section 4851(a) of this title for diplomatic construction or design projects each fiscal year shall be allocated to the extent practicable for contracts with American small business contractors.

(f) Limitation on subcontracting

With respect to a diplomatic construction project, a prime contractor may not subcontract more than 50 percent of the total value of its contract for that project.

Sec. 4853. Security requirements for contractors

Not later than 90 days after August 27, 1986, the Secretary of State shall issue regulations to—

(1) strengthen the security procedures applicable to contractors and subcontractors involved in any way with any diplomatic construction or design project; and

(2) permit a contractor or subcontractor to have access to any design or blueprint relating to such a project only in accordance with those procedures.

Sec. 4854. Qualifications of persons hired for diplomatic construction program

In carrying out the diplomatic construction program referred to in section 4851(a) of this title, the Secretary of State shall employ as professional staff (by appointment, contract, or otherwise) only those persons with a demonstrated specialized background in the fields of construction, construction law, or contract management. In filling such positions, the Secretary shall actively recruit women and members of minority groups.

Sec. 4855. Cost overruns

Any amount required to complete any capital project described in the Department of State's Supplemental Diplomatic Security Program, as justified to the Congress for the respective fiscal year, which is in excess of the amount made available for that project pursuant to section 4851(a)(1) or (3) shall be treated as a reprogramming of funds under section 2706 of this title and shall not be available for obligation or expenditure except in compliance with the procedures applicable to such reprogrammings.

Sec. 4856. Efficiency in contracting

(a) Bonuses and penalties

The Director of the Office of Foreign Buildings shall provide for a contract system of bonuses and penalties for the diplomatic construction program funded pursuant to the authorizations of appropriations provided in this subchapter. Not later than 3 months after August 27, 1986, the Director shall submit a report to the Congress on the implementation of this section.

(b) Surety bonds and guarantees

The Director of the Office of Foreign Buildings shall require each person awarded a contract for work under the diplomatic construction program to post a surety bond or guarantee, in such amount as the Director may determine, to assure performance under such contract.

(c) Disqualification of contractors

No person doing business with Libya may be eligible for any contract awarded pursuant to this Act.

Sec. 4857. Advisory Panel on Overseas Security

Not later than 90 days after August 27, 1986, the Secretary of State shall submit a report to the Congress on the implementation of the 91 recommendations contained in the final report of the Advisory Panel on Overseas Security. If any such recommendation has been rejected, the Secretary shall provide the reasons why that recommendation was rejected.

Sec. 4858. Training to improve perimeter security at United States diplomatic missions abroad

(a) Training

It is the sense of Congress that the President should use the authority under chapter 8 of title II of the Foreign Assistance Act of 1961 (22 U.S.C. 2349aa et seq.) (relating to antiterrorism assistance) to improve perimeter security of United States diplomatic missions abroad.

Sec. 4859. Protection of public entrances of United States diplomatic missions abroad

The Secretary of State shall install and maintain a walk-through metal detector or other advanced screening system at public entrances of each United States diplomatic mission abroad.

Sec. 4860. Reimbursement of Department of the Treasury

The Secretary of State shall reimburse the appropriate appropriations account of the Department of the Treasury out of funds appropriated pursuant to section 4851(a)(1) of this title for the actual costs incurred by the United States Secret Service, as agreed to by the Secretary of the Treasury, for providing protection for the spouses of foreign heads of state during fiscal years 1986 and 1987.

Sec. 4861. Inspector General for Department of State

(a) Direction to establish

The Congress directs the Secretary of State to proceed immediately to establish an Office of Inspector General of the Department of State not later than October 1, 1986. Not later than January 31, 1987, the Secretary of State shall submit a report to the Committee on Foreign Relations of the Senate and the Committee on Foreign Affairs of the House of Representatives on the progress in establishing that office. Such report shall include an accounting of the obligation of funds for fiscal year 1987 for that office.

(b) Duties and responsibilities

The Inspector General of the Department of State (as established by the amendment made by section 150(a) of the Foreign Relations Authorization Act, Fiscal Years 1986 and 1987) is authorized to perform all duties and responsibilities, and to exercise the authorities, stated in section 3929 of this title and in the Inspector General Act of 1978.

(c) Earmark

Of the amounts made available for fiscal year 1987 for salaries and expenses under the heading "Administration of Foreign Affairs," not less than $6,500,000 shall be used for the sole purpose of establishing and maintaining the Office of Inspector General of the Department of State.

(d) Limitation on appointment

No career member of the Foreign Service, as defined by section 3903 of this title, may be appointed Inspector General of the Department of State.

Sec. 4862. Prohibition on use of funds for facilities in Israel, Jerusalem, or West Bank

None of the funds authorized to be appropriated by this Act may be obligated or expended for site acquisition, development, or construction of any facility in Israel, Jerusalem, or the West Bank.

Sec. 4863. Use of cleared personnel to ensure secure maintenance and repair of diplomatic facilities abroad

(a) Policies and regulations

The Secretary of State shall develop and implement policies and regulations to provide for the use of persons who have been granted an appropriate United States security clearance to ensure that the security of areas intended for the storage of classified materials or the conduct of classified activities in a United States diplomatic mission or consular post abroad is not compromised in the performance of maintenance and repair services in those areas.

(b) Study and report

The Secretary of State shall conduct a study of the feasibility and necessity of requiring that, in the case of certain United States diplomatic facilities abroad, no contractor shall be hired to perform maintenance or repair services in an area intended for the storage of classified materials or the conduct of classified activities unless such contractor has been granted an appropriate United States security clearance. Such study shall include, but is not limited to, United States facilities located in Cairo, New Delhi, Riyadh, and Tokyo. Not later than 180 days after February 16, 1990, the Secretary of State shall report the results of such study to the Chairman of the Committee on Foreign Relations of the Senate and the Committee on Foreign Affairs of the House of Representatives.

Sec. 4864. Increased participation of United States contractors in local guard contracts abroad under diplomatic security program

(a) Findings

The Congress makes the following findings:

(1) State Department policy concerning the advertising of security contracts at Foreign Service buildings has been inconsistent over the years. In many cases, diplomatic and consular posts abroad have been given the responsibility to determine the manner in which the private sector was notified concerning an invitation for bids or a request for proposals with respect to a local guard contract. Some United States foreign missions have only chosen to advertise locally the availability of a local security guard contract abroad.

(2) As a result, many United States security firms that provide local guard services abroad have been unaware that local guard contracts were available for bidding abroad and such firms have been disadvantaged as a result.

(3) Undoubtedly, United States security firms would be interested in bidding on more local guard contracts abroad if such firms knew of the opportunity to bid on such contracts.

(b) Objective

It is the objective of this section to improve the efficiency of the local guard programs abroad administered by the Bureau of Diplomatic Security of the Department of State and to ensure maximum competition for local guard contracts abroad concerning Foreign Service buildings.

(c) Participation of United States contractors in local guard contracts abroad
With respect to local guard contracts for a Foreign Service building which exceed $250,000 and are entered into after February 16, 1990, the Secretary of State shall—

(1) establish procedures to ensure that all solicitations for such contracts are adequately advertised in the Commerce and Business Daily;

(2) absent compelling reasons, award such contracts through the competitive process;

(3) in evaluating proposals for such contracts, award contracts to the technically acceptable firm offering the lowest evaluated price, except that proposals of United States persons and qualified United States joint venture persons (as defined in subsection (d) of this section) shall be evaluated by reducing the bid price by 10 percent;

(4) in countries where contract denomination and/or payment in local currencies constitutes a barrier to competition by United States firms—

(A) allow solicitations to be bid in United States dollars; and

(B) allow contracts awarded to United States firms to be paid in United States dollars;

(5) ensure that United States diplomatic and consular posts assist United States firms in obtaining local licenses and permits; and

(6) establish procedures to ensure that appropriate measures are taken by diplomatic and consular post management to assure that United States persons and qualified United States joint venture persons are not disadvantaged during the solicitation and bid evaluation process.

(d) Definitions
For the purposes of this section—

(1) the term "United States person" means a person which—

(A) is incorporated or legally organized under the laws of the United States, including the laws of any State, locality, or the District of Columbia;

(B)   has its principal place of business in the United States;

(C)   has been incorporated or legally organized in the United States for more than 2 years before the issuance date of the invitation for bids or request for proposals with respect to the contract under subsection (c) of this section;

(D)   has performed within the United States or overseas security services similar in complexity to the contract being bid;

(E)   with respect to the contract under subsection (c) of this section, has achieved a total business volume equal to or greater than the value of the project being bid in 3 years of the 5-year period before the date specified in subparagraph (C);

(F)

(i)   employs United States citizens in at least 80 percent of its principal management positions in the United States; and

(ii)   employs United States citizens in more than half of its permanent, full-time positions in the United States; and

(G)   has the existing technical and financial resources in the United States to perform the contract;

(2)   the term "qualified United States joint venture person" means a joint venture in which a United States person or persons owns at least 51 percent of the assets of the joint venture;

(3)   the term "Foreign Service building" means any building or grounds of the United States which is in a foreign country and is under the jurisdiction and control of the Secretary of State, including residences of United States personnel assigned overseas under the authority of the Ambassador; and

(4)   the term "barrier to local competition" means—

(A)   conditions of extreme currency volatility;

(B)   restrictions on repatriation of profits;

(C)   multiple exchange rates which significantly disadvantage United States firms;

(D)   government restrictions inhibiting the free convertibility of foreign exchange; or

(E) conditions of extreme local political instability.

(e) United States minority contractors

Not less than 10 percent of the amount of funds obligated for local guard contracts for Foreign Service buildings subject to subsection (c) of this section shall be allocated to the extent practicable for contracts with United States minority small business contractors.

(f) United States small business contractors

Not less than 10 percent of the amount of funds obligated for local guard contracts for Foreign Service buildings subject to subsection (c) of this section shall be allocated to the extent practicable for contracts with United States small business contractors.

(g) Limitation of subcontracting

With respect to local guard contracts subject to subsection (c) of this section, a prime contractor may not subcontract more than 50 percent of the total value of its contract for that project.

Sec. 4865. Security requirements for United States diplomatic facilities

(a) In general

The following security requirements shall apply with respect to United States diplomatic facilities and specified personnel:

(1) Threat assessment

(A) Emergency Action Plan

The Emergency Action Plan (EAP) of each United States mission shall address the threat of large explosive attacks from vehicles and the safety of employees during such an explosive attack. Such plan shall be reviewed and updated annually.

(B) Security Environment Threat List

The Security Environment Threat List shall contain a section that addresses potential acts of international terrorism against United States diplomatic facilities based on threat identification criteria that emphasize the threat of transnational terrorism and include the local security environment, host government support, and other relevant factors such as cultural realities. Such plan shall be reviewed and updated every six months.

(2) Site selection

(A) In general
In selecting a site for any new United States diplomatic facility abroad, the Secretary shall ensure that all United States Government personnel at the post (except those under the command of an area military commander) will be located on the site.

(B) Waiver authority

(i) In general
Subject to clause (ii), the Secretary of State may waive subparagraph (A) if the Secretary, together with the head of each agency employing personnel that would not be located at the site, determine that security considerations permit and it is in the national interest of the United States.

(ii) Chancery or consulate building

(I) Authority not delegable
The Secretary may not delegate the waiver authority under clause (i) with respect to a chancery or consulate building.

(II) Congressional notification
Not less than 15 days prior to implementing the waiver authority under clause (i) with respect to a chancery or consulate building, the Secretary shall notify the appropriate congressional committees in writing of the waiver and the reasons for the determination.

(iii) Report to Congress
The Secretary shall submit to the appropriate congressional committees an annual report of all waivers under this subparagraph.

(3) Perimeter distance

(A) Requirement
Each newly acquired United States diplomatic facility shall be sited not less than 100 feet from the perimeter of the property on which the facility is to be situated.

(B) Waiver authority

(i) In general
Subject to clause (ii), the Secretary of State may waive subparagraph (A) if the Secretary determines that secu-

rity considerations permit and it is in the national interest of the United States.

(ii) Chancery or consulate building

(I)   Authority not delegable
The Secretary may not delegate the waiver authority under clause (i) with respect to a chancery or consulate building.

(II)   Congressional notification
Not less than 15 days prior to implementing the waiver authority under subparagraph (A) with respect to a chancery or consulate building, the Secretary shall notify the appropriate congressional committees in writing of the waiver and the reasons for the determination.

(iii) Report to Congress
The Secretary shall submit to the appropriate congressional committees an annual report of all waivers under this subparagraph.

(4) Crisis management training

(A) Training of headquarters staff
The appropriate personnel of the Department of State headquarters staff shall undertake crisis management training for mass casualty and mass destruction incidents relating to diplomatic facilities for the purpose of bringing about a rapid response to such incidents from Department of State headquarters in Washington, D.C.

(B) Training of personnel abroad
A program of appropriate instruction in crisis management shall be provided to personnel at United States diplomatic facilities abroad at least on an annual basis.

(5) Diplomatic security training
Not later than six months after November 29, 1999, the Secretary of State shall—

(A) develop annual physical fitness standards for all diplomatic security agents to ensure that the agents are prepared to carry out all of their official responsibilities; and

(B) provide for an independent evaluation by an outside entity of the overall adequacy of current new agent, in-service, and management training programs to prepare agents to carry out the full scope of diplomatic security responsibilities, including preventing attacks on United States personnel and facilities.

(6) State Department support

(A) Foreign Emergency Support Team
The Foreign Emergency Support Team (FEST) of the Department of State shall receive sufficient support from the Department, including—

(i) conducting routine training exercises of the FEST;

(ii) providing personnel identified to serve on the FEST as a collateral duty;

(iii) providing personnel to assist in activities such as security, medical relief, public affairs, engineering, and building safety; and

(iv) providing such additional support as may be necessary to enable the FEST to provide support in a post-crisis environment involving mass casualties and physical damage.

(B) FEST aircraft

(i) Replacement aircraft
The President shall develop a plan to replace on a priority basis the current FEST aircraft funded by the Department of Defense with a dedicated, capable, and reliable replacement aircraft and backup aircraft to be operated and maintained by the Department of Defense.

(ii) Report
Not later than 60 days after November 29, 1999, the President shall submit a report to the appropriate congressional committees describing the aircraft selected pursuant to clause (i) and the arrangements for the funding, operation, and maintenance of such aircraft.

(iii) Authority to lease aircraft to respond to a terrorist attack abroad
Subject to the availability of appropriations, when the Attorney General of the Department of Justice exercises the Attorney General's authority to lease commercial air-

craft to transport equipment and personnel in response to a terrorist attack abroad if there have been reasonable efforts to obtain appropriate Department of Defense aircraft and such aircraft are unavailable, the Attorney General shall have the authority to obtain indemnification insurance or guarantees if necessary and appropriate.

(7) Rapid response procedures

The Secretary of State shall enter into a memorandum of understanding with the Secretary of Defense setting out rapid response procedures for mobilization of personnel and equipment of their respective departments to provide more effective assistance in times of emergency with respect to United States diplomatic facilities.

(8) Storage of emergency equipment and records

All United States diplomatic facilities shall have emergency equipment and records required in case of an emergency situation stored at an off-site facility.

(b) Statutory construction

Nothing in this section alters or amends existing security requirements not addressed by this section.

Chapter 61—Anti-Terrorism—PLO

Sec. 5201. Findings; determinations

(a) Findings

The Congress finds that—

(1) Middle East terrorism accounted for 60 percent of total international terrorism in 1985;

(2) the Palestine Liberation Organization (hereafter in this chapter referred to as the "PLO") was directly responsible for the murder of an American citizen on the Achille Lauro cruise liner in 1985, and a member of the PLO's Executive Committee is under indictment in the United States for the murder of that American citizen;

(3) the head of the PLO has been implicated in the murder of a United States Ambassador overseas;

(4) the PLO and its constituent groups have taken credit for, and been implicated in, the murders of dozens of American citizens abroad;

(5) the PLO covenant specifically states that "armed struggle is the only way to liberate Palestine, thus it is an overall strategy, not merely a tactical phase";

(6) the PLO rededicated itself to the "continuing struggle in all its armed forms" at the Palestine National Council meeting in April 1987; and

(7) the Attorney General has stated that "various elements of the Palestine Liberation Organization and its allies and affiliates are in the thick of international terror."

(b) Determinations

Therefore, the Congress determines that the PLO and its affiliates are a terrorist organization and a threat to the interests of the United States, its allies, and to international law and should not benefit from operating in the United States.

Sec. 5202. Prohibitions regarding PLO

It shall be unlawful, if the purpose be to further the interests of the Palestine Liberation Organization or any of its constituent groups, any successor to any of those, or any agents thereof, on or after the effective date of this chapter—

(1) to receive anything of value except informational material from the PLO or any of its constituent groups, any successor thereto, or any agents thereof;

(2) to expend funds from the PLO or any of its constituent groups, any successor thereto, or any agents thereof; or

(3) notwithstanding any provision of law to the contrary, to establish or maintain an office, headquarters, premises, or other facilities or establishments within the jurisdiction of the United States at the behest or direction of, or with funds provided by the Palestine Liberation Organization or any of its constituent groups, any successor to any of those, or any agents thereof.

Sec. 5203. Enforcement

(a) Attorney General

The Attorney General shall take the necessary steps and institute the necessary legal action to effectuate the policies and provisions of this chapter.

(b) Relief

Any district court of the United States for a district in which a violation of this chapter occurs shall have authority, upon petition of relief by the Attorney General, to grant injunctive and such other equitable relief as it shall deem necessary to enforce the provisions of this chapter.

Chapter 64—United States Response to Terrorism Affecting Americans Abroad

Sec. 5501. International negotiations concerning aviation security

(a) United States policy

It is the policy of the United States—

(1) to seek bilateral agreements to achieve United States aviation security objectives with foreign governments;

(2) to continue to press vigorously for security improvements through the Foreign Airport Security Act[1] and the foreign airport assessment program; and

Aviation Organization to improve aviation security internationally.

(b) Negotiations for aviation security

(1) The Department of State, in consultation with the Department of Transportation, shall be responsible for negotiating requisite aviation security agreements with foreign governments concerning the implementation of United States rules and regulations which affect the foreign operations of United States air carriers, foreign air carriers, and foreign international airports. The Secretary of State is directed to enter, expeditiously, into negotiations for bilateral and multilateral agreements—

(A) for enhanced aviation security objectives;

(B) to implement the Foreign Airport Security Act and the foreign airport assessment program to the fullest extent practicable; and

(C) to achieve improved availability of passenger manifest information.

(2) A principal objective of bilateral and multilateral negotiations with foreign governments and the International Civil Aviation Organization shall be improved availability of passenger manifest information.

Sec. 5502. Coordinator for Counterterrorism

The Coordinator for Counterterrorism shall be responsible for the coordination of international aviation security for the Department of State.

Sec. 5503. Department of State notification of families of victims

(a) Department of State policy

It is the policy of the Department of State pursuant to section 2715 of this title to directly and promptly notify the families of victims of aviation disasters abroad concerning citizens of the United States directly affected by such a disaster, including timely written notice. The Secretary of State shall ensure that such notification by the Department of State is carried out notwithstanding notification by any other person.

(b) Department of State guidelines

Not later than 60 days after November 16, 1990, the Secretary of State shall issue such regulations, guidelines, and circulars as are necessary to ensure that the policy under subsection (a) of this section is fully implemented.

Sec. 5504. Designation of State Department-family liaison and toll-free family communications system

(a) Designation of State Department-family liaison

Not later than 60 days after November 16, 1990, the Secretary of State shall issue such rules and guidelines as are necessary to provide that in the event of an aviation disaster directly involving United States citizens abroad, if possible, the Department of State will assign a specific individual, and an alternate, as the Department of State liaison for the family of each such citizen.

(b) Toll-free communications system

In the establishment of the Department of State toll-free communications system to facilitate inquiries concerning the affect of any disaster abroad on United States citizens residing or traveling abroad, the Secretary of State shall ensure that a toll-free telephone number is reserved for the exclusive use of the families of citizens who have been determined to be directly involved in any such disaster.

Sec. 5505. Disaster training for State Department personnel

(a) Additional training

The Secretary of State shall institute a supplemental program of training in disaster management for all consular officers.

(b) Training improvements

(1) In expanding the training program under subsection (a) of this section, the Secretary of State shall consult with death and bereavement counselors concerning the particular demands posed by aviation tragedies and terrorist activities.

(2) In providing such additional training under subsection (a) of this section the Secretary of State shall consider supplementing the current training program through—

(A) providing specialized training to create a team of "disaster specialists" to deploy immediately in a crisis; or

(B) securing outside experts to be brought in during the initial phases to assist consular personnel.

Sec. 5506. Department of State responsibilities and procedures at international disaster site

(a) Dispatch of senior State Department official to site

Not later than 60 days after November 16, 1990, the Secretary of State shall issue such rules and guidelines as are necessary to provide that in the event of an international disaster, particularly an aviation tragedy, directly involving significant numbers of United States citizens abroad not less than one senior officer from the Bureau of Consular Affairs of the Department of State shall be dispatched to the site of such disaster.

(b) Criteria for Department of State staffing at disaster site

Not later than 60 days after November 16, 1990, the Secretary of State shall promulgate criteria for Department of State staffing of disaster sites abroad. Such criteria shall define responsibility for staffing decisions and shall consider the deployment of crisis teams under subsection (d) of this section. The Secretary of State shall promptly issue such rules and guidelines as are necessary to implement criteria developed pursuant to this subsection.

(c) State Department ombudsman

Not later than 60 days after November 16, 1990, the Secretary of State shall issue such rules and guidelines as are necessary to provide that in the event of an international aviation disaster involving significant numbers of United States citizens abroad not less than one officer or employee of the Department of State shall be dispatched to the disaster site to provide on-site assistance to families who may visit the site and to act as an ombudsman in matters involving the foreign local government authorities and social service agencies.

(d) Crisis teams
Not later than 60 days after November 16, 1990, the Secretary of State shall promulgate procedures for the deployment of a "crisis team," which may include public affairs, forensic, and bereavement experts, to the site of any international disaster involving United States citizens abroad to augment in-country Embassy and consulate staff. The Secretary of State shall promptly issue such rules and guidelines as are necessary to implement procedures developed pursuant to this subsection.

Sec. 5507. Recovery and disposition of remains and personal effects

It is the policy of the Department of State (pursuant to section 2715 of this title) to provide liaison with foreign governments and persons and with United States air carriers concerning arrangements for the preparation and transport to the United States of the remains of citizens who die abroad, as well as the disposition of personal effects. The Secretary of State shall ensure that regulations and guidelines of the Department of State reflect such policy and that such assistance is rendered to the families of United States citizens who are killed in terrorist incidents and disasters abroad.

Sec. 5508. Assessment of Lockerbie experience

(a) Assessment
The Secretary of State shall compile an assessment of the Department of State response to the Pan American Airways Flight 103 aviation disaster over Lockerbie, Scotland, on December 21, 1988.

(b) Guidelines
The Secretary of State shall establish, based on the assessment compiled under subsection (a) of this section and other relevant factors, guidelines for future Department of State responses to comparable disasters and shall distribute such guidelines to all United States diplomatic and consular posts abroad.

Sec. 5509. Official Department of State recognition

Not later than 60 days after November 16, 1990, the Secretary of State shall promulgate guidelines for appropriate ceremonies or other official expressions of respect and support for the families of United States citizens who are killed through acts of terrorism abroad.

Sec. 5510. United States Government compensation for victims of terrorism

(a) Compensation
The President shall submit to the Congress, not later than one year after November 16, 1990, recommendations on whether or not legislation should be enacted to authorize the United States to provide monetary and tax relief as compensation to United States citizens who are victims of terrorism.

(b) Board
The President may establish a board to develop criteria for compensation and to recommend changes to existing laws to establish a single comprehensive approach to victim compensation for terrorist acts.

(c) Income tax benefit for victims of Lockerbie terrorism

(1) In general
Subject to paragraph (2), in the case of any individual whose death was a direct result of the Pan American Airways Flight 103 terrorist disaster over Lockerbie, Scotland, on December 21, 1988, any tax imposed by subtitle A of title 26 shall not apply—

(A) with respect to the taxable year which includes December 21, 1988, and (B) with respect to the prior taxable year.

(2) Limitation
In no case may the tax benefit pursuant to paragraph (1) for any taxable year, for any individual, exceed an amount equal to 28 percent of the annual rate of basic pay at Level V of the Executive Schedule of the United States as of December 21, 1988.

Sec. 5511. Overseas Security Electronic Bulletin Board

Not later than 60 days after November 16, 1990, the Secretary of State shall issue such rules and regulations as may be necessary to establish, under the Bureau of Consular Affairs, an electronic bulletin board accessible to the general public. Such bulletin board shall contain all information, updated daily, which is available on the Overseas Security Electronic Bulletin Board of the Bureau of Diplomatic Security.

Sec. 5512. Antiterrorism measures

(a) Guidelines for international aviation travelers
For the purpose of notifying the public, the Secretary of State, in consultation with the Secretary of Transportation, shall develop and publish guidelines for thwarting efforts by international terrorists to enlist the unwitting assistance of international aviation travelers in terrorist activities. Notices concerning such guidelines shall be posted and prominently displayed domestically and abroad in international airports.

(b) Development of international standards
The Secretary of State and the Secretary of Transportation in all appropriate fora, particularly talks and meetings related to international civil aviation, shall enter into negotiations with other nations for the establishment of international standards regarding guidelines for thwarting efforts by international terrorists to enlist the unwitting assistance of international aviation travelers in terrorist activities.

(c) Publication of rewards for terrorism-related information
For the purpose of notifying the public, the Secretary of State shall publish the availability of United States Government rewards for information on international terrorist-related activities, including rewards available under section 2708(a) of this title and chapter 204 of title 18. To the extent appropriate and feasible, notices making such publication shall be posted and prominently displayed domestically and abroad in international airports.

(d) Sense of Congress
It is the sense of Congress that the Secretary of Transportation should take appropriate measures to utilize and train properly the officers and employees of other United States Government agencies who have functions at international airports in the United States and abroad in the detection of explosives and firearms which could be a threat to international civil aviation.

Sec. 5513. Proposal for consideration by International Civil Aviation Organization

Not later than 60 days after November 16, 1990, the Secretary of State, in consultation with the Secretary of Transportation, shall propose to the International Civil Aviation Organization the establishment of a comprehensive aviation security program which shall include (1) training for airport security personnel, (2) grants for security equipment acquisition for certain nations, and (3) expansion of the appropriate utilization of canine teams in the detection of explosive devices in all airport areas, including use in passenger screening areas and nonpublic baggage assembly and processing areas.

Chapter 65—Control and Elimination of Chemical and Biological Weapons

Sec. 5601. Purposes

The purposes of this chapter are—

(1) to mandate United States sanctions, and to encourage international sanctions, against countries that use chemical or biological weapons in violation of international law or use lethal chemical or biological weapons against their own nationals, and to impose sanctions against companies that aid in the proliferation of chemical and biological weapons;

(2) to support multilaterally coordinated efforts to control the proliferation of chemical and biological weapons;

(3) to urge continued close cooperation with the Australia Group and cooperation with other supplier nations to devise ever more effective controls on the transfer of materials, equipment, and technology applicable to chemical or biological weapons production; and

(4) to require Presidential reports on efforts that threaten United States interests or regional stability by Iran, Iraq, Syria, Libya, and others to acquire the materials and technology to develop, produce, stockpile, deliver, transfer, or use chemical or biological weapons.

Sec. 5602. Multilateral efforts

(a) Multilateral controls on proliferation
It is the policy of the United States to seek multilaterally coordinated

efforts with other countries to control the proliferation of chemical and biological weapons. In furtherance of this policy, the United States shall—

(1) promote agreements banning the transfer of missiles suitable for armament with chemical or biological warheads;

(2) set as a top priority the early conclusion of a comprehensive global agreement banning the use, development, production, and stockpiling of chemical weapons;

(3) seek and support effective international means of monitoring and reporting regularly on commerce in equipment, materials, and technology applicable to the attainment of a chemical or biological weapons capability; and

(4) pursue and give full support to multilateral sanctions pursuant to United Nations Security Council Resolution 620, which declared the intention of the Security Council to give immediate consideration to imposing "appropriate and effective" sanctions against any country which uses chemical weapons in violation of international law.

(b) Multilateral controls on chemical agents, precursors, and equipment
It is also the policy of the United States to strengthen efforts to control chemical agents, precursors, and equipment by taking all appropriate multilateral diplomatic measures—

(1) to continue to seek a verifiable global ban on chemical weapons at the 40 nation Conference on Disarmament in Geneva;

(2) to support the Australia Group's objective to support the norms and restraints against the spread and the use of chemical warfare, to advance the negotiation of a comprehensive ban on chemical warfare by taking appropriate measures, and to protect the Australia Group's domestic industries against inadvertent association with supply of feedstock chemical equipment that could be misused to produce chemical weapons;

(3) to implement paragraph (2) by proposing steps complementary to, and not mutually exclusive of, existing multilateral efforts seeking a verifiable ban on chemical weapons, such as the establishment of—

(A) a harmonized list of export control rules and regulations to prevent relative commercial advantage and disadvantages accruing to Australia Group members,

(B)   liaison officers to the Australia Group's coordinating entity from within the diplomatic missions,

(C)   a close working relationship between the Australia Group and industry,

(D)   a public unclassified warning list of controlled chemical agents, precursors, and equipment,

(E)   information-exchange channels of suspected proliferants,

(F)   a "denial" list of firms and individuals who violate the Australia Group's export control provisions, and

(G)   broader cooperation between the Australia Group and other countries whose political commitment to stem the proliferation of chemical weapons is similar to that of the Australia Group; and

(4)   to adopt the imposition of stricter controls on the export of chemical agents, precursors, and equipment and to adopt tougher multilateral sanctions against firms and individuals who violate these controls or against countries that use chemical weapons.

Sec. 5603.   United States export controls

The President shall—

(1)   use the authorities of the Arms Export Control Act (22 U.S.C. 2751 et seq.) to control the export of those defense articles and defense services, and

(2)   use the authorities of the Export Administration Act of 1979 (50 App. U.S.C. 2401 et seq.) to control the export of those goods and technology, that the President determines would assist the government of any foreign country in acquiring the capability to develop, produce, stockpile, deliver, or use chemical or biological weapons.

Sec. 5604.   Determinations regarding use of chemical or biological weapons

(a)   Determination by President

(1)   When determination required; nature of determination
Whenever persuasive information becomes available to the executive branch indicating the substantial possibility that, on or after

October 28, 1991, the government of a foreign country has made substantial preparation to use or has used chemical or biological weapons, the President shall, within 60 days after the receipt of such information by the executive branch, determine whether that government, on or after October 28, 1991, has used chemical or biological weapons in violation of international law or has used lethal chemical or biological weapons against its own nationals. Section 5605 of this title applies if the President determines that that government has so used chemical or biological weapons.

(2) Matters to be considered
In making the determination under paragraph (1), the President shall consider the following:

(A) All physical and circumstantial evidence available bearing on the possible use of such weapons.

(B) All information provided by alleged victims, witnesses, and independent observers.

(C) The extent of the availability of the weapons in question to the purported user.

(D) All official and unofficial statements bearing on the possible use of such weapons.

(E) Whether, and to what extent, the government in question is willing to honor a request from the Secretary General of the United Nations to grant timely access to a United Nations fact-finding team to investigate the possibility of chemical or biological weapons use or to grant such access to other legitimate outside parties.

(3) Determination to be reported to Congress
Upon making a determination under paragraph (1), the President shall promptly report that determination to the Congress. If the determination is that a foreign government had used chemical or biological weapons as described in that paragraph, the report shall specify the sanctions to be imposed pursuant to section 5605 of this title.

(b) Congressional requests; report

(1) Request
The Chairman of the Committee on Foreign Relations of the Senate (upon consultation with the ranking minority member of such com-

mittee) or the Chairman of the Committee on Foreign Affairs of the House of Representatives (upon consultation with the ranking minority member of such committee) may at any time request the President to consider whether a particular foreign government, on or after December 4, 1991, has used chemical or biological weapons in violation of international law or has used lethal chemical or biological weapons against its own nationals.

(2) Report to Congress
Not later than 60 days after receiving such a request, the President shall provide to the Chairman of the Committee on Foreign Relations of the Senate and the Chairman of the Committee on Foreign Affairs of the House of Representatives a written report on the information held by the executive branch which is pertinent to the issue of whether the specified government, on or after December 4, 1991, has used chemical or biological weapons in violation of international law or has used lethal chemical or biological weapons against its own nationals. This report shall contain an analysis of each of the items enumerated in subsection (a)(2) of this section.

Sec. 5605. Sanctions against use of chemical or biological weapons

(a) Initial sanctions
If, at any time, the President makes a determination pursuant to section 5604(a)(1) of this title with respect to the government of a foreign country, the President shall forthwith impose the following sanctions:

(1) Foreign assistance
The United States Government shall terminate assistance to that country under the Foreign Assistance Act of 1961 (22 U.S.C. 2151 et seq.), except for urgent humanitarian assistance and food or other agricultural commodities or products.

(2) Arms sales
The United States Government shall terminate—

(A) sales to that country under the Arms Export Control Act (22 U.S.C. 2751 et seq.) of any defense articles, defense services, or design and construction services, and

(B) licenses for the export to that country of any item on the United States Munitions List.

(3) Arms sales financing

The United States Government shall terminate all foreign military financing for that country under the Arms Export Control Act.

(4) Denial of United States Government credit or other financial assistance

The United States Government shall deny to that country any credit, credit guarantees, or other financial assistance by any department, agency, or instrumentality of the United States Government, including the Export-Import Bank of the United States.

(5) Exports of national security-sensitive goods and technology

The authorities of section 2405 of title 50, Appendix, shall be used to prohibit the export to that country of any goods or technology on that part of the control list established under section 2404(c)(1) of title 50, Appendix.

(b) Additional sanctions if certain conditions not met

(1) Presidential determination

Unless, within 3 months after making a determination pursuant to section 5604(a)(1) of this title with respect to a foreign government, the President determines and certifies in writing to the Congress that—

(A) that government is no longer using chemical or biological weapons in violation of international law or using lethal chemical or biological weapons against its own nationals,

(B) that government has provided reliable assurances that it will not in the future engage in any such activities, and

(C) that government is willing to allow on-site inspections by United Nations observers or other internationally recognized, impartial observers, or other reliable means exist, to ensure that that government is not using chemical or biological weapons in violation of international law and is not using lethal chemical or biological weapons against its own nationals, then the President, after consultation with the Congress, shall impose on that country the sanctions set forth in at least 3 of subparagraphs (A) through (F) of paragraph (2).

(2) Sanctions

The sanctions referred to in paragraph (1) are the following:

(A) Multilateral development bank assistance

The United States Government shall oppose, in accordance

with section 262d of this title, the extension of any loan or financial or technical assistance to that country by international financial institutions.

(B) Bank loans
The United States Government shall prohibit any United States bank from making any loan or providing any credit to the government of that country, except for loans or credits for the purpose of purchasing food or other agricultural commodities or products.

(C) Further export restrictions
The authorities of section 2405 of title 50, Appendix, shall be used to prohibit exports to that country of all other goods and technology (excluding food and other agricultural commodities and products).

(D) Import restrictions
Restrictions shall be imposed on the importation into the United States of articles (which may include petroleum or any petroleum product) that are the growth, product, or manufacture of that country.

(E) Diplomatic relations
The President shall use his constitutional authorities to downgrade or suspend diplomatic relations between the United States and the government of that country.

(F) Presidential action regarding aviation

(i)

(I)   The President is authorized to notify the government of a country with respect to which the President has made a determination pursuant to section 5604(a)(1) of this title of his intention to suspend the authority of foreign air carriers owned or controlled by the government of that country to engage in foreign air transportation to or from the United States.

(II)   Within 10 days after the date of notification of a government under subclause (I), the Secretary of Transportation shall take all steps necessary to suspend at the earliest possible date the authority of any foreign air carrier owned or controlled, directly or indirectly, by that government to engage in foreign air transportation to or from the United States, notwithstanding any agreement relating to air services.

(ii)

(I)   The President may direct the Secretary of State to terminate any air service agreement between the United States and a country with respect to which the President has made a determination pursuant to section 5604(a)(1) of this title, in accordance with the provisions of that agreement.

(II)   Upon termination of an agreement under this clause, the Secretary of Transportation shall take such steps as may be necessary to revoke at the earliest possible date the right of any foreign air carrier owned, or controlled, directly or indirectly, by the government of that country to engage in foreign air transportation to or from the United States.

(iii) The Secretary of Transportation may provide for such exceptions from clauses (i) and (ii) as the Secretary considers necessary to provide for emergencies in which the safety of an aircraft or its crew or passengers is threatened.

(iv) For purposes of this subparagraph, the terms "air transportation," "air carrier," "foreign air carrier," and "foreign air transportation" have the meanings such terms have under section 40102(a) of title 49.

(c)   Removal of sanctions
The President shall remove the sanctions imposed with respect to a country pursuant to this section if the President determines and so certifies to the Congress, after the end of the 12-month period beginning on the date on which sanctions were initially imposed on that country pursuant to subsection (a) of this section, that—

(1) the government of that country has provided reliable assurances that it will not use chemical or biological weapons in violation of international law and will not use lethal chemical or biological weapons against its own nationals;

(2) that government is not making preparations to use chemical or biological weapons in violation of international law or to use lethal chemical or biological weapons against its own nationals;

(3) that government is willing to allow on-site inspections by United Nations observers or other internationally recognized, impartial observers to verify that it is not making preparations to use chemical or biological weapons in violation of international law or to use lethal chemical or biological weapons against its own nationals, or other reliable means exist to verify that it is not making such preparations; and

(4) that government is making restitution to those affected by any use of chemical or biological weapons in violation of international law or by any use of lethal chemical or biological weapons against its own nationals.

(d) Waiver

(1) Criteria for waiver
The President may waive the application of any sanction imposed with respect to a country pursuant to this section—

(A) if—

(i) in the case of any sanction other than a sanction specified in subsection (b)(2)(D) of this section (relating to import restrictions) or (b)(2)(E) of this section (relating to the downgrading or suspension of diplomatic relations), the President determines and certifies to the Congress that such waiver is essential to the national security interests of the United States, and if the President notifies the Committee on Foreign Relations of the Senate and the Committee on Foreign Affairs of the House of Representatives of his determination and certification at least 15 days before the waiver takes effect, in accordance with the procedures applicable to reprogramming notifications under section 634A of the Foreign Assistance Act of 1961 (22 U.S.C. 2394-1), or

(ii) in the case of any sanction specified in subsection (b)(2)(D) of this section (relating to import restrictions), the President determines and certifies to the Congress that such waiver is essential to the national security interest of the United States, and if the President notifies the

Committee on Finance of the Senate and the Committee on Ways and Means of the House of Representatives of his determination and certification at least 15 days before the waiver takes effect; or

(B) if the President determines and certifies to the Congress that there has been a fundamental change in the leadership and policies of the government of that country, and if the President notifies the Congress at least 20 days before the waiver takes effect.

(2) Report

In the event that the President decides to exercise the waiver authority provided in paragraph (1) with respect to a country, the President's notification to the Congress under such paragraph shall include a report fully articulating the rationale and circumstances which led the President to exercise that waiver authority, including a description of the steps which the government of that country has taken to satisfy the conditions set forth in paragraphs (1) through (4) of subsection (c) of this section.

(e) Contract sanctity

(1) Sanctions not applied to existing contracts

(A) A sanction described in paragraph (4) or (5) of subsection (a) of this section or in any of subparagraphs (A) through (D) of subsection (b)(2) of this section shall not apply to any activity pursuant to any contract or international agreement entered into before the date of the presidential determination under section 5604(a)(1) of this title unless the President determines, on a case-by-case basis, that to apply such sanction to that activity would prevent the performance of a contract or agreement that would have the effect of assisting a country in using chemical or biological weapons in violation of international law or in using lethal chemical or biological weapons against its own nationals.

(B) The same restrictions of subsection (p) of section 2405 of title 50, Appendix, as that subsection is so redesignated by section 304(b) of this title, which are applicable to exports prohibited under section 2405 of title 50, Appendix, shall apply to exports prohibited under subsection (a)(5) or (b)(2)(C) of this section. For purposes of this subparagraph, any contract or agreement the performance of which (as determined by the President) would have the effect of assisting a foreign government in using chemical or biological weapons in violation of international law or in using lethal chemical or biological weapons against its own nationals shall be treated as constituting a breach of the peace that poses a serious and direct threat to the strategic interest of the United States, within the meaning of subparagraph (A) of section 2405(p) of title 50, Appendix.

(2) Sanctions applied to existing contracts

The sanctions described in paragraphs (1), (2), and (3) of subsection (a) of this section shall apply to contracts, agreements, and licenses without regard to the date the contract or agreement was entered into or the license was issued (as the case may be), except that such sanctions shall not apply to any contract or agreement entered into or license issued before the date of the presidential determination under section 5604(a)(1) of this title if the President determines that the application of such sanction would be detrimental to the national security interests of the United States.

Sec. 5606. Presidential reporting requirements

(a) Reports to Congress

Not later than 90 days after December 4, 1991, and every 12 months thereafter, the President shall transmit to the Congress a report which shall include—

(1) a description of the actions taken to carry out this chapter, including the amendments made by this chapter;

(2) a description of the current efforts of foreign countries and subnational groups to acquire equipment, materials, or technology to develop, produce, or use chemical or biological weapons, together with an assessment of the current and likely future capabilities of such countries and groups to develop, produce, stockpile, deliver, transfer, or use such weapons;

(3) a description of—

(A) the use of chemical weapons by foreign countries in violation of international law,

(B) the use of chemical weapons by subnational groups,

(C) substantial preparations by foreign countries and subnational groups to do so, and

(D) the development, production, stockpiling, or use of biological weapons by foreign countries and subnational groups; and

(4) a description of the extent to which foreign persons or governments have knowingly and materially assisted third countries or subnational groups to acquire equipment, material, or technology intended to develop, produce, or use chemical or biological weapons.

(b) Protection of classified information

To the extent practicable, reports submitted under subsection (a) of this section or any other provision of this chapter should be based on unclassified information. Portions of such reports may be classified.

Title 28—Judiciary and Judicial Procedure

Chapter 97—Jurisdictional Immunities of Foreign States

Sec. 1602. Findings and declaration of purpose

The Congress finds that the determination by United States courts of the claims of foreign states to immunity from the jurisdiction of such courts would serve the interests of justice and would protect the rights of both foreign states and litigants in United States courts. Under international law, states are not immune from the jurisdiction of foreign courts insofar as their commercial activities are concerned, and their commercial property may be levied upon for the satisfaction of judgments rendered against them in connection with their commercial activities. Claims of foreign states to immunity should henceforth be decided by courts of the United States and of the States in conformity with the principles set forth in this chapter.

Sec. 1603. Definitions

For purposes of this chapter—

(a) A "foreign state," except as used in section 1608 of this title, includes a political subdivision of a foreign state or an agency or instrumentality of a foreign state as defined in subsection (b).

(b) An "agency or instrumentality of a foreign state" means any entity—

(1) which is a separate legal person, corporate or otherwise, and

(2) which is an organ of a foreign state or political subdivision thereof, or a majority of whose shares or other ownership interest is owned by a foreign state or political subdivision thereof, and

(3) which is neither a citizen of a State of the United States as defined in section 1332 (c) and (d) of this title, nor created under the laws of any third country.

(c) The "United States" includes all territory and waters, continental or insular, subject to the jurisdiction of the United States.

(d) A "commercial activity" means either a regular course of commercial conduct or a particular commercial transaction or act. The commercial character of an activity shall be determined by reference to the nature of the course of conduct or particular transaction or act, rather than by reference to its purpose.

(e) A "commercial activity carried on in the United States by a foreign state" means commercial activity carried on by such state and having substantial contact with the United States.

Sec. 1604. Immunity of a foreign state from jurisdiction

Subject to existing international agreements to which the United States is a party at the time of enactment of this Act a foreign state shall be immune from the jurisdiction of the courts of the United States and of the States except as provided in sections 1605 to 1607 of this chapter.

Sec. 1605. General exceptions to the jurisdictional immunity of a foreign state

(a) A foreign state shall not be immune from the jurisdiction of courts of the United States or of the States in any case—

(1) in which the foreign state has waived its immunity either explicitly or by implication, notwithstanding any withdrawal of the waiver which the foreign state may purport to effect except in accordance with the terms of the waiver;

(2) in which the action is based upon a commercial activity carried on in the United States by the foreign state; or upon an act performed in the United States in connection with a commercial activity of the foreign state elsewhere; or upon an act outside the territory of the United States in connection with a commercial activity of the foreign state elsewhere and that act causes a direct effect in the United States;

(3) in which rights in property taken in violation of international law are in issue and that property or any property exchanged for such property is present in the United States in connection with a commercial activity carried on in the United States by the foreign state; or that property or any property exchanged for such property is owned or operated by an agency or instrumentality of the foreign state and that agency or instrumentality is engaged in a commercial activity in the United States;

(4) in which rights in property in the United States acquired by succession or gift or rights in immovable property situated in the United States are in issue;

(5) not otherwise encompassed in paragraph (2) above, in which money damages are sought against a foreign state for personal injury or death, or damage to or loss of property, occurring in the United States and caused by the tortious act or omission of that foreign state or of any official or employee of that foreign state while acting within the scope of his office or employment; except this paragraph shall not apply to—

(A) any claim based upon the exercise or performance or the failure to exercise or perform a discretionary function regardless of whether the discretion be abused, or

(B) any claim arising out of malicious prosecution, abuse of process, libel, slander, misrepresentation, deceit, or interference with contract rights;

(6) in which the action is brought, either to enforce an agreement made by the foreign state with or for the benefit of a private party to submit to arbitration all or any differences which have arisen or which may arise between the parties with respect to a defined legal relationship, whether contractual or not, concerning a subject matter capable of settlement by arbitration under the laws of the United States, or to confirm an award made pursuant to such an agreement to arbitrate, if (A) the arbitration takes place or is intended to take place in the United States, (B) the agreement or award is or may be governed by a treaty or other international agreement in force for the United States calling for the recognition and enforcement of arbitral awards, (C) the underlying claim, save for the agreement to arbitrate, could have been brought in a United States court under this section or section1607, or (D) paragraph (1) of this subsection is otherwise applicable; or

(7) not otherwise covered by paragraph (2), in which money damages are sought against a foreign state for personal injury or death that was caused by an act of torture, extrajudicial killing, aircraft sabotage, hostage taking, or the provision of material support or resources (as defined in section 2339A of title 18) for such an act if such act or provision of material support is engaged in by an official, employee, or agent of such foreign state while acting within

the scope of his or her office, employment, or agency, except that the court shall decline to hear a claim under this paragraph—

(A) if the foreign state was not designated as a state sponsor of terrorism under section 6(j) of the Export Administration Act of 1979 (50 U.S.C. App. 2405(j)) or section 620A of the Foreign Assistance Act of 1961 (22 U.S.C. 2371) at the time the act occurred, unless later so designated as a result of such act; and

(B) even if the foreign state is or was so designated, if—

(i) the act occurred in the foreign state against which the claim has been brought and the claimant has not afforded the foreign state a reasonable opportunity to arbitrate the claim in accordance with accepted international rules of arbitration; or

(ii) neither the claimant nor the victim was a national of the United States (as that term is defined in section 101(a)(22) of the Immigration and Nationality Act) when the act upon which the claim is based occurred.

(b) A foreign state shall not be immune from the jurisdiction of the courts of the United States in any case in which a suit in admiralty is brought to enforce a maritime lien against a vessel or cargo of the foreign state, which maritime lien is based upon a commercial activity of the foreign state: Provided, That—

(1) notice of the suit is given by delivery of a copy of the summons and of the complaint to the person, or his agent, having possession of the vessel or cargo against which the maritime lien is asserted; and if the vessel or cargo is arrested pursuant to process obtained on behalf of the party bringing the suit, the service of process of arrest shall be deemed to constitute valid delivery of such notice, but the party bringing the suit shall be liable for any damages sustained by the foreign state as a result of the arrest if the party bringing the suit had actual or constructive knowledge that the vessel or cargo of a foreign state was involved; and

(2) notice to the foreign state of the commencement of suit as provided in section 1608 of this title is initiated within ten days either of the delivery of notice as provided in paragraph (1) of this subsection or, in the case of a party who was unaware that the vessel or cargo of a foreign state was involved, of the date such party determined the existence of the foreign state's interest.

(c) Whenever notice is delivered under subsection (b)(1), the suit to enforce a maritime lien shall thereafter proceed and shall be heard and determined according to the principles of law and rules of practice of suits in rem whenever it appears that, had the vessel been privately owned and possessed, a suit in rem might have been maintained. A decree against the foreign state may include costs of the suit and, if the decree is for a money judgment, interest as ordered by the court, except that the court may not award judgment against the foreign state in an amount greater than the value of the vessel or cargo upon which the maritime lien arose. Such value shall be determined as of the time notice is served under subsection (b)(1). Decrees shall be subject to appeal and revision as provided in other cases of admiralty and maritime jurisdiction. Nothing shall preclude the plaintiff in any proper case from seeking relief in personam in the same action brought to enforce a maritime lien as provided in this section.

(d) A foreign state shall not be immune from the jurisdiction of the courts of the United States in any action brought to foreclose a preferred mortgage, as defined in the Ship Mortgage Act, 1920 (46 U.S.C. 911 and following). Such action shall be brought, heard, and determined in accordance with the provisions of that Act and in accordance with the principles of law and rules of practice of suits in rem, whenever it appears that had the vessel been privately owned and possessed a suit in rem might have been maintained.

(e) For purposes of paragraph (7) of subsection (a)—

(1) the terms "torture" and "extrajudicial killing" have the meaning given those terms in section 3 of the Torture Victim Protection Act of 1991;

(2) the term "hostage taking" has the meaning given that term in Article 1 of the International Convention Against the Taking of Hostages; and

(3) the term "aircraft sabotage" has the meaning given that term in Article 1 of the Convention for the Suppression of Unlawful Acts Against the Safety of Civil Aviation.

(f) No action shall be maintained under subsection (a)(7) unless the action is commenced not later than 10 years after the date on which the cause of action arose. All principles of equitable tolling, including the period during which the foreign state was immune from suit, shall apply in calculating this limitation period.

(g) Limitation on Discovery.—

(1) In general.—(A) Subject to paragraph (2), if an action is filed that would otherwise be barred by section 1604, but for subsection (a)(7), the court, upon request of the Attorney General, shall stay any request, demand, or order for discovery on the United States that the Attorney General certifies would significantly interfere with a criminal investigation or prosecution, or a national security operation, related to the incident that gave rise to the cause of action, until such time as the Attorney General advises the court that such request, demand, or order will no longer so interfere.

(B) A stay under this paragraph shall be in effect during the 12-month period beginning on the date on which the court issues the order to stay discovery. The court shall renew the order to stay discovery for additional 12-month periods upon motion by the United States if the Attorney General certifies that discovery would significantly interfere with a criminal investigation or prosecution, or a national security operation, related to the incident that gave rise to the cause of action.

(2) Sunset.—(A) Subject to subparagraph (B), no stay shall be granted or continued in effect under paragraph (1) after the date that is 10 years after the date on which the incident that gave rise to the cause of action occurred.

(B) After the period referred to in subparagraph (A), the court, upon request of the Attorney General, may stay any request, demand, or order for discovery on the United States that the court finds a substantial likelihood would—

(i) create a serious threat of death or serious bodily injury to any person;

(ii) adversely affect the ability of the United States to work in cooperation with foreign and international law enforcement agencies in investigating violations of United States law; or

(iii) obstruct the criminal case related to the incident that gave rise to the cause of action or undermine the potential for a conviction in such case.

(3) Evaluation of evidence.—The court's evaluation of any request for a stay under this subsection filed by the Attorney General shall be conducted ex parte and in camera.

(4) Bar on motions to dismiss.—A stay of discovery under this subsection shall constitute a bar to the granting of a motion to dismiss under rules 12(b)(6) and 56 of the Federal Rules of Civil Procedure.

(5) Construction.—Nothing in this subsection shall prevent the United States from seeking protective orders or asserting privileges ordinarily available to the United States.

Sec. 1606. Extent of liability

As to any claim for relief with respect to which a foreign state is not entitled to immunity under section 1605 or 1607 of this chapter, the foreign state shall be liable in the same manner and to the same extent as a private individual under like circumstances; but a foreign state except for an agency or instrumentality thereof shall not be liable for punitive damages, except any action under section 1605(a)(7) or 1610(f); if, however, in any case wherein death was caused, the law of the place where the action or omission occurred provides, or has been construed to provide, for damages only punitive in nature, the foreign state shall be liable for actual or compensatory damages measured by the pecuniary injuries resulting from such death which were incurred by the persons for whose benefit the action was brought.

Sec. 1607. Counterclaims

In any action brought by a foreign state, or in which a foreign state intervenes, in a court of the United States or of a State, the foreign state shall not be accorded immunity with respect to any counterclaim—

(a) for which a foreign state would not be entitled to immunity under section 1605 of this chapter had such claim been brought in a separate action against the foreign state; or

(b) arising out of the transaction or occurrence that is the subject matter of the claim of the foreign state; or

(c) to the extent that the counterclaim does not seek relief exceeding in amount or differing in kind from that sought by the foreign state.

Sec. 1608. Service; time to answer; default

(a) Service in the courts of the United States and of the States shall be made upon a foreign state or political subdivision of a foreign state:

(1) by delivery of a copy of the summons and complaint in accordance with any special arrangement for service between the plaintiff and the foreign state or political subdivision; or

(2) if no special arrangement exists, by delivery of a copy of the summons and complaint in accordance with an applicable international convention on service of judicial documents; or

(3) if service cannot be made under paragraphs (1) or (2), by sending a copy of the summons and complaint and a notice of suit, together with a translation of each into the official language of the foreign state, by any form of mail requiring a signed receipt, to be addressed and dispatched by the clerk of the court to the head of the ministry of foreign affairs of the foreign state concerned, or

(4) if service cannot be made within 30 days under paragraph (3), by sending two copies of the summons and complaint and a notice of suit, together with a translation of each into the official language of the foreign state, by any form of mail requiring a signed receipt, to be addressed and dispatched by the clerk of the court to the Secretary of State in Washington, District of Columbia, to the attention of the Director of Special Consular Services—and the Secretary shall transmit one copy of the papers through diplomatic channels to the foreign state and shall send to the clerk of the court a certified copy of the diplomatic note indicating when the papers were transmitted. As used in this subsection, a "notice of suit" shall mean a notice addressed to a foreign state and in a form prescribed by the Secretary of State by regulation.

(b) Service in the courts of the United States and of the States shall be made upon an agency or instrumentality of a foreign state:

(1) by delivery of a copy of the summons and complaint in accordance with any special arrangement for service between the plaintiff and the agency or instrumentality; or

(2) if no special arrangement exists, by delivery of a copy of the summons and complaint either to an officer, a managing or general agent, or to any other agent authorized by appointment or by law to receive service of process in the United States; or in accordance with an applicable international convention on service of judicial documents; or

(3) if service cannot be made under paragraphs (1) or (2), and if reasonably calculated to give actual notice, by delivery of a copy of

the summons and complaint, together with a translation of each into the official language of the foreign state—

(A) as directed by an authority of the foreign state or political subdivision in response to a letter rogatory or request or

(B) by any form of mail requiring a signed receipt, to be addressed and dispatched by the clerk of the court to the agency or instrumentality to be served, or

(C) as directed by order of the court consistent with the law of the place where service is to be made.

(c) Service shall be deemed to have been made—

(1) in the case of service under subsection (a)(4), as of the date of transmittal indicated in the certified copy of the diplomatic note; and

(2) in any other case under this section, as of the date of receipt indicated in the certification, signed and returned postal receipt, or other proof of service applicable to the method of service employed.

(d) In any action brought in a court of the United States or of a State, a foreign state, a political subdivision thereof, or an agency or instrumentality of a foreign state shall serve an answer or other responsive pleading to the complaint within sixty days after service has been made under this section.

(e) No judgment by default shall be entered by a court of the United States or of a State against a foreign state, a political subdivision thereof, or an agency or instrumentality of a foreign state, unless the claimant establishes his claim or right to relief by evidence satisfactory to the court. A copy of any such default judgment shall be sent to the foreign state or political subdivision in the manner prescribed for service in this section.

Sec. 1609. Immunity from attachment and execution of property of a foreign state

Subject to existing international agreements to which the United States is a party at the time of enactment of this Act the property in the United States of a foreign state shall be immune from attachment arrest and execution except as provided in sections 1610 and 1611 of this chapter.

Sec. 1610 Exceptions to the immunity from attachment or execution

(a) The property in the United States of a foreign state, as defined in section 1603(a) of this chapter, used for a commercial activity in the United States, shall not be immune from attachment in aid of execution, or from execution, upon a judgment entered by a court of the United States or of a State after the effective date of this Act, if—

(1) the foreign state has waived its immunity from attachment in aid of execution or from execution either explicitly or by implication, notwithstanding any withdrawal of the waiver the foreign state may purport to effect except in accordance with the terms of the waiver, or

(2) the property is or was used for the commercial activity upon which the claim is based, or

(3) the execution relates to a judgment establishing rights in property which has been taken in violation of international law or which has been exchanged for property taken in violation of international law, or

(4) the execution relates to a judgment establishing rights in property—

(A) which is acquired by succession or gift, or

(B) which is immovable and situated in the United States: Provided, That such property is not used for purposes of maintaining a diplomatic or consular mission or the residence of the Chief of such mission, or

(5) the property consists of any contractual obligation or any proceeds from such a contractual obligation to indemnify or hold harmless the foreign state or its employees under a policy of automobile or other liability or casualty insurance covering the claim which merged into the judgment, or

(6) the judgment is based on an order confirming an arbitral award rendered against the foreign state, provided that attachment in aid of execution, or execution, would not be inconsistent with any provision in the arbitral agreement, or

(7) the judgment relates to a claim for which the foreign state is not immune under section 1605(a)(7), regardless of whether the property is or was involved with the act upon which the claim is based.

(b) In addition to subsection (a), any property in the United States of an agency or instrumentality of a foreign state engaged in commercial activity in the United States shall not be immune from attachment in aid of execution, or from execution, upon a judgment entered by a court of the United States or of a State after the effective date of this Act, if—

(1) the agency or instrumentality has waived its immunity from attachment in aid of execution or from execution either explicitly or implicitly, notwithstanding any withdrawal of the waiver the agency or instrumentality may purport to effect except in accordance with the terms of the waiver, or

(2) the judgment relates to a claim for which the agency or instrumentality is not immune by virtue of section 1605(a)(2), (3), or (5), or 1605(b) of this section, regardless of whether the property is or was involved in the act upon which the claim is based.

(c) No attachment or execution referred to in subsections (a) and (b) of this section shall be permitted until the court has ordered such attachment and execution after having determined that a reasonable period of time has elapsed following the entry of judgment and the giving of any notice required under section 1608(e) of this chapter.

(d) The property of a foreign state, as defined in section 1603(a) of this chapter, used for a commercial activity in the United States, shall not be immune from attachment prior to the entry of judgment in any action brought in a court of the United States or of a State, or prior to the elapse of the period of time provided in subsection (c) of this section, if—

(1) the foreign state has explicitly waived its immunity from attachment prior to judgment, notwithstanding any withdrawal of the waiver the foreign state may purport to effect except in accordance with the terms of the waiver, and

(2) the purpose of the attachment is to secure satisfaction of a judgment that has been or may ultimately be entered against the foreign state, and not to obtain jurisdiction.

(e) The vessels of a foreign state shall not be immune from arrest in rem, interlocutory sale, and execution in actions brought to foreclose a preferred mortgage as provided in section 1605(d).

(f) (1)

(A) Notwithstanding any other provision of law, including but not limited to section 208(f) of the Foreign Missions Act (22

U.S.C. 4308(f)), and except as provided in subparagraph (B), any property with respect to which financial transactions are prohibited or regulated pursuant to section 5(b) of the Trading with the Enemy Act (50 U.S.C. App. 5(b)), section 620(a) of the Foreign Assistance Act of 1961 (22 U.S.C. 2370(a)), sections 202 and 203 of the International Emergency Economic Powers Act (50 U.S.C. 1701–1702), or any other proclamation, order, regulation, or license issued pursuant thereto, shall be subject to execution or attachment in aid of execution of any judgment relating to a claim for which a foreign state (including any agency or instrumentality or such state) claiming such property is not immune under section 1605(a)(7).

(B)   Subparagraph (A) shall not apply if, at the time the property is expropriated or seized by the foreign state, the property has been held in title by a natural person or, if held in trust, has been held for the benefit of a natural person or persons.

(2)

(A)   At the request of any party in whose favor a judgment has been issued with respect to a claim for which the foreign state is not immune under section 1605(a)(7), the Secretary of the Treasury and the Secretary of State shall fully, promptly, and effectively assist any judgment creditor or any court that has issued any such judgment in identifying, locating, and executing against the property of that foreign state or any agency or instrumentality of such state.

(B)   In providing such assistance, the Secretaries—

(i)   may provide such information to the court under seal; and

(ii)   shall provide the information in a manner sufficient to allow the court to direct the United States Marshall's office to promptly and effectively execute against that property.

Sec. 1611. Certain types of property immune from execution

(a)   Notwithstanding the provisions of section 1610 of this chapter, the property of those organizations designated by the President as being entitled to enjoy the privileges, exemptions, and immunities provided by the International Organizations Immunities Act shall not be subject to attachment or any other judicial process impeding the disbursement of funds to, or on the order of, a foreign state as the result of an action brought in the courts of the United States or of the States.

(b) Notwithstanding the provisions of section 1610 of this chapter, the property of a foreign state shall be immune from attachment and from execution, if—

(1) the property is that of a foreign central bank or monetary authority held for its own account, unless such bank or authority, or its parent foreign government, has explicitly waived its immunity from attachment in aid of execution, or from execution, notwithstanding any withdrawal of the waiver which the bank, authority or government may purport to effect except in accordance with the terms of the waiver; or

(2) the property is, or is intended to be, used in connection with a military activity and

(A) is of a military character, or

(B) is under the control of a military authority or defense agency.

(c) Notwithstanding the provisions of section 1610 of this chapter, the property of a foreign state shall be immune from attachment and from execution in an action brought under section 302 of the Cuban Liberty and Democratic Solidarity (LIBERTAD) Act of 1996 to the extent that the property is a facility or installation used by an accredited diplomatic mission for official purposes.

Notes to United States Code, Title 28—Judiciary and Judicial Procedure

Note to 28 U.S.C. 524—Availability of Appropriations

Counterterrorism Fund

Pub.L. 104–19, Title III, July 27, 1995, 109 Stat. 249, provided in part that: "There is hereby established the Counterterrorism Fund which shall remain available without fiscal year limitation. For necessary expenses, as determined by the Attorney General, $34,220,000, to remain available until expended, is appropriated to the Counterterrorism Fund to reimburse any Department of Justice organization for the costs incurred in reestablishing the operational capability of an office or facility which has been damaged or destroyed as the result of the bombing of the Alfred P. Murrah Federal Building in Oklahoma City or any domestic or international terrorism event: *Provided*, That funds from this appropriation also may be used to reimburse the appropriation account of any Department of Justice agency engaged in, or providing support to, countering, investigation or prosecuting domestic or international terrorism, including payment of rewards in connection with these activities, and to conduct a terrorism threat assessment of Federal agencies and their facilities: *Provided further*, That any amount obligated from appropriations under this heading may be used under the authorities available to the organization reimbursed from this appropriation: *Provided further*, That amounts in excess of the $10,555,000 made available for extraordinary expenses incurred in the Oklahoma City bombing for fiscal year 1995, shall be available only after the Attorney General notifies the Committees on Appropriations of the House of Representatives and the Senate in accordance with section 605 of Public Law 103–317 [not classified to the Code]: *Provided further*, That the entire amount is designated by Congress as an emergency requirement pursuant to section 251(b)(2)(D)(i) of the Balanced Budget and Emergency Deficit Control Act of 1985 [section 901(b)(2)(D)(i) of Title 2, The Congress], as amended: *Provided further*, That the amount not previously designated by the President as an emergency requirement shall be available only to the extent an official budget request, for a specific dollar amount that includes designation of the entire amount of the request as an emergency requirement, as defined in the Balanced Budge and Emergency Deficit Control Act of 1985, as amended [Pub.L. 99–177, Dec. 12, 1985, 99 Stat. 1037, for classifications of which to the Code see Tables], is transmitted to Congress."

Note to 28 U.S.C. 531—Federal Bureau of Investigation

Federal Bureau of Investigation Funding Authorizations

Pub.L. 104–132, Title VIII, § 811, Apr. 24, 1996, 110 Stat. 1312, provided that: "(a) In general.—With funds made available pursuant to subsection (c)—

(1) The Attorney General shall—

(B) create a Federal Bureau of Investigation counterterrorism and counterintelligence fund for costs associated with the investigation of cases involving cases of terrorism.

Notes to 28 U.S.C. 994—Duties of the United States Sentencing Commission

Deterrent Against Terrorist Activity Damaging a Federal Interest Computer.

Pub.L. 104–132, Title VIII, § 805, Apr. 24, 1996, 110 Stat. 1305 provided that:

(a) Review.—Not later than 60 calendar days after the date of enactment of this Act, the United States Sentencing Commission shall review the deterrent effect of existing guideline levels as they apply to paragraphs (4) and (5) of section 1030(a) of title 18, United States Code.

(b) Report.—The United States Sentencing Commission shall prepare and transmit a report to the Congress on the findings under the study conducted under subsection (a).

(c) Amendment of Guidelines.—Pursuant to its authority under section 994(p) of title 28, United States Code, the United States Sentencing Commission shall amend the sentencing guidelines to ensure any individual convicted of a violation of paragraph (4) or (5) of section 1030(a) of title 18, United States Code, is imprisoned for not less than 6 months.

International Terrorism; Amendment of Sentencing Guidelines

Pub.L. 104–132, Title VII, § 730, Apr. 24, 1996, 110 Stat. 1303, provided that:

The United States Sentencing Commission shall forthwith, in accordance with the procedures set forth in section 21(a) of the Sentencing Act of 1987, as though the authority under that section had not expired, amend the sentencing guidelines so that the chapter 3 adjustment relating to international terrorism only applies to Federal crimes of terrorism, as defined in section 2332b(g) of title 18, United States Code.

Sentencing Guidelines Increase for Terrorist Crimes

Section 120004 of Pub.L. 103–332 provided that: "The United States Sentencing Commission is directed to amend its sentencing guidelines to provide an appropriate enhancement for any felony, whether committed within or outside the United States, that involves or is intended to promote international terrorism, unless such involvement or intent is itself an element of the crime."

Note to 28 U.S.C. 1605—General exceptions to the jurisdictional immunity of a foreign state

Civil Liability for Acts of State Sponsored Terrorism

Pub.L. 104–208, Div. A, Title I, § 101(c) [Title V, § 589], Sept. 30, 1996, 110 Stat. 3009–172, provided that:

"(a) An official, employee, or agent of a foreign state designated as a state sponsor of terrorism designated under section 6(j) of the Export Administration Act of 1979 [section 2405(j) of the Appendix to Title 50, War and National Defense] while acting within the scope of his or her office, employment, or agency shall be liable to a United States national or the national's legal representative for personal injury or death caused by acts of that official, employee, or agent for which the courts of the United States may maintain jurisdiction under section 1605(a)(7) of title 28, United States Code for money damages which may include economic damages, solatium, pain, and suffering, and punitive damages if the acts were among those described in section 1605(a)(7).

"(b) Provisions related to statute of limitations and limitations on discover that would apply to an action brought under 28 U.S.C. 1605(f) and (g) shall also apply to actions brought under this section. No action shall be maintained under this action [sic] if an official, employee, or agent of the United States, while acting within the scope of his or her office, employment, or agency would not be liable for such acts if carried out within the United States."

Title 46 Appendix—Shipping

Chapter 37—International Maritime and Port Security

Sec. 1801. International measures for seaport and shipboard security

The Congress encourages the President to continue to seek agreement through the International Maritime Organization on matters of international seaport and shipboard security, and commends him on his efforts to date. In developing such agreement, each member country of the International Maritime Organization should consult with appropriate private sector interests in that country. Such agreement would establish seaport and vessel security measures and could include—

(1) seaport screening of cargo and baggage similar to that done at airports;

(2) security measures to restrict access to cargo, vessels, and dockside property to authorized personnel only;

(3) additional security on board vessels;

(4) licensing or certification of compliance with appropriate security standards; and

(5) other appropriate measures to prevent unlawful acts against passengers and crews on board vessels.

Sec. 1802. Threat of terrorism to United States ports and vessels

Not later than February 28, 1987, and annually thereafter, the Secretary of Transportation shall report to the Congress on the threat from acts of terrorism to United States ports and vessels operating from those ports.

Sec. 1803. Security standards at foreign ports

(a) Assessment of security measures

The Secretary of Transportation shall develop and implement a plan to assess the effectiveness of the security measures maintained at those foreign ports which the Secretary, in consultation with the Secretary of State, determines pose a high risk of acts of terrorism directed against passenger vessels.

(b) Consultation with Secretary of State

In carrying out subsection (a) of this section, the Secretary of Transportation shall consult the Secretary of State with respect to the terrorist threat which exists in each country and poses a high risk of acts of terrorism directed against passenger vessels.

(c) Report of assessments

Not later than 6 months after August 27, 1986, the Secretary of Transportation shall report to the Congress on the plan developed pursuant to subsection (a) of this section and how the Secretary will implement the plan.

(d) Determination and notification to foreign country

If, after implementing the plan in accordance with subsection (a) of this section, the Secretary of Transportation determines that a port does not maintain and administer effective security measures, the Secretary of State (after being informed by the Secretary of Transportation) shall notify the appropriate government authorities of the country in which the port is located of such determination, and shall recommend the steps necessary to bring the security measures in use at that port up to the standard used by the Secretary of Transportation in making such assessment.

(e) Antiterrorism assistance related to maritime security

The President is encouraged to provide antiterrorism assistance related to maritime security under chapter 8 of part II of the Foreign Assistance Act of 1961 (22 U.S.C. 2349aa et seq.) to foreign countries, especially with respect to a port which the Secretary of Transportation determines under subsection (d) of this section does not maintain and administer effective security measures.

Sec. 1804. Travel advisories concerning security at foreign ports

(a) Travel advisory

Upon being notified by the Secretary of Transportation that the Secretary has determined that a condition exists that threatens the safety or security of passengers, passenger vessels, or crew traveling to or from a foreign port which the Secretary of Transportation has determined pursuant to section 1803(d) of this Appendix to be a port which does not maintain and administer effective security measures, the Secretary of State shall immediately issue a travel advisory with respect to that port. The Secretary of State shall take the necessary steps to widely publicize that travel advisory.

(b) Lifting of travel advisory

The travel advisory required to be issued under subsection (a) of this section may be lifted only if the Secretary of Transportation, in consultation with the Secretary of State, has determined that effective security measures are maintained and administered at the port with respect to which the Secretary of Transportation had made the determination described in section 1803(d) of this Appendix.

(c) Notification to Congress

The Secretary of State shall immediately notify the Congress of any change in the status of a travel advisory imposed pursuant to this section.

Sec. 1805. Suspension of passenger service

(a) President's determination

Whenever the President determines that a foreign nation permits the use of territory under its jurisdiction as a base of operations or training for, or as a sanctuary for, or in any way arms, aids, or abets, any terrorist or terrorist group which knowingly uses the illegal seizure of passenger vessels or the threat thereof as an instrument of policy, the President may, without notice or hearing and for as long as the President determines necessary to assure the security of passenger vessels against unlawful seizure, suspend the right of any passenger vessel common carrier to operate to and from, and the right of any passenger vessel of the United States to utilize, any port in that foreign nation for passenger service.

(b) Prohibition

It shall be unlawful for any passenger vessel common carrier, or any passenger vessel of the United States, to operate in violation of the suspension of rights by the President under this section.

(c) Penalty

(1) If a person operates a vessel in violation of this section, the Secretary of the department in which the Coast Guard is operating may deny the vessels of that person entry to United States ports.

(2) A person violating this section is liable to the United States Government for a civil penalty of not more than $50,000. Each day a vessel utilizes a prohibited port shall be a separate violation of this section.

Sec. 1806. Sanctions for seizure of vessels by terrorists

The Congress encourages the President—

(1) to review the adequacy of domestic and international sanctions against terrorists who seize or attempt to seize vessels; and

(2) to strengthen where necessary, through bilateral and multilateral efforts, the effectiveness of such sanctions. Not later than one year after August 27, 1986, the President shall submit a report to the Congress which includes the review of such sanctions and the efforts to improve such sanctions.

Sec. 1807. Definitions

For purposes of this chapter—

(1) the term "common carrier" has the same meaning given such term in section 1702(6) of this Appendix; and

(2) the terms "passenger vessel" and "vessel of the United States" have the same meaning given such terms in section 2101 of title 46.

Sec. 1808. Authorization of Appropriations

There are authorized to be appropriated $12,500,000 for each of the fiscal years 1987 through 1991, to be available to the Secretary of Transportation to carry out this chapter.

Sec. 1809. Reports

(a) Consolidation
To the extent practicable, the reports required under sections 903, 905, and 907 (46 App. U.S.C. 1801 note, 1802, 1803) shall be consolidated into a single document before being submitted to the Congress. Any classified material in those reports shall be submitted separately as an addendum to the consolidated report.

(b) Submission to committees
The reports required to be submitted to the Congress under this chapter shall be submitted to the Committee on Foreign Affairs and the Committee on Merchant Marine and Fisheries of the House of Representatives and the Committee on Foreign Relations and the Committee on Commerce, Science and Transportation of the Senate.

Title 49—Transportation

Chapter 449—Security

Sec. 44901. Screening passengers and property

(a) General Requirements.—The Administrator of the Federal Aviation Administration shall prescribe regulations requiring screening of all passengers and property that will be carried in a cabin of an aircraft in air transportation or intrastate air transportation. The screening must take place before boarding and be carried out by a weapon-detecting facility or procedure used or operated by an employee or agent of an air carrier, intrastate air carrier, or foreign air carrier.

(b) Amending Regulations.—Notwithstanding subsection (a) of this section, the Administrator may amend a regulation prescribed under subsection (a) to require screening only to ensure security against criminal violence and aircraft piracy in air transportation and intrastate air transportation.

(c) Exemptions and Advising Congress on Regulations.—The Administrator—

(1) may exempt from this section air transportation operations, except scheduled passenger operations of an air carrier providing air transportation under a certificate issued under section 41102 of this title or a permit issued under section 41302 of this title; and

(2) shall advise Congress of a regulation to be prescribed under this section at least 30 days before the effective date of the regulation, unless the Administrator decides an emergency exists requiring the regulation to become effective in fewer than 30 days and notifies Congress of that decision.

Sec. 44902. Refusal to transport passengers and property

(a) Mandatory Refusal.—The Administrator of the Federal Aviation Administration shall prescribe regulations requiring an air carrier, intrastate air carrier, or foreign air carrier to refuse to transport—

(1) a passenger who does not consent to a search under section 44901(a) of this title establishing whether the passenger is carrying

unlawfully a dangerous weapon, explosive, or other destructive substance; or

(2) property of a passenger who does not consent to a search of the property establishing whether the property unlawfully contains a dangerous weapon, explosive, or other destructive substance.

(b) Permissive Refusal.—Subject to regulations of the Administrator, an air carrier, intrastate air carrier, or foreign air carrier may refuse to transport a passenger or property the carrier decides is, or might be, inimical to safety.

(c) Agreeing to Consent to Search.—An agreement to carry passengers or property in air transportation or intrastate air transportation by an air carrier, intrastate air carrier, or foreign air carrier is deemed to include an agreement that the passenger or property will not be carried if consent to search the passenger or property for a purpose referred to in this section is not given.

Sec. 44903. Air transportation security

(a) Definition.—In this section, "law enforcement personnel" means individuals—

(1) authorized to carry and use firearms;

(2) vested with the degree of the police power of arrest the Administrator of the Federal Aviation Administration considers necessary to carry out this section; and

(3) identifiable by appropriate indicia of authority.

(b) Protection Against Violence and Piracy.—The Administrator shall prescribe regulations to protect passengers and property on an aircraft operating in air transportation or intrastate air transportation against an act of criminal violence or aircraft piracy. When prescribing a regulation under this subsection, the Administrator shall—

(1) consult with the Secretary of Transportation, the Attorney General, the heads of other departments, agencies, and instrumentalities of the United States Government, and State and local authorities;

(2) consider whether a proposed regulation is consistent with—

(A) protecting passengers; and

(B) the public interest in promoting air transportation and intrastate air transportation;

(3) to the maximum extent practicable, require a uniform procedure for searching and detaining passengers and property to ensure—

(A) their safety; and

(B) courteous and efficient treatment by an air carrier, an agent or employee of an air carrier, and Government, State, and local law enforcement personnel carrying out this section; and

(4) consider the extent to which a proposed regulation will carry out this section.

(c) Security Programs.—(1) The Administrator shall prescribe regulations under subsection (b) of this section that require each operator of an airport regularly serving an air carrier holding a certificate issued by the Secretary of Transportation to establish an air transportation security program that provides a law enforcement presence and capability at each of those airports that is adequate to ensure the safety of passengers. The regulations shall authorize the operator to use the services of qualified State, local, and private law enforcement personnel. When the Administrator decides, after being notified by an operator in the form the Administrator prescribes, that not enough qualified State, local, and private law enforcement personnel are available to carry out subsection (b), the Administrator may authorize the operator to use, on a reimbursable basis, personnel employed by the Administrator, or by another department, agency, or instrumentality of the Government with the consent of the head of the department, agency, or instrumentality, to supplement State, local, and private law enforcement personnel. When deciding whether additional personnel are needed, the Administrator shall consider the number of passengers boarded at the airport, the extent of anticipated risk of criminal violence or aircraft piracy at the airport or to the air carrier aircraft operations at the airport, and the availability of qualified State or local law enforcement personnel at the airport.

(2)

(A) The Administrator may approve a security program of an airport operator, or an amendment in an existing program, that incorporates a security program of an airport tenant (except an air carrier separately complying with part 108 or 129 of title 14, Code of Federal Regulations) having access to a secured area of the airport, if the program or amendment incorporates—

(i) the measures the tenant will use, within the tenant's leased areas or areas designated for the tenant's exclusive use under an agreement with the airport operator, to carry out the security requirements imposed by the Administrator on the airport operator under the access control system requirements of section 107.14 of title 14, Code of Federal Regulations, or under other requirements of part 107 of title 14; and

(ii) the methods the airport operator will use to monitor and audit the tenant's compliance with the security requirements and provides that the tenant will be required to pay monetary penalties to the airport operator if the tenant fails to carry out a security requirement under a contractual provision or requirement imposed by the airport operator.

(B) If the Administrator approves a program or amendment described in subparagraph (A) of this paragraph, the airport operator may not be found to be in violation of a requirement of this subsection or subsection (b) of this section when the airport operator demonstrates that the tenant or an employee, permittee, or invitee of the tenant is responsible for the violation and that the airport operator has complied with all measures in its security program for securing compliance with its security program by the tenant.

(d) Authorizing Individuals To Carry Firearms and Make Arrests.—With the approval of the Attorney General and the Secretary of State, the Secretary of Transportation may authorize an individual who carries out air transportation security duties—

(1) to carry firearms; and

(2) to make arrests without warrant for an offense against the United States committed in the presence of the individual or for a felony under the laws of the United States, if the individual reasonably believes the individual to be arrested has committed or is committing a felony.

(e) Exclusive Responsibility Over Passenger Safety.—The Administrator has the exclusive responsibility to direct law enforcement activity related to the safety of passengers on an aircraft involved in an offense under section 46502 of this title from the moment all external doors of the aircraft are closed following boarding until those doors are opened to allow passengers to leave the aircraft. When requested by the Administrator, other departments, agencies, and instrumentalities of the Government shall provide assistance necessary to carry out this subsection.

Sec. 44904. Domestic air transportation system security

(a) Assessing Threats.—The Administrator of the Federal Aviation Administration and the Director of the Federal Bureau of Investigation jointly shall assess current and potential threats to the domestic air transportation system. The assessment shall include consideration of the extent to which there are individuals with the capability and intent to carry out terrorist or related unlawful acts against that system and the ways in which those individuals might carry out those acts. The Administrator and the Director jointly shall decide on and carry out the most effective method for continuous analysis and monitoring of security threats to that system.

(b) Assessing Security.—In coordination with the Director, the Administrator shall carry out periodic threat and vulnerability assessments on security at each airport that is part of the domestic air transportation system. Each assessment shall include consideration of—

(1) the adequacy of security procedures related to the handling and transportation of checked baggage and cargo;

(2) space requirements for security personnel and equipment;

(3) separation of screened and unscreened passengers, baggage, and cargo;

(4) separation of the controlled and uncontrolled areas of airport facilities; and

(5) coordination of the activities of security personnel of the Administration, the United States Customs Service, the Immigration and Naturalization Service, and air carriers, and of other law enforcement personnel.

(c) Improving Security.—The Administrator shall take necessary actions to improve domestic air transportation security by correcting any deficiencies in that security discovered in the assessments, analyses, and monitoring carried out under this section.

Sec. 44905. Information about threats to civil aviation

(a) Providing Information.—Under guidelines the Secretary of Transportation prescribes, an air carrier, airport operator, ticket agent, or individual employed by an air carrier, airport operator, or ticket agent, receiving information (except a communication directed by the United States Government) about a threat to civil aviation shall provide the information promptly to the Secretary.

(b) Flight Cancellation.—If a decision is made that a particular threat cannot be addressed in a way adequate to ensure, to the extent feasible, the safety of passengers and crew of a particular flight or series of flights, the Administrator of the Federal Aviation Administration shall cancel the flight or series of flights.

(c) Guidelines on Public Notice.—(1) The President shall develop guidelines for ensuring that public notice is provided in appropriate cases about threats to civil aviation. The guidelines shall identify officials responsible for—

> (A) deciding, on a case-by-case basis, if public notice of a threat is in the best interest of the United States and the traveling public;

> (B) ensuring that public notice is provided in a timely and effective way, including the use of a toll-free telephone number; and

> (C) canceling the departure of a flight or series of flights under subsection (b) of this section.

(2) The guidelines shall provide for consideration of—

> (A) the specificity of the threat;

> (B) the credibility of intelligence information related to the threat;

> (C) the ability to counter the threat effectively;

> (D) the protection of intelligence information sources and methods;

> (E) cancellation, by an air carrier or the Administrator, of a flight or series of flights instead of public notice;

> (F) the ability of passengers and crew to take steps to reduce the risk to their safety after receiving public notice of a threat; and

> (G) other factors the Administrator considers appropriate.

(d) Guidelines on Notice to Crews.—The Administrator shall develop guidelines for ensuring that notice in appropriate cases of threats to the security of an air carrier flight is provided to the flight crew and cabin crew of that flight.

(e) Limitation on Notice to Selective Travelers.—Notice of a threat to civil aviation may be provided to selective potential travelers only if the threat applies only to those travelers.

(f) Restricting Access to Information.—In cooperation with the departments, agencies, and instrumentalities of the Government that collect, receive, and analyze intelligence information related to aviation security, the Administrator shall develop procedures to minimize the number of individuals who have access to information about threats. However, a restriction on access to that information may be imposed only if the restriction does not diminish the ability of the Government to carry out its duties and powers related to aviation security effectively, including providing notice to the public and flight and cabin crews under this section.

(g) Distribution of Guidelines.—The guidelines developed under this section shall be distributed for use by appropriate officials of the Department of Transportation, the Department of State, the Department of Justice, and air carriers.

Sec. 44906. Foreign air carrier security programs

The Administrator of the Federal Aviation Administration shall continue in effect the requirement of section 129.25 of title 14, Code of Federal Regulations, that a foreign air carrier must adopt and use a security program approved by the Administrator. The Administrator shall not approve a security program of a foreign air carrier under section *129*.25, or any successor regulation, unless the security program requires the foreign air carrier in its operations to and from airports in the United States to adhere to the identical security measures that the Administrator requires air carriers serving the same airports to adhere to. The foregoing requirement shall not be interpreted to limit the ability of the Administrator to impose additional security measures on a foreign air carrier or an air carrier when the Administrator determines that a specific threat warrants such additional measures. The Administrator shall prescribe regulations to carry out this section.

Sec. 44907. Security standards at foreign airports

(a) Assessment.—(1) At intervals the Secretary of Transportation considers necessary, the Secretary shall assess the effectiveness of the security measures maintained at—

(A) a foreign airport—

(i) served by an air carrier;

(ii) from which a foreign air carrier serves the United States; or

(iii) that poses a high risk of introducing danger to international air travel; and

(B) other foreign airports the Secretary considers appropriate.

(2) The Secretary of Transportation shall conduct an assessment under paragraph (1) of this subsection—

(A) in consultation with appropriate aeronautic authorities of the government of a foreign country concerned and each air carrier serving the foreign airport for which the Secretary is conducting the assessment;

(B) to establish the extent to which a foreign airport effectively maintains and carries out security measures; and

(C) by using a standard that will result in an analysis of the security measures at the airport based at least on the standards and appropriate recommended practices contained in Annex 17 to the Convention on International Civil Aviation in effect on the date of the assessment.

(3) Each report to Congress required under section 44938(b) of this title shall contain a summary of the assessments conducted under this subsection.

(b) Consultation.—In carrying out subsection (a) of this section, the Secretary of Transportation shall consult with the Secretary of State—

(1) on the terrorist threat that exists in each country; and

(2) to establish which foreign airports are not under the de facto control of the government of the foreign country in which they are located and pose a high risk of introducing danger to international air travel.

(c) Notifying Foreign Authorities.—When the Secretary of Transportation, after conducting an assessment under subsection (a) of this section, decides that an airport does not maintain and carry out effective security measures, the Secretary of Transportation, after advising the Secretary of State, shall notify the appropriate authorities of the government of the foreign country of the decision and recommend the steps necessary to bring the security measures in use at the airport up to the standard used by the Secretary of Transportation in making the assessment.

(d) Actions When Airports Not Maintaining and Carrying Out Effective Security Measures.—(1) When the Secretary of Transportation decides under this section that an airport does not maintain and carry out effective security measures—

> (A) the Secretary of Transportation shall—
>
> > (i) publish the identity of the airport in the Federal Register;
> >
> > (ii) have the identity of the airport posted and displayed prominently at all United States airports at which scheduled air carrier operations are provided regularly; and
> >
> > (iii) notify the news media of the identity of the airport;
>
> (B) each air carrier and foreign air carrier providing transportation between the United States and the airport shall provide written notice of the decision, on or with the ticket, to each passenger buying a ticket for transportation between the United States and the airport;
>
> (C) notwithstanding section 40105(b) of this title, the Secretary of Transportation, after consulting with the appropriate aeronautic authorities of the foreign country concerned and each air carrier serving the airport and with the approval of the Secretary of State, may withhold, revoke, or prescribe conditions on the operating authority of an air carrier or foreign air carrier that uses that airport to provide foreign air transportation; and
>
> (D) the President may prohibit an air carrier or foreign air carrier from providing transportation between the United States and any other foreign airport that is served by aircraft flying to or from the airport with respect to which a decision is made under this section.

(2)

> (A) Paragraph (1) of this subsection becomes effective—
>
> > (i) 90 days after the government of a foreign country is notified under subsection (c) of this section if the Secretary of Transportation finds that the government has not brought the security measures at the airport up to the

standard the Secretary used in making an assessment under subsection (a) of this section; or

(ii) immediately on the decision of the Secretary of Transportation under subsection (c) of this section if the Secretary of Transportation decides, after consulting with the Secretary of State, that a condition exists that threatens the safety or security of passengers, aircraft, or crew traveling to or from the airport.

(B) The Secretary of Transportation immediately shall notify the Secretary of State of a decision under subparagraph (A)(ii) of this paragraph so that the Secretary of State may issue a travel advisory required under section 44908(a) of this title.

(3) The Secretary of Transportation promptly shall submit to Congress a report (and classified annex if necessary) on action taken under paragraph (1) or (2) of this subsection, including information on attempts made to obtain the cooperation of the government of a foreign country in meeting the standard the Secretary used in assessing the airport under subsection (a) of this section.

(4) An action required under paragraph (1)(A) and (B) of this subsection is no longer required only if the Secretary of Transportation, in consultation with the Secretary of State, decides that effective security measures are maintained and carried out at the airport. The Secretary of Transportation shall notify Congress when the action is no longer required to be taken.

(e) Suspensions.—Notwithstanding sections 40105(b) and 40106(b) of this title, the Secretary of Transportation, with the approval of the Secretary of State and without notice or a hearing, shall suspend the right of an air carrier or foreign air carrier to provide foreign air transportation, and the right of a person to operate aircraft in foreign air commerce, to or from a foreign airport when the Secretary of Transportation decides that—

(1) a condition exists that threatens the safety or security of passengers, aircraft, or crew traveling to or from that airport; and

(2) the public interest requires an immediate suspension of transportation between the United States and that airport.

(f) Condition of Carrier Authority.—This section is a condition to authority the Secretary of Transportation grants under this part to an air carrier or foreign air carrier.

Sec. 44908. Travel advisory and suspension of foreign assistance

(a) Travel Advisories.—On being notified by the Secretary of Transportation that the Secretary of Transportation has decided under section 44907(d)(2)(A)(ii) of this title that a condition exists that threatens the safety or security of passengers, aircraft, or crew traveling to or from a foreign airport that the Secretary of Transportation has decided under section 44907 of this title does not maintain and carry out effective security measures, the Secretary of State—

(1) immediately shall issue a travel advisory for that airport; and

(2) shall publicize the advisory widely.

(b) Suspending Assistance.—The President shall suspend assistance provided under the Foreign Assistance Act of 1961 (22 U.S.C. 2151 et seq.) or the Arms Export Control Act (22 U.S.C. 2751 et seq.) to a country in which is located an airport with respect to which section 44907(d)(1) of this title becomes effective if the Secretary of State decides the country is a high terrorist threat country. The President may waive this subsection if the President decides, and reports to Congress, that the waiver is required because of national security interests or a humanitarian emergency.

(c) Actions No Longer Required.—An action required under this section is no longer required only if the Secretary of Transportation has made a decision as provided under section 44907(d)(4) of this title. The Secretary shall notify Congress when the action is no longer required to be taken.

Sec. 44909. Passenger manifests

(a) Air Carrier Requirements.—(1) Not later than March 16, 1991, the Secretary of Transportation shall require each air carrier to provide a passenger manifest for a flight to an appropriate representative of the Secretary of State—

(A) not later than one hour after that carrier is notified of an aviation disaster outside the United States involving that flight; or

(B) if it is not technologically feasible or reasonable to comply with clause (A) of this paragraph, then as expeditiously as possible, but not later than 3 hours after the carrier is so notified.

(2) The passenger manifest shall include the following information:

(A) the full name of each passenger.

(B) the passport number of each passenger, if required for travel.

(C) the name and telephone number of a contact for each passenger.

(3) In carrying out this subsection, the Secretary of Transportation shall consider the necessity and feasibility of requiring air carriers to collect passenger manifest information as a condition for passengers boarding a flight of the carrier.

(b) Foreign Air Carrier Requirements.—The Secretary of Transportation shall consider imposing a requirement on foreign air carriers comparable to that imposed on air carriers under subsection (a)(1) and (2) of this section.

Sec. 44910. Agreements on aircraft sabotage, aircraft hijacking, and airport security

The Secretary of State shall seek multilateral and bilateral agreement on strengthening enforcement measures and standards for compliance related to aircraft sabotage, aircraft hijacking, and airport security.

Sec. 44911. Intelligence

(a) Definition.—In this section, "intelligence community" means the intelligence and intelligence-related activities of the following units of the United States Government:

(1) the Department of State.

(2) the Department of Defense.

(3) the Department of the Treasury.

(4) the Department of Energy.

(5) the Departments of the Army, Navy, and Air Force.

(6) the Central Intelligence Agency.

(7) the National Security Agency.

(8) the Defense Intelligence Agency.

(9) the Federal Bureau of Investigation.

(10) the Drug Enforcement Administration.

(b) Policies and Procedures on Report Availability.—The head of each unit in the intelligence community shall prescribe policies and procedures to ensure that intelligence reports about international terrorism are made available, as appropriate, to the heads of other units in the intelligence community, the Secretary of Transportation, and the Administrator of the Federal Aviation Administration.

(c) Unit for Strategic Planning on Terrorism.—The heads of the units in the intelligence community shall consider placing greater emphasis on strategic intelligence efforts by establishing a unit for strategic planning on terrorism.

(d) Designation of Intelligence Officer.—At the request of the Secretary, the Director of Central Intelligence shall designate at least one intelligence officer of the Central Intelligence Agency to serve in a senior position in the Office of the Secretary.

(e) Written Working Agreements.—The heads of units in the intelligence community, the Secretary, and the Administrator shall review and, as appropriate, revise written working agreements between the intelligence community and the Administrator.

Sec. 44912. Research and development

(a) Program Requirement.—(1) The Administrator of the Federal Aviation Administration shall establish and carry out a program to accelerate and expand the research, development, and implementation of technologies and procedures to counteract terrorist acts against civil aviation. The program shall provide for developing and having in place, not later than November 16, 1993, new equipment and procedures necessary to meet the technological challenges presented by terrorism. The program shall include research on, and development of, technological improvements and ways to enhance human performance.

(2) In designing and carrying out the program established under this subsection, the Administrator shall—

(A) consult and coordinate activities with other departments, agencies, and instrumentalities of the United States Government doing similar research;

(B) identify departments, agencies, and instrumentalities that would benefit from that research; and

(C) seek cost-sharing agreements with those departments, agencies, and instrumentalities.

(3) In carrying out the program established under this subsection, the Administrator shall review and consider the annual reports the Secretary of Transportation submits to Congress on transportation security and intelligence.

(4) The Administrator may—

(A) make grants to institutions of higher learning and other appropriate research facilities with demonstrated ability to carry out research described in paragraph (1) of this subsection, and fix the amounts and terms of the grants; and

(B) make cooperative agreements with governmental authorities the Administrator decides are appropriate.

(b) Review of Threats.—(1) The Administrator shall complete an intensive review of threats to civil aviation, with particular focus on—

(A) explosive material that presents the most significant threat to civil aircraft;

(B) the minimum amounts, configurations, and types of explosive material that can cause, or would reasonably be expected to cause, catastrophic damage to commercial aircraft in service and expected to be in service in the 10-year period beginning on November 16, 1990;

(C) the amounts, configurations, and types of explosive material that can be detected reliably by existing, or reasonably anticipated, near-term explosive detection technologies;

(D) the feasibility of using various ways to minimize damage caused by explosive material that cannot be detected reliably by existing, or reasonably anticipated, near-term explosive detection technologies;

(E) the ability to screen passengers, carry-on baggage, checked baggage, and cargo; and

(F) the technologies that might be used in the future to attempt to destroy or otherwise threaten commercial aircraft and the way in which those technologies can be countered effectively.

(2) The Administrator shall use the results of the review under this subsection to develop the focus and priorities of the program established under subsection (a) of this section.

(c) Scientific Advisory Panel.—The Administrator shall establish a scientific advisory panel, as a subcommittee of the Research, Engineering and Development Advisory Committee, to review, comment on, advise on the progress of, and recommend modifications in, the program established under subsection (a) of this section, including the need for long-range research programs to detect and prevent catastrophic damage to commercial aircraft by the next generation of terrorist weapons. The panel shall consist of individuals with scientific and technical expertise in—

(1) the development and testing of effective explosive detection systems;

(2) aircraft structure and experimentation to decide on the type and minimum weights of explosives that an effective technology must be capable of detecting;

(3) technologies involved in minimizing airframe damage to aircraft from explosives; and

(4) other scientific and technical areas the Administrator considers appropriate.

Sec. 44913. Explosive detection

(a) Deployment and Purchase of Equipment.—(1) A deployment or purchase of explosive detection equipment under section 108.7(b)(8) or 108.20 of title 14, Code of Federal Regulations, or similar regulation is required only if the Administrator of the Federal Aviation Administration certifies that the equipment alone, or as part of an integrated system, can detect under realistic air carrier operating conditions the amounts, configurations, and types of explosive material that would likely be used to cause catastrophic damage to commercial aircraft. The Administrator shall base the certification on the results of tests conducted under protocols developed in consultation with expert scientists outside of the Administration. Those tests shall be completed not later than April 16, 1992.

(2) Before completion of the tests described in paragraph (1) of this subsection, but not later than April 16, 1992, the Administrator may require deployment of explosive detection equipment described in paragraph (1) if the Administrator decides that deployment will enhance aviation security significantly. In making that decision, the Administrator shall consider factors such as the ability of the equipment alone, or as part of an integrated system, to detect under realistic air carrier operating conditions the amounts, configurations,

and types of explosive material that would likely be used to cause catastrophic damage to commercial aircraft. The Administrator shall notify the Committee on Commerce, Science, and Transportation of the Senate and the Committee on Transportation and Infrastructure of the House of Representatives of a deployment decision made under this paragraph.

(3) Until such time as the Administrator determines that equipment certified under paragraph (1) is commercially available and has successfully completed operational testing as provided in paragraph (1), the Administrator shall facilitate the deployment of such approved commercially available explosive detection devices as the Administrator determines will enhance aviation security significantly. The Administrator shall require that equipment deployed under this paragraph be replaced by equipment certified under paragraph (1) when equipment certified under paragraph (1) becomes commercially available. The Administrator is authorized, based on operational considerations at individual airports, to waive the required installation of commercially available equipment under paragraph (1) in the interests of aviation security. The Administrator may permit the requirements of this paragraph to be met at airports by the deployment of dogs or other appropriate animals to supplement equipment for screening passengers, baggage, mail, or cargo for explosives or weapons.

(4) This subsection does not prohibit the Administrator from purchasing or deploying explosive detection equipment described in paragraph (1) of this subsection.

(b) Grants.—The Secretary of Transportation may provide grants to continue the Explosive Detection K-9 Team Training Program to detect explosives at airports and on aircraft.

Sec. 44914. Airport construction guidelines

In consultation with air carriers, airport authorities, and others the Administrator of the Federal Aviation Administration considers appropriate, the Administrator shall develop guidelines for airport design and construction to allow for maximum security enhancement. In developing the guidelines, the Administrator shall consider the results of the assessment carried out under section 44904(a) of this title.

Sec. 44915. Exemptions

The Administrator of the Federal Aviation Administration may exempt from sections 44901, 44903(a)–(c) and (e), 44906, 44935, and 44936 of this title airports in Alaska served only by air carriers that—

(1) hold certificates issued under section 41102 of this title;

(2) operate aircraft with certificates for a maximum gross takeoff weight of less than 12,500 pounds; and

(3) board passengers, or load property intended to be carried in an aircraft cabin, that will be screened under section 44901 of this title at another airport in Alaska before the passengers board, or the property is loaded on, an aircraft for a place outside Alaska.

Sec. 44916. Assessments and evaluations

(a) Periodic Assessments.—The Administrator shall require each air carrier and airport (including the airport owner or operator in cooperation with the air carriers and vendors serving each airport) that provides for intrastate, interstate, or foreign air transportation to conduct periodic vulnerability assessments of the security systems of that air carrier or airport, respectively. The Administration shall perform periodic audits of such assessments.

(b) Investigations.—The Administrator shall conduct periodic and unannounced inspections of security systems of airports and air carriers to determine the effectiveness and vulnerabilities of such systems. To the extent allowable by law, the Administrator may provide for anonymous tests of those security systems.

Sec. 44931. Director of Intelligence and Security

(a) Organization.—There is in the Office of the Secretary of Transportation a Director of Intelligence and Security. The Director reports directly to the Secretary.

(b) Duties and Powers.—The Director shall—

(1) receive, assess, and distribute intelligence information related to long-term transportation security;

(2) develop policies, strategies, and plans for dealing with threats to transportation security;

(3) make other plans related to transportation security, including

coordinating countermeasures with appropriate departments, agencies, and instrumentalities of the United States Government;

(4) serve as the primary liaison of the Secretary to the intelligence and law enforcement communities; and

(5) carry out other duties and powers the Secretary decides are necessary to ensure, to the extent possible, the security of the traveling public.

Sec. 44932. Assistant Administrator for Civil Aviation Security

(a) Organization.—There is an Assistant Administrator for Civil Aviation Security. The Assistant Administrator reports directly to the Administrator of the Federal Aviation Administration and is subject to the authority of the Administrator.

(b) Duties and Powers.—The Assistant Administrator shall—

(1) on a day-to-day basis, manage and provide operational guidance to the field security resources of the Administration, including Federal Security Managers as provided by section 44933 of this title;

(2) enforce security-related requirements;

(3) identify the research and development requirements of security-related activities;

(4) inspect security systems;

(5) report information to the Director of Intelligence and Security that may be necessary to allow the Director to carry out assigned duties and powers;

(6) assess threats to civil aviation; and

(7) carry out other duties and powers the Administrator considers appropriate.

(c) Review and Development of Ways To Strengthen Security.—The Assistant Administrator shall review and, as necessary, develop ways to strengthen air transportation security, including ways—

(1) to strengthen controls over checked baggage in air transportation, including ways to ensure baggage reconciliation and inspection of items in passenger baggage that could potentially contain explosive devices;

(2) to strengthen control over individuals having access to aircraft;

(3) to improve testing of security systems;

(4) to ensure the use of the best available x-ray equipment for air transportation security purposes; and

(5) to strengthen preflight screening of passengers.

Sec. 44933. Federal Security Managers

(a) Establishment, Designation, and Stationing.—The Administrator of the Federal Aviation Administration shall establish the position of Federal Security Manager at each airport in the United States at which the Administrator decides a Manager is necessary for air transportation security. The Administrator shall designate individuals as Managers for, and station those Managers at, those airports. The Administrator may designate a current field employee of the Administration as a Manager. A Manager reports directly to the Assistant Administrator for Civil Aviation Security. The Administrator shall station an individual as Manager at each airport in the United States that the Secretary of Transportation designates as a category X airport.

(b) Duties and Powers.—The Manager at each airport shall—

(1) receive intelligence information related to aviation security;

(2) ensure, and assist in, the development of a comprehensive security plan for the airport that—

(A) establishes the responsibilities of each air carrier and airport operator for air transportation security at the airport; and

(B) includes measures to be taken during periods of normal airport operations and during periods when the Manager decides that there is a need for additional airport security, and identifies the individuals responsible for carrying out those measures;

(3) oversee and enforce the carrying out by air carriers and airport operators of United States Government security requirements, including the security plan under clause (2) of this subsection;

(4) serve as the on-site coordinator of the Administrator's response to terrorist incidents and threats at the airport;

(5) coordinate the day-to-day Government aviation security activities at the airport;

(6) coordinate efforts related to aviation security with local law enforcement; and

(7) coordinate activities with other Managers.

(c) Limitation.—A Civil Aviation Security Field Officer may not be assigned security duties and powers at an airport having a Manager.

Sec. 44934. Foreign Security Liaison Officers

(a) Establishment, Designation, and Stationing.—The Administrator of the Federal Aviation Administration shall establish the position of Foreign Security Liaison Officer for each airport outside the United States at which the Administrator decides an Officer is necessary for air transportation security. In coordination with the Secretary of State, the Administrator shall designate an Officer for each of those airports. In coordination with the Secretary, the Administrator shall designate an Officer for each of those airports where extraordinary security measures are in place. The Secretary shall give high priority to stationing those Officers.

(b) Duties and Powers.—An Officer reports directly to the Assistant Administrator for Civil Aviation Security. The Officer at each airport shall—

(1) serve as the liaison of the Assistant Administrator to foreign security authorities (including governments of foreign countries and foreign airport authorities) in carrying out United States Government security requirements at that airport; and

(2) to the extent practicable, carry out duties and powers referred to in section 44933(b) of this title.

(c) Coordination of Activities.—The activities of each Officer shall be coordinated with the chief of the diplomatic mission of the United States to which the Officer is assigned. Activities of an Officer under this section shall be consistent with the duties and powers of the Secretary and the chief of mission to a foreign country under section 103 of the Omnibus Diplomatic Security and Antiterrorism Act of 1986 (22 U.S.C. 4802) and section 207 of the Foreign Service Act of 1980 (22 U.S.C. 3927).

Sec. 44935. Employment standards and training

(a) Employment Standards.—The Administrator of the Federal Aviation Administration shall prescribe standards for the employment and continued employment of, and contracting for, air carrier personnel and, as appropriate, airport security personnel. The standards shall include—

(1) minimum training requirements for new employees;

(2) retraining requirements;

(3) minimum staffing levels;

(4) minimum language skills; and

(5) minimum education levels for employees, when appropriate.

(b) Review and Recommendations.—In coordination with air carriers, airport operators, and other interested persons, the Administrator shall review issues related to human performance in the aviation security system to maximize that performance. When the review is completed, the Administrator shall recommend guidelines and prescribe appropriate changes in existing procedures to improve that performance.

(c) Security Program Training, Standards, and Qualifications.—

(1) The Administrator—

(A) may train individuals employed to carry out a security program under section 44903(c) of this title; and

(B) shall prescribe uniform training standards and uniform minimum qualifications for individuals eligible for that training.

(2) The Administrator may authorize reimbursement for travel, transportation, and subsistence expenses for security training of non-United States Government domestic and foreign individuals whose services will contribute significantly to carrying out civil aviation security programs. To the extent practicable, air travel reimbursed under this paragraph shall be on air carriers.

(d) Education and Training Standards for Security Coordinators, Supervisory Personnel, and Pilots.—(1) The Administrator shall prescribe standards for educating and training—

(A) ground security coordinators;

(B) security supervisory personnel; and

(C) airline pilots as in-flight security coordinators.

(2) The standards shall include initial training, retraining, and continuing education requirements and methods. Those requirements and methods shall be used annually to measure the performance of ground security coordinators and security supervisory personnel.

Sec. 44936. Employment investigations and restrictions

(a) Employment Investigation Requirement.—(1)(A) The Administrator of the Federal Aviation Administration shall require by regulation that an employment investigation, including a criminal history record check, shall be conducted, as the Administrator decides is necessary to ensure air transportation security, of each individual employed in, or applying for, a position in which the individual has unescorted access, or may permit other individuals to have unescorted access, to—

(i) aircraft of an air carrier or foreign air carrier; or

(ii) a secured area of an airport in the United States the Administrator designates that serves an air carrier or foreign air carrier.

(B) The Administrator shall require by regulation that an employment investigation (including a criminal history record check in any case described in subparagraph (C)) be conducted for—

(i) individuals who will be responsible for screening passengers or property under section 44901 of this title;

(ii) supervisors of the individuals described in clause (i); and

(iii) such other individuals who exercise security functions associated with baggage or cargo, as the Administrator determines is necessary to ensure air transportation security.

(C) Under the regulations issued under subparagraph (B), a criminal history record check shall be conducted in any case in which—

(i) an employment investigation reveals a gap in employment of 12 months or more that the individual who is the subject of the investigation does not satisfactorily account for;

(ii) such individual is unable to support statements made on the application of such individual;

(iii) there are significant inconsistencies in the information provided on the application of such individual; or

(iv) information becomes available during the employment investigation indicating a possible conviction for one of the crimes listed in subsection (b)(1)(B).

(D) If an individual requires a criminal history record check under subparagraph (C), the individual may be employed as a screener until the check is completed if the individual is subject to supervision.

(2) An air carrier, foreign air carrier, or airport operator that employs, or authorizes or makes a contract for the services of, an individual in a position described in paragraph (1) of this subsection shall ensure that the investigation the Administrator requires is conducted.

(3) The Administrator shall provide for the periodic audit of the effectiveness of criminal history record checks conducted under paragraph (1) of this subsection.

(b) Prohibited Employment.—(1) Except as provided in paragraph (3) of this subsection, an air carrier, foreign air carrier, or airport operator may not employ, or authorize or make a contract for the services of, an individual in a position described in subsection (a)(1) of this section if—

(A) the investigation of the individual required under this section has not been conducted; or

(B) the results of that investigation establish that, in the 10-year period ending on the date of the investigation, the individual was convicted of—

(i) a crime referred to in section 46306, 46308, 46312, 46314, or 46315 or chapter 465 of this title or section 32 of title 18;

(ii) murder;

(iii) assault with intent to murder;

(iv) espionage;

(v) sedition;

(vi) treason;

(vii) rape;

(viii) kidnapping;

(ix) unlawful possession, sale, distribution, or manufacture of an explosive or weapon;

(x) extortion;

(xi) armed robbery;

(xii) distribution of, or intent to distribute, a controlled substance; or

(xiii) conspiracy to commit any of the acts referred to in clauses (i)–(xii) of this paragraph.

(2) The Administrator may specify other factors that are sufficient to prohibit the employment of an individual in a position described in subsection (a)(1) of this section.

(3) An air carrier, foreign air carrier, or airport operator may employ, or authorize or contract for the services of, an individual in a position described in subsection (a)(1) of this section without carrying out the investigation required under this section, if the Administrator approves a plan to employ the individual that provides alternate security arrangements.

(c) Fingerprinting and Record Check Information.—(1) If the Administrator requires an identification and criminal history record check, to be conducted by the Attorney General, as part of an investigation under this section, the Administrator shall designate an individual to obtain fingerprints and submit those fingerprints to the Attorney General. The Attorney General may make the results of a check available to an individual the Administrator designates. Before designating an individual to obtain and submit fingerprints or receive results of a check, the Administrator shall consult with the Attorney General.

(2) The Administrator shall prescribe regulations on—

(A) procedures for taking fingerprints; and

(B) requirements for using information received from the Attorney General under paragraph (1) of this subsection—

(i) to limit the dissemination of the information; and

(ii) to ensure that the information is used only to carry out this section.

(3) If an identification and criminal history record check is conducted as part of an investigation of an individual under this section, the individual—

(A) shall receive a copy of any record received from the Attorney General; and

(B) may complete and correct the information contained in the check before a final employment decision is made based on the check.

(d) Fees and Charges.—The Administrator and the Attorney General shall establish reasonable fees and charges to pay expenses incurred in carrying out this section. The employer of the individual being investigated shall pay the costs of a record check of the individual. Money collected under this section shall be credited to the account in the Treasury from which the expenses were incurred and are available to the Administrator and the Attorney General for those expenses.

(e) When Investigation or Record Check Not Required.—This section does not require an investigation or record check when the investigation or record check is prohibited by a law of a foreign country.

(f) Records of Employment of Pilot Applicants.—

(1) In general.—Subject to paragraph (14), before allowing an individual to begin service as a pilot, an air carrier shall request and receive the following information:

(A) FAA records.—From the Administrator of the Federal Aviation Administration, records pertaining to the individual that are maintained by the Administrator concerning—

(i) current airman certificates (including airman medical certificates) and associated type ratings, including any limitations to those certificates and ratings; and

(ii) summaries of legal enforcement actions resulting in a finding by the Administrator of a violation of this title or a regulation prescribed or order issued under this title that was not subsequently overturned.

(B) Air carrier and other records.—From any air carrier or other person that has employed the individual as a pilot of a civil or public aircraft at any time during the 5-year period preceding the date of the employment application of the individual, or from the trustee in bankruptcy for such air carrier or person—

(i) records pertaining to the individual that are maintained by an air carrier (other than records relating to flight time, duty time, or rest time) under regulations set forth in—

(I) section 121.683 of title 14, Code of Federal Regulations;

(II) paragraph (A) of section VI, appendix I, part 121 of such title;

(III) paragraph (A) of section IV, appendix J, part 121 of such title;

(IV) section 125.401 of such title; and

(V) section 135.63(a)(4) of such title; and

(ii) other records pertaining to the individual that are maintained by the air carrier or person concerning—

(I) the training, qualifications, proficiency, or professional competence of the individual, including comments and evaluations made by a check airman designated in accordance with section 121.411, 125.295, or 135.337 of such title;

(II) any disciplinary action taken with respect to the individual that was not subsequently overturned; and

(III) any release from employment or resignation, termination, or disqualification with respect to employment.

(C) National driver register records.—In accordance with section 30305(b)(8) of this title, from the chief driver licensing official of a State, information concerning the motor vehicle driving record of the individual.

(2) Written consent; release from liability.—An air carrier making a request for records under paragraph (1)—

(A) shall be required to obtain written consent to the release of those records from the individual that is the subject of the records requested; and

(B) may, notwithstanding any other provision of law or agreement to the contrary, require the individual who is the subject of the records to request to execute a release from liability for any claim arising from the furnishing of such records to or the use of such records by such air carrier (other than a claim arising from furnishing information known to be false and maintained in violation of a criminal statute).

(3) 5-year reporting period.—A person shall not furnish a record in response to a request made under paragraph (1) if the record was entered more than 5 years before the date of the request, unless the information concerns a revocation or suspension of an airman certificate or motor vehicle license that is in effect on the date of the request.

(4) Requirement to maintain records.—The Administrator and air carriers shall maintain pilot records described in paragraphs (1)(A) and (1)(B) for a period of at least 5 years.

(5) Receipt of consent; provision of information.—A person shall not furnish a record in response to a request made under paragraph (1) without first obtaining a copy of the written consent of the individual who is the subject of the records requested. A person who receives a request for records under this subsection shall furnish a copy of all of such requested records maintained by the person not later than 30 days after receiving the request.

(6) Right to receive notice and copy of any record furnished.—A person who receives a request for records under paragraph (1) shall provide to the individual who is the subject of the records—

(A) on or before the 20th day following the date of receipt of the request, written notice of the request and of the individual's right to receive a copy of such records; and

(B) in accordance with paragraph (10), a copy of such records, if requested by the individual.

(7) Reasonable charges for processing requests and furnishing copies.—A person who receives a request under paragraph (1) or

(6) may establish a reasonable charge for the cost of processing the request and furnishing copies of the requested records.

(8) Standard forms.—The Administrator shall promulgate—

(A) standard forms that may be used by an air carrier to request records under paragraph (1); and

(B) standard forms that may be used by an air carrier to—

(i) obtain the written consent of the individual who is the subject of a request under paragraph (1); and

(ii) inform the individual of—

(I) the request; and

(II) the individual right of that individual to receive a copy of any records furnished in response to the request.

(9) Right to correct inaccuracies.—An air carrier that maintains or requests and receives the records of an individual under paragraph (1) shall provide the individual with a reasonable opportunity to submit written comments to correct any inaccuracies contained in

the records before making a final hiring decision with respect to the individual.

(10) Right of pilot to review certain records.—Notwithstanding any other provision of law or agreement, an air carrier shall, upon written request from a pilot who is or has been employed by such carrier, make available, within a reasonable time, but not later than 30 days after the date of the request, to the pilot for review, any and all employment records referred to in paragraph (1)(B)(i) or (ii) pertaining to the employment of the pilot.

(11) Privacy protections.—An air carrier that receives the records of an individual under paragraph (1) may use such records only to assess the qualifications of the individual in deciding whether or not to hire the individual as a pilot. The air carrier shall take such actions as may be necessary to protect the privacy of the pilot and the confidentiality of the records, including ensuring that information contained in the records is not divulged to any individual that is not directly involved in the hiring decision.

(12) Periodic review.—Not later than 18 months after the date of the enactment of the Pilot Records Improvement Act of 1996, and at least once every 3 years thereafter, the Administrator shall transmit to Congress a statement that contains, taking into account recent developments in the aviation industry—

(A) recommendations by the Administrator concerning proposed changes to Federal Aviation Administration records, air carrier records, and other records required to be furnished under subparagraphs (A) and (B) of paragraph (1); or

(B) reasons why the Administrator does not recommend any proposed changes to the records referred to in subparagraph (A).

(13) Regulations.—The Administrator may prescribe such regulations as may be necessary—

(A) to protect—

(i) the personal privacy of any individual whose records are requested under paragraph (1); and

(ii) the confidentiality of those records;

(B) to preclude the further dissemination of records received under paragraph (1) by the person who requested those records; and

(C) to ensure prompt compliance with any request made under paragraph (1).

(14)Special rules with respect to certain pilots.—

(A) Pilots of certain small aircraft.—Notwithstanding paragraph (1), an air carrier, before receiving information requested about an individual under paragraph (1), may allow the individual to begin service for a period not to exceed 90 days as a pilot of an aircraft with a maximum payload capacity (as defined in section 119.3 of title 14, Code of Federal Regulations) of 7,500 pounds or less, or a helicopter, on a flight that is not a scheduled operation (as defined in such section). Before the end of the 90-day period, the air carrier shall obtain and evaluate such information. The contract between the carrier and the individual shall contain a term that provides that the continuation of the individual's employment, after the last day of the 90-day period, depends on a satisfactory evaluation.

(B) Good faith exception.—Notwithstanding paragraph (1), an air carrier, without obtaining information about an individual under paragraph (1)(B) from an air carrier or other person that no longer exists, may allow the individual to begin service as a pilot if the air carrier required to request the information has made a documented good faith attempt to obtain such information.

(g) Limitation on Liability; Preemption of State Law.—

(1) Limitation on liability.—No action or proceeding may be brought by or on behalf of an individual who has applied for or is seeking a position with an air carrier as a pilot and who has signed a release from liability, as provided for under paragraph

(2), against—

(A) the air carrier requesting the records of that individual under subsection (f)(1);

(B) a person who has complied with such request;

(C) a person who has entered information contained in the individual's records; or

(D) an agent or employee of a person described in subparagraph (A) or (B); in the nature of an action for defamation, invasion of privacy, negligence, interference with contract, or otherwise, or under any Federal or State law with respect to the furnishing or use of such records in accordance with subsection (f).

(2) Preemption.—No State or political subdivision thereof may enact, prescribe, issue, continue in effect, or enforce any law (including any regulation, standard, or other provision having the force and effect of law) that prohibits, penalizes, or imposes liability for furnishing or using records in accordance with subsection (f).

(3) Provision of knowingly false information.—Paragraphs (1) and (2) shall not apply with respect to a person who furnishes information in response to a request made under subsection (f)(1), that—

(A) the person knows is false; and

(B) was maintained in violation of a criminal statute of the United States.

(h) Limitation on Statutory Construction.—Nothing in subsection (f) shall be construed as precluding the availability of the records of a pilot in an investigation or other proceeding concerning an accident or incident conducted by the Administrator, the National Transportation Safety Board, or a court.

Sec. 44937. Prohibition on transferring duties and powers

Except as specifically provided by law, the Administrator of the Federal Aviation Administration may not transfer a duty or power under section 44903(a), (b), (c), or (e), 44906, 44912, 44935, 44936, or 44938(b)(3) of this title to another department, agency, or instrumentality of the United States Government.

Sec. 44938. Reports

(a) Transportation Security.—Not later than March 31 of each year, the Secretary of Transportation shall submit to Congress a report on transportation security with recommendations the Secretary considers appropriate. The report shall be prepared in conjunction with the biennial report the Administrator of the Federal Aviation Administration submits under subsection (b) of this section in each year the Administrator submits the biennial report, but may not duplicate the information submitted under subsection (b) or section 44907(a)(3) of this title. The

Secretary may submit the report in classified and unclassified parts. The report shall include—

(1) an assessment of trends and developments in terrorist activities, methods, and other threats to transportation;

(2) an evaluation of deployment of explosive detection devices;

(3) recommendations for research, engineering, and development activities related to transportation security, except research engineering and development activities related to aviation security to the extent those activities are covered by the national aviation research plan required under section 44501(c) of this title;

(4) identification and evaluation of cooperative efforts with other departments, agencies, and instrumentalities of the United States Government;

(5) an evaluation of cooperation with foreign transportation and security authorities;

(6) the status of the extent to which the recommendations of the President's Commission on Aviation Security and Terrorism have been carried out and the reasons for any delay in carrying out those recommendations;

(7) a summary of the activities of the Director of Intelligence and Security in the 12-month period ending on the date of the report;

(8) financial and staffing requirements of the Director;

(9) an assessment of financial and staffing requirements, and attainment of existing staffing goals, for carrying out duties and powers of the Administrator related to security; and

(10) appropriate legislative and regulatory recommendations.

(b) Screening and Foreign Air Carrier and Airport Security.—The Administrator shall submit biennially to Congress a report—

(1) on the effectiveness of procedures under section 44901 of this title;

(2) that includes a summary of the assessments conducted under section 44907(a)(1) and (2) of this title; and

(3) that includes an assessment of the steps being taken, and the progress being made, in ensuring compliance with section 44906 of this title for each foreign air carrier security program at airports outside the United States—

(A)   at which the Administrator decides that Foreign Security Liaison Officers are necessary for air transportation security; and

(B)   for which extraordinary security measures are in place.

Title 50—War and National Defense

Chapter 36—Foreign Intelligence Surveillance

Subchapter I—Electronic Surveillance

Sec. 1801. Definitions

As used in this subchapter:

(a) "Foreign power" means—

(1) a foreign government or any component thereof, whether or not recognized by the United States;

(2) a faction of a foreign nation or nations, not substantially composed of United States persons;

(3) an entity that is openly acknowledged by a foreign government or governments to be directed and controlled by such foreign government or governments;

(4) a group engaged in international terrorism or activities in preparation therefor;

(5) a foreign-based political organization, not substantially composed of United States persons; or

(6) an entity that is directed and controlled by a foreign government or governments.

(b) "Agent of a foreign power" means—

(1) any person other than a United States person, who—

(A) acts in the United States as an officer or employee of a foreign power, or as a member of a foreign power as defined in subsection (a)(4) of this section;

(B) acts for or on behalf of a foreign power which engages in clandestine intelligence activities in the United States contrary to the interests of the United States, when the circumstances of such person's presence in the United States indicate that such person may engage in such activities in the United States, or when such person knowingly aids or abets any person in the conduct of such activities or knowingly conspires with any person to engage in such activities; or

(2) any person who—

(A) knowingly engages in clandestine intelligence gathering activities for or on behalf of a foreign power, which activities involve or may involve a violation of the criminal statutes of the United States;

(B) pursuant to the direction of an intelligence service or network of a foreign power, knowingly engages in any other clandestine intelligence activities for or on behalf of such foreign power, which activities involve or are about to involve a violation of the criminal statutes of the United States;

(C) knowingly engages in sabotage or international terrorism, or activities that are in preparation therefor, for or on behalf of a foreign power;

(D) knowingly enters the United States under a false or fraudulent identity for or on behalf of a foreign power or, while in the United States, knowingly assumes a false or fraudulent identity for or on behalf of a foreign power; or

(E) knowingly aids or abets any person in the conduct of activities described in subparagraph (A), (B), or (C) or knowingly conspires with any person to engage in activities described in subparagraph (A), (B), or (C).

(c) "International terrorism" means activities that—

(1) involve violent acts or acts dangerous to human life that are a violation of the criminal laws of the United States or of any State, or that would be a criminal violation if committed within the jurisdiction of the United States or any State;

(2) appear to be intended—

(A) to intimidate or coerce a civilian population;

(B) to influence the policy of a government by intimidation or coercion; or

(C) to affect the conduct of a government by assassination or kidnapping; and

(3) occur totally outside the United States, or transcend national boundaries in terms of the means by which they are accomplished, the persons they appear intended to coerce or intimidate, or the locale in which their perpetrators operate or seek asylum.

(d) "Sabotage" means activities that involve a violation of chapter 105 of title 18, or that would involve such a violation if committed against the United States.

(e) "Foreign intelligence information" means—

(1) information that relates to, and if concerning a United States person is necessary to, the ability of the United States to protect against—

(A) actual or potential attack or other grave hostile acts of a foreign power or an agent of a foreign power;

(B) sabotage or international terrorism by a foreign power or an agent of a foreign power; or

(C) clandestine intelligence activities by an intelligence service or network of a foreign power or by an agent of a foreign power; or

(2) information with respect to a foreign power or foreign territory that relates to, and if concerning a United States person is necessary to—

(A) the national defense or the security of the United States; or

(B) the conduct of the foreign affairs of the United States.

(f) "Electronic surveillance" means—

(1) the acquisition by an electronic, mechanical, or other surveillance device of the contents of any wire or radio communication sent by or intended to be received by a particular, known United States person who is in the United States, if the contents are acquired by intentionally targeting that United States person, under circumstances in which a person has a reasonable expectation of privacy and a warrant would be required for law enforcement purposes;

(2) the acquisition by an electronic, mechanical, or other surveillance device of the contents of any wire communication to or from a person in the United States, without the consent of any party thereto, if such acquisition occurs in the United States;

(3) the intentional acquisition by an electronic, mechanical, or other surveillance device of the contents of any radio communication,

under circumstances in which a person has a reasonable expectation of privacy and a warrant would be required for law enforcement purposes, and if both the sender and all intended recipients are located within the United States; or

(4) the installation or use of an electronic, mechanical, or other surveillance device in the United States for monitoring to acquire information, other than from a wire or radio communication, under circumstances in which a person has a reasonable expectation of privacy and a warrant would be required for law enforcement purposes.

(g) "Attorney General" means the Attorney General of the United States (or Acting Attorney General) or the Deputy Attorney General.

(h) "Minimization procedures," with respect to electronic surveillance, means—

(1) specific procedures, which shall be adopted by the Attorney General, that are reasonably designed in light of the purpose and technique of the particular surveillance, to minimize the acquisition and retention, and prohibit the dissemination, of nonpublicly available information concerning unconsenting United States persons consistent with the need of the United States to obtain, produce, and disseminate foreign intelligence information;

(2) procedures that require that nonpublicly available information, which is not foreign intelligence information, as defined in subsection (e)(1) of this section, shall not be disseminated in a manner that identifies any United States person, without such person's consent, unless such person's identity is necessary to understand foreign intelligence information or assess its importance;

(3) notwithstanding paragraphs (1) and (2), procedures that allow for the retention and dissemination of information that is evidence of a crime which has been, is being, or is about to be committed and that is to be retained or disseminated for law enforcement purposes; and

(4) notwithstanding paragraphs (1), (2), and (3), with respect to any electronic surveillance approved pursuant to section 1802(a) of this title, procedures that require that no contents of any communication to which a United States person is a party shall be disclosed, disseminated, or used for any purpose or retained for longer than twenty-four hours unless a court order under section 1805 of this title is obtained or unless the Attorney General determines that the

information indicates a threat of death or serious bodily harm to any person.

(i) "United States person" means a citizen of the United States, an alien lawfully admitted for permanent residence (as defined in section 1101(a)(20) of title 8), an unincorporated association a substantial number of members of which are citizens of the United States or aliens lawfully admitted for permanent residence, or a corporation which is incorporated in the United States, but does not include a corporation or an association which is a foreign power, as defined in subsection (a)(1), (2), or (3) of this section.

(j) "United States," when used in a geographic sense, means all areas under the territorial sovereignty of the United States and the Trust Territory of the Pacific Islands.

(k) "Aggrieved person" means a person who is the target of an electronic surveillance or any other person whose communications or activities were subject to electronic surveillance.

(l) "Wire communication" means any communication while it is being carried by a wire, cable, or other like connection furnished or operated by any person engaged as a common carrier in providing or operating such facilities for the transmission of interstate or foreign communications.

(m) "Person" means any individual, including any officer or employee of the Federal Government, or any group, entity, association, corporation, or foreign power.

(n) "Contents," when used with respect to a communication, includes any information concerning the identity of the parties to such communication or the existence, substance, purport, or meaning of that communication.

(o) "State" means any State of the United States, the District of Columbia, the Commonwealth of Puerto Rico, the Trust Territory of the Pacific Islands, and any territory or possession of the United States.

Sec. 1802. Electronic surveillance authorization without court order; certification by Attorney General; reports to Congressional committees; transmittal under seal; duties and compensation of communication common carrier; applications; jurisdiction of court

(a)

(1) Notwithstanding any other law, the President, through the Attorney General, may authorize electronic surveillance without a court order under this subchapter to acquire foreign intelligence information for periods of up to one year if the Attorney General certifies in writing under oath that—

(A) the electronic surveillance is solely directed at—

(i) the acquisition of the contents of communications transmitted by means of communications used exclusively between or among foreign powers, as defined in section 1801(a)(1), (2), or (3) of this title; or

(ii) the acquisition of technical intelligence, other than the spoken communications of individuals, from property or premises under the open and exclusive control of a foreign power, as defined in section 1801(a)(1), (2), or (3) of this title;

(B) there is no substantial likelihood that the surveillance will acquire the contents of any communication to which a United States person is a party; and

(C) the proposed minimization procedures with respect to such surveillance meet the definition of minimization procedures under section 1801(h) of this title; and if the Attorney General reports such minimization procedures and any changes thereto to the House Permanent Select Committee on Intelligence and the Senate Select Committee on Intelligence at least thirty days prior to their effective date, unless the Attorney General determines immediate action is required and notifies the committees immediately of such minimization procedures and the reason for their becoming effective immediately.

(2) An electronic surveillance authorized by this subsection may be conducted only in accordance with the Attorney General's certification and the minimization procedures adopted by him. The Attorney General shall assess compliance with such procedures and

shall report such assessments to the House Permanent Select Committee on Intelligence and the Senate Select Committee on Intelligence under the provisions of section 1808(a) of this title.

(3) The Attorney General shall immediately transmit under seal to the court established under section 1803(a) of this title a copy of his certification. Such certification shall be maintained under security measures established by the Chief Justice with the concurrence of the Attorney General, in consultation with the Director of Central Intelligence, and shall remain sealed unless—

(A) an application for a court order with respect to the surveillance is made under sections 1801(h)(4) and 1804 of this title; or

(B) the certification is necessary to determine the legality of the surveillance under section 1806(f) of this title.

(4) With respect to electronic surveillance authorized by this subsection, the Attorney General may direct a specified communication common carrier to—

(A) furnish all information, facilities, or technical assistance necessary to accomplish the electronic surveillance in such a manner as will protect its secrecy and produce a minimum of interference with the services that such carrier is providing its customers; and

(B) maintain under security procedures approved by the Attorney General and the Director of Central Intelligence any records concerning the surveillance or the aid furnished which such carrier wishes to retain. The Government shall compensate, at the prevailing rate, such carrier for furnishing such aid.

(b) Applications for a court order under this subchapter are authorized if the President has, by written authorization, empowered the Attorney General to approve applications to the court having jurisdiction under section 1803 of this title, and a judge to whom an application is made may, notwithstanding any other law, grant an order, in conformity with section 1805 of this title, approving electronic surveillance of a foreign power or an agent of a foreign power for the purpose of obtaining foreign intelligence information, except that the court shall not have jurisdiction to grant any order approving electronic surveillance directed solely as described in paragraph (1)(A) of subsection (a) of this section unless such surveillance may involve the acquisition of communications of any United States person.

Sec. 1803. Designation of judges

(a) Court to hear applications and grant orders; record of denial; transmittal to court of review

The Chief Justice of the United States shall publicly designate seven district court judges from seven of the United States judicial circuits who shall constitute a court which shall have jurisdiction to hear applications for and grant orders approving electronic surveillance anywhere within the United States under the procedures set forth in this chapter, except that no judge designated under this subsection shall hear the same application for electronic surveillance under this chapter which has been denied previously by another judge designated under this subsection. If any judge so designated denies an application for an order authorizing electronic surveillance under this chapter, such judge shall provide immediately for the record a written statement of each reason of his decision and, on motion of the United States, the record shall be transmitted, under seal, to the court of review established in subsection (b) of this section.

(b) Court of review; record, transmittal to Supreme Court

The Chief Justice shall publicly designate three judges, one of whom shall be publicly designated as the presiding judge, from the United States district courts or courts of appeals who together shall comprise a court of review which shall have jurisdiction to review the denial of any application made under this chapter. If such court determines that the application was properly denied, the court shall immediately provide for the record a written statement of each reason for its decision and, on petition of the United States for a writ of certiorari, the record shall be transmitted under seal to the Supreme Court, which shall have jurisdiction to review such decision.

(c) Expeditious conduct of proceedings; security measures for maintenance of records

Proceedings under this chapter shall be conducted as expeditiously as possible. The record of proceedings under this chapter, including applications made and orders granted, shall be maintained under security measures established by the Chief Justice in consultation with the Attorney General and the Director of Central Intelligence.

(d) Tenure

Each judge designated under this section shall so serve for a maximum of seven years and shall not be eligible for redesignation, except that the judges first designated under subsection (a) of this section shall be designated for terms of from one to seven years so that one term expires each year, and that judges first designated under subsection (b) of this section shall be designated for terms of three, five, and seven years.

Sec. 1804. Applications for court orders

(a) Submission by Federal officer; approval of Attorney General; contents

Each application for an order approving electronic surveillance under this subchapter shall be made by a Federal officer in writing upon oath or affirmation to a judge having jurisdiction under section 1803 of this title. Each application shall require the approval of the Attorney General based upon his finding that it satisfies the criteria and requirements of such application as set forth in this subchapter. It shall include—

(1) the identity of the Federal officer making the application;

(2) the authority conferred on the Attorney General by the President of the United States and the approval of the Attorney General to make the application;

(3) the identity, if known, or a description of the target of the electronic surveillance;

(4) a statement of the facts and circumstances relied upon by the applicant to justify his belief that—

(A) the target of the electronic surveillance is a foreign power or an agent of a foreign power; and

(B) each of the facilities or places at which the electronic surveillance is directed is being used, or is about to be used, by a foreign power or an agent of a foreign power;

(5) a statement of the proposed minimization procedures;

(6) a detailed description of the nature of the information sought and the type of communications or activities to be subjected to the surveillance;

(7) a certification or certifications by the Assistant to the President for National Security Affairs or an executive branch official or officials designated by the President from among those executive officers employed in the area of national security or defense and appointed by the President with the advice and consent of the Senate—

(A) that the certifying official deems the information sought to be foreign intelligence information;

(B) that the purpose of the surveillance is to obtain foreign intelligence information;

(C) that such information cannot reasonably be obtained by normal investigative techniques;

(D) that designates the type of foreign intelligence information being sought according to the categories described in section 1801(e) of this title; and

(E) including a statement of the basis for the certification that—

    (i) the information sought is the type of foreign intelligence information designated; and

    (ii) such information cannot reasonably be obtained by normal investigative techniques;

(8) a statement of the means by which the surveillance will be effected and a statement whether physical entry is required to effect the surveillance;

(9) a statement of the facts concerning all previous applications that have been made to any judge under this subchapter involving any of the persons, facilities, or places specified in the application, and the action taken on each previous application;

(10) a statement of the period of time for which the electronic surveillance is required to be maintained, and if the nature of the intelligence gathering is such that the approval of the use of electronic surveillance under this subchapter should not automatically terminate when the described type of information has first been obtained, a description of facts supporting the belief that additional information of the same type will be obtained thereafter; and

(11) whenever more than one electronic, mechanical or other surveillance device is to be used with respect to a particular proposed electronic surveillance, the coverage of the devices involved and what minimization procedures apply to information acquired by each device.

(b) Exclusion of certain information respecting foreign power targets
Whenever the target of the electronic surveillance is a foreign power, as defined in section 1801(a)(1), (2), or (3) of this title, and each of the

facilities or places at which the surveillance is directed is owned, leased, or exclusively used by that foreign power, the application need not contain the information required by paragraphs (6), (7)(E), (8), and (11) of subsection (a) of this section, but shall state whether physical entry is required to effect the surveillance and shall contain such information about the surveillance techniques and communications or other information concerning United States persons likely to be obtained as may be necessary to assess the proposed minimization procedures.

(c) Additional affidavits or certifications

The Attorney General may require any other affidavit or certification from any other officer in connection with the application.

(d) Additional information

The judge may require the applicant to furnish such other information as may be necessary to make the determinations required by section 1805 of this title.

Sec. 1805. Issuance of order

(a) Necessary findings

Upon an application made pursuant to section 1804 of this title, the judge shall enter an ex parte order as requested or as modified approving the electronic surveillance if he finds that—

(1) the President has authorized the Attorney General to approve applications for electronic surveillance for foreign intelligence information;

(2) the application has been made by a Federal officer and approved by the Attorney General;

(3) on the basis of the facts submitted by the applicant there is probable cause to believe that—

(A) the target of the electronic surveillance is a foreign power or an agent of a foreign power: Provided, That no United States person may be considered a foreign power or an agent of a foreign power solely upon the basis of activities protected by the first amendment to the Constitution of the United States; and

(B) each of the facilities or places at which the electronic surveillance is directed is being used, or is about to be used, by a foreign power or an agent of a foreign power;

(4) the proposed minimization procedures meet the definition of minimization procedures under section 1804(h) of this title; and

(5) the application which has been filed contains all statements and certifications required by section 1804 of this title and, if the target is a United States person, the certification or certifications are not clearly erroneous on the basis of the statement made under section 1804(a)(7)(E) of this title and any other information furnished under section 1804(d) of this title.

(b) Specifications and directions of orders

An order approving an electronic surveillance under this section shall—

(1) specify—

(A) the identity, if known, or a description of the target of the electronic surveillance;

(B) the nature and location of each of the facilities or places at which the electronic surveillance will be directed;

(C) the type of information sought to be acquired and the type of communications or activities to be subjected to the surveillance;

(D) the means by which the electronic surveillance will be effected and whether physical entry will be used to effect the surveillance;

(E) the period of time during which the electronic surveillance is approved; and

(F) whenever more than one electronic, mechanical, or other surveillance device is to be used under the order, the authorized coverage of the devices involved and what minimization procedures shall apply to information subject to acquisition by each device; and

(2) direct—

(A) that the minimization procedures be followed;

(B) that, upon the request of the applicant, a specified communication or other common carrier, landlord, custodian, or other specified person furnish the applicant forthwith all information, facilities, or technical assistance necessary to accomplish the electronic surveillance in such a manner as will protect its secrecy and produce a minimum of interference with the services that such carrier, landlord, custodian, or other person is providing that target of electronic surveillance;

(C) that such carrier, landlord, custodian, or other person maintain under security procedures approved by the Attorney General and the Director of Central Intelligence any records concerning the surveillance or the aid furnished that such person wishes to retain; and

(D) that the applicant compensate, at the prevailing rate, such carrier, landlord, custodian, or other person for furnishing such aid.

(c) Exclusion of certain information respecting foreign power targets

Whenever the target of the electronic surveillance is a foreign power, as defined in section 1801(a)(1), (2), or (3) of this title, and each of the facilities or places at which the surveillance is directed is owned, leased, or exclusively used by that foreign power, the order need not contain the information required by subparagraphs (C), (D), and (F) of subsection (b)(1) of this section, but shall generally describe the information sought, the communications or activities to be subjected to the surveillance, and the type of electronic surveillance involved, including whether physical entry is required.

(d) Duration of order; extensions; review of circumstances under which information was acquired, retained or disseminated

(1) An order issued under this section may approve an electronic surveillance for the period necessary to achieve its purpose, or for ninety days, whichever is less, except that an order under this section shall approve an electronic surveillance targeted against a foreign power, as defined in section 1801(a)(1), (2), or (3) of this title, for the period specified in the application or for one year, whichever is less.

(2) Extensions of an order issued under this subchapter may be granted on the same basis as an original order upon an application for an extension and new findings made in the same manner as required for an original order, except that an extension of an order under this chapter for a surveillance targeted against a foreign power, as defined in section 1801(a)(5) or (6) of this title, or against a foreign power as defined in section 1801(a)(4) of this title that is not a United States person, may be for a period not to exceed one year if the judge finds probable cause to believe that no communication of any individual United States person will be acquired during the period.

(3) At or before the end of the period of time for which electronic surveillance is approved by an order or an extension, the judge may assess compliance with the minimization procedures by reviewing the circumstances under which information concerning United States persons was acquired, retained, or disseminated.

(e) Emergency orders

Notwithstanding any other provision of this subchapter, when the Attorney General reasonably determines that—

(1) an emergency situation exists with respect to the employment of electronic surveillance to obtain foreign intelligence information before an order authorizing such surveillance can with due diligence be obtained; and

(2) the factual basis for issuance of an order under this subchapter to approve such surveillance exists; he may authorize the emergency employment of electronic surveillance if a judge having jurisdiction under section 1803 of this title is informed by the Attorney General or his designee at the time of such authorization that the decision has been made to employ emergency electronic surveillance and if an application in accordance with this subchapter is made to that judge as soon as practicable, but not more than twenty-four hours after the Attorney General authorizes such surveillance. If the Attorney General authorizes such emergency employment of electronic surveillance, he shall require that the minimization procedures required by this subchapter for the issuance of a judicial order be followed. In the absence of a judicial order approving such electronic surveillance, the surveillance shall terminate when the information sought is obtained, when the application for the order is denied, or after the expiration of twenty-four hours from the time of authorization by the Attorney General, whichever is earliest. In the event that such application for approval is denied, or in any other case where the electronic surveillance is terminated and no order is issued approving the surveillance, no information obtained or evidence derived from such surveillance shall be received in evidence or otherwise disclosed in any trial, hearing, or other proceeding in or before any court, grand jury, department, office, agency, regulatory body, legislative committee, or other authority of the United States, a State, or political subdivision thereof, and no information concerning any United States person acquired from such surveillance shall subsequently be used or disclosed in any other manner

by Federal officers or employees without the consent of such person, except with the approval of the Attorney General if the information indicates a threat of death or serious bodily harm to any person. A denial of the application made under this subsection may be reviewed as provided in section 1803 of this title.

(f) Testing of electronic equipment; discovering unauthorized electronic surveillance; training of intelligence personnel

Notwithstanding any other provision of this subchapter, officers, employees, or agents of the United States are authorized in the normal course of their official duties to conduct electronic surveillance not targeted against the communications of any particular person or persons, under procedures approved by the Attorney General, solely to—

(1) test the capability of electronic equipment, if—

(A) it is not reasonable to obtain the consent of the persons incidentally subjected to the surveillance;

(B) the test is limited in extent and duration to that necessary to determine the capability of the equipment;

(C) the contents of any communication acquired are retained and used only for the purpose of determining the capability of the equipment, are disclosed only to test personnel, and are destroyed before or immediately upon completion of the test; and:

(D) Provided, That the test may exceed ninety days only with the prior approval of the Attorney General;

(2) determine the existence and capability of electronic surveillance equipment being used by persons not authorized to conduct electronic surveillance, if—

(A) it is not reasonable to obtain the consent of persons incidentally subjected to the surveillance;

(B) such electronic surveillance is limited in extent and duration to that necessary to determine the existence and capability of such equipment; and

(C) any information acquired by such surveillance is used only to enforce chapter 119 of title 18, or section 605 of title 47, or to protect information from unauthorized surveillance; or

(3) train intelligence personnel in the use of electronic surveillance equipment, if—

(A) it is not reasonable to—

(i) obtain the consent of the persons incidentally subjected to the surveillance;

(ii) train persons in the course of surveillances otherwise authorized by this subchapter; or

(iii) train persons in the use of such equipment without engaging in electronic surveillance;

(B) such electronic surveillance is limited in extent and duration to that necessary to train the personnel in the use of the equipment; and

(C) no contents of any communication acquired are retained or disseminated for any purpose, but are destroyed as soon as reasonably possible.

(g) Retention of certifications, applications and orders

Certifications made by the Attorney General pursuant to section 1802(a) of this title and applications made and orders granted under this subchapter shall be retained for a period of at least ten years from the date of the certification or application.

Sec. 1806. Use of information

(a) Compliance with minimization procedures; privileged communications; lawful purposes

Information acquired from an electronic surveillance conducted pursuant to this subchapter concerning any United States person may be used and disclosed by Federal officers and employees without the consent of the United States person only in accordance with the minimization procedures required by this subchapter. No otherwise privileged communication obtained in accordance with, or in violation of, the provisions of this subchapter shall lose its privileged character. No information acquired from an electronic surveillance pursuant to this subchapter may be used or disclosed by Federal officers or employees except for lawful purposes.

(b) Statement for disclosure

No information acquired pursuant to this subchapter shall be disclosed for law enforcement purposes unless such disclosure is accompanied by a statement that such information, or any information derived therefrom, may only be used in a criminal proceeding with the advance authorization of the Attorney General.

(c) Notification by United States

Whenever the Government intends to enter into evidence or otherwise use or disclose in any trial, hearing, or other proceeding in or before any court, department, officer, agency, regulatory body, or other authority of the United States, against an aggrieved person, any information obtained or derived from an electronic surveillance of that aggrieved person pursuant to the authority of this subchapter, the Government shall, prior to the trial, hearing, or other proceeding or at a reasonable time prior to an effort to so disclose or so use that information or submit it in evidence, notify the aggrieved person and the court or other authority in which the information is to be disclosed or used that the Government intends to so disclose or so use such information.

(d) Notification by States or political subdivisions

Whenever any State or political subdivision thereof intends to enter into evidence or otherwise use or disclose in any trial, hearing, or other proceeding in or before any court, department, officer, agency, regulatory body, or other authority of a State or a political subdivision thereof, against an aggrieved person any information obtained or derived from an electronic surveillance of that aggrieved person pursuant to the authority of this subchapter, the State or political subdivision thereof shall notify the aggrieved person, the court or other authority in which the information is to be disclosed or used, and the Attorney General that the State or political subdivision thereof intends to so disclose or so use such information.

(e) Motion to suppress

Any person against whom evidence obtained or derived from an electronic surveillance to which he is an aggrieved person is to be, or has been, introduced or otherwise used or disclosed in any trial, hearing, or other proceeding in or before any court, department, officer, agency, regulatory body, or other authority of the United States, a State, or a political subdivision thereof, may move to suppress the evidence obtained or derived from such electronic surveillance on the grounds that—

(1) the information was unlawfully acquired; or

(2) the surveillance was not made in conformity with an order of authorization or approval. Such a motion shall be made before the trial, hearing, or other proceeding unless there was no opportunity to make such a motion or the person was not aware of the grounds of the motion.

(f) In camera and ex parte review by district court
Whenever a court or other authority is notified pursuant to subsection (c) or (d) of this section, or whenever a motion is made pursuant to subsection (e) of this section, or whenever any motion or request is made by an aggrieved person pursuant to any other statute or rule of the United States or any State before any court or other authority of the United States or any State to discover or obtain applications or orders or other materials relating to electronic surveillance or to discover, obtain, or suppress evidence or information obtained or derived from electronic surveillance under this chapter, the United States district court or, where the motion is made before another authority, the United States district court in the same district as the authority, shall, notwithstanding any other law, if the Attorney General files an affidavit under oath that disclosure or an adversary hearing would harm the national security of the United States, review in camera and ex parte the application, order, and such other materials relating to the surveillance as may be necessary to determine whether the surveillance of the aggrieved person was lawfully authorized and conducted. In making this determination, the court may disclose to the aggrieved person, under appropriate security procedures and protective orders, portions of the application, order, or other materials relating to the surveillance only where such disclosure is necessary to make an accurate determination of the legality of the surveillance.

(g) Suppression of evidence; denial of motion
If the United States district court pursuant to subsection (f) of this section determines that the surveillance was not lawfully authorized or conducted, it shall, in accordance with the requirements of law, suppress the evidence which was unlawfully obtained or derived from electronic surveillance of the aggrieved person or otherwise grant the motion of the aggrieved person. If the court determines that the surveillance was lawfully authorized and conducted, it shall deny the motion of the aggrieved person except to the extent that due process requires discovery or disclosure.

(h) Finality of orders
Orders granting motions or requests under subsection (g) of this section, decisions under this section that electronic surveillance was not lawfully authorized or conducted, and orders of the United States district court requiring review or granting disclosure of applications, orders, or other materials relating to a surveillance shall be final orders and binding upon all courts of the United States and the several States except a United States court of appeals and the Supreme Court.

(i) Destruction of unintentionally acquired information

In circumstances involving the unintentional acquisition by an electronic, mechanical, or other surveillance device of the contents of any radio communication, under circumstances in which a person has a reasonable expectation of privacy and a warrant would be required for law enforcement purposes, and if both the sender and all intended recipients are located within the United States, such contents shall be destroyed upon recognition, unless the Attorney General determines that the contents indicate a threat of death or serious bodily harm to any person.

(j) Notification of emergency employment of electronic surveillance; contents; postponement, suspension or elimination

If an emergency employment of electronic surveillance is authorized under section 1805(e) of this title and a subsequent order approving the surveillance is not obtained, the judge shall cause to be served on any United States person named in the application and on such other United States persons subject to electronic surveillance as the judge may determine in his discretion it is in the interest of justice to serve, notice of—

(1) the fact of the application;

(2) the period of the surveillance; and

(3) the fact that during the period information was or was not obtained. On an ex parte showing of good cause to the judge the serving of the notice required by this subsection may be postponed or suspended for a period not to exceed ninety days. Thereafter, on a further ex parte showing of good cause, the court shall forego ordering the serving of the notice required under this subsection.

Sec. 1807. Report to Administrative Office of the United States Court and to Congress

In April of each year, the Attorney General shall transmit to the Administrative Office of the United States Court and to Congress a report setting forth with respect to the preceding calendar year—

(a) the total number of applications made for orders and extensions of orders approving electronic surveillance under this subchapter; and

(b) the total number of such orders and extensions either granted, modified, or denied.

Sec. 1808. Report of Attorney General to Congressional committees; limitation on authority or responsibility of information gathering activities of Congressional committees; report of Congressional committees to Congress

(a) On a semiannual basis the Attorney General shall fully inform the House Permanent Select Committee on Intelligence and the Senate Select Committee on Intelligence concerning all electronic surveillance under this subchapter. Nothing in this subchapter shall be deemed to limit the authority and responsibility of the appropriate committees of each House of Congress to obtain such information as they may need to carry out their respective functions and duties.

(b) On or before one year after October 25, 1978, and on the same day each year for four years thereafter, the Permanent Select Committee on Intelligence and the Senate Select Committee on Intelligence shall report respectively to the House of Representatives and the Senate, concerning the implementation of this chapter. Said reports shall include but not be limited to an analysis and recommendations concerning whether this chapter should be (1) amended, (2) repealed, or (3) permitted to continue in effect without amendment.

Sec. 1809. Criminal sanctions

(a) Prohibited activities
A person is guilty of an offense if he intentionally—

(1) engages in electronic surveillance under color of law except as authorized by statute; or

(2) discloses or uses information obtained under color of law by electronic surveillance, knowing or having reason to know that the information was obtained through electronic surveillance not authorized by statute.

(b) Defense
It is a defense to a prosecution under subsection (a) of this section that the defendant was a law enforcement or investigative officer engaged in the course of his official duties and the electronic surveillance was authorized by and conducted pursuant to a search warrant or court order of a court of competent jurisdiction.

(c) Penalties
An offense described in this section is punishable by a fine of not more than $10,000 or imprisonment for not more than five years, or both.

(d) Federal jurisdiction
There is Federal jurisdiction over an offense under this section if the person committing the offense was an officer or employee of the United States at the time the offense was committed.

Sec. 1810. Civil liability

An aggrieved person, other than a foreign power or an agent of a foreign power, as defined in section 1801(a) or (b)(1)(A) of this title, respectively, who has been subjected to an electronic surveillance or about whom information obtained by electronic surveillance of such person has been disclosed or used in violation of section 1809 of this title shall have a cause of action against any person who committed such violation and shall be entitled to recover—

(a) actual damages, but not less than liquidated damages of $1,000 or $100 per day for each day of violation, whichever is greater;

(b) punitive damages; and

(c) reasonable attorney's fees and other investigation and litigation costs reasonably incurred.

Sec. 1811. Authorization during time of war

Notwithstanding any other law, the President, through the Attorney General, may authorize electronic surveillance without a court order under this subchapter to acquire foreign intelligence information for a period not to exceed fifteen calendar days following a declaration of war by the Congress.

Subchapter II—Physical Searches

Sec. 1821. Definitions

As used in this subchapter:

(1) The terms "foreign power," "agent of a foreign power," "international terrorism," "sabotage," "foreign intelligence information," "Attorney General," "United States person," "United States," "per-

son," and "State" shall have the same meanings as in section 1801 of this title, except as specifically provided by this subchapter.

(2) "Aggrieved person" means a person whose premises, property, information, or material is the target of physical search or any other person whose premises, property, information, or material was subject to physical search.

(3) "Foreign Intelligence Surveillance Court" means the court established by section 1803(a) of this title.

(4) "Minimization procedures" with respect to physical search, means—

(A) specific procedures, which shall be adopted by the Attorney General, that are reasonably designed in light of the purposes and technique of the particular physical search, to minimize the acquisition and retention, and prohibit the dissemination, of nonpublicly available information concerning unconsenting United States persons consistent with the need of the United States to obtain, produce, and disseminate foreign intelligence information;

(B) procedures that require that nonpublicly available information, which is not foreign intelligence information, as defined in section 1801(e)(1) of this title, shall not be disseminated in a manner that identifies any United States person, without such person's consent, unless such person's identity is necessary to understand such foreign intelligence information or assess its importance;

(C) notwithstanding subparagraphs (A) and (B), procedures that allow for the retention and dissemination of information that is evidence of a crime which has been, is being, or is about to be committed and that is to be retained or disseminated for law enforcement purposes; and

(D) notwithstanding subparagraphs (A), (B), and (C), with respect to any physical search approved pursuant to section 1822(a) of this title, procedures that require that no information, material, or property of a United States person shall be disclosed, disseminated, or used for any purpose or retained for longer than 24 hours unless a court order under section 1824 of this title is obtained or unless the Attorney General determines that the information indicates a threat of death or serious bodily harm to any person.

(5) "Physical search" means any physical intrusion within the United States into premises or property (including examination of the interior of property by technical means) that is intended to result in a seizure, reproduction, inspection, or alteration of information, material, or property, under circumstances in which a person has a reasonable expectation of privacy and a warrant would be required for law enforcement purposes, but does not include (A) "electronic surveillance," as defined in section 1801(f) of this title, or (B) the acquisition by the United States Government of foreign intelligence information from international or foreign communications, or foreign intelligence activities conducted in accordance with otherwise applicable Federal law involving a foreign electronic communications system, utilizing a means other than electronic surveillance as defined in section 1801(f) of this title.

Sec. 1822. Authorization of physical searches for foreign intelligence purposes

(a) Presidential authorization

(1) Notwithstanding any other provision of law, the President, acting through the Attorney General, may authorize physical searches without a court order under this subchapter to acquire foreign intelligence information for periods of up to one year if—

(A) the Attorney General certifies in writing under oath that—

(i) the physical search is solely directed at premises, information, material, or property used exclusively by, or under the open and exclusive control of, a foreign power or powers (as defined in section 1801(a)(1), (2), or (3) of this title);

(ii) there is no substantial likelihood that the physical search will involve the premises, information, material, or property of a United States person; and

(iii) the proposed minimization procedures with respect to such physical search meet the definition of minimization procedures under paragraphs (1) through (4) of section 1821(4) of this title; and any changes thereto to the Permanent Select committee on Intelligence of the House of Representatives and the Select Committee on Intelligence of the Senate at least 30 days before their effective date, unless the Attorney General determines that immediate action is required and notifies the committees immediately of such minimization procedures and the reason for their becoming effective immediately.

(2) A physical search authorized by this subsection may be conducted only in accordance with the certification and minimization procedures adopted by the Attorney General. The Attorney General shall assess compliance with such procedures and shall report such assessments to the Permanent Select Committee on Intelligence of the House of Representatives and the Select Committee on Intelligence of the Senate under the provisions of section 1826 of this title.

(3) The Attorney General shall immediately transmit under seal to the Foreign Intelligence Surveillance Court a copy of the certification. Such certification shall be maintained under security measures established by the Chief Justice of the United States with the concurrence of the Attorney General, in consultation with the Director of Central Intelligence, and shall remain sealed unless—

(A) an application for a court order with respect to the physical search is made under section 1821(4) of this title and section 1823 of this title; or

(B) the certification is necessary to determine the legality of the physical search under section 1825(g) of this title.

(4)

(A) With respect to physical searches authorized by this subsection, the Attorney General may direct a specified landlord, custodian, or other specified person to—

(i) furnish all information, facilities, or assistance necessary to accomplish the physical search in such a manner as will protect its secrecy and produce a minimum of interference with the services that such landlord, custodian, or other person is providing the target of the physical search; and

(ii) maintain under security procedures approved by the Attorney General and the Director of Central Intelligence any records concerning the search or the aid furnished that such person wishes to retain.

(B) The Government shall compensate, at the prevailing rate, such landlord, custodian, or other person for furnishing such aid.

(b) Application for order; authorization

Applications for a court order under this subchapter are authorized if the President has, by written authorization, empowered the Attorney General to approve applications to the Foreign Intelligence Surveillance Court. Notwithstanding any other provision of law, a judge of the court to whom application is made may grant an order in accordance with section 1824 of this title approving a physical search in the United States of the premises, property, information, or material of a foreign power or an agent of a foreign power for the purpose of collecting foreign intelligence information.

(c) Jurisdiction of Foreign Intelligence Surveillance Court

The Foreign Intelligence Surveillance Court shall have jurisdiction to hear applications for and grant orders approving a physical search for the purpose of obtaining foreign intelligence information anywhere within the United States under the procedures set forth in this subchapter, except that no judge shall hear the same application which has been denied previously by another judge designated under section 1803(a) of this title. If any judge so designated denies an application for an order authorizing a physical search under this subchapter, such judge shall provide immediately for the record a written statement of each reason for such decision and, on motion of the United States, the record shall be transmitted, under seal, to the court of review established under section 1803(b) of this title.

(d) Court of review; record; transmittal to Supreme Court

The court of review established under section 1803(b) of this title shall have jurisdiction to review the denial of any application made under this subchapter. If such court determines that the application was properly denied, the court shall immediately provide for the record a written statement of each reason for its decision and, on petition of the United States for a writ of certiorari, the record shall be transmitted under seal to the Supreme Court, which shall have jurisdiction to review such decision.

(e) Expeditious conduct of proceedings; security measures for maintenance of records

Judicial proceedings under this subchapter shall be concluded as expeditiously as possible. The record of proceedings under this subchapter, including applications made and orders granted, shall be maintained under security measures established by the Chief Justice of the United States in consultation with the Attorney General and the Director of Central Intelligence.

Sec. 1823. Application for order

(a) Submission by Federal officer; approval of Attorney General; contents
Each application for an order approving a physical search under this subchapter shall be made by a Federal officer in writing upon oath or affirmation to a judge of the Foreign Intelligence Surveillance Court. Each application shall require the approval of the Attorney General based upon the Attorney General's finding that it satisfies the criteria and requirements for such application as set forth in this subchapter. Each application shall include—

(1) the identity of the Federal officer making the application;

(2) the authority conferred on the Attorney General by the President and the approval of the Attorney General to make the application;

(3) the identity, if known, or a description of the target of the search, and a detailed description of the premises or property to be searched and of the information, material, or property to be seized, reproduced, or altered;

(4) a statement of the facts and circumstances relied upon by the applicant to justify the applicant's belief that—

(A) the target of the physical search is a foreign power or an agent of a foreign power;

(B) the premises or property to be searched contains foreign intelligence information; and

(C) the premises or property to be searched is owned, used, possessed by, or is in transit to or from a foreign power or an agent of a foreign power;

(5) a statement of the proposed minimization procedures;

(6) a statement of the nature of the foreign intelligence sought and the manner in which the physical search is to be conducted;

(7) a certification or certifications by the Assistant to the President for National Security Affairs or an executive branch official or officials designated by the President from among those executive branch

officers employed in the area of national security or defense and appointed by the President, by and with the advice and consent of the Senate—

(A) that the certifying official deems the information sought to be foreign intelligence information;

(B) that the purpose of the search is to obtain foreign intelligence information;

(C) that such information cannot reasonably be obtained by normal investigative techniques;

(D) that designates the type of foreign intelligence information being sought according to the categories described in section 1801(e) of this title; and

(E) includes a statement explaining the basis for the certifications required by subparagraphs (C) and (D);

(8) where the physical search involves a search of the residence of a United States person, the Attorney General shall state what investigative techniques have previously been utilized to obtain the foreign intelligence information concerned and the degree to which these techniques resulted in acquiring such information; and

(9) a statement of the facts concerning all previous applications that have been made to any judge under this subchapter involving any of the persons, premises, or property specified in the application, and the action taken on each previous application.

(b) Additional affidavits or certifications

The Attorney General may require any other affidavit or certification from any other officer in connection with the application.

(c) Additional information

The judge may require the applicant to furnish such other information as may be necessary to make the determinations required by section 1824 of this title.

Sec. 1824. Issuance of order

(a) Necessary findings

Upon an application made pursuant to section 1823 of this title, the judge shall enter an ex parte order as requested or as modified approving the physical search if the judge finds that—

(1) the President has authorized the Attorney General to approve applications for physical searches for foreign intelligence purposes;

(2) the application has been made by a Federal officer and approved by the Attorney General;

(3) on the basis of the facts submitted by the applicant there is probable cause to believe that—

(A) the target of the physical search is a foreign power or an agent of a foreign power, except that no United States person may be considered an agent of a foreign power solely upon the basis of activities protected by the first amendment to the Constitution of the United States; and

(B) the premises or property to be searched is owned, used, possessed by, or is in transit to or from an agent of a foreign power or a foreign power;

(4) the proposed minimization procedures meet the definition of minimization contained in this subchapter; and

(5) the application which has been filed contains all statements and certifications required by section 1823 of this title, and, if the target is a United States person, the certification or certifications are not clearly erroneous on the basis of the statement made under section 1823(a)(7)(E) of this title and any other information furnished under section 1823(c) of this title.

(b) Specifications and directions of orders

An order approving a physical search under this section shall—

(1) specify—

(A) the identity, if known, or a description of the target of the physical search;

(B) the nature and location of each of the premises or property to be searched;

(C) the type of information, material, or property to be seized, altered, or reproduced;

(D) a statement of the manner in which the physical search is to be conducted and, whenever more than one physical search is authorized under the order, the authorized scope of each search and what minimization procedures shall apply to the information acquired by each search; and

(E) the period of time during which physical searches are approved; and

(2) direct—

(A) that the minimization procedures be followed;

(B) that, upon the request of the applicant, a specified landlord, custodian, or other specified person furnish the applicant forthwith all information, facilities, or assistance necessary to accomplish the physical search in such a manner as will protect its secrecy and produce a minimum of interference with the services that such landlord, custodian, or other person is providing the target of the physical search;

(C) that such landlord, custodian, or other person maintain under security procedures approved by the Attorney General and the Director of Central Intelligence any records concerning the search or the aid furnished that such person wishes to retain;

(D) that the applicant compensate, at the prevailing rate, such landlord, custodian, or other person for furnishing such aid; and

(E) that the Federal officer conducting the physical search promptly report to the court the circumstances and results of the physical search.

(c) Duration of order; extensions; assessment of compliance

(1) An order issued under this section may approve a physical search for the period necessary to achieve its purpose, or for forty-five days, whichever is less, except that an order under this section shall approve a physical search targeted against a foreign power, as defined in paragraph (1), (2), or (3) of section 1801(a) of this title, for the period specified in the application or for one year, whichever is less.

(2) Extensions of an order issued under this subchapter may be granted on the same basis as the original order upon an application for an extension and new findings made in the same manner as required for the original order, except that an extension of an order under this chapter for a physical search targeted against a foreign power, as defined in section 1801(a)(5) or (6) of this title, or against a foreign power, as defined in section 1801(a)(4) of this title, that is not a United States person, may be for a period not to exceed one year if the judge finds probable cause to believe that no property of any individual United States person will be acquired during the period.

(3) At or before the end of the period of time for which a physical search is approved by an order or an extension, or at any time after a physical search is carried out, the judge may assess compliance with the minimization procedures by reviewing the circumstances under which information concerning United States persons was acquired, retained, or disseminated.

(d) Emergency orders

(1)

(A) Notwithstanding any other provision of this subchapter, whenever the Attorney General reasonably makes the determination specified in subparagraph (B), the Attorney General may authorize the execution of an emergency physical search if—

(i) a judge having jurisdiction under section 1803 of this title is informed by the Attorney General or the Attorney General's designee at the time of such authorization that the decision has been made to execute an emergency search, and

(ii) an application in accordance with this subchapter is made to that judge as soon as practicable but not more than 24 hours after the Attorney General authorizes such search.

(B) The determination referred to in subparagraph (A) is a determination that—

(i) an emergency situation exists with respect to the execution of a physical search to obtain foreign intelligence information before an order authorizing such search can with due diligence be obtained, and

(ii) the factual basis for issuance of an order under this subchapter to approve such a search exists.

(2) If the Attorney General authorizes an emergency search under paragraph (1), the Attorney General shall require that the minimization procedures required by this subchapter for the issuance of a judicial order be followed.

(3) In the absence of a judicial order approving such a physical search, the search shall terminate the earlier of—

(A) the date on which the information sought is obtained;

(B) the date on which the application for the order is denied; or

(C) the expiration of 24 hours from the time of authorization by the Attorney General.

(4) In the event that such application for approval is denied, or in any other case where the physical search is terminated and no order is issued approving the search, no information obtained or evidence derived from such search shall be received in evidence or otherwise disclosed in any trial, hearing, or other proceeding in or before any court, grand jury, department, office, agency, regulatory body, legislative committee, or other authority of the United States, a State, or political subdivision thereof, and no information concerning any United States person acquired from such search shall subsequently be used or disclosed in any other manner by Federal officers or employees without the consent of such person, except with the approval of the Attorney General, if the information indicates a threat of death or serious bodily harm to any person. A denial of the application made under this subsection may be reviewed as provided in section 1822 of this title.

(e) Retention of applications and orders
Applications made and orders granted under this subchapter shall be retained for a period of at least 10 years from the date of the application.

Sec. 1825. Use of information

(a) Compliance with minimization procedures; lawful purposes
Information acquired from a physical search conducted pursuant to this subchapter concerning any United States person may be used and disclosed by Federal officers and employees without the consent of the United States person only in accordance with the minimization procedures required by this subchapter. No information acquired from a physical search pursuant to this subchapter may be used or disclosed by Federal officers or employees except for lawful purposes.

(b) Notice of search and identification of property seized, altered, or reproduced
Where a physical search authorized and conducted pursuant to section 1824 of this title involves the residence of a United States person, and, at any time after the search the Attorney General determines there is no national security interest in continuing to maintain the secrecy of the search, the Attorney General shall provide notice to the United States

person whose residence was searched of the fact of the search conducted pursuant to this chapter and shall identify any property of such person seized, altered, or reproduced during such search.

(c) Statement for disclosure

No information acquired pursuant to this subchapter shall be disclosed for law enforcement purposes unless such disclosure is accompanied by a statement that such information, or any information derived therefrom, may only be used in a criminal proceeding with the advance authorization of the Attorney General.

(d) Notification by United States

Whenever the United States intends to enter into evidence or otherwise use or disclose in any trial, hearing, or other proceeding in or before any court, department, officer, agency, regulatory body, or other authority of the United States, against an aggrieved person, any information obtained or derived from a physical search pursuant to the authority of this subchapter, the United States shall, prior to the trial, hearing, or the other proceeding or at a reasonable time prior to an effort to so disclose or so use that information or submit it in evidence, notify the aggrieved person and the court or other authority in which the information is to be disclosed or used that the United States intends to so disclose or so use such information.

(e) Notification by States or political subdivisions

Whenever any State or political subdivision thereof intends to enter into evidence or otherwise use or disclose in any trial, hearing, or other proceeding in or before any court, department, officer, agency, regulatory body, or other authority of a State or a political subdivision thereof against an aggrieved person any information obtained or derived from a physical search pursuant to the authority of this subchapter, the State or political subdivision thereof shall notify the aggrieved person, the court or other authority in which the information is to be disclosed or used, and the Attorney General that the State or political subdivision thereof intends to so disclose or so use such information.

(f) Motion to suppress

(1) Any person against whom evidence obtained or derived from a physical search to which he is an aggrieved person is to be, or has been, introduced or otherwise used or disclosed in any trial, hearing, or other proceeding in or before any court, department, officer, agency, regulatory body, or other authority of the United States,

a State, or a political subdivision thereof, may move to suppress the evidence obtained or derived from such search on the grounds that—

(A) the information was unlawfully acquired; or

(B) the physical search was not made in conformity with an order of authorization or approval.

(2) Such a motion shall be made before the trial, hearing, or other proceeding unless there was no opportunity to make such a motion or the person was not aware of the grounds of the motion.

(g) In camera and ex parte review by district court
Whenever a court or other authority is notified pursuant to subsection (d) or (e) of this section, or whenever a motion is made pursuant to subsection (f) of this section, or whenever any motion or request is made by an aggrieved person pursuant to any other statute or rule of the United States or any State before any court or other authority of the United States or any State to discover or obtain applications or orders or other materials relating to a physical search authorized by this subchapter or to discover, obtain, or suppress evidence or information obtained or derived from a physical search authorized by this subchapter, the United States district court or, where the motion is made before another authority, the United States district court in the same district as the authority shall, notwithstanding any other provision of law, if the Attorney General files an affidavit under oath that disclosure or any adversary hearing would harm the national security of the United States, review in camera and ex parte the application, order, and such other materials relating to the physical search as may be necessary to determine whether the physical search of the aggrieved person was lawfully authorized and conducted. In making this determination, the court may disclose to the aggrieved person, under appropriate security procedures and protective orders, portions of the application, order, or other materials relating to the physical search, or may require the Attorney General to provide to the aggrieved person a summary of such materials, only where such disclosure is necessary to make an accurate determination of the legality of the physical search.

(h) Suppression of evidence; denial of motion
If the United States district court pursuant to subsection (g) of this section determines that the physical search was not lawfully authorized or conducted, it shall, in accordance with the requirements of law, suppress the evidence which was unlawfully obtained or derived from the physi-

cal search of the aggrieved person or otherwise grant the motion of the aggrieved person. If the court determines that the physical search was lawfully authorized or conducted, it shall deny the motion of the aggrieved person except to the extent that due process requires discovery or disclosure.

(i) Finality of orders

Orders granting motions or requests under subsection (h) of this section, decisions under this section that a physical search was not lawfully authorized or conducted, and orders of the United States district court requiring review or granting disclosure of applications, orders, or other materials relating to the physical search shall be final orders and binding upon all courts of the United States and the several States except a United States Court of Appeals or the Supreme Court.

(j) Notification of emergency execution of physical search; contents; postponement, suspension, or elimination

(1) If an emergency execution of a physical search is authorized under section 1824(d) of this title and a subsequent order approving the search is not obtained, the judge shall cause to be served on any United States person named in the application and on such other United States persons subject to the search as the judge may determine in his discretion it is in the interests of justice to serve, notice of—

(A) the fact of the application;

(B) the period of the search; and

(C) the fact that during the period information was or was not obtained.

(2) On an ex parte showing of good cause to the judge, the serving of the notice required by this subsection may be postponed or suspended for a period not to exceed 90 days. Thereafter, on a further ex parte showing of good cause, the court shall forego ordering the serving of the notice required under this subsection.

Sec. 1826. Congressional oversight

On a semiannual basis the Attorney General shall fully inform the Permanent Select Committee on Intelligence of the House of Representatives and the Select Committee on Intelligence of the Senate concerning all physical searches conducted pursuant to this subchapter.

On a semiannual basis the Attorney General shall also provide to those committees and the Committees on the Judiciary of the House of Representatives and the Senate a report setting forth with respect to the preceding six-month period—

(1) the total number of applications made for orders approving physical searches under this subchapter;

(2) the total number of such orders either granted, modified, or denied; and

(3) the number of physical searches which involved searches of the residences, offices, or personal property of United States persons, and the number of occasions, if any, where the Attorney General provided notice pursuant to section 1825(b) of this title.

Sec. 1827. Penalties

(a) Prohibited activities

A person is guilty of an offense if he intentionally—

(1) under color of law for the purpose of obtaining foreign intelligence information, executes a physical search within the United States except as authorized by statute; or

(2) discloses or uses information obtained under color of law by physical search within the United States, knowing or having reason to know that the information was obtained through physical search not authorized by statute, for the purpose of obtaining intelligence information.

(b) Defense

It is a defense to a prosecution under subsection (a) of this section that the defendant was a law enforcement or investigative officer engaged in the course of his official duties and the physical search was authorized by and conducted pursuant to a search warrant or court order of a court of competent jurisdiction.

(c) Fine or imprisonment

An offense described in this section is punishable by a fine of not more than $10,000 or imprisonment for not more than five years, or both.

(d) Federal jurisdiction

There is Federal jurisdiction over an offense under this section if the person committing the offense was an officer or employee of the United States at the time the offense was committed.

Sec. 1828. Civil liability

An aggrieved person, other than a foreign power or an agent of a foreign power, as defined in section 1801(a) or (b)(1)(A), respectively, of this title, whose premises, property, information, or material has been subjected to a physical search within the United States or about whom information obtained by such a physical search has been disclosed or used in violation of section 1827 of this title shall have a cause of action against any person who committed such violation and shall be entitled to recover—

(1) actual damages, but not less than liquidated damages of $1,000 or $100 per day for each day of violation, whichever is greater;

(2) punitive damages; and

(3) reasonable attorney's fees and other investigative and litigation costs reasonably incurred.

Sec. 1829. Authorization during time of war

Notwithstanding any other provision of law, the President, through the Attorney General, may authorize physical searches without a court order under this subchapter to acquire foreign intelligence information for a period not to exceed 15 calendar days following a declaration of war by the Congress.

Subchapter III—Pen Registers and Trap and Trace Devices for Foreign Intelligence Purposes

Sec. 1841. Definitions

As used in this subchapter:

(1) The terms "foreign power," "agent of a foreign power," "international terrorism," "foreign intelligence information," "Attorney General," "United States person," "United States," "person," and "State" shall have the same meanings as in section 1801 of this title.

(2) The terms "pen register" and "trap and trace device" have the meanings given such terms in section 3127 of title 18.

(3) The term "aggrieved person" means any person—

(A) whose telephone line was subject to the installation or use of a pen register or trap and trace device authorized by this subchapter; or

(B) whose communication instrument or device was subject to the use of a pen register or trap and trace device authorized by this subchapter to capture incoming electronic or other communications impulses.

Sec. 1842. Pen registers and trap and trace devices for foreign intelligence and international terrorism investigations

(a) Application for authorization or approval

(1) Notwithstanding any other provision of law, the Attorney General or a designated attorney for the Government may make an application for an order or an extension of an order authorizing or approving the installation and use of a pen register or trap and trace device for any investigation to gather foreign intelligence information or information concerning international terrorism which is being conducted by the Federal Bureau of Investigation under such guidelines as the Attorney General approves pursuant to Executive Order No. 12333, or a successor order.

(2) The authority under paragraph (1) is in addition to the authority under subchapter I of this chapter to conduct the electronic surveillance referred to in that paragraph.

(b) Form of application; recipient

Each application under this section shall be in writing under oath or affirmation to—

(1) a judge of the court established by section 1803(a) of this title; or

(2) a United States Magistrate Judge under chapter 43 of title 28 who is publicly designated by the Chief Justice of the United States to have the power to hear applications for and grant orders approving the installation and use of a pen register or trap and trace device on behalf of a judge of that court.

(c) Executive approval; contents of application

Each application under this section shall require the approval of the Attorney General, or a designated attorney for the Government, and shall include—

(1) the identity of the Federal officer seeking to use the pen register or trap and trace device covered by the application;

(2) a certification by the applicant that the information likely to be obtained is relevant to an ongoing foreign intelligence or international terrorism investigation being conducted by the Federal Bureau of Investigation under guidelines approved by the Attorney General; and

(3) information which demonstrates that there is reason to believe that the telephone line to which the pen register or trap and trace device is to be attached, or the communication instrument or device to be covered by the pen register or trap and trace device, has been or is about to be used in communication with—

(A) an individual who is engaging or has engaged in international terrorism or clandestine intelligence activities that involve or may involve a violation of the criminal laws of the United States; or

(B) a foreign power or agent of a foreign power under circumstances giving reason to believe that the communication concerns or concerned international terrorism or clandestine intelligence activities that involve or may involve a violation of the criminal laws of the United States.

(d) Ex parte judicial order of approval

(1) Upon an application made pursuant to this section, the judge shall enter an ex parte order as requested, or as modified, approving the installation and use of a pen register or trap and trace device if the judge finds that the application satisfies the requirements of this section.

(2) An order issued under this section—

(A) shall specify—

(i) the identity, if known, of the person who is the subject of the foreign intelligence or international terrorism investigation;

(ii) in the case of an application for the installation and use of a pen register or trap and trace device with respect to a telephone line—

(I) the identity, if known, of the person to whom is leased or in whose name the telephone line is listed; and

(II) the number and, if known, physical location of the telephone line; and

(iii) in the case of an application for the use of a pen register or trap and trace device with respect to a communication instrument or device not covered by clause (ii)—

(I) the identity, if known, of the person who owns or leases the instrument or device or in whose name the instrument or device is listed; and

(II) the number of the instrument or device; and

(B) shall direct that—

(i) upon request of the applicant, the provider of a wire or electronic communication service, landlord, custodian, or other person shall furnish any information, facilities, or technical assistance necessary to accomplish the installation and operation of the pen register or trap and trace device in such a manner as will protect its secrecy and produce a minimum amount of interference with the services that such provider, landlord, custodian, or other person is providing the person concerned;

(ii) such provider, landlord, custodian, or other person—

(I) shall not disclose the existence of the investigation or of the pen register or trap and trace device to any person unless or until ordered by the court; and

(II) shall maintain, under security procedures approved by the Attorney General and the Director of Central Intelligence pursuant to section 1805(b)(2)(C) of this title, any records concerning the pen register or trap and trace device or the aid furnished; and

(iii) the applicant shall compensate such provider, landlord, custodian, or other person for reasonable expenses incurred by such provider, landlord, custodian, or other person in providing such information, facilities, or technical assistance.

(e) Time limitation

An order issued under this section shall authorize the installation and use of a pen register or trap and trace device for a period not to exceed

90 days. Extensions of such an order may be granted, but only upon an application for an order under this section and upon the judicial finding required by subsection (d) of this section. The period of extension shall be for a period not to exceed 90 days.

(f) Cause of action barred

No cause of action shall lie in any court against any provider of a wire or electronic communication service, landlord, custodian, or other person (including any officer, employee, agent, or other specified person thereof) that furnishes any information, facilities, or technical assistance under subsection (d) of this section in accordance with the terms of a court under this section.

(g) Furnishing of results

Unless otherwise ordered by the judge, the results of a pen register or trap and trace device shall be furnished at reasonable intervals during regular business hours for the duration of the order to the authorized Government official or officials.

Sec. 1843. Authorization during emergencies

(a) Requirements for authorization

Notwithstanding any other provision of this subchapter, when the Attorney General makes a determination described in subsection (b) of this section, the Attorney General may authorize the installation and use of a pen register or trap and trace device on an emergency basis to gather foreign intelligence information or information concerning international terrorism if—

> (1) a judge referred to in section 1842(b) of this title is informed by the Attorney General or his designee at the time of such authorization that the decision has been made to install and use the pen register or trap and trace device, as the case may be, on an emergency basis; and

> (2) an application in accordance with section 1842 of this title is made to such judge as soon as practicable, but not more than 48 hours, after the Attorney General authorizes the installation and use of the pen register or trap and trace device, as the case may be, under this section.

(b) Determination of emergency and factual basis

A determination under this subsection is a reasonable determination by the Attorney General that—

(1) an emergency requires the installation and use of a pen register or trap and trace device to obtain foreign intelligence information or information concerning international terrorism before an order authorizing the installation and use of the pen register or trap and trace device, as the case may be, can with due diligence be obtained under section 1842 of this title; and

(2) the factual basis for issuance of an order under such section 1842 of this title to approve the installation and use of the pen register or trap and trace device, as the case may be, exists.

(c) Effect of absence of order

(1) In the absence of an order applied for under subsection (a)(2) of this section approving the installation and use of a pen register or trap and trace device authorized under this section, the installation and use of the pen register or trap and trace device, as the case may be, shall terminate at the earlier of—

(A) when the information sought is obtained;

(B) when the application for the order is denied under section 1842 of this title; or

(C) 48 hours after the time of the authorization by the Attorney General.

(2) In the event that an application for an order applied for under subsection (a)(2) of this section is denied, or in any other case where the installation and use of a pen register or trap and trace device under this section is terminated and no order under section 1842 of this title is issued approving the installation and use of the pen register or trap and trace device, as the case may be, no information obtained or evidence derived from the use of the pen register or trap and trace device, as the case may be, shall be received in evidence or otherwise disclosed in any trial, hearing, or other proceeding in or before any court, grand jury, department, office, agency, regulatory body, legislative committee, or other authority of the United States, a State, or political subdivision thereof, and no information concerning any United States person acquired from the use of the pen register or trap and trace device, as the case may be, shall subsequently be used or disclosed in any other manner by Federal officers or employees without the consent of such person, except with the approval of the Attorney General if the information indicates a threat of death or serious bodily harm to any person.

Sec. 1844. Authorization during time of war

Notwithstanding any other provision of law, the President, through the Attorney General, may authorize the use of a pen register or trap and trace device without a court order under this subchapter to acquire foreign intelligence information for a period not to exceed 15 calendar days following a declaration of war by Congress.

Sec. 1845. Use of information

(a) In general

(1) Information acquired from the use of a pen register or trap and trace device installed pursuant to this subchapter concerning any United States person may be used and disclosed by Federal officers and employees without the consent of the United States person only in accordance with the provisions of this section.

(2) No information acquired from a pen register or trap and trace device installed and used pursuant to this subchapter may be used or disclosed by Federal officers or employees except for lawful purposes.

(b) Disclosure for law enforcement purposes

No information acquired pursuant to this subchapter shall be disclosed for law enforcement purposes unless such disclosure is accompanied by a statement that such information, or any information derived therefrom, may only be used in a criminal proceeding with the advance authorization of the Attorney General.

(c) Notification of intended disclosure by United States

Whenever the United States intends to enter into evidence or otherwise use or disclose in any trial, hearing, or other proceeding in or before any court, department, officer, agency, regulatory body, or other authority of the United States against an aggrieved person any information obtained or derived from the use of a pen register or trap and trace device pursuant to this subchapter, the United States shall, before the trial, hearing, or the other proceeding or at a reasonable time before an effort to so disclose or so use that information or submit it in evidence, notify the aggrieved person and the court or other authority in which the information is to be disclosed or used that the United States intends to so disclose or so use such information.

(d) Notification of intended disclosure by State or political subdivision

Whenever any State or political subdivision thereof intends to enter into evidence or otherwise use or disclose in any trial, hearing, or other proceeding in or before any court, department, officer, agency, regulatory body, or other authority of the State or political subdivision thereof against an aggrieved person any information obtained or derived from the use of a pen register or trap and trace device pursuant to this subchapter, the State or political subdivision thereof shall notify the aggrieved person, the court or other authority in which the information is to be disclosed or used, and the Attorney General that the State or political subdivision thereof intends to so disclose or so use such information.

(e) Motion to suppress

(1) Any aggrieved person against whom evidence obtained or derived from the use of a pen register or trap and trace device is to be, or has been, introduced or otherwise used or disclosed in any trial, hearing, or other proceeding in or before any court, department, officer, agency, regulatory body, or other authority of the United States, or a State or political subdivision thereof, may move to suppress the evidence obtained or derived from the use of the pen register or trap and trace device, as the case may be, on the grounds that—

(A) the information was unlawfully acquired; or

(B) the use of the pen register or trap and trace device, as the case may be, was not made in conformity with an order of authorization or approval under this subchapter.

(2) A motion under paragraph (1) shall be made before the trial, hearing, or other proceeding unless there was no opportunity to make such a motion or the aggrieved person concerned was not aware of the grounds of the motion.

(f) In camera and ex parte review

(1) Whenever a court or other authority is notified pursuant to subsection (c) or (d) of this section, whenever a motion is made pursuant to subsection (e) of this section, or whenever any motion or request is made by an aggrieved person pursuant to any other statute or rule of the United States or any State before any court or other authority of the United States or any State to discover or obtain applications or orders or other materials relating to the use of a pen register or trap and trace device authorized by this subchapter or to discover, obtain, or suppress evidence or information obtained or derived from the use of a pen register or trap and trace device authorized by this subchapter, the United States district court

or, where the motion is made before another authority, the United States district court in the same district as the authority shall, notwithstanding any other provision of law and if the Attorney General files an affidavit under oath that disclosure or any adversary hearing would harm the national security of the United States, review in camera and ex parte the application, order, and such other materials relating to the use of the pen register or trap and trace device, as the case may be, as may be necessary to determine whether the use of the pen register or trap and trace device, as the case may be, was lawfully authorized and conducted.

(2) In making a determination under paragraph (1), the court may disclose to the aggrieved person, under appropriate security procedures and protective orders, portions of the application, order, or other materials relating to the use of the pen register or trap and trace device, as the case may be, or may require the Attorney General to provide to the aggrieved person a summary of such materials, only where such disclosure is necessary to make an accurate determination of the legality of the use of the pen register or trap and trace device, as the case may be.

(g) Effect of determination of lawfulness

(1) If the United States district court determines pursuant to subsection (f) of this section that the use of a pen register or trap and trace device was not lawfully authorized or conducted, the court may, in accordance with the requirements of law, suppress the evidence which was unlawfully obtained or derived from the use of the pen register or trap and trace device, as the case may be, or otherwise grant the motion of the aggrieved person.

(2) If the court determines that the use of the pen register or trap and trace device, as the case may be, was lawfully authorized or conducted, it may deny the motion of the aggrieved person except to the extent that due process requires discovery or disclosure.

(h) Binding final orders

Orders granting motions or requests under subsection (g) of this section, decisions under this section that the use of a pen register or trap and trace device was not lawfully authorized or conducted, and orders of the United States district court requiring review or granting disclosure of applications, orders, or other materials relating to the installation and use of a pen register or trap and trace device shall be final orders and binding upon all courts of the United States and the several States except a United States Court of Appeals or the Supreme Court.

Sec. 1846. Congressional oversight

(a) On a semiannual basis, the Attorney General shall fully inform the Permanent Select Committee on Intelligence of the House of Representatives and the Select Committee on Intelligence of the Senate concerning all uses of pen registers and trap and trace devices pursuant to this subchapter.

(b) On a semiannual basis, the Attorney General shall also provide to the committees referred to in subsection (a) of this section and to the Committees on the Judiciary of the House of Representatives and the Senate a report setting forth with respect to the preceding 6-month period—

(1) the total number of applications made for orders approving the use of pen registers or trap and trace devices under this subchapter; and

(2) the total number of such orders either granted, modified, or denied.

Subchapter IV—Access to Certain Business Records for Foreign Intelligence Purposes

Sec. 1861. Definitions

As used in this subchapter:

(1) The terms "foreign power," "agent of a foreign power," "foreign intelligence information," "international terrorism," and "Attorney General" shall have the same meanings as in section 1801 of this title.

(2) The term "common carrier" means any person or entity transporting people or property by land, rail, water, or air for compensation.

(3) The term "physical storage facility" means any business or entity that provides space for the storage of goods or materials, or services related to the storage of goods or materials, to the public or any segment thereof.

(4) The term "public accommodation facility" means any inn, hotel, motel, or other establishment that provides lodging to transient guests.

(5) The term "vehicle rental facility" means any person or entity that provides vehicles for rent, lease, loan, or other similar use to the public or any segment thereof

Sec. 1862. Access to certain business records for foreign intelligence and international terrorism investigations

(a) Application for authorization
The Director of the Federal Bureau of Investigation or a designee of the Director (whose rank shall be no lower than Assistant Special Agent in Charge) may make an application for an order authorizing a common carrier, public accommodation facility, physical storage facility, or vehicle rental facility to release records in its possession for an investigation to gather foreign intelligence information or an investigation concerning international terrorism which investigation is being conducted by the Federal Bureau of Investigation under such guidelines as the Attorney General approves pursuant to Executive Order No. 12333, or a successor order.

(b) Recipient and contents of application
Each application under this section—

(1) shall be made to—

(A) a judge of the court established by section 1803(a) of this title; or

(B) a United States Magistrate Judge under chapter 43 of title 28 who is publicly designated by the Chief Justice of the United States to have the power to hear applications and grant orders for the release of records under this section on behalf of a judge of that court; and

(2) shall specify that—

(A) the records concerned are sought for an investigation described in subsection (a) of this section; and

(B) there are specific and articulable facts giving reason to believe that the person to whom the records pertain is a foreign power or an agent of a foreign power.

(c) Ex parte judicial order of approval

(1) Upon application made pursuant to this section, the judge shall enter an ex parte order as requested, or as modified, approving the release of records if the judge finds that the application satisfies the requirements of this section.

(2) An order under this subsection shall not disclose that it is issued for purposes of an investigation described in subsection (a) of this section.

(d) Compliance; nondisclosure

(1) Any common carrier, public accommodation facility, physical storage facility, or vehicle rental facility shall comply with an order under subsection (c) of this section.

(2) No common carrier, public accommodation facility, physical storage facility, or vehicle rental facility, or officer, employee, or agent thereof, shall disclose to any person (other than those officers, agents, or employees of such common carrier, public accommodation facility, physical storage facility, or vehicle rental facility necessary to fulfill the requirement to disclose information to the Federal Bureau of Investigation under this section) that the Federal Bureau of Investigation has sought or obtained records pursuant to an order under this section.

Sec. 1863. Congressional oversight

(a) On a semiannual basis, the Attorney General shall fully inform the Permanent Select Committee on Intelligence of the House of Representatives and the Select Committee on Intelligence of the Senate concerning all requests for records under this subchapter.

(b) On a semiannual basis, the Attorney General shall provide to the Committees on the Judiciary of the House of Representatives and the Senate a report setting forth with respect to the preceding 6-month period—

(1) the total number of applications made for orders approving requests for records under this subchapter; and

(2) the total number of such orders either granted, modified, or denied.

Chapter 39—Spoils of War

Sec. 2202. Prohibition on transfers to countries which support terrorism

Spoils of war in the possession, custody, or control of the United States may not be transferred to any country determined by the Secretary of State, for purposes of section 2780 of title 22, to be a nation whose government has repeatedly provided support for acts of international terrorism.

Chapter 40—Defense Against Weapons of Mass Destruction

Sec. 2301. Findings

Congress makes the following findings:

(1) Weapons of mass destruction and related materials and technologies are increasingly available from worldwide sources. Technical information relating to such weapons is readily available on the Internet, and raw materials for chemical, biological, and radiological weapons are widely available for legitimate commercial purposes.

(2) The former Soviet Union produced and maintained a vast array of nuclear, biological, and chemical weapons of mass destruction.

(3) Many of the states of the former Soviet Union retain the facilities, materials, and technologies capable of producing additional quantities of weapons of mass destruction.

(4) The disintegration of the former Soviet Union was accompanied by disruptions of command and control systems, deficiencies in accountability for weapons, weapons-related materials and technologies, economic hardships, and significant gaps in border control among the states of the former Soviet Union. The problems of organized crime and corruption in the states of the former Soviet Union increase the potential for proliferation of nuclear, radiological, biological, and chemical weapons and related materials.

(5) The conditions described in paragraph (4) have substantially increased the ability of potentially hostile nations, terrorist groups, and individuals to acquire weapons of mass destruction and related materials and technologies from within the states of the former

Soviet Union and from unemployed scientists who worked on those programs.

(6) As a result of such conditions, the capability of potentially hostile nations and terrorist groups to acquire nuclear, radiological, biological, and chemical weapons is greater than at any time in history.

(7) The President has identified North Korea, Iraq, Iran, and Libya as hostile states which already possess some weapons of mass destruction and are developing others.

(8) The acquisition or the development and use of weapons of mass destruction is well within the capability of many extremist and terrorist movements, acting independently or as proxies for foreign states.

(9) Foreign states can transfer weapons to or otherwise aid extremist and terrorist movements indirectly and with plausible deniability.

(10) Terrorist groups have already conducted chemical attacks against civilian targets in the United States and Japan, and a radiological attack in Russia.

(11) The potential for the national security of the United States to be threatened by nuclear, radiological, chemical, or biological terrorism must be taken seriously.

(12) There is a significant and growing threat of attack by weapons of mass destruction on targets that are not military targets in the usual sense of the term.

(13) Concomitantly, the threat posed to the citizens of the United States by nuclear, radiological, biological, and chemical weapons delivered by unconventional means is significant and growing.

(14) Mass terror may result from terrorist incidents involving nuclear, radiological, biological, or chemical materials.

(15) Facilities required for production of radiological, biological, and chemical weapons are much smaller and harder to detect than nuclear weapons facilities, and biological and chemical weapons can be deployed by alternative delivery means other than long-range ballistic missiles.

(16) Covert or unconventional means of delivery of nuclear, radiological, biological, and chemical weapons include cargo ships, pas-

senger aircraft, commercial and private vehicles and vessels, and commercial cargo shipments routed through multiple destinations.

(17) Traditional arms control efforts assume large state efforts with detectable manufacturing programs and weapons production programs, but are ineffective in monitoring and controlling smaller, though potentially more dangerous, unconventional proliferation efforts.

(18) Conventional counterproliferation efforts would do little to detect or prevent the rapid development of a capability to suddenly manufacture several hundred chemical or biological weapons with nothing but commercial supplies and equipment.

(19) The United States lacks adequate planning and countermeasures to address the threat of nuclear, radiological, biological, and chemical terrorism.

(20) The Department of Energy has established a Nuclear Emergency Response Team which is available in case of nuclear or radiological emergencies, but no comparable units exist to deal with emergencies involving biological or chemical weapons or related materials.

(21) State and local emergency response personnel are not adequately prepared or trained for incidents involving nuclear, radiological, biological, or chemical materials.

(22) Exercises of the Federal, State, and local response to nuclear, radiological, biological, or chemical terrorism have revealed serious deficiencies in preparedness and severe problems of coordination.

(23) The development of, and allocation of responsibilities for, effective countermeasures to nuclear, radiological, biological, or chemical terrorism in the United States requires well-coordinated participation of many Federal agencies, and careful planning by the Federal Government and State and local governments.

(24) Training and exercises can significantly improve the preparedness of State and local emergency response personnel for emergencies involving nuclear, radiological, biological, or chemical weapons or related materials.

(25) Sharing of the expertise and capabilities of the Department of Defense, which traditionally has provided assistance to Federal, State, and local officials in neutralizing, dismantling, and disposing of explosive ordnance, as well as radiological, biological, and chemical

materials, can be a vital contribution to the development and deployment of countermeasures against nuclear, biological, and chemical weapons of mass destruction.

(26) The United States lacks effective policy coordination regarding the threat posed by the proliferation of weapons of mass destruction.

Sec. 2302. Definitions

In this chapter:

(1) The term "weapon of mass destruction" means any weapon or device that is intended, or has the capability, to cause death or serious bodily injury to a significant number of people through the release, dissemination, or impact of—

(A) toxic or poisonous chemicals or their precursors;

(B) a disease organism; or

(C) radiation or radioactivity.

(2) The term "independent states of the former Soviet Union" has the meaning given that term in section 5801 of title 22.

(3) The term "highly enriched uranium" means uranium enriched to 20 percent or more in the isotope U-235.

Subchapter I—Domestic Preparedness

Sec. 2311. Response to threats of terrorist use of weapons of mass destruction

(a) Enhanced response capability

In light of the potential for terrorist use of weapons of mass destruction against the United States, the President shall take immediate action—

(1) to enhance the capability of the Federal Government to prevent and respond to terrorist incidents involving weapons of mass destruction; and

(2) to provide enhanced support to improve the capabilities of State and local emergency response agencies to prevent and respond to such incidents at both the national and the local level.

(b) Report required

Not later than January 31, 1997, the President shall transmit to Congress a report containing—

(1) an assessment of the capabilities of the Federal Government to prevent and respond to terrorist incidents involving weapons of mass destruction and to support State and local prevention and response efforts;

(2) requirements for improvements in those capabilities; and

(3) the measures that should be taken to achieve such improvements, including additional resources and legislative authorities that would be required.

Sec. 2312. Emergency response assistance program

(a) Program required

(1) The Secretary of Defense shall carry out a program to provide civilian personnel of Federal, State, and local agencies with training and expert advice regarding emergency responses to a use or threatened use of a weapon of mass destruction or related materials.

(2) The President may designate the head of an agency other than the Department of Defense to assume the responsibility for carrying out the program on or after October 1, 1999, and relieve the Secretary of Defense of that responsibility upon the assumption of the responsibility by the designated official.

(3) In this section, the official responsible for carrying out the program is referred to as the "lead official."

(b) Coordination

In carrying out the program, the lead official shall coordinate with each of the following officials who is not serving as the lead official:

(1) The Director of the Federal Emergency Management Agency.

(2) The Secretary of Energy.

(3) The Secretary of Defense.

(4) The heads of any other Federal, State, and local government agencies that have an expertise or responsibilities relevant to emergency responses described in subsection (a)(1) of this section.

(c) Eligible participants

The civilian personnel eligible to receive assistance under the program are civilian personnel of Federal, State, and local agencies who have emergency preparedness responsibilities.

(d) Involvement of other Federal agencies

(1) The lead official may use personnel and capabilities of Federal agencies outside the agency of the lead official to provide training and expert advice under the program.

(2)

(A) Personnel used under paragraph (1) shall be personnel who have special skills relevant to the particular assistance that the personnel are to provide.

(B) Capabilities used under paragraph (1) shall be capabilities that are especially relevant to the particular assistance for which the capabilities are used.

(3) If the lead official is not the Secretary of Defense, and requests assistance from the Department of Defense that, in the judgment of the Secretary of Defense would affect military readiness or adversely affect national security, the Secretary of Defense may appeal the request for Department of Defense assistance by the lead official to the President.

(e) Available assistance

Assistance available under this program shall include the following:

(1) Training in the use, operation, and maintenance of equipment for—

(A) detecting a chemical or biological agent or nuclear radiation;

(B) monitoring the presence of such an agent or radiation;

(C) protecting emergency personnel and the public; and

(D) decontamination.

(2) Establishment of a designated telephonic link (commonly referred to as a "hot line") to a designated source of relevant data and expert advice for the use of State or local officials responding to emergencies involving a weapon of mass destruction or related materials.

(3) Use of the National Guard and other reserve components for purposes authorized under this section that are specified by the lead

official (with the concurrence of the Secretary of Defense if the Secretary is not the lead official).

(4) Loan of appropriate equipment.

(f) Limitations on Department of Defense assistance to law enforcement agencies

Assistance provided by the Department of Defense to law enforcement agencies under this section shall be provided under the authority of, and subject to the restrictions provided in, chapter 18 of title 10.

(g) Administration of Department of Defense assistance

The Secretary of Defense shall designate an official within the Department of Defense to serve as the executive agent of the Secretary for the coordination of the provision of Department of Defense assistance under this section.

(h) Funding

(1) Of the total amount authorized to be appropriated under section 301, 35,000,000 is available for the program required under this section.

(2) Of the amount available for the program pursuant to paragraph (1), $10,500,000 is available for use by the Secretary of Defense to assist the Secretary of Health and Human Services in the establishment of metropolitan emergency medical response teams (commonly referred to as "Metropolitan Medical Strike Force Teams") to provide medical services that are necessary or potentially necessary by reason of a use or threatened use of a weapon of mass destruction.

(3) The amount available for the program under paragraph (1) is in addition to any other amounts authorized to be appropriated for the program under section 301.

Sec. 2313. Nuclear, chemical, and biological emergency response

(a) Department of Defense

The Secretary of Defense shall designate an official within the Department of Defense as the executive agent for—

(1) the coordination of Department of Defense assistance to Federal, State, and local officials in responding to threats involving biological or chemical weapons or related materials or technologies, including assistance in identifying, neutralizing, dismantling, and

disposing of biological and chemical weapons and related materials and technologies; and

(2) the coordination of Department of Defense assistance to the Department of Energy in carrying out that department's responsibilities under subsection (b) of this section.

(b) Department of Energy
The Secretary of Energy shall designate an official within the Department of Energy as the executive agent for—

(1) the coordination of Department of Energy assistance to Federal, State, and local officials in responding to threats involving nuclear, chemical, and biological weapons or related materials or technologies, including assistance in identifying, neutralizing, dismantling, and disposing of nuclear weapons and related materials and technologies; and

(2) the coordination of Department of Energy assistance to the Department of Defense in carrying out that department's responsibilities under subsection (a) of this section.

(c) Funding
Of the total amount authorized to be appropriated under section 301, $15,000,000 is available for providing assistance described in subsection (a) of this section.

Sec. 2314. Chemical-biological emergency response team

(a) Department of Defense rapid response team
The Secretary of Defense shall develop and maintain at least one domestic terrorism rapid response team composed of members of the Armed Forces and employees of the Department of Defense who are capable of aiding Federal, State, and local officials in the detection, neutralization, containment, dismantlement, and disposal of weapons of mass destruction containing chemical, biological, or related materials.

(b) Addition to Federal response plan
Not later than December 31, 1997, the Director of the Federal Emergency Management Agency shall develop and incorporate into existing Federal emergency response plans and programs prepared under section 5196(b) of title 42 guidance on the use and deployment of the rapid response teams established under this section to respond to emergencies involving weapons of mass destruction. The Director shall carry out this

subsection in consultation with the Secretary of Defense and the heads of other Federal agencies involved with the emergency response plans.

Sec. 2315. Testing of preparedness for emergencies involving nuclear, radiological, chemical, and biological weapons

(a) Emergencies involving chemical or biological weapons

(1) The Secretary of Defense shall develop and carry out a program for testing and improving the responses of Federal, State, and local agencies to emergencies involving biological weapons and related materials and emergencies involving chemical weapons and related materials.

(2) The program shall include exercises to be carried out during each of five successive fiscal years beginning with fiscal year 1997.

(3) In developing and carrying out the program, the Secretary shall coordinate with the Director of the Federal Bureau of Investigation, the Director of the Federal Emergency Management Agency, the Secretary of Energy, and the heads of any other Federal, State, and local government agencies that have an expertise or responsibilities relevant to emergencies described in paragraph (1).

(b) Emergencies involving nuclear and radiological weapons

(1) The Secretary of Energy shall develop and carry out a program for testing and improving the responses of Federal, State, and local agencies to emergencies involving nuclear and radiological weapons and related materials.

(2) The program shall include exercises to be carried out during each of five successive fiscal years beginning with fiscal year 1997.

(3) In developing and carrying out the program, the Secretary shall coordinate with the Director of the Federal Bureau of Investigation, the Director of the Federal Emergency Management Agency, the Secretary of Defense, and the heads of any other Federal, State, and local government agencies that have an expertise or responsibilities relevant to emergencies described in paragraph (1).

(c) Annual revisions of programs

The official responsible for carrying out a program developed under subsection (a) or (b) of this section shall revise the program not later than June 1 in each fiscal year covered by the program. The revisions shall include adjustments that the official determines necessary or appropriate on the basis of the lessons learned from the exercise or exercises carried out under the program in the fiscal year, including lessons learned regarding coordination problems and equipment deficiencies.

(d) Option to transfer responsibility

(1) The President may designate the head of an agency outside the Department of Defense to assume the responsibility for carrying out the program developed under subsection (a) of this section beginning on or after October 1, 1999, and relieve the Secretary of Defense of that responsibility upon the assumption of the responsibility by the designated official.

(2) The President may designate the head of an agency outside the Department of Energy to assume the responsibility for carrying out the program developed under subsection (b) of this section beginning on or after October 1, 1999, and relieve the Secretary of Energy of that responsibility upon the assumption of the responsibility by the designated official.

(e) Funding

Of the total amount authorized to be appropriated under section 301, $15,000,000 is available for the development and execution of the programs required by this section, including the participation of State and local agencies in exercises carried out under the programs.

Sec. 2316. Actions to increase civilian expertise

(a) to (c) Omitted

(d) Civilian expertise

The President shall take reasonable measures to reduce the reliance of civilian law enforcement officials on Department of Defense resources to counter the threat posed by the use or potential use of biological and chemical weapons of mass destruction within the United States. The measures shall include—

(1) actions to increase civilian law enforcement expertise to counter such a threat; and

(2) actions to improve coordination between civilian law enforcement officials and other civilian sources of expertise, within and outside the Federal Government, to counter such a threat.

(e) Reports

The President shall submit to Congress the following reports:

(1) Not later than 90 days after September 23, 1996, a report describing the respective policy functions and operational roles of Federal agencies in countering the threat posed by the use or potential use of biological and chemical weapons of mass destruction within the United States.

(2) Not later than one year after September 23, 1996, a report describing—

(A) the actions planned to be taken to carry out subsection (d) of this section; and

(B) the costs of such actions.

(3) Not later than three years after September 23, 1996, a report updating the information provided in the reports submitted pursuant to paragraphs (1) and (2), including the measures taken pursuant to subsection (d) of this section.

Sec. 2317. Rapid response information system

(a) Inventory of rapid response assets

(1) The head of each Federal Response Plan agency shall develop and maintain an inventory of physical equipment and assets under the jurisdiction of that agency that could be made available to aid State and local officials in search and rescue and other disaster management and mitigation efforts associated with an emergency involving weapons of mass destruction. The agency head shall submit a copy of the inventory, and any updates of the inventory, to the Director of the Federal Emergency Management Agency for inclusion in the master inventory required under subsection (b) of this section.

(2) Each inventory shall include a separate listing of any equipment that is excess to the needs of that agency and could be considered for disposal as excess or surplus property for use for response and training with regard to emergencies involving weapons of mass destruction.

(b) Master inventory

The Director of the Federal Emergency Management Agency shall compile and maintain a comprehensive listing of all inventories prepared under subsection (a) of this section. The first such master list shall be completed not later than December 31, 1997, and shall be updated annually thereafter.

(c) Addition to Federal response plan

Not later than December 31, 1997, the Director of the Federal Emergency Management Agency shall develop and incorporate into existing Federal emergency response plans and programs prepared under section 5196(b) of title 42 guidance on accessing and using the physical equipment and assets included in the master list developed under subsection to respond to emergencies involving weapons of mass destruction.

(b) of this section."

(d) Database on chemical and biological materials

The Director of the Federal Emergency Management Agency, in consultation with the Secretary of Defense, shall prepare a database on chemical and biological agents and munitions characteristics and safety precautions for civilian use. The initial design and compilation of the database shall be completed not later than December 31, 1997.

(e) Access to inventory and database

The Director of the Federal Emergency Management Agency shall design and maintain a system to give Federal, State, and local officials access to the inventory listing and database maintained under this section in the event of an emergency involving weapons of mass destruction or to prepare and train to respond to such an emergency. The system shall include a secure but accessible emergency response hotline to access information and request assistance.

Subchapter II—Interdiction of Weapons of Mass Destruction and Related Materials

Sec. 2331. Procurement of detection equipment for United States border security

Of the amount authorized to be appropriated by section 301, $15,000,000 is available for the procurement of—

(1) equipment capable of detecting the movement of weapons of mass destruction and related materials into the United States;

(2) equipment capable of interdicting the movement of weapons of mass destruction and related materials into the United States; and

(3) materials and technologies related to use of equipment described in paragraph (1) or (2).

Sec. 2332. Sense of Congress concerning criminal penalties

(a) Sense of Congress concerning inadequacy of sentencing guidelines
It is the sense of Congress that the sentencing guidelines prescribed by the United States Sentencing Commission for the offenses of importation, attempted importation, exportation, and attempted exportation of nuclear, biological, and chemical weapons materials constitute inadequate punishment for such offenses.

(b) Urging of revision to guidelines
Congress urges the United States Sentencing Commission to revise the relevant sentencing guidelines to provide for increased penalties for offenses relating to importation, attempted importation, exportation, and attempted exportation of nuclear, biological, or chemical weapons or related materials or technologies under the following provisions of law:

(1) Section 2410 of the Appendix to this title.

(2) Sections 2778 and 2780 of title 22.

(3) The International Emergency Economic Powers Act (50 U.S.C. 1701 et seq.).

(4) Section 2139a(c) of title 42.

Sec. 2333. International border security

(a) Secretary of Defense responsibility
The Secretary of Defense, in consultation and cooperation with the Commissioner of Customs, shall carry out programs for assisting customs officials and border guard officials in the independent states of the former Soviet Union, the Baltic states, and other countries of Eastern Europe in preventing unauthorized transfer and transportation of nuclear, biological, and chemical weapons and related materials. Training, expert advice, maintenance of equipment, loan of equipment, and audits may be provided under or in connection with the programs.

(b) Funding
Of the total amount authorized to be appropriated by section 301, $15,000,000 is available for carrying out the programs referred to in subsection (a) of this section.

(c) Assistance to states of former Soviet Union
Assistance under programs referred to in subsection (a) of this section may (notwithstanding any provision of law prohibiting the extension of foreign assistance to any of the newly independent states of the former

Soviet Union) be extended to include an independent state of the former Soviet Union if the President certifies to Congress that it is in the national interest of the United States to extend assistance under this section to that state.

Subchapter III—Control and Disposition of Weapons of Mass Destruction and Related Materials Threatening the United States

Sec. 2341. Elimination of plutonium production

(a) Replacement program

The Secretary of Energy, in consultation with the Secretary of Defense, shall develop a cooperative program with the Government of Russia to eliminate the production of weapons grade plutonium by modifying or replacing the reactor cores at Tomsk-7 and Krasnoyarsk-26 with reactor cores that are less suitable for the production of weapons-grade plutonium.

(b) Program requirements

(1) The program shall be designed to achieve completion of the modifications or replacements of the reactor cores within three years after the modification or replacement activities under the program are begun.

(2) The plan for the program shall—

(A) specify—

(i) successive steps for the modification or replacement of the reactor cores; and

(ii) clearly defined milestones to be achieved; and

(B) include estimates of the costs of the program.

(c) Submission of program plan to Congress

Not later than 180 days after September 23, 1996, the Secretary of Defense shall submit to Congress—

(1) a plan for the program under subsection (a) of this section;

(2) an estimate of the United States funding that is necessary for carrying out the activities under the program for each fiscal year covered by the program; and

(3) a comparison of the benefits of the program with the benefits of other nonproliferation programs.

Subchapter IV—Coordination of Policy and Countermeasures Against Proliferation of Weapons of Mass Destruction

Sec. 2351. National coordinator on nonproliferation

(a) Designation of position

The President shall designate an individual to serve in the Executive Office of the President as the National Coordinator for Nonproliferation Matters.

(b) Duties

The Coordinator, under the direction of the National Security Council, shall advise and assist the President by—

(1) advising the President on nonproliferation of weapons of mass destruction, including issues related to terrorism, arms control, and international organized crime;

(2) chairing the Committee on Nonproliferation of the National Security Council; and

(3) taking such actions as are necessary to ensure that there is appropriate emphasis in, cooperation on, and coordination of, nonproliferation research efforts of the United States, including activities of Federal agencies as well as activities of contractors funded by the Federal Government.

(c) Allocation of funds

Of the total amount authorized to be appropriated under section 301, $2,000,000 is available to the Department of Defense for carrying out research referred to in subsection (b)(3) of this section.

Sec. 2352. National Security Council Committee on Nonproliferation

(a) Establishment

The Committee on Nonproliferation (in this section referred to as the "Committee") is established as a committee of the National Security Council.

(b) Membership

(1) The Committee shall be composed of representatives of the following:

(A) The Secretary of State.

(B) The Secretary of Defense.

(C) The Director of Central Intelligence.

(D) The Attorney General.

(E) The Secretary of Energy.

(F) The Administrator of the Federal Emergency Management Agency.

(G) The Secretary of the Treasury.

(H) The Secretary of Commerce.

(I) Such other members as the President may designate.

(2) The National Coordinator for Nonproliferation Matters shall chair the Committee on Nonproliferation.

(c) Responsibilities

The Committee has the following responsibilities:

(1) To review and coordinate Federal programs, policies, and directives relating to the proliferation of weapons of mass destruction and related materials and technologies, including matters relating to terrorism and international organized crime.

(2) To make recommendations through the National Security Council to the President regarding the following:

(A) Integrated national policies for countering the threats posed by weapons of mass destruction.

(B) Options for integrating Federal agency budgets for countering such threats.

(C) Means to ensure that Federal, State, and local governments have adequate capabilities to manage crises involving nuclear, radiological, biological, or chemical weapons or related materials or technologies, and to manage the consequences of a use of such weapon or related materials or technologies, and that use of those capabilities is coordinated.

(D) Means to ensure appropriate cooperation on, and coordination of, the following:

(i) Preventing the smuggling of weapons of mass destruction and related materials and technologies.

(ii) Promoting domestic and international law enforcement efforts against proliferation-related efforts.

(iii) Countering the involvement of organized crime groups in proliferation-related activities.

(iv) Safeguarding weapons of mass destruction materials and related technologies.

(v) Improving coordination and cooperation among intelligence activities, law enforcement, and the Departments of Defense, State, Commerce, and Energy in support of nonproliferation and counterproliferation efforts.

(vi) Improving export controls over materials and technologies that can contribute to the acquisition of weapons of mass destruction.

(vii) Reducing proliferation of weapons of mass destruction and related materials and technologies.

Sec. 2353. Comprehensive preparedness program

(a) Program required

The President, acting through the Committee on Nonproliferation established under section 2352 of this title, shall develop a comprehensive program for carrying out this chapter.

(b) Content of program

The program set forth in the report shall include specific plans as follows:

(1) Plans for countering proliferation of weapons of mass destruction and related materials and technologies.

(2) Plans for training and equipping Federal, State, and local officials for managing a crisis involving a use or threatened use of a weapon of mass destruction, including the consequences of the use of such a weapon.

(3) Plans for providing for regular sharing of information among intelligence, law enforcement, and customs agencies.

(4) Plans for training and equipping law enforcement units, customs services, and border security personnel to counter the smuggling of weapons of mass destruction and related materials and technologies.

(5) Plans for establishing appropriate centers for analyzing seized nuclear, radiological, biological, and chemical weapons, and related materials and technologies.

(6) Plans for establishing in the United States appropriate legal controls and authorities relating to the exporting of nuclear, radiological, biological, and chemical weapons, and related materials and technologies.

(7) Plans for encouraging and assisting governments of foreign countries to implement and enforce laws that set forth appropriate penalties for offenses regarding the smuggling of weapons of mass destruction and related materials and technologies.

(8) Plans for building the confidence of the United States and Russia in each other's controls over United States and Russian nuclear weapons and fissile materials, including plans for verifying the dismantlement of nuclear weapons.

(9) Plans for reducing United States and Russian stockpiles of excess plutonium, reflecting—

> (A) consideration of the desirability and feasibility of a United States-Russian agreement governing fissile material disposition and the specific technologies and approaches to be used for disposition of excess plutonium; and

> (B) an assessment of the options for United States cooperation with Russia in the disposition of Russian plutonium.

(10) Plans for studying the merits and costs of establishing a global network of means for detecting and responding to terroristic or other criminal use of biological agents against people or other forms of life in the United States or any foreign country.

(c) Report

(1) At the same time that the President submits the budget for fiscal year 1998 to Congress pursuant to section 1105(a) of title 31, the President shall submit to Congress a report that sets forth the comprehensive program developed under subsection (a) of this section.

(2) The report shall include the following:

> (A) The specific plans for the program that are required under subsection (b) of this section.

> (B) Estimates of the funds necessary, by agency or department, for carrying out such plans in fiscal year 1998 and the following five fiscal years.

(3) The report shall be in an unclassified form. If there is a classified version of the report, the President shall submit the classified version at the same time.

Sec. 2354. Termination

After September 30, 1999, the President—

(1) is not required to maintain a National Coordinator for Nonproliferation Matters under section 2351 of this title; and

(2) may terminate the Committee on Nonproliferation established under section 2352 of this title.

Subchapter V—Miscellaneous

Sec. 2361. Sense of Congress concerning contracting policy

It is the sense of Congress that the Secretary of Defense, the Secretary of Energy, the Secretary of the Treasury, and the Secretary of State, to the extent authorized by law, should—

(1) contract directly with suppliers in independent states of the former Soviet Union when such action would—

(A) result in significant savings of the programs referred to in subchapter III of this chapter; and

(B) substantially expedite completion of the programs referred to in subchapter III of this chapter; and

(2) seek means to use innovative contracting approaches to avoid delay and increase the effectiveness of such programs and of the exercise of such authorities.

Sec. 2362. Transfers of allocations among cooperative threat reduction programs

Congress finds that—

(1) the various Cooperative Threat Reduction programs are being carried out at different rates in the various countries covered by such programs; and

(2) it is necessary to authorize transfers of funding allocations among the various programs in order to maximize the effectiveness of United States efforts under such programs.

Sec. 2363. Sense of Congress concerning assistance to states of former Soviet Union

It is the sense of Congress that—

(1) the Cooperative Threat Reduction programs and other United States programs authorized in title XIV of the National Defense Authorization Act for Fiscal Year 1993 (Public Law 102–484; 22 U.S.C. 5901 et seq.) should be expanded by offering assistance under those programs to other independent states of the former Soviet Union in addition to Russia, Ukraine, Kazakhstan, and Belarus; and

(2) the President should offer assistance to additional independent states of the former Soviet Union in each case in which the participation of such states would benefit national security interests of the United States by improving border controls and safeguards over materials and technology associated with weapons of mass destruction.

Sec. 2364. Purchase of low-enriched uranium derived from Russian highly enriched uranium

(a) Sense of Congress

It is the sense of Congress that the allies of the United States and other nations should participate in efforts to ensure that stockpiles of weapons-grade nuclear material are reduced.

(b) Actions by Secretary of State

Congress urges the Secretary of State to encourage, in consultation with the Secretary of Energy, other countries to purchase low-enriched uranium that is derived from highly enriched uranium extracted from Russian nuclear weapons.

Sec. 2365. Sense of Congress concerning purchase, packaging, and transportation of fissile materials at risk of theft

It is the sense of Congress that—

(1) the Secretary of Defense, the Secretary of Energy, the Secretary of the Treasury, and the Secretary of State should purchase, package, and transport to secure locations weapons-grade nuclear materials from a stockpile of such materials if such officials determine that—

(A) there is a significant risk of theft of such materials; and

(B) there is no reasonable and economically feasible alternative for securing such materials; and

(2) if it is necessary to do so in order to secure the materials, the materials should be imported into the United States, subject to the laws and regulations that are applicable to the importation of such materials into the United States.

Sec. 2366. Reports on acquisition of technology relating to weapons of mass destruction and advanced conventional munitions

(a) Reports

Not later than 6 months after October 11, 1996, and every 6 months thereafter, the Director of Central Intelligence shall submit to Congress a report on—

(1) the acquisition by foreign countries during the preceding 6 months of dual-use and other technology useful for the development or production of weapons of mass destruction (including nuclear weapons, chemical weapons, and biological weapons) and advanced conventional munitions; and

(2) trends in the acquisition of such technology by such countries.

(b) Form of reports

The reports submitted under subsection (a) of this section shall be submitted in unclassified form, but may include a classified annex.

Sec. 2367. Annual report on threat posed to United States by weapons of mass destruction, ballistic missiles, and cruise missiles

(a) Annual report

The Secretary of Defense shall submit to Congress by January 30 of each year a report on the threats posed to the United States and allies of the United States—

(1) by weapons of mass destruction, ballistic missiles, and cruise missiles; and

(2) by the proliferation of weapons of mass destruction, ballistic missiles, and cruise missiles.

(b) Consultation

Each report submitted under subsection (a) of this section shall be prepared in consultation with the Director of Central Intelligence.

(c) Matters to be included

Each report submitted under subsection (a) of this section shall include the following:

(1) Identification of each foreign country and non-State organization that possesses weapons of mass destruction, ballistic missiles, or cruise missiles, and a description of such weapons and missiles with respect to each such foreign country and non-State organization.

(2) A description of the means by which any foreign country and non-State organization that has achieved capability with respect to weapons of mass destruction, ballistic missiles, or cruise missiles has achieved that capability, including a description of the international network of foreign countries and private entities that provide assistance to foreign countries and non-State organizations in achieving that capability.

(3) An examination of the doctrines that guide the use of weapons of mass destruction in each foreign country that possesses such weapons.

(4) An examination of the existence and implementation of the control mechanisms that exist with respect to nuclear weapons in each foreign country that possesses such weapons.

(5) Identification of each foreign country and non-State organization that seeks to acquire or develop (indigenously or with foreign assistance) weapons of mass destruction, ballistic missiles, or cruise missiles, and a description of such weapons and missiles with respect to each such foreign country and non-State organization.

(6) An assessment of various possible timelines for the achievement by foreign countries and non-State organizations of capability with respect to weapons of mass destruction, ballistic missiles, and cruise missiles, taking into account the probability of whether the Russian Federation and the People's Republic of China will comply with the Missile Technology Control Regime, the potential availability of assistance from foreign technical specialists, and the potential for independent sales by foreign private entities without authorization from their national governments.

(7) For each foreign country or non-State organization that has not achieved the capability to target the United States or its territories with weapons of mass destruction, ballistic missiles, or cruise

missiles as of November 18, 1997, an estimate of how far in advance the United States is likely to be warned before such foreign country or non-State organization achieves that capability.

(8) For each foreign country or non-State organization that has not achieved the capability to target members of the United States Armed Forces deployed abroad with weapons of mass destruction, ballistic missiles, or cruise missiles as of November 18, 1997, an estimate of how far in advance the United States is likely to be warned before such foreign country or non-State organization achieves that capability.

(d) Classification
Each report under subsection (a) of this section shall be submitted in classified and unclassified form.

Title 50 Appendix—
War and National Defense—
Export Regulation

§ 2405. Foreign policy controls

(a) Authority.

(1) In order to carry out the policy set forth in paragraph (2)(B), (7), (8), or (13) of section 3 of this Act [50 USCS Appx. § 2402 (2)(B), (7), (8), or (13)], the President may prohibit or curtail the exportation of any goods, technology, or other information subject to the jurisdiction of the United States or exported by any person subject to the jurisdiction of the United States, to the extent necessary to further significantly the foreign policy of the United States or to fulfill its declared international obligations. The authority granted by this subjection shall be exercised by the Secretary, in consultation with the Secretary of State, the Secretary of Defense, the Secretary of Agriculture, the Secretary of the Treasury, the United States Trade Representative, and such other departments and agencies as the Secretary considers appropriate, and shall be implemented by means of export licenses issued by the Secretary.

(2) Any export control imposed under this section shall apply to any transaction or activity undertaken with the intent to evade that export control, even if that export control would not otherwise apply to that transaction or activity.

(3) Export controls maintained for foreign policy purposes shall expire on December 31, 1979, or one year after imposition, whichever is later, unless extended by the President in accordance with subsections (b) and (f). Any such extension and any subsequent extension shall not be for a period of more than one year.

(4) Whenever the Secretary denies any export license under this subsection, the Secretary shall specify in the notice to the applicant of the denial of such license that the license was denied under the authority contained in this subsection, and the reasons for such denial, with reference to the criteria set forth in subsection (b) of

this section. The Secretary shall also include in such notice what, if any, modifications in or restrictions on the goods or technology for which the license was sought would allow such export to be compatible with controls implemented under this section, or the Secretary shall indicate in such notice which officers and employees of the Department of Commerce who are familiar with the application will be made reasonably available to the applicant for consultation with regard to such modifications or restrictions, if appropriate.

(5) In accordance with the provisions of section 10 of this Act [50 USCS Appx. § 2409], the Secretary of State shall have the right to review any export license application under this section which the Secretary of State requests to review.

(6) Before imposing, expanding, or extending export controls under this section on exports to a country which can use goods, technology, or information available from foreign sources and so incur little or no economic costs as a result of the controls, the President should, through diplomatic means, employ alternatives to export controls which offer opportunities of distinguishing the United States from, and expressing the displeasure of the United States with, the specific actions of that country in response to which the controls are proposed. Such alternatives include private discussions with foreign leaders, public statements in situations where private diplomacy is unavailable or not effective, withdrawal of ambassadors, and reduction of the size of the diplomatic staff that the country involved is permitted to have in the United States.

(b) Criteria.

(1) Subject to paragraph (2) of this subsection, the President may impose, extend, or expand export controls under this section only if the President determines that—

(A) such controls are likely to achieve the intended foreign policy purpose, in light of other factors, including the availability from other countries of the goods or technology proposed for such controls, and that foreign policy purpose cannot be achieved through negotiations or other alternative means;

(B) the proposed controls are compatible with the foreign policy objectives of the United States and with overall United States policy toward the country to which exports are to be subject to the proposed controls;

(C) the reaction of other countries to the imposition, extension, or expansion of such export controls by the United States is not likely to render the controls ineffective in achieving the intended foreign policy purpose or to be counterproductive to United States foreign policy interests;

(D) the effect of the proposed controls on the export performance of the United States, the competitive position of the United States in the international economy, the international reputation of the United States as a supplier of goods and technology, or on the economic well-being of individual United States companies and their employees and communities does not exceed the benefit to United States foreign policy objectives; and

(E) the United States has the ability to enforce the proposed controls effectively.

(2) With respect to those export controls in effect under this section on the date of the enactment of the Export Administration Amendments Act of 1985 [enacted July 12, 1985], the President, in determining whether to extend those controls, as required by subsection (a)(3) of this section, shall consider the criteria set forth in paragraph (1) of this subsection and shall consider the foreign policy consequences of modifying the export controls.

(c) Consultation with industry. The Secretary in every possible instance shall consult with and seek advice from affected United States industries and appropriate advisory committees established under section 135 of the Trade Act of 1974 [19 USCS § 2155] before imposing any export control under this section. Such consultation and advice shall be with respect to the criteria set forth in subsection (b)(1) and such other matters as the Secretary considers appropriate.

(d) Consultation with other countries. When imposing export controls under this section, the President shall, at the earliest appropriate opportunity, consult with the countries with which the United States maintains export controls cooperatively, and with such other countries as the President considers appropriate, with respect to the criteria set forth in subsection (b)(1) and such other matters as the President considers appropriate.

(e) Alternative means. Before resorting to the imposition of export controls under this section, the President shall determine that reasonable efforts have been made to achieve the purposes of the controls through negotiations or other alternative means.

(f) Consultation with the Congress.

(1) The President may impose or expand export controls under this section, or extend such controls as required by subsection (a)(3) of this section, only after consultation with the Congress, including the Committee on Foreign Affairs of the House of Representatives and the Committee on Banking, Housing, and Urban Affairs of the Senate.

(2) The President may not impose, expand, or extend export controls under this section until the President has submitted to the Congress a report—

(A) specifying the purpose of the controls;

(B) specifying the determinations of the President (or, in the case of those export controls described in subsection (b)(2), the considerations of the President) with respect to each of the criteria set forth in subsection (b)(1), the bases for such determinations (or considerations), and any possible adverse foreign policy consequences of the controls;

(C) describing the nature, the subjects, and the results of, or the plans for, the consultation with industry pursuant to subsection (c) and with other countries pursuant to subsection (d);

(D) specifying the nature and results of any alternative means attempted under subsection (e), or the reasons for imposing, expanding, or extending the controls without attempting any such alternative means; and

(E) describing the availability from other countries of goods or technology comparable to the goods or technology subject to the proposed export controls, and describing the nature and results of the efforts made pursuant to subsection (h) to secure the cooperation of foreign governments in controlling the foreign availability of such comparable goods or technology.

Such report shall also indicate how such controls will further significantly the foreign policy of the United States or will further its declared international obligations.

(3) To the extent necessary to further the effectiveness of the export controls, portions of a report required by paragraph (2) may be submitted to the Congress on a classified basis, and shall be subject to the provisions of section 12(c) of this Act [50 USCS Appx § 2411(c)].

(4) In the case of export controls under this section which prohibit or curtail the export of any agricultural commodity, a report submitted pursuant to paragraph (2) shall be deemed to be the report required by section 7(g)(3)(A) of this Act [50 USCS Appx § 2406(g)(3)(A)].

(5) In addition to any written report required under this section, the Secretary, not less frequently than annually, shall present in oral testimony before the Committee on Banking, Housing, and Urban Affairs of the Senate and the Committee on Foreign Affairs of the House of Representatives a report on policies and actions taken by the Government to carry out the provisions of the section.

(g) Exclusion for medicine and medical supplies and for certain food exports. This section does not authorize export controls on medicine or medical supplies. This section also does not authorize export controls on donations of goods (including, but not limited to, food, educational materials, seeds and hand tools, medicines and medical supplies, water resources equipment, clothing and shelter materials, and basic household supplies) that are intended to meet basic human needs. Before export controls on food are imposed, expanded, or extended under this section, the Secretary shall notify the Secretary of State in the case of export controls applicable with respect to any developed country and shall notify the Administrator of the Agency for International Development in the case of export controls applicable with respect to any developing country. The Secretary of State with respect to developed countries, and the Administrator with respect to developing countries, shall determine whether the proposed export controls on food would cause measurable malnutrition and shall inform the Secretary of that determination. If the Secretary is informed that the proposed export controls on food would cause measurable malnutrition, then those controls may not be imposed, expanded, or extended, as the case may be, unless the President determines that those controls are necessary to protect the national security interests of the United States, or unless the President determines that arrangements are insufficient to ensure that the food will reach those most in need. Each such determination by the Secretary of State or the Administrator of the Agency for International Development, and any such determination by the President, shall be reported to the Congress, together with a statement of the reasons for that determination. It is the intent of Congress that the President not impose export controls under this section on any goods or technology if he determines that the principal effect of the export of such goods or technology would be to help meet basic human needs. This subsection shall not be construed to prohibit the President from imposing restrictions on the export of medicine or medical supplies or of food under the International Emergency Economic Powers Act [50 USCS §§ 1701 et seq.]. This subsection shall not apply to any export control on medicine, medical supplies, or food, except for donations, which is in effect on the date of the enactment of the Export Administration Amendments Act of 1985 [enacted July 12, 1985]. Notwithstanding the preceding provisions of this subsection, the President may impose export controls under this section on medicine, medical supplies, food, and donations of goods in order to carry out the policy set forth in paragraph (13) of section 3 of this Act [50 USCS Appx § 2402(13)].

(h) Foreign availability.

> (1) In applying export controls under this section, the President shall take all feasible steps to initiate and conclude negotiations with appropriate foreign governments for the purpose of securing the cooperation of such foreign governments in controlling the export to countries and consignees to which the United States export controls apply of any goods or technology comparible to goods or technology controlled under this section.

> (2) Before extending any export control pursuant to subsection (a)(3) of this section, the President shall evaluate the results of his actions under paragraph (1) of this subsection and shall include the results of that evaluation in his report to the Congress pursuant to subsection (f) of this section.

> (3) If, within 6 months after the date on which export controls under this section are imposed or expanded, or within 6 months after the date of the enactment of the Export Administration Amendments Act of 1985 [enacted July 12, 1985] in the case of export controls in effect on such date of enactment [enacted July 12, 1985], the President's efforts under paragraph (1) are not successful in securing the cooperation of foreign governments described in paragraph (1) with respect to those export controls, the Secretary shall thereafter take into account the foreign availability of the goods or technology subject to the export controls. If the Secretary affirmatively determines that a good or technology subject to the export controls is available in sufficient quantity and comparable quality

from sources outside the United States to countries subject to the export controls so that denial of an export license would be ineffective in achieving the purposes of the controls, then the Secretary shall, during the period of such foreign availability, approve any license application which is required for the export of the good or technology and which meets all requirements for such a license. The Secretary shall remove the good or technology from the list established pursuant to subsection (l) of this section if the Secretary determines that such action is appropriate.

(4) In making a determination of foreign availability under paragraph (3) of this subsection, the Secretary shall follow the procedures set forth in section 5(f)(3) of this Act [50 USCS Appx § 2404(f)(3)].

(i) International obligations. The provisions of subsections (b), (c), (d), (e), (g), and (h) shall not apply in any case in which the President exercises the authority contained in this section to impose export controls, or to approve or deny export license applications, in order to fulfill obligations of the United States pursuant to treaties to which the United States is a party or pursuant to other international agreements.

(j) Countries supporting international terrorism.

(1) A validated license shall be required for the export of goods or technology to a country if the Secretary of State has made the following determinations:

(A) The government of such country has repeatedly provided support for acts of international terrorism.

(B) The export of such goods or technology could make a significant contribution to the military potential of such country, including its military logistics capability, or could enhance the ability of such country to support acts of international terrorism.

(2) The Secretary and the Secretary of State shall notify the Committee on Foreign Affairs of the House of Representatives and the Committee on Banking, Housing, and Urban Affairs and the Committee on Foreign Relations of the Senate at least 30 days before issuing any validated license required by paragraph (1).

(3) Each determination of the Secretary of State under paragraph (1)(A), including each determination in effect on the date of the enactment of the Antiterrorism and Arms Export Amendments Act

of 1989 [enacted Dec. 12, 1989], shall be published in the Federal Register.

(4) A determination made by the Secretary of State under paragraph (1)(A) may not be rescinded unless the President submits to the Speaker of the House of Representatives and the chairman of the Committee on Banking, Housing, and Urban Affairs and the chairman of the Committee on Foreign Relations of the Senate—

(A) before the proposed rescission would take effect, a report certifying that—

(i) there has been a fundamental change in the leadership and policies of the government of the country concerned;

(ii) that government is not supporting acts of international terrorism; and

(iii) that government has provided assurances that it will not support acts of international terrorism in the future; or

(B) at least 45 days before the proposed rescission would take effect, a report justifying the rescission and certifying that—

(i) the government concerned has not provided any support for international terrorism during the preceding 6-month period; and

(ii) the government concerned has provided assurances that it will not support acts of international terrorism in the future.

(5) The Secretary and the Secretary of State shall include in the notification required by paragraph (2)—

(A) a detailed description of the goods or services to be offered, including a brief description of the capabilities of any article for which a license to export is sought;

(B) the reasons why the foreign country or international organization to which the export or transfer is proposed to be made needs the goods or services which are the subject of such export or transfer and a description of the manner in which such country or organization intends to use such articles, services, or design and construction services;

(C) the reasons why the proposed export or transfer is in the national interest of the United States;

(D) an analysis of the impact of the proposed export or transfer on the military capabilities of the foreign country or international organization to which such export or transfer would be made;

(E) an analysis of the manner in which the proposed export would affect the relative military strengths of countries in the region to which the goods or services which are the subject of such export would be delivered and whether other countries in the region have comparable kinds and amounts of articles, services, or design and construction services; and

(F) an analysis of the impact of the proposed export or transfer on the United States relations with the countries in the region to which the goods or services which are the subject of such export would be delivered.

(k) Negotiations with other countries.

(1) Countries participating in certain agreements. The Secretary of State, in consultation with the Secretary, the Secretary of Defense, and the heads of other appropriate departments and agencies, shall be responsible for conducting negotiations with those countries participating in the groups known as the Coordinating Committee, the Missile Technology Control Regime, the Australia Group, and the Nuclear Suppliers' Group, regarding their cooperation in restricting the export of goods and technology in order to carry out—

(A) the policy set forth in section 3(2)(B) of this Act [50 USCS Appx. § 2402(2)(B)], and

(B) United States policy opposing the proliferation of chemical, biological, nuclear, and other weapons and their delivery systems, and effectively restricting the export of dual use components of such weapons and their delivery systems, in accordance with this subsection and subsections (a) and (1).

Such negotiations shall cover, among other issues, which goods and technology should be subject to multilaterally agreed export restrictions, and the implementation of the restrictions consistent with the principles identified in section 5(b)(2)(C) of this Act [50 USCS Appx. § 2404(b)(2)(C)].

(2) Other countries. The Secretary of State, in consultation with the Secretary, the Secretary of Defense, and the heads of other appropriate departments and agencies, shall be responsible for conduct-

ing negotiations with countries and groups of countries not referred to in paragraph (1) regarding their cooperation in restricting the export of goods and technology consistent with purposes set forth in paragraph (1). In cases where such negotiations produce agreements on export restrictions that the Secretary, in consultation with the Secretary of State and the Secretary of Defense, determines to be consistent with the principles identified in section 5(b)(2)(C) of this Act [50 USCS Appx. § 2404(b)(2)(C)], the Secretary may treat exports, whether by individual or multiple licenses, to countries party to such agreements in the same manner as exports are treated to countries that are MTCR adherents.

(3) Review of determinations. The Secretary shall annually review any determination under paragraph (2) with respect to a country. For each such country which the Secretary determines is not meeting the requirements of an effective export control system in accordance with section 5(b)(2)(C) [50 USCS Appx. 2404(b)(2)(C)], the Secretary shall restrict or eliminate any preferential licensing treatment for exports to that country provided under this subsection.

(l) Missile technology.

(1) Determination of controlled items. The Secretary, in consultation with the Secretary of State, the Secretary of Defense, and the heads of other appropriate departments and agencies—

(A) shall establish and maintain, as part of the control list established under this section, a list of all dual use goods and technology on the MTCR Annex; and

(B) may include, as part of the control list established under this section, goods and technology that would provide a direct and immediate impact on the development of missile delivery systems and are not included in the MTCR Annex but which the United States is proposing to the other MTCR adherents to have included in the MTCR Annex.

(2) Requirement of individual validated licenses. The Secretary shall require an individual validated license for—

(A) any export of goods or technology on the list established under paragraph (1) to any country; and

(B) any export of goods or technology that the exporter knows is destined for a project or facility for the design, development, or manufacture of a missile in a country that is not an MTCR adherent.

(3) Policy of denial of licenses.

(A) Licenses under paragraph (2) should in general be denied if the ultimate consignee of the goods or technology is a facility in a country that is not an adherent to the Missile Technology Control Regime and the facility is designed to develop or build missiles.

(B) Licenses under paragraph (2) shall be denied if the ultimate consignee of the goods or technology is a facility in a country the government of which has been determined under subsection (j) to have repeatedly provided support for acts of international terrorism.

(4) Consultation with other departments.

(A) A determination of the Secretary to approve an export license under paragraph (2) for the export of goods or technology to a country of concern regarding missile proliferation may be made only after consultation with the Secretary of Defense and the Secretary of State for a period of 20 days. The countries of concern referred to in the preceding sentence shall be maintained on a classified list by the Secretary of State, in consultation with the Secretary and the Secretary of Defense.

(B) Should the Secretary of Defense disagree with the determination of the Secretary to approve an export license to which subparagraph (A) applies, the Secretary of Defense shall so notify the Secretary within the 20 days provided for consultation on the determination. The Secretary of Defense shall at the same time submit the matter to the President for resolution of the dispute. The Secretary shall also submit the Secretary's recommendation to the President on the license application.

(C) The President shall approve or disapprove the export license application within 20 days after receiving the submission of the Secretary of Defense under subparagraph (B).

(D) Should the Secretary of Defense fail to notify the Secretary within the time period prescribed in subparagraph (B), the Secretary may approve the license application without awaiting the notification by the Secretary of Defense. Should the President fail to notify the Secretary of his decision on the export license application within the time period prescribed in subparagraph (C), the Secretary may approve the license application without awaiting the President's decision on the license application.

(E) Within 10 days after an export license is issued under this subsection, the Secretary shall provide to the Secretary of Defense and the Secretary of State the license application and accompanying documents issued to the applicant, to the extent that the relevant Secretary indicates the need to receive such application and documents.

(5) Information sharing. The Secretary shall establish a procedure for information sharing with appropriate officials of the intelligence community, as determined by the Director of Central Intelligence, and other appropriate Government agencies, that will ensure effective monitoring of transfers of MTCR equipment or technology and other missile technology.

(m) Chemical and biological weapons.

(1) Establishment of list. The Secretary, in consultation with the Secretary of State, the Secretary of Defense, and the heads of other appropriate departments and agencies, shall establish and maintain, as part of the list maintained under this section, a list of goods and technology that would directly and substantially assist a foreign government or group in acquiring the capability to develop, produce, stockpile, or deliver chemical or biological weapons, the licensing of which would be effective in barring acquisition or enhancement of such capability.

(2) Requirement for validated licenses. The Secretary shall require a validated license for any export of goods or technology on the list established under paragraph (1) to any country of concern.

(3) Countries of concern. For purposes of paragraph (2), the term "country of concern" means any country other than—

(A) a country with whose government the United States has entered into a bilateral or multilateral arrangement for the control of goods or technology on the list established under paragraph (1); and

(B) such other countries as the Secretary of State, in consultation with the Secretary and the Secretary of Defense, shall designate consistent with the purposes of the Chemical and Biological Weapons Control and Warfare Elimination Act of 1991.

(n) Crime control instruments.

(1) Crime control and detection instruments and equipment shall be approved for export by the Secretary only pursuant to a validated export license. Notwithstanding any other provision of this Act—

(A) any determination of the Secretary of what goods or technology shall be included on the list established pursuant to subsection (l) of this section as a result of the export restrictions imposed by this subsection shall be made with the concurrence of the Secretary of State, and

(B) any determination of the Secretary to approve or deny an export license application to export crime control or detection instruments or equipment shall be made in concurrence with the recommendations of the Secretary of State submitted to the Secretary with respect to the application pursuant to section 10(e) of this Act [50 USCS Appx § 2409(e)], except that, if the Secretary does not agree with the Secretary of State with respect to any determination under subparagraph (A) or (B), the matter shall be referred to the President for resolution.

(2) The provisions of this subsection shall not apply with respect to exports to countries which are members of the North Atlantic Treaty Organization or to Japan, Australia, or New Zealand, or to such other countries as the President shall designate consistent with the purposes of this subsection and section 502B of the Foreign Assistance Act of 1961 [22 USCS § 2304].

(o) Control list. The Secretary shall establish and maintain, as part of the control list, a list of any goods or technology subject to export controls under this section, and the countries to which such controls apply. The Secretary shall clearly identify on the control list which goods or technology, and which countries or destinations, are subject to which types of controls under this section. Such list shall consist of goods and technology identified by the Secretary of State, with the concurrence of the Secretary. If the Secretary and the Secretary of State are unable to agree on the list, the matter shall be referred to the President. Such list shall be reviewed not less frequently than every three years in the case of controls maintained cooperatively with other countries, and annually in the case of all other controls, for the purpose of making such revisions as are necessary in order to carry out this section. During the course of such review, an assessment shall be made periodically of the availability from sources outside the United States or any of its territories or possessions, of goods and technology comparable to those controlled for export from the United States under this section.

(p) Effect on existing contracts and licenses. The President may not, under this section, prohibit or curtail the export or reexport of goods, technology, or other information—

(1) in performance of a contract or agreement entered into before the date on which the President reports to the Congress, pursuant to subsection (f) of this section, his intention to impose controls on the export or reexport of such goods, technology, or other information, or

(2) under a validated license or other authorization issued under this Act, unless and until the President determines and certifies to the Congress that—

(A) a breach of the peace poses a serious and direct threat to the strategic interest of the United States,

(B) the prohibition or curtailment of such contracts, agreements, licenses, or authorizations will be instrumental in remedying the situation posing the direct threat, and

(C) the export controls will continue only so long as the direct threat persists.

(q) Extension of certain controls. Those export controls imposed under this section with respect to South Africa which were in effect on February 28, 1982, and ceased to be effective on March 1, 1982, September 15, 1982, or January 20, 1983, shall become effective on the date of the enactment of this subsection [enacted July 12, 1985], and shall remain in effect until 1 year after such date of enactment [enacted July 12, 1985]. At the end of that 1-year period, any of those controls made effective by this subsection may be extended by the President in accordance with subsections (b) and (f) of this section.

(r) Expanded authority to impose controls.

(1) In any case in which the President determines that it is necessary to impose controls under this section without any limitation contained in subsection (c), (d), (e), (g), (h), or (m) of this section,

the President may impose those controls only if the President submits that determination to the Congress, together with a report pursuant to subsection (f) of this section with respect to the proposed controls, and only if a law is enacted authorizing the imposition of those controls. If a joint resolution authorizing the imposition of those controls is introduced in either House of Congress within 30 days after the Congress receives the determination and report of the President, that joint resolution shall be referred to the Committee on Banking, Housing, and Urban Affairs of the Senate and to the appropriate committee of the House of Representatives. If either such committee has not reported the joint resolution at the end of 30 days after its referral, the committee shall be discharged from further consideration of the joint resolution.

(2) For purposes of this subsection, the term "joint resolution" means a joint resolution the matter after the resolving clause of which is as follows: "That the Congress, having received on a determination of the President under section 6(o)(1) of the Export Administration Act of 1979 with respect to the export controls which are set forth in the report submitted to the Congress with that determination, authorizes the President to impose those export controls.", with the date of the receipt of the determination and report inserted in the blank.

(3) In the computation of the periods of 30 days referred to in paragraph (1), there shall be excluded the days on which either House of Congress is not in session because of an adjournment of more than 3 days to a day certain or because of an adjournment of the Congress sine die.

(s) Spare parts.

(1) At the same time as the President imposes or expands export controls under this section, the President shall determine whether such export controls will apply to replacement parts for parts in goods subject to such export controls.

(2) With respect to export controls imposed under this section before the date of the enactment of this subsection [enacted Aug. 23, 1988], an individual validated export license shall not be required for replacement parts which are exported to replace on a one-for-one basis parts that were in a good that was lawfully exported from the United States, unless the President determines that such a license should be required for such parts.

Sentencing Guidelines for the United States Courts

Part A—Victim-Related Adjustments

18 USCS Appendix § 3A1.4 (2001)

§ 3A1.4. Terrorism

(a) If the offense is a felony that involved, or was intended to promote, a federal crime of **terrorism**, increase by 12 levels; but if the resulting offense level is less than level 32, increase to level 32.

(b) In each such case, the defendant's criminal history category from Chapter Four (Criminal History and Criminal Livelihood) shall be Category VI.

Commentary

Application Notes

1. Subsection (a) increases the offense level if the offense involved, or was intended to promote, a federal crime of **terrorism**. "Federal crime of **terrorism**" is defined at 18 U.S.C. § 2332b(g).

2. Under subsection (b), if the defendant's criminal history category as determined under Chapter Four (Criminal History and Criminal Livelihood) is less than Category VI, it shall be increased to Category VI.

History:

Historical Note: Effective November 1, 1995 (see Appendix C, amendment 526). Amended effective November 1, 1996 (see Appendix C, amendment 539); November 1, 1997 (see Appendix C, amendment 565)

Treason

§ 2M1.1. Treason

(a) Base Offense Level:

(1) **43**, if the conduct is tantamount to waging war against the United States;

(2) the offense level applicable to the most analogous offense, otherwise.

Commentary

Statutory Provision

18 U.S.C. § 2381.

Background

Treason is a rarely prosecuted offense that could encompass a relatively broad range of conduct, including many of the more specific offenses in this Part. The guideline contemplates imposition of the maximum penalty in the most serious cases, with reference made to the most analogous offense guideline in lesser cases.

Historical Note

Effective November 1, 1987.

Sabotage

§ 2M2.1. Destruction of, or Production of Defective, War Material, Premises, or Utilities

(a) Base Offense Level: **32**

Commentary

Statutory Provisions

18 U.S.C. § 2153, 2154; 42 U.S.C. § 2284.

Application Note

1. Violations of 42 U.S.C. § 2284 are included in this section where the defendant was convicted of acting with intent to injure the United States or aid a foreign nation.

Historical Note

Effective November 1, 1987. Amended effective November 1, 1993 (see Appendix C, amendment 481).

§ 2M2.3. Destruction of, or Production of Defective, National Defense Material, Premises, or Utilities

(a) Base Offense Level: **26**

Commentary

Statutory Provisions

18 U.S.C. §§ 2155, 2156; 42 U.S.C. § 2284.

Application Note

1. Violations of 42 U.S.C. § 2284 not included in § 2M2.1 are included in this section.

Historical Note

Effective November 1, 1987. Amended effective November 1, 1993 (see Appendix C, amendment 481).

Espionage and Related Offenses

§ 2M3.1. Gathering or Transmitting National Defense Information to Aid a Foreign Government

(a) Base Offense Level:

    (1) **42**, if top secret information was gathered or transmitted; or

    (2) **37**, otherwise.

Commentary

Statutory Provisions

18 U.S.C. § 794; 42 U.S.C. §§ 2274(a), (b), 2275.

Application Notes

1. "Top secret information" is information that, if disclosed, "reasonably could be expected to cause exceptionally grave damage to the national security." Executive Order 12356.

2. The Commission has set the base offense level in this subpart on the assumption that the information at issue bears a significant relation to the nation's security, and that the revelation will significantly and adversely affect security interests. When revelation is likely to cause little or no harm, a downward departure may be warranted. See Chapter Five, Part K (Departures).

3. The court may depart from the guidelines upon representation by the President or his duly authorized designee that the imposition of a sanction other than authorized by the guideline is necessary to protect national security or further the objectives of the nation's foreign policy.

Background

Offense level distinctions in this subpart are generally based on the classification of the information gathered or transmitted. This classification, in turn, reflects the importance of the information to the national security.

Historical Note

Effective November 1, 1987.

§ 2M3.2. Gathering National Defense Information

(a) Base Offense Level:

(1) **35**, if top secret information was gathered; or

(2) **30**, otherwise.

Commentary

Statutory Provisions

18 U.S.C. § 793(a), (b), (c), (d), (e), (g). For additional statutory provision(s), see Appendix A (Statutory Index).

Application Notes

1. See Commentary to § 2M3.1.

2. If the defendant is convicted under 18 U.S.C. § 793(d) or (e), § 2M3.3 may apply. See Commentary to § 2M3.3.

Background

The statutes covered in this section proscribe diverse forms of obtaining and transmitting national defense information with intent or reason to believe the information would injure the United States or be used to the advantage of a foreign government.

Historical Note

Effective November 1, 1987.

§ 2M3.3. Transmitting National Defense Information; Disclosure of Classified Cryptographic Information; Unauthorized Disclosure to a Foreign Government or a Communist Organization of Classified Information by Government Employee; Unauthorized Receipt of Classified Information

(a) Base Offense Level:

  (1) **29**, if top secret information; or

  (2) **24**, otherwise.

Commentary

Statutory Provisions

18 U.S.C. §§ 793(d), (e), (g), 798; 50 U.S.C. § 783(b), (c).

Application Notes

1. See Commentary to § 2M3.1.

2. If the defendant was convicted of 18 U.S.C. § 793(d) or (e) for the willful transmission or communication of intangible information with reason to believe that it could be used to the injury of the United States or the advantage of a foreign nation, apply § 2M3.2.

Background

The statutes covered in this section proscribe willfully transmitting or communicating to a person not entitled to receive it a document, writing, code book, signal book, sketch, photograph, photographic negative, blueprint, plan, map, model, instrument, appliance, or note relating to the national defense. Proof that the item was communicated with reason to believe that it could be used to the injury of the United States or the advantage of a foreign nation is required only where intangible information is communicated under 18 U.S.C. § 793(d) or (e).

This section also covers statutes that proscribe the disclosure of classified information concerning cryptographic or communication intelligence to the detriment of the United States or for the benefit of a foreign government, the unauthorized disclosure to a foreign government or a communist organization of classified information by a government employee, and the unauthorized receipt of classified information.

Historical Note

Effective November 1, 1987. Amended effective November 1, 1993 (see Appendix C, amendment 481).

§ 2M3.4. Losing National Defense Information

(a) Base Offense Level:

(1) **18**, if top secret information was lost; or

(2) **13**, otherwise.

Commentary

Statutory Provision

18 U.S.C. § 793(f).

Application Note

1. See Commentary to § 2M3.1.

Background

Offenses prosecuted under this statute generally do not involve subversive conduct on behalf of a foreign power, but rather the loss of classified information by the gross negligence of an employee of the federal government or a federal contractor.

Historical Note

Effective November 1, 1987.

§ 2M3.5. Tampering with Restricted Data Concerning Atomic Energy

(a) Base Offense Level: **24**

Commentary

Statutory Provision

42 U.S.C. § 2276.

Application Note

1. See Commentary to § 2M3.1.

Historical Note

Effective November 1, 1987

§ 2M3.9. Disclosure of Information Identifying a Covert Agent

(a) Base Offense Level:

(1) **30**, if the information was disclosed by a person with, or who had authorized access to classified information identifying a covert agent; or

(2) **25**, if the information was disclosed by a person with authorized access only to other classified information.

Commentary

Statutory Provision

50 U.S.C. § 421.

Application Notes

1. See Commentary to § 2M3.1.

2. This guideline applies only to violations of 50 U.S.C. § 421 by persons who have or previously had authorized access to classified information. This guideline does not apply to violations of 50 U.S.C. § 421 by defendants, including journalists, who disclosed such information without having or having had authorized access to classified information. Violations of 50 U.S.C. § 421 not covered by this guideline may vary in the degree of harm they inflict, and the court should impose a sentence that reflects such harm. See § 2X5.1 (Other Offenses).

Background

The alternative base offense levels reflect a statutory distinction by providing a greater base offense level for a violation of 50 U.S.C. § 421 by an official who has or had authorized access to classified information identifying a covert agent than for a violation by an official with authorized access only to other classified information. This guideline does not apply to violations of 50 U.S.C. § 421 by defendants who disclosed such information without having, or having had, authorized access to classified information.

Historical Note

Effective November 1, 1987.

Evasion of Military Service

§ 2M4.1. Failure to Register and Evasion of Military Service

(a) Base Offense Level: **6**

(b) Specific Offense Characteristic

(1) If the offense occurred at a time when persons were being inducted for compulsory military service, increase by **6** levels.

Commentary

Statutory Provision

50 U.S.C. App. § 462.

Application Note

1. Subsection (b)(1) does not distinguish between whether the offense was committed in peacetime or during time of war or armed conflict. If the offense was committed when persons were being inducted for compulsory military service during time of war or armed conflict, an upward departure may be warranted.

Historical Note

Effective November 1, 1987. Amended effective November 1, 1990 (see Appendix C, amendment 336).

Prohibited Financial Transactions and Exports

§ 2M5.1. Evasion of Export Controls

(a) Base Offense Level (Apply the greater):

(1) **22**, if national security or nuclear proliferation controls were evaded; or

(2) **14**.

Commentary

Statutory Provisions

50 U.S.C. App. §§ 2401–2420.

Application Notes

1. In the case of a violation during time of war or armed conflict, an upward departure may be warranted.

2. In determining the sentence within the applicable guideline range, the court may consider the degree to which the violation threatened a security interest of the United States, the volume of commerce involved, the extent of planning or sophistication, and whether there were multiple occurrences. Where such factors are present in an extreme form, a departure from the guidelines may be warranted. See Chapter Five, Part K (Departures).

3. In addition to the provisions for imprisonment, 50 U.S.C. App. § 2410 contains provisions for criminal fines and forfeiture as well as civil penalties. The maximum fine for individual defendants is $250,000. In the case of corporations, the maximum fine is five times the value of the exports involved or $1 million, whichever is greater. When national security controls are violated, in addition to any other sanction, the defendant is subject to forfeiture of any interest in, security of, or claim against: any goods or tangible items that were the subject of the violation; property used to export or attempt to export that was the subject of the violation; and any proceeds obtained directly or indirectly as a result of the violation.

Historical Note

Effective November 1, 1987.

§ 2M5.2. Exportation of Arms, Munitions, or Military Equipment or Services Without Required Validated Export License

(a) Base Offense Level:

(1) **22**, except as provided in subdivision (2) below;

(2) **14**, if the offense involved only non-fully automatic small arms (rifles, handguns, or shotguns), and the number of weapons did not exceed ten.

Commentary

Statutory Provisions

22 U.S.C. §§ 2778, 2780.

Application Notes

1. Under 22 U.S.C. § 2778, the President is authorized, through a licensing system administered by the Department of State, to control exports of defense articles and defense services that he deems critical to a security or foreign policy interest of the United States. The items subject to control constitute the United States Munitions List, which is set out in 22 C.F.R. Part 121.1. Included in this list are such things as military aircraft, helicopters, artillery, shells, missiles, rockets, bombs, vessels of war, explosives, military and space electronics, and certain firearms.

   The base offense level assumes that the offense conduct was harmful or had the potential to be harmful to a security or foreign policy interest of the United States. In the unusual case where the offense conduct posed no such risk, a downward departure may be warranted. In the case of a violation during time of war or armed conflict, an upward departure may be warranted. See Chapter Five, Part K (Departures).

2. In determining the sentence within the applicable guideline range, the court may consider the degree to which the violation threatened a security or foreign policy interest of the United States, the volume of commerce involved, the extent of planning or sophistication, and whether there were multiple occurrences. Where such factors are present in an extreme form, a departure from the guidelines may be warranted.

Historical Note

Effective November 1, 1987. Amended effective November 1, 1990 (see Appendix C, amendment 337).

Atomic Energy

§ 2M6.1. Unlawful Acquisition, Alteration, Use, Transfer, or Possession of Nuclear Material, Weapons, or Facilities

(a) Base Offense Level: **30**

(b) Specific Offense Characteristic

(1) If the offense was committed with intent to injure the United States or to aid a foreign nation, increase by **12** levels.

Commentary

Statutory Provisions

42 U.S.C. §§ 2077(b), 2122, 2131. Also, 18 U.S.C. § 831 (only where the conduct is similar to that proscribed by the aforementioned statutory provisions). For additional statutory provision(s), see Appendix A (Statutory Index).

Historical Note

Effective November 1, 1987.

§ 2M6.2. Violation of Other Federal Atomic Energy Agency Statutes, Rules, and Regulations

(a) Base Offense Level (Apply the greater):

(1) **30**, if the offense was committed with intent to injure the United States or to aid a foreign nation; or

(2) **6**.

Commentary

Statutory Provision

42 U.S.C. § 2273.

Background

This section applies to offenses related to nuclear energy not specifically addressed elsewhere. This provision covers, for example, violations of statutes dealing with rules and regulations, license conditions, and orders of the Nuclear Regulatory Commission and the Department of Energy.

Historical Note

Effective November 1, 1987. Amended effective November 1, 1990 (see Appendix C, amendment 359).

Rules for the Alien Terrorist Removal Court of the United States

Rule 1. Name of Court

This Court, established pursuant to the Antiterrorism and Effective Death Penalty Act of 1996, Pub. L. No. 104–132, Title IV, 110 Stat. 1214, 1258, (Title V of the Immigration and Nationality Act), and as amended by the Omnibus Consolidated Appropriations Act for 1997, Public Law No. 104–208, Title I, § 354, 110 Stat. 3009, shall be known as the Alien Terrorist Removal Court of the United States (8 U.S.C. § 1531 et seq.).

Rule 2. Seal

The seal of the Court shall contain the words "Alien Terrorist Removal Court" in the upper sector of space included within the two outer concentric circles and the words "of the United States of America" in the lower sector, and shall contain the standardized eagle rampant in the center.

Rule 3. Situs

The situs of the Court shall be at the United States Courthouse, Washington, D.C., 20001.

Rule 4. Clerk

(a) The Clerk of the District Court for the District of Columbia shall be the Clerk of this Court.

(b) The Clerk shall supply a deputy clerk and other personnel as the business of this Court may require.

(c) Personnel responsible for filing and maintaining records of this Court containing classified information shall have appropriate levels of security clearance in compliance with Executive Branch procedures governing classified information.

Rule 5. Application for Removal

(a) The Attorney General, acting on behalf of the United States as applicant, shall file an original and two copies of an application seeking removal of an alleged alien, named as respondent.

(b) The application shall be submitted ex parte and in camera and shall be filed under seal with the Clerk of this Court.

(c) The application shall state, to the extent known, the level of classified information, if any, that the Attorney General will present in support of removal.

(d) The application shall state whether the respondent is a permanent resident alien.

Rule 6. Assignment of Cases

(a) The Clerk shall promptly advise the Chief Judge, by a secured means, of the filing of an application. The Chief Judge shall thereupon make an assignment of the case to a member of the Court for consideration and determination of that case.

(b) Cases shall be assigned to judges of the Court in such a manner that each judge, if available for an assignment, shall receive an assignment before any other judge receives a second or successive assignment.

Rule 7. Service of an Order Granting an Application and Notice of a Removal Hearing

(a) If an order is entered granting an ex parte application, an authorized representative of the Attorney General shall serve the respondent who is the subject of the application with a copy of the order, excluding any classified information in the order, together with a Notice pursuant to 8 U.S.C. § 1534(b). The Notice shall also set an expeditious date for the Removal Hearing.

(b) The Attorney General shall file with the Clerk a certificate of service of the order and Notice.

(c) Retained counsel for a respondent shall promptly file an appearance with the Clerk.

(d) If a respondent is financially unable to obtain adequate representation, the respondent may request appointment of counsel from the Criminal Justice Panel for United States District Court for the District of Columbia, as provided for in Section 3006A of Title 18 (Criminal Justice Act).

Rule 8. Interim Hearing

(a) For the convenience of the assigned judge and the parties, the judge may conduct an Interim Hearing or Hearings for the purpose of resolving issues relating to representation of the respondent, special issues relating to a permanent resident alien respondent, issues relating to classified information, or if required by statute. When appropriate, the Interim Hearing will be conducted ex parte and in camera.

(b) Any Interim Hearing shall be conducted in the United States Courthouse in Washington, D.C.

Rule 9. Place of Conducting Removal Hearing

The Removal Hearing shall be held in the United States Courthouse in Washington, D.C. The Removal Hearing shall be conducted publicly, except that any part of the argument that refers to evidence received in camera and ex parte, shall be heard in camera and ex parte.

Rule 10. Verbatim Record of Proceedings

All ex parte, in camera, and public hearings of the Court shall be recorded verbatim by a reporter retained pursuant to 28 U.S.C. § 753, by short-hand, mechanical means, electronic sound recording, or any other method, subject to regulations promulgated by the Judicial Conference of the United States.

Rule 11. Motions

(a) Any motion shall include or be accompanied by a statement of the specific points of law and authority that support the motion, including where appropriate a concise statement of facts. If a table of cases is provided, counsel shall place asterisks in the margin to the left of those cases or authorities on which counsel chiefly relies.

(b) Within 15 days of the date of service or at such other time as the assigned judge may direct, an opposing party shall serve and file a memorandum of points and authorities in opposition to the motion. If such a memorandum is not filed within the prescribed time, the judge may treat the motion as uncontested.

(c) Each motion shall be accompanied by a proposed order.

(d) Within 10 days after service of the memorandum in opposition, the moving party may serve and file a reply memorandum.

(e) A memorandum of points and authorities in support of or in opposition to a motion shall not exceed 15 pages and a reply memorandum shall not exceed 10 pages, without prior approval of the assigned judge.

(f) A party may in a motion or opposition request oral argument, but its allowance shall be within the discretion of the assigned judge.

Rule 12. Subpoenas

Except for good cause shown, requests for issuance of a subpoena pursuant to 8 U.S.C. § 1534(d) by either the respondent or applicant, shall be made at least 10 days prior to the date of the removal hearing.

Rule 13. Classified Information

(a) The ex parte and in camera examination of any classified information, pursuant to 8 U.S.C. § 1534(e)(3)(A)–(E), and of the proposed unclassified summary of specific information shall both be conducted on the day of the Interim Hearing unless the assigned judge otherwise directs.

(b) The unclassified summary, following approval by the judge, shall be delivered to the respondent without delay.

(c) When the respondent is a lawful permanent resident alien, who is denied an unclassified summary pursuant to 8 U.S.C. § 1534(e)(3)(F), the judge shall designate a special attorney to assist the respondent by reviewing the classified information.

(d) When the appointed special attorney moves to challenge the veracity of the evidence contained in the classified information pursuant to 8 U.S.C. § 1534(e)(3)(F)(i)(II), the assigned judge shall schedule an in camera proceeding prior to the Removal Hearing to consider the motion.

Rule 14. Removal Hearing Memorandum

Seven days prior to the Removal Hearing, counsel for the applicant and the respondent shall file with the Clerk and serve on each other a Hearing Memorandum setting forth any legal issues to be raised, a summary of the anticipated testimony (exclusive of classified information), and copies of exhibits (exclusive of classified information). The names of individuals involved in the investigation and prospective witnesses need not be included in the material filed with the Court.

PART II

USA Patriot Act of 2001

Uniting and Strengthening America by Providing Appropriate Tools Required to Intercept and Obstruct Terrorism Act of 2001

(USA PATRIOT ACT)

H.R. 3162

One Hundred Seventh Congress of the United States of America

AT THE FIRST SESSION

Begun and held at the City of Washington on Wednesday, the third day of January, two thousand and one

An Act

To deter and punish terrorist acts in the United States and around the world, to enhance law enforcement investigatory tools, and for other purposes.

Be it enacted by the Senate and House of Representatives of the United States of America in Congress assembled,

Sec. 1. Short Title and Table of Contents.

(a) SHORT TITLE—This Act may be cited as the 'Uniting and Strengthening America by Providing Appropriate Tools Required to Intercept and Obstruct Terrorism (USA PATRIOT ACT) Act of 2001'.

(b) TABLE OF CONTENTS—The table of contents for this Act is as follows:

TITLE III—INTERNATIONAL MONEY LAUNDERING ABATEMENT AND ANTI-TERRORIST FINANCING ACT OF 2001

TITLE IV—PROTECTING THE BORDER

TITLE V—REMOVING OBSTACLES TO INVESTIGATING TERRORISM

TITLE VI—PROVIDING FOR VICTIMS OF TERRORISM, PUBLIC SAFETY OFFICERS, AND THEIR FAMILIES

TITLE VII—INCREASED INFORMATION SHARING FOR CRITICAL INFRASTRUCTURE PROTECTION

TITLE VIII—STRENGTHENING THE CRIMINAL LAWS AGAINST TERRORISM

Sec. 2. Construction; Severability.

Any provision of this Act held to be invalid or unenforceable by its terms, or as applied to any person or circumstance, shall be construed so as to give it the maximum effect permitted by law, unless such holding shall be one of utter invalidity or unenforceability, in which event such provision shall be deemed severable from this Act and shall not affect the remainder thereof or the application of such provision to other persons not similarly situated or to other, dissimilar circumstances.

Title I—Enhancing Domestic Security Against Terrorism

Sec. 101. Counterterrorism Fund.

(a) ESTABLISHMENT; AVAILABILITY—There is hereby established in the Treasury of the United States a separate fund to be known as the 'Counterterrorism Fund', amounts in which shall remain available without fiscal year limitation—

(1) to reimburse any Department of Justice component for any costs incurred in connection with—

(A) reestablishing the operational capability of an office or facility that has been damaged or destroyed as the result of any domestic or international terrorism incident;

(B) providing support to counter, investigate, or prosecute domestic or international terrorism, including, without limitation, paying rewards in connection with these activities; and

(C) conducting terrorism threat assessments of Federal agencies and their facilities; and

(2) to reimburse any department or agency of the Federal Government for any costs incurred in connection with detaining in foreign countries individuals accused of acts of terrorism that violate the laws of the United States.

(b) NO EFFECT ON PRIOR APPROPRIATIONS—Subsection (a) shall not be construed to affect the amount or availability of any appropriation to the Counterterrorism Fund made before the date of the enactment of this Act.

Sec. 102. Sense of Congress Condemning Discrimination Against Arab and Muslim Americans.

(a) FINDINGS—Congress makes the following findings:

(1) Arab Americans, Muslim Americans, and Americans from South Asia play a vital role in our Nation and are entitled to nothing less than the full rights of every American.

(2) The acts of violence that have been taken against Arab and Muslim Americans since the September 11, 2001, attacks against the United States should be and are condemned by all Americans who value freedom.

(3) The concept of individual responsibility for wrongdoing is sacrosanct in American society, and applies equally to all religious, racial, and ethnic groups.

(4) When American citizens commit acts of violence against those who are, or are perceived to be, of Arab or Muslim descent, they should be punished to the full extent of the law.

(5) Muslim Americans have become so fearful of harassment that many Muslim women are changing the way they dress to avoid becoming targets.

(6) Many Arab Americans and Muslim Americans have acted heroically during the attacks on the United States, including Mohammed Salman Hamdani, a 23-year-old New Yorker of Pakistani descent, who is believed to have gone to the World Trade Center to offer rescue assistance and is now missing.

(b) SENSE OF CONGRESS—It is the sense of Congress that—

(1) the civil rights and civil liberties of all Americans, including Arab Americans, Muslim Americans, and Americans from South Asia, must be protected, and that every effort must be taken to preserve their safety;

(2) any acts of violence or discrimination against any Americans be condemned; and

(3) the Nation is called upon to recognize the patriotism of fellow citizens from all ethnic, racial, and religious backgrounds.

Sec. 103. Increased Funding for the Technical Support Center at the Federal Bureau of Investigation.

There are authorized to be appropriated for the Technical Support Center established in section 811 of the Antiterrorism and Effective Death Penalty Act of 1996 (Public Law 104–132) to help meet the demands for activities to combat terrorism and support and enhance the technical support and tactical operations of the FBI, $200,000,000 for each of the fiscal years 2002, 2003, and 2004.

Sec. 104. Requests for Military Assistance to Enforce Prohibition in Certain Emergencies.

Section 2332e of title 18, United States Code, is amended—

(1) by striking '2332c' and inserting '2332a'; and

(2) by striking 'chemical'.

Sec. 105. Expansion of National Electronic Crime Task Force Initiative.

The Director of the United States Secret Service shall take appropriate actions to develop a national network of electronic crime task forces, based on the New York Electronic Crimes Task Force model, throughout the United States, for the purpose of preventing, detecting, and investigating various forms of electronic crimes, including potential terrorist attacks against critical infrastructure and financial payment systems.

Sec. 106. Presidential Authority.

Section 203 of the International Emergency Powers Act (50 U.S.C. 1702) is amended—

(1) in subsection (a)(1)—

(A) at the end of subparagraph (A) (flush to that subparagraph), by striking '; and' and inserting a comma and the following:

'by any person, or with respect to any property, subject to the jurisdiction of the United States;';

(B) in subparagraph (B)—

(i) by inserting ', block during the pendency of an investigation' after 'investigate'; and

(ii) by striking 'interest;' and inserting 'interest by any person, or with respect to any property, subject to the jurisdiction of the United States; and';

(C) by striking 'by any person, or with respect to any property, subject to the jurisdiction of the United States'; and

(D) by inserting at the end the following:

'(C) when the United States is engaged in armed hostilities or has been attacked by a foreign country or foreign nationals, confiscate any property, subject to the jurisdiction of the United States, of any foreign person, foreign organization, or foreign country that he determines has planned, authorized, aided, or engaged in such hostilities or attacks against the United States; and all right, title, and interest in any property so confiscated shall vest, when, as, and upon the terms directed by the President, in such agency or person as the President may designate from time to time, and upon such terms and conditions as the President may prescribe, such interest or property shall be held, used, administered, liquidated, sold, or otherwise dealt with in the interest of and for the benefit of the United States, and such designated agency or person may perform any and all acts incident to the accomplishment or furtherance of these purposes.'; and

(2) by inserting at the end the following:

'(c) CLASSIFIED INFORMATION—In any judicial review of a determination made under this section, if the determination was based on classified information (as defined in section 1(a) of the Classified Information Procedures Act) such information may be submitted to the reviewing court ex parte and in camera. This subsection does not confer or imply any right to judicial review.'.

Title II—Enhanced Surveillance Procedures

Sec. 201. Authority to Intercept Wire, Oral, and Electronic Communications Relating to Terrorism.

Section 2516(1) of title 18, United States Code, is amended—

(1) by redesignating paragraph (p), as so redesignated by section 434(2) of the Antiterrorism and Effective Death Penalty Act of 1996 (Public Law 104–132; 110 Stat. 1274), as paragraph (r); and

(2) by inserting after paragraph (p), as so redesignated by section 201(3) of the Illegal Immigration Reform and Immigrant Responsibility Act of 1996 (division C of Public Law 104–208; 110 Stat. 3009–565), the following new paragraph:

'(q) any criminal violation of section 229 (relating to chemical weapons); or sections 2332, 2332a, 2332b, 2332d, 2339A, or 2339B of this title (relating to terrorism); or'.

Sec. 202. Authority to Intercept Wire, Oral, and Electronic Communications Relating to Computer Fraud and Abuse Offenses.

Section 2516(1)(c) of title 18, United States Code, is amended by striking 'and section 1341 (relating to mail fraud),' and inserting 'section 1341 (relating to mail fraud), a felony violation of section 1030 (relating to computer fraud and abuse),'.

Sec. 203. Authority to Share Criminal Investigative Information.

(a) AUTHORITY TO SHARE GRAND JURY INFORMATION-

(1) IN GENERAL—Rule 6(e)(3)(C) of the Federal Rules of Criminal Procedure is amended to read as follows:

'(C)(i) Disclosure otherwise prohibited by this rule of matters occurring before the grand jury may also be made—

'(I) when so directed by a court preliminarily to or in connection with a judicial proceeding;

'(II) when permitted by a court at the request of the defendant, upon a showing that grounds may exist for a motion to dismiss the indictment because of matters occurring before the grand jury;

'(III) when the disclosure is made by an attorney for the government to another Federal grand jury;

'(IV) when permitted by a court at the request of an attorney for the government, upon a showing that such matters may disclose a violation of State criminal law, to an appropriate official of a State or subdivision of a State for the purpose of enforcing such law; or

'(V) when the matters involve foreign intelligence or counterintelligence (as defined in section 3 of the National Security Act of 1947 (50 U.S.C. 401a)), or foreign intelligence information (as defined in clause (iv) of this subparagraph), to any Federal law enforcement, intelligence, protective, immigration, national defense, or national security official in order to assist the official receiving that information in the performance of his official duties.

'(ii) If the court orders disclosure of matters occurring before the grand jury, the disclosure shall be made in such manner, at such time, and under such conditions as the court may direct.

'(iii) Any Federal official to whom information is disclosed pursuant to clause (i)(V) of this subparagraph may use that information only as necessary in the conduct of that person's official duties subject to any limitations on the unauthorized disclosure of such information. Within a reasonable time after such disclosure, an attorney for the government shall file under seal a notice with the court stating the fact that such information was disclosed and the departments, agencies, or entities to which the disclosure was made.

'(iv) In clause (i)(V) of this subparagraph, the term 'foreign intelligence information' means—

'(I) information, whether or not concerning a United States person, that relates to the ability of the United States to protect against—

'(aa) actual or potential attack or other grave

hostile acts of a foreign power or an agent of a foreign power;

'(bb) sabotage or international terrorism by a foreign power or an agent of a foreign power; or

'(cc) clandestine intelligence activities by an intelligence service or network of a foreign power or by an agent of foreign power; or

'(II) information, whether or not concerning a United States person, with respect to a foreign power or foreign territory that relates to—

'(aa) the national defense or the security of the United States; or

'(bb) the conduct of the foreign affairs of the United States.'.

(2) CONFORMING AMENDMENT—Rule 6(e)(3)(D) of the Federal Rules of Criminal Procedure is amended by striking '(e)(3)(C)(i)' and inserting '(e)(3)(C)(i)(I)'.

(b) AUTHORITY TO SHARE ELECTRONIC, WIRE, AND ORAL INTERCEPTION INFORMATION-

(1) LAW ENFORCEMENT—Section 2517 of title 18, United States Code, is amended by inserting at the end the following:

'(6) Any investigative or law enforcement officer, or attorney for the Government, who by any means authorized by this chapter, has obtained knowledge of the contents of any wire, oral, or electronic communication, or evidence derived therefrom, may disclose such contents to any other Federal law enforcement, intelligence, protective, immigration, national defense, or national security official to the extent that such contents include foreign intelligence or counterintelligence (as defined in section 3 of the National Security Act of 1947 (50 U.S.C. 401a)), or foreign intelligence information (as defined in subsection (19) of section 2510 of this title), to assist the official who is to receive that information in the performance of his official duties. Any Federal official who receives information pursuant to this provision may use that information only as necessary in the conduct of that person's official duties subject to any limitations on the unauthorized disclosure of such information.'.

(2) DEFINITION—Section 2510 of title 18, United States Code, is amended by—

(A) in paragraph (17), by striking 'and' after the semicolon;

(B) in paragraph (18), by striking the period and inserting '; and'; and

(C) by inserting at the end the following:

'(19) 'foreign intelligence information' means—

'(A) information, whether or not concerning a United States person, that relates to the ability of the United States to protect against—

'(i) actual or potential attack or other grave hostile acts of a foreign power or an agent of a foreign power;

'(ii) sabotage or international terrorism by a foreign power or an agent of a foreign power; or

'(iii) clandestine intelligence activities by an intelligence service or network of a foreign power or by an agent of a foreign power; or

'(B) information, whether or not concerning a United States person, with respect to a foreign power or foreign territory that relates to—

'(i) the national defense or the security of the United States; or

'(ii) the conduct of the foreign affairs of the United States.'.

(c) PROCEDURES—The Attorney General shall establish procedures for the disclosure of information pursuant to section 2517(6) and Rule 6(e)(3)(C)(i)(V) of the Federal Rules of Criminal Procedure that identifies a United States person, as defined in section 101 of the Foreign Intelligence Surveillance Act of 1978 (50 U.S.C. 1801)).

(d) FOREIGN INTELLIGENCE INFORMATION-

(1) IN GENERAL—Notwithstanding any other provision of law, it shall be lawful for foreign intelligence or counterintelligence (as defined in section 3 of the National Security Act of 1947 (50 U.S.C. 401a)) or foreign intelligence information obtained as part of a criminal investigation to be disclosed to any Federal law enforcement, intelligence, protective, immigration, national defense, or national security official in order to assist the official receiving that information in the performance of his official duties. Any Federal official

who receives information pursuant to this provision may use that information only as necessary in the conduct of that person's official duties subject to any limitations on the unauthorized disclosure of such information.

(2) DEFINITION—In this subsection, the term 'foreign intelligence information' means—

(A) information, whether or not concerning a United States person, that relates to the ability of the United States to protect against—

(i) actual or potential attack or other grave hostile acts of a foreign power or an agent of a foreign power;

(ii) sabotage or international terrorism by a foreign power or an agent of a foreign power; or

(iii) clandestine intelligence activities by an intelligence service or network of a foreign power or by an agent of a foreign power; or

(B) information, whether or not concerning a United States person, with respect to a foreign power or foreign territory that relates to—

(i) the national defense or the security of the United States; or

(ii) the conduct of the foreign affairs of the United States.

Sec. 204. Clarification of Intelligence Exceptions from Limitations on Interception and Disclosure of Wire, Oral, and Electronic Communications.

Section 2511(2)(f) of title 18, United States Code, is amended—

(1) by striking 'this chapter or chapter 121' and inserting 'this chapter or chapter 121 or 206 of this title'; and

(2) by striking 'wire and oral' and inserting 'wire, oral, and electronic'.

Sec. 205. Employment of Translators by the Federal Bureau of Investigation.

(a) AUTHORITY—The Director of the Federal Bureau of Investigation is authorized to expedite the employment of personnel as translators to support counterterrorism investigations and operations without regard to applicable Federal personnel requirements and limitations.

(b) SECURITY REQUIREMENTS—The Director of the Federal Bureau of Investigation shall establish such security requirements as are necessary for the personnel employed as translators under subsection (a).

(c) REPORT—The Attorney General shall report to the Committees on the Judiciary of the House of Representatives and the Senate on—

(1) the number of translators employed by the FBI and other components of the Department of Justice;

(2) any legal or practical impediments to using translators employed by other Federal, State, or local agencies, on a full, part-time, or shared basis; and

(3) the needs of the FBI for specific translation services in certain languages, and recommendations for meeting those needs.

Sec. 206. Roving Surveillance Authority Under the Foreign Intelligence Surveillance Act of 1978.

Section 105(c)(2)(B) of the Foreign Intelligence Surveillance Act of 1978 (50 U.S.C. 1805(c)(2)(B)) is amended by inserting ', or in circumstances where the Court finds that the actions of the target of the application may have the effect of thwarting the identification of a specified person, such other persons,' after 'specified person'.

Sec. 207. Duration of Fisa Surveillance of Non-United States Persons Who Are Agents of a Foreign Power.

(a) DURATION-

(1) SURVEILLANCE—Section 105(e)(1) of the Foreign Intelligence Surveillance Act of 1978 (50 U.S.C. 1805(e)(1)) is amended by—

(A) inserting '(A)' after 'except that'; and

(B) inserting before the period the following: ', and (B) an order under this Act for a surveillance targeted against an agent of a foreign power, as defined in section 101(b)(1)(A) may be for the period specified in the application or for 120 days, whichever is less'.

(2) PHYSICAL SEARCH—Section 304(d)(1) of the Foreign Intelligence Surveillance Act of 1978 (50 U.S.C. 1824(d)(1)) is amended by—

(A) striking 'forty-five' and inserting '90';

(B) inserting '(A)' after 'except that'; and

(C) inserting before the period the following: ', and (B) an order under this section for a physical search targeted against an agent of a foreign power as defined in section 101(b)(1)(A) may be for the period specified in the application or for 120 days, whichever is less'.

(b) EXTENSION-

(1) IN GENERAL—Section 105(d)(2) of the Foreign Intelligence Surveillance Act of 1978 (50 U.S.C. 1805(d)(2)) is amended by—

(A) inserting '(A)' after 'except that'; and

(B) inserting before the period the following: ', and (B) an extension of an order under this Act for a surveillance targeted against an agent of a foreign power as defined in section 101(b)(1)(A) may be for a period not to exceed 1 year'.

(2) DEFINED TERM—Section 304(d)(2) of the Foreign Intelligence Surveillance Act of 1978 (50 U.S.C. 1824(d)(2) is amended by inserting after 'not a United States person,' the following: 'or against an agent of a foreign power as defined in section 101(b)(1)(A),'.

Sec. 208. Designation of Judges.

Section 103(a) of the Foreign Intelligence Surveillance Act of 1978 (50 U.S.C. 1803(a)) is amended by—

(1) striking 'seven district court judges' and inserting '11 district court judges'; and

(2) inserting 'of whom no fewer than 3 shall reside within 20 miles of the District of Columbia' after 'circuits'.

Sec. 209. Seizure of Voice-Mail Messages Pursuant to Warrants.

Title 18, United States Code, is amended—

(1) in section 2510—

(A) in paragraph (1), by striking beginning with 'and such' and all that follows through 'communication'; and

(B) in paragraph (14), by inserting 'wire or' after 'transmission of'; and

(2) in subsections (a) and (b) of section 2703—

(A) by striking 'CONTENTS OF ELECTRONIC' and inserting 'CONTENTS OF WIRE OR ELECTRONIC' each place it appears;

(B) by striking 'contents of an electronic' and inserting 'contents of a wire or electronic' each place it appears; and

(C) by striking 'any electronic' and inserting 'any wire or electronic' each place it appears.

Sec. 210. Scope of Subpoenas for Records of Electronic Communications.

Section 2703(c)(2) of title 18, United States Code, as redesignated by section 212, is amended—

(1) by striking 'entity the name, address, local and long distance telephone toll billing records, telephone number or other subscriber number or identity, and length of service of a subscriber' and inserting the following: 'entity the—

'(A) name;

'(B) address;

'(C) local and long distance telephone connection records, or records of session times and durations;

'(D) length of service (including start date) and types of service utilized;

'(E) telephone or instrument number or other subscriber number or identity, including any temporarily assigned network address; and

'(F) means and source of payment for such service (including any credit card or bank account number), of a subscriber'; and

(2) by striking 'and the types of services the subscriber or customer utilized,'.

Sec. 211. Clarification of Scope.

Section 631 of the Communications Act of 1934 (47 U.S.C. 551) is amended—

(1) in subsection (c)(2)—

(A) in subparagraph (B), by striking 'or';

(B) in subparagraph (C), by striking the period at the end and inserting '; or'; and

(C) by inserting at the end the following:

'(D) to a government entity as authorized under chapters 119, 121, or 206 of title 18, United States Code, except that such disclosure shall not include records revealing cable subscriber selection of video programming from a cable operator.'; and

(2) in subsection (h), by striking 'A governmental entity' and inserting 'Except as provided in subsection (c)(2)(D), a governmental entity'.

Sec. 212. Emergency Disclosure of Electronic Communications to Protect Life and Limb.

(a) DISCLOSURE OF CONTENTS-

(1) IN GENERAL—Section 2702 of title 18, United States Code, is amended—

(A) by striking the section heading and inserting the following:

'Sec. 2702. Voluntary disclosure of customer communications or records';

(B) in subsection (a)—

(i) in paragraph (2)(A), by striking 'and' at the end;

(ii) in paragraph (2)(B), by striking the period and inserting '; and'; and

(iii) by inserting after paragraph (2) the following:

'(3) a provider of remote computing service or electronic communication service to the public shall not knowingly divulge a record or other information pertaining to a subscriber to or customer of such service (not including the contents of communications covered by paragraph (1) or (2)) to any governmental entity.';

(C) in subsection (b), by striking 'EXCEPTIONS—A person or entity' and inserting 'EXCEPTIONS FOR DISCLOSURE OF COMMUNICATIONS—A provider described in subsection (a)';

(D) in subsection (b)(6)—

(i) in subparagraph (A)(ii), by striking 'or';

(ii) in subparagraph (B), by striking the period and inserting '; or'; and

(iii) by adding after subparagraph (B) the following:

'(C) if the provider reasonably believes that an emergency involving immediate danger of death or serious physical injury to any person requires disclosure of the information without delay.'; and

(E) by inserting after subsection (b) the following:

'(c) EXCEPTIONS FOR DISCLOSURE OF CUSTOMER RECORDS —A provider described in subsection (a) may divulge a record or other information pertaining to a subscriber to or customer of such service (not including the contents of communications covered by subsection (a)(1) or (a)(2))—

'(1) as otherwise authorized in section 2703;

'(2) with the lawful consent of the customer or subscriber;

'(3) as may be necessarily incident to the rendition of the service or to the protection of the rights or property of the provider of that service;

'(4) to a governmental entity, if the provider reasonably believes that an emergency involving immediate danger of death or serious physical injury to any person justifies disclosure of the information; or

'(5) to any person other than a governmental entity.'.

(2) TECHNICAL AND CONFORMING AMENDMENT—The table of sections for chapter 121 of title 18, United States Code, is amended by striking the item relating to section 2702 and inserting the following:

'2702. Voluntary disclosure of customer communications or records.'.

(b) REQUIREMENTS FOR GOVERNMENT ACCESS-

(1) IN GENERAL—Section 2703 of title 18, United States Code, is amended—

(A) by striking the section heading and inserting the following: 'Sec. 2703. Required disclosure of customer communications or records';

(B) in subsection (c) by redesignating paragraph (2) as paragraph (3);

(C) in subsection (c)(1)—

(i) by striking '(A) Except as provided in subparagraph (B), a provider of electronic communication service or remote computing service may' and inserting 'A governmental entity may require a provider of electronic communication service or remote computing service to';

(ii) by striking 'covered by subsection (a) or (b) of this section) to any person other than a governmental entity.

'(B) A provider of electronic communication service or remote computing service shall disclose a record or other information pertaining to a subscriber to or customer of such service (not including the contents of communications covered by subsection (a) or (b) of this section) to a governmental entity' and inserting ')';

(iii) by redesignating subparagraph (C) as paragraph (2);

(iv) by redesignating clauses (i), (ii), (iii), and (iv) as subparagraphs (A), (B), (C), and (D), respectively;

(v) in subparagraph (D) (as redesignated) by striking the period and inserting '; or'; and

(vi) by inserting after subparagraph (D) (as redesignated) the following:

'(E) seeks information under paragraph (2).'; and

(D) in paragraph (2) (as redesignated) by striking 'subparagraph (B)' and insert 'paragraph (1)'.

(2) TECHNICAL AND CONFORMING AMENDMENT—The table of sections for chapter 121 of title 18, United States Code, is amended by striking the item relating to section 2703 and inserting the following:

'2703. Required disclosure of customer communications or records.'.

Sec. 213. Authority for Delaying Notice of the Execution of a Warrant.

Section 3103a of title 18, United States Code, is amended—

(1) by inserting '(a) IN GENERAL—' before 'In addition'; and

(2) by adding at the end the following:

'(b) DELAY—With respect to the issuance of any warrant or court order under this section, or any other rule of law, to search for and seize any property or material that constitutes evidence of a criminal offense in violation of the laws of the United States, any notice required, or that may be required, to be given may be delayed if—

'(1) the court finds reasonable cause to believe that providing immediate notification of the execution of the warrant may have an adverse result (as defined in section 2705);

'(2) the warrant prohibits the seizure of any tangible property, any wire or electronic communication (as defined in section 2510), or, except as expressly provided in chapter 121, any stored wire or electronic information, except where the court finds reasonable necessity for the seizure; and

'(3) the warrant provides for the giving of such notice within a reasonable period of its execution, which period may thereafter be extended by the court for good cause shown.'.

Sec. 214. Pen Register and Trap and Trace Authority Under Fisa.

(a) APPLICATIONS AND ORDERS—Section 402 of the Foreign Intelligence Surveillance Act of 1978 (50 U.S.C. 1842) is amended—

(1) in subsection (a)(1), by striking 'for any investigation to gather foreign intelligence information or information concerning international terrorism' and inserting 'for any investigation to obtain foreign intelligence information not concerning a United States person or to protect against international terrorism or clandestine intelligence activities, provided that such investigation of a United States person is not conducted solely upon the basis of activities protected by the first amendment to the Constitution';

(2) by amending subsection (c)(2) to read as follows:

'(2) a certification by the applicant that the information likely to be obtained is foreign intelligence information not concerning a United States person or is relevant to an ongoing investigation to protect against international terrorism or clandestine intelligence activities, provided that such investigation of a United States person is not conducted solely upon the basis of activities protected by the first amendment to the Constitution.';

(3) by striking subsection (c)(3); and

(4) by amending subsection (d)(2)(A) to read as follows:

'(A) shall specify—

'(i) the identity, if known, of the person who is the subject of the investigation;

'(ii) the identity, if known, of the person to whom is leased or in whose name is listed the telephone line or other facility to which the pen register or trap and trace device is to be attached or applied;

'(iii) the attributes of the communications to which the order applies, such as the number or other identifier, and, if known, the location of the telephone line or other facility to which the pen register or trap and trace device is to be attached or applied and, in the case of a trap and trace device, the geographic limits of the trap and trace order.'.

(b) AUTHORIZATION DURING EMERGENCIES—Section 403 of the Foreign Intelligence Surveillance Act of 1978 (50 U.S.C. 1843) is amended—

(1) in subsection (a), by striking 'foreign intelligence information or information concerning international terrorism' and inserting 'foreign intelligence information not concerning a United States person or information to protect against international terrorism or clandestine intelligence activities, provided that such investigation of a United States person is not conducted solely upon the basis of activities protected by the first amendment to the Constitution'; and

(2) in subsection (b)(1), by striking 'foreign intelligence information or information concerning international terrorism' and inserting 'foreign intelligence information not concerning a United States person or information to protect against international terrorism or clandestine intelligence activities, provided that such investigation of a United States person is not conducted solely upon the basis of activities protected by the first amendment to the Constitution'.

Sec. 215. Access to Records and Other Items Under the Foreign Intelligence Surveillance Act.

Title V of the Foreign Intelligence Surveillance Act of 1978 (50 U.S.C. 1861 et seq.) is amended by striking sections 501 through 503 and inserting the following:

'Sec. 501. Access to Certain Business Records for Foreign Intelligence and International Terrorism Investigations.

'(a)(1) The Director of the Federal Bureau of Investigation or a designee of the Director (whose rank shall be no lower than Assistant Special Agent in Charge) may make an application for an order requiring the production of any tangible things (including books, records, papers, documents, and other items) for an investigation to protect against international terrorism or clandestine intelligence activities, provided that such investigation of a United States person is not conducted solely upon the basis of activities protected by the first amendment to the Constitution.

'(2) An investigation conducted under this section shall—

'(A) be conducted under guidelines approved by the Attorney General under Executive Order 12333 (or a successor order); and

'(B) not be conducted of a United States person solely upon the basis of activities protected by the first amendment to the Constitution of the United States.

'(b) Each application under this section—

'(1) shall be made to—

'(A) a judge of the court established by section 103(a); or

'(B) a United States Magistrate Judge under chapter 43 of title 28, United States Code, who is publicly designated by the Chief Justice of the United States to have the power to hear applications and grant orders for the production of tangible things under this section on behalf of a judge of that court; and

'(2) shall specify that the records concerned are sought for an authorized investigation conducted in accordance with subsection (a)(2) to obtain foreign intelligence information not concerning a United States person or to protect against international terrorism or clandestine intelligence activities.

'(c)(1) Upon an application made pursuant to this section, the judge shall enter an ex parte order as requested, or as modified, approving the release of records if the judge finds that the application meets the requirements of this section.

'(2) An order under this subsection shall not disclose that it is issued for purposes of an investigation described in subsection (a).

'(d) No person shall disclose to any other person (other than those persons necessary to produce the tangible things under this section) that the Federal Bureau of Investigation has sought or obtained tangible things under this section.

'(e) A person who, in good faith, produces tangible things under an order pursuant to this section shall not be liable to any other person for such production. Such production shall not be deemed to constitute a waiver of any privilege in any other proceeding or context.

'Sec. 502. Congressional Oversight.

'(a) On a semiannual basis, the Attorney General shall fully inform the Permanent Select Committee on Intelligence of the House of Representatives and the Select Committee on Intelligence of the Senate concerning all requests for the production of tangible things under section 402.

'(b) On a semiannual basis, the Attorney General shall provide to the Committees on the Judiciary of the House of Representatives and the Senate a report setting forth with respect to the preceding 6-month period—

'(1) the total number of applications made for orders approving requests for the production of tangible things under section 402; and

'(2) the total number of such orders either granted, modified, or denied.'.

Sec. 216. Modification of Authorities Relating to Use of Pen Registers and Trap and Trace Devices.

(a) GENERAL LIMITATIONS—Section 3121(c) of title 18, United States Code, is amended—

(1) by inserting 'or trap and trace device' after 'pen register';

(2) by inserting ', routing, addressing,' after 'dialing'; and

(3) by striking 'call processing' and inserting 'the processing and transmitting of wire or electronic communications so as not to include the contents of any wire or electronic communications'.

(b) ISSUANCE OF ORDERS-

(1) IN GENERAL—Section 3123(a) of title 18, United States Code, is amended to read as follows:

'(a) IN GENERAL-

'(1) ATTORNEY FOR THE GOVERNMENT—Upon an application made under section 3122(a)(1), the court shall enter an ex parte order authorizing the installation and use of a pen register or trap and trace device anywhere within the United States, if the court finds that the attorney for the Government has certified to the court that the information likely to be obtained by such installation and use is relevant to an ongoing criminal investigation. The order, upon service of that order, shall apply to any person or entity providing wire or electronic communication service in the United States whose assistance may facilitate the execution of the order. Whenever such an order is served on any person or entity not specifically named in the order, upon request of such person or entity, the attorney for the Government or law enforcement or investigative officer that is serving the order shall provide written or electronic certification that the order applies to the person or entity being served.

'(2) STATE INVESTIGATIVE OR LAW ENFORCEMENT OFFICER—Upon an application made under section 3122(a)(2), the court shall enter an ex parte order authorizing the installation and use of a pen register or trap and trace device within the jurisdiction of the court, if the court finds that the State law enforcement or investigative officer has certified to the court that the information likely to be obtained by such installation and use is relevant to an ongoing criminal investigation.

'(3)(A) Where the law enforcement agency implementing an ex parte order under this subsection seeks to do so by installing and using its own pen register or trap and trace device on a packet-switched data network of a provider of electronic communication service to the public, the agency shall ensure that a record will be maintained which will identify—

'(i) any officer or officers who installed the device and any officer or officers who accessed the device to obtain information from the network;

'(ii) the date and time the device was installed, the date and time the device was uninstalled, and the date, time, and duration of each time the device is accessed to obtain information;

'(iii) the configuration of the device at the time of its installation and any subsequent modification thereof; and

'(iv) any information which has been collected by the device. To the extent that the pen register or trap and trace device can be set automatically to record this information electronically, the record shall be maintained electronically throughout the installation and use of such device.

'(B) The record maintained under subparagraph (A) shall be provided ex parte and under seal to the court which entered the ex parte order authorizing the installation and use of the device within 30 days after termination of the order (including any extensions thereof).'.

(2) CONTENTS OF ORDER—Section 3123(b)(1) of title 18, United States Code, is amended—

(A) in subparagraph (A)—

(i) by inserting 'or other facility' after 'telephone line'; and

(ii) by inserting before the semicolon at the end 'or applied'; and

(B) by striking subparagraph (C) and inserting the following:

'(C) the attributes of the communications to which the order applies, including the number or other identifier and, if known, the location of the telephone line or other facility to which the pen register or trap and trace device is to be attached or applied, and, in the case of an order authorizing installation and use of a trap and trace device under subsection (a)(2), the geographic limits of the order; and'.

(3) NONDISCLOSURE REQUIREMENTS—Section 3123(d)(2) of title 18, United States Code, is amended—

(A) by inserting 'or other facility' after 'the line'; and

(B) by striking ', or who has been ordered by the court' and inserting 'or applied, or who is obligated by the order'.

(c) DEFINITIONS-

(1) COURT OF COMPETENT JURISDICTION—Section 3127(2) of title 18, United States Code, is amended by striking subparagraph (A) and inserting the following:

'(A) any district court of the United States (including a magistrate judge of such a court) or any United States court of appeals having jurisdiction over the offense being investigated; or'.

(2) PEN REGISTER—Section 3127(3) of title 18, United States Code, is amended—

(A) by striking 'electronic or other impulses' and all that follows through 'is attached' and inserting 'dialing, routing, addressing, or signaling information transmitted by an instrument or facility from which a wire or electronic communication is transmitted, provided, however, that such information shall not include the contents of any communication'; and

(B) by inserting 'or process' after 'device' each place it appears.

(3) TRAP AND TRACE DEVICE—Section 3127(4) of title 18, United States Code, is amended—

(A) by striking 'of an instrument' and all that follows through the semicolon and inserting 'or other dialing, routing, addressing, and signaling information reasonably likely to identify the source of a wire or electronic communication, provided, however, that such information shall not include the contents of any communication;'; and

(B) by inserting 'or process' after 'a device'.

(4) CONFORMING AMENDMENT—Section 3127(1) of title 18, United States Code, is amended—

(A) by striking 'and'; and

(B) by inserting ', and 'contents' after 'electronic communication service'.

(5) TECHNICAL AMENDMENT—Section 3124(d) of title 18, United States Code, is amended by striking 'the terms of'.

(6) CONFORMING AMENDMENT—Section 3124(b) of title 18, United States Code, is amended by inserting 'or other facility' after 'the appropriate line'.

Sec. 217. Interception of Computer Trespasser Communications.

Chapter 119 of title 18, United States Code, is amended—

(1) in section 2510—

(A) in paragraph (18), by striking 'and' at the end;

(B) in paragraph (19), by striking the period and inserting a semicolon; and

(C) by inserting after paragraph (19) the following:

'(20) 'protected computer' has the meaning set forth in section 1030; and

'(21) 'computer trespasser'—

'(A) means a person who accesses a protected computer without authorization and thus has no reasonable expectation of privacy in any communication transmitted to, through, or from the protected computer; and

'(B) does not include a person known by the owner or operator of the protected computer to have an existing contractual relationship with the owner or operator of the protected computer for access to all or part of the protected computer.'; and

(2) in section 2511(2), by inserting at the end the following:

'(i) It shall not be unlawful under this chapter for a person acting under color of law to intercept the wire or electronic communications of a computer trespasser transmitted to, through, or from the protected computer, if—

'(I) the owner or operator of the protected computer authorizes the interception of the computer trespasser's communications on the protected computer;

'(II) the person acting under color of law is lawfully engaged in an investigation;

'(III) the person acting under color of law has reasonable grounds to believe that the contents of the computer trespasser's communications will be relevant to the investigation; and

'(IV) such interception does not acquire communications other than those transmitted to or from the computer trespasser.'.

Sec. 218. Foreign Intelligence Information.

Sections 104(a)(7)(B) and section 303(a)(7)(B) (50 U.S.C. 1804(a)(7)(B) and 1823(a)(7)(B)) of the Foreign Intelligence Surveillance Act of 1978 are each amended by striking 'the purpose' and inserting 'a significant purpose'.

Sec. 219. Single-Jurisdiction Search Warrants for Terrorism.

Rule 41(a) of the Federal Rules of Criminal Procedure is amended by inserting after 'executed' the following: 'and (3) in an investigation of domestic terrorism or international terrorism (as defined in section 2331 of title 18, United States Code), by a Federal magistrate judge in any district in which activities related to the terrorism may have occurred, for a search of property or for a person within or outside the district'.

Sec. 220. Nationwide Service of Search Warrants for Electronic Evidence.

(a) IN GENERAL—Chapter 121 of title 18, United States Code, is amended—

(1) in section 2703, by striking 'under the Federal Rules of Criminal Procedure' every place it appears and inserting 'using the procedures described in the Federal Rules of Criminal Procedure by a court with jurisdiction over the offense under investigation'; and

(2) in section 2711—

(A) in paragraph (1), by striking 'and';

(B) in paragraph (2), by striking the period and inserting '; and'; and

(C) by inserting at the end the following:

'(3) the term 'court of competent jurisdiction' has the meaning assigned by section 3127, and includes any Federal court within that definition, without geographic limitation.'.

(b) CONFORMING AMENDMENT—Section 2703(d) of title 18, United States Code, is amended by striking 'described in section 3127(2)(A)'.

Sec. 221. Trade Sanctions.

(a) IN GENERAL—The Trade Sanctions Reform and Export

Enhancement Act of 2000 (Public Law 106–387; 114 Stat. 1549A-67) is amended—

(1) by amending section 904(2)(C) to read as follows:

'(C) used to facilitate the design, development, or production of chemical or biological weapons, missiles, or weapons of mass destruction.';

(2) in section 906(a)(1)—

(A) by inserting ', the Taliban or the territory of Afghanistan controlled by the Taliban,' after 'Cuba'; and

(B) by inserting ', or in the territory of Afghanistan controlled by the Taliban,' after 'within such country'; and

(3) in section 906(a)(2), by inserting ', or to any other entity in Syria or North Korea' after 'Korea'.

(b) APPLICATION OF THE TRADE SANCTIONS REFORM AND EXPORT ENHANCEMENT ACT—Nothing in the Trade Sanctions Reform and Export Enhancement Act of 2000 shall limit the application or scope of any law establishing criminal or civil penalties, including any Executive order or regulation promulgated pursuant to such laws (or similar or successor laws), for the unlawful export of any agricultural commodity, medicine, or medical device to—

(1) a foreign organization, group, or person designated pursuant to Executive Order No. 12947 of January 23, 1995, as amended;

(2) a Foreign Terrorist Organization pursuant to the Antiterrorism and Effective Death Penalty Act of 1996 (Public Law 104–132);

(3) a foreign organization, group, or person designated pursuant to Executive Order No. 13224 (September 23, 2001);

(4) any narcotics trafficking entity designated pursuant to Executive Order No. 12978 (October 21, 1995) or the Foreign Narcotics Kingpin Designation Act (Public Law 106–120); or

(5) any foreign organization, group, or persons subject to any restriction for its involvement in weapons of mass destruction or missile proliferation.

Sec. 222. Assistance to Law Enforcement Agencies.

Nothing in this Act shall impose any additional technical obligation or requirement on a provider of a wire or electronic communication service or other person to furnish facilities or technical assistance. A provider of a wire or electronic communication service, landlord, custodian, or other person who furnishes facilities or technical assistance pursuant to section 216 shall be reasonably compensated for such reasonable expenditures incurred in providing such facilities or assistance.

Sec. 223. Civil Liability for Certain Unauthorized Disclosures.

(a) Section 2520 of title 18, United States Code, is amended—

(1) in subsection (a), after 'entity', by inserting ', other than the United States,';

(2) by adding at the end the following:

'(f) ADMINISTRATIVE DISCIPLINE—If a court or appropriate department or agency determines that the United States or any of its departments or agencies has violated any provision of this chapter, and the court or appropriate department or agency finds that the circumstances surrounding the violation raise serious questions about whether or not an officer or employee of the United States acted willfully or intentionally with respect to the violation, the department or agency shall, upon receipt of a true and correct copy of the decision and findings of the court or appropriate department or agency promptly initiate a proceeding to determine whether disciplinary action against the officer or employee is warranted. If the head of the department or agency involved determines that disciplinary action is not warranted, he or she shall notify the Inspector General with jurisdiction over the department or agency concerned and shall provide the Inspector General with the reasons for such determination.'; and

(3) by adding a new subsection (g), as follows:

'(g) IMPROPER DISCLOSURE IS VIOLATION—Any willful disclosure or use by an investigative or law enforcement officer or governmental entity of information beyond the extent permitted by section 2517 is a violation of this chapter for purposes of section 2520(a).'.

(b) Section 2707 of title 18, United States Code, is amended—

(1) in subsection (a), after 'entity', by inserting ', other than the United States,';

(2) by striking subsection (d) and inserting the following:

'(d) ADMINISTRATIVE DISCIPLINE—If a court or appropriate department or agency determines that the United States or any of its departments or agencies has violated any provision of this chapter, and the court or appropriate department or agency finds that the circumstances surrounding the violation raise serious questions about whether or not an officer or employee of the United States acted willfully or intentionally with respect to the violation, the department or agency shall, upon receipt of a true and correct copy of the decision and findings of the court or appropriate department or agency promptly initiate a proceeding to determine whether disciplinary action against the officer or employee is warranted. If the head of the department or agency involved determines that disciplinary action is not warranted, he or she shall notify the Inspector General with jurisdiction over the department or agency concerned and shall provide the Inspector General with the reasons for such determination.'; and

(3) by adding a new subsection (g), as follows:

'(g) IMPROPER DISCLOSURE—Any willful disclosure of a 'record', as that term is defined in section 552a(a) of title 5, United States Code, obtained by an investigative or law enforcement officer, or a governmental entity, pursuant to section 2703 of this title, or from a device installed pursuant to section 3123 or 3125 of this title, that is not a disclosure made in the proper performance of the official functions of the officer or governmental entity making the disclosure, is a violation of this chapter. This provision shall not apply to information previously lawfully disclosed (prior to the commencement of any civil or administrative proceeding under this chapter) to the public by a Federal, State, or local governmental entity or by the plaintiff in a civil action under this chapter.'.

(c)(1) Chapter 121 of title 18, United States Code, is amended by adding at the end the following:

'Sec. 2712. Civil actions against the United States

'(a) IN GENERAL—Any person who is aggrieved by any willful violation of this chapter or of chapter 119 of this title or of sections 106(a), 305(a), or 405(a) of the Foreign Intelligence Surveillance Act of 1978 (50 U.S.C. 1801 et seq.) may commence an action in United States District Court against the United States to recover money damages. In any such action, if a person who is aggrieved successfully establishes such a violation of this chapter or of chapter 119 of this title or of the above specific provisions of title 50, the Court may assess as damages—

'(1) actual damages, but not less than $10,000, whichever amount is greater; and

'(2) litigation costs, reasonably incurred.

'(b) PROCEDURES—(1) Any action against the United States under this section may be commenced only after a claim is presented to the appropriate department or agency under the procedures of the Federal Tort Claims Act, as set forth in title 28, United States Code.

'(2) Any action against the United States under this section shall be forever barred unless it is presented in writing to the appropriate Federal agency within 2 years after such claim accrues or unless action is begun within 6 months after the date of mailing, by certified or registered mail, of notice of final denial of the claim by the agency to which it was presented. The claim shall accrue on the date upon which the claimant first has a reasonable opportunity to discover the violation.

'(3) Any action under this section shall be tried to the court without a jury.

'(4) Notwithstanding any other provision of law, the procedures set forth in section 106(f), 305(g), or 405(f) of the Foreign Intelligence Surveillance Act of 1978 (50 U.S.C. 1801 et seq.) shall be the exclusive means by which materials governed by those sections may be reviewed.

'(5) An amount equal to any award against the United States under this section shall be reimbursed by the department or agency concerned to the fund described in section 1304 of title 31, United States Code, out of any appropriation, fund, or other account (excluding any part of such appropriation, fund, or account that is available for the enforcement of any Federal law) that is available for the operating expenses of the department or agency concerned.

'(c) ADMINISTRATIVE DISCIPLINE—If a court or appropriate department or agency determines that the United States or any of its departments or agencies has violated any provision of this chapter, and the court or appropriate department or agency finds that the circumstances surrounding the violation raise serious questions about whether or not an officer or employee of the United States acted willfully or intentionally with respect to the violation, the department or agency shall, upon receipt of a true and correct copy of the decision and findings of the court or appropriate department or agency promptly initiate a proceeding to determine whether disciplinary action against the officer or employee is warranted. If the head of the department or agency involved determines that disciplinary action is not warranted, he or she shall notify the Inspector General with jurisdiction over the department or agency concerned and shall provide the Inspector General with the reasons for such determination.

'(d) EXCLUSIVE REMEDY—Any action against the United States under this subsection shall be the exclusive remedy against the United States for any claims within the purview of this section.

'(e) STAY OF PROCEEDINGS—(1) Upon the motion of the United States, the court shall stay any action commenced under this section if the court determines that civil discovery will adversely affect the ability of the Government to conduct a related investigation or the prosecution of a related criminal case. Such a stay shall toll the limitations periods of paragraph (2) of subsection (b).

'(2) In this subsection, the terms 'related criminal case' and 'related investigation' mean an actual prosecution or investigation in progress at the time at which the request for the stay or any subsequent motion to lift the stay is made. In determining whether an investigation or a criminal case is related to an action commenced under this section, the court shall consider the degree of similarity between the parties, witnesses, facts, and circumstances involved in the 2 proceedings, without requiring that any one or more factors be identical.

'(3) In requesting a stay under paragraph (1), the Government may, in appropriate cases, submit evidence ex parte in order to avoid disclosing any matter that may adversely affect a related investigation or a related criminal case. If the Government makes such an ex parte submission, the plaintiff shall be given an opportunity to make a submission to the court, not ex parte, and the court may, in its discretion, request further information from either party.'.

(2) The table of sections at the beginning of chapter 121 is amended to read as follows:

'2712. Civil action against the United States.'.

Sec. 224. Sunset.

(a) IN GENERAL—Except as provided in subsection (b), this title and the amendments made by this title (other than sections 203(a), 203(c),

205, 208, 210, 211, 213, 216, 219, 221, and 222, and the amendments made by those sections) shall cease to have effect on December 31, 2005.

(b) EXCEPTION—With respect to any particular foreign intelligence investigation that began before the date on which the provisions referred to in subsection (a) cease to have effect, or with respect to any particular offense or potential offense that began or occurred before the date on which such provisions cease to have effect, such provisions shall continue in effect.

Sec. 225. Immunity for Compliance With Fisa Wiretap.

Section 105 of the Foreign Intelligence Surveillance Act of 1978 (50 U.S.C. 1805) is amended by inserting after subsection (g) the following:

'(h) No cause of action shall lie in any court against any provider of a wire or electronic communication service, landlord, custodian, or other person (including any officer, employee, agent, or other specified person thereof) that furnishes any information, facilities, or technical assistance in accordance with a court order or request for emergency assistance under this Act.'.

TITLE III—INTERNATIONAL MONEY LAUNDERING ABATEMENT AND ANTI-TERRORIST FINANCING ACT OF 2001

Sec. 301. Short Title.

This title may be cited as the 'International Money Laundering Abatement and Financial Anti-Terrorism Act of 2001'.

Sec. 302. Findings and Purposes.

(a) FINDINGS—The Congress finds that—

(1) money laundering, estimated by the International Monetary Fund to amount to between 2 and 5 percent of global gross domestic product, which is at least $600,000,000,000 annually, provides the financial fuel that permits transnational criminal enterprises to conduct and expand their operations to the detriment of the safety and security of American citizens;

(2) money laundering, and the defects in financial transparency on which money launderers rely, are critical to the financing of global terrorism and the provision of funds for terrorist attacks;

(3) money launderers subvert legitimate financial mechanisms and banking relationships by using them as protective covering for the movement of criminal proceeds and the financing of crime and terrorism, and, by so doing, can threaten the safety of United States citizens and undermine the integrity of United States financial institutions and of the global financial and trading systems upon which prosperity and growth depend;

(4) certain jurisdictions outside of the United States that offer 'offshore' banking and related facilities designed to provide anonymity, coupled with weak financial supervisory and enforcement regimes, provide essential tools to disguise ownership and movement of criminal funds, derived from, or used to commit, offenses ranging from narcotics trafficking, terrorism, arms smuggling, and trafficking in human beings, to financial frauds that prey on law-abiding citizens;

(5) transactions involving such offshore jurisdictions make it difficult for law enforcement officials and regulators to follow the trail of money earned by criminals, organized international criminal enterprises, and global terrorist organizations;

(6) correspondent banking facilities are one of the banking mechanisms susceptible in some circumstances to manipulation by foreign banks to permit the laundering of funds by hiding the identity of real parties in interest to financial transactions;

(7) private banking services can be susceptible to manipulation by money launderers, for example corrupt foreign government officials, particularly if those services include the creation of offshore accounts and facilities for large personal funds transfers to channel funds into accounts around the globe;

(8) United States anti-money laundering efforts are impeded by outmoded and inadequate statutory provisions that make investigations, prosecutions, and forfeitures more difficult, particularly in cases in which money laundering involves foreign persons, foreign banks, or foreign countries;

(9) the ability to mount effective counter-measures to international money launderers requires national, as well as bilateral and multilateral action, using tools specially designed for that effort; and

(10) the Basle Committee on Banking Regulation and Supervisory Practices and the Financial Action Task Force on Money Laundering, of both of which the United States is a member, have each adopted international anti-money laundering principles and recommendations.

(b) PURPOSES—The purposes of this title are—

(1) to increase the strength of United States measures to prevent, detect, and prosecute international money laundering and the financing of terrorism;

(2) to ensure that—

(A) banking transactions and financial relationships and the conduct of such transactions and relationships, do not contravene the purposes of subchapter II of chapter 53 of title 31, United States Code, section 21 of the Federal Deposit Insurance Act, or chapter 2 of title I of Public Law 91–508 (84 Stat. 1116), or facilitate the evasion of any such provision; and

(B) the purposes of such provisions of law continue to be fulfilled, and such provisions of law are effectively and efficiently administered;

(3) to strengthen the provisions put into place by the Money Laundering Control Act of 1986 (18 U.S.C. 981 note), especially with respect to crimes by non-United States nationals and foreign financial institutions;

(4) to provide a clear national mandate for subjecting to special scrutiny those foreign jurisdictions, financial institutions operating outside of the United States, and classes of international transactions or types of accounts that pose particular, identifiable opportunities for criminal abuse;

(5) to provide the Secretary of the Treasury (in this title referred to as the 'Secretary') with broad discretion, subject to the safeguards provided by the Administrative Procedure Act under title 5, United States Code, to take measures tailored to the particular money laundering problems presented by specific foreign jurisdictions, financial institutions operating outside of the United States, and classes of international transactions or types of accounts;

(6) to ensure that the employment of such measures by the Secretary permits appropriate opportunity for comment by affected financial institutions;

(7) to provide guidance to domestic financial institutions on particular foreign jurisdictions, financial institutions operating outside of the United States, and classes of international transactions that are of primary money laundering concern to the United States Government;

(8) to ensure that the forfeiture of any assets in connection with the anti-terrorist efforts of the United States permits for adequate challenge consistent with providing due process rights;

(9) to clarify the terms of the safe harbor from civil liability for filing suspicious activity reports;

(10) to strengthen the authority of the Secretary to issue and administer geographic targeting orders, and to clarify that violations of such orders or any other requirement imposed under the authority contained in chapter 2 of title I of Public Law 91–508 and subchapters II and III of chapter 53 of title 31, United States Code, may result in criminal and civil penalties;

(11) to ensure that all appropriate elements of the financial services industry are subject to appropriate requirements to report potential money laundering transactions to proper authorities, and that jurisdictional disputes do not hinder examination of compliance by financial institutions with relevant reporting requirements;

(12) to strengthen the ability of financial institutions to maintain the integrity of their employee population; and

(13) to strengthen measures to prevent the use of the United States financial system for personal gain by corrupt foreign officials and to facilitate the repatriation of any stolen assets to the citizens of countries to whom such assets belong.

Sec. 303. 4-Year Congressional Review; Expedited Consideration.

(a) IN GENERAL—Effective on and after the first day of fiscal year 2005, the provisions of this title and the amendments made by this title shall terminate if the Congress enacts a joint resolution, the text after the resolving clause of which is as follows: 'That provisions of the International Money Laundering Abatement and Anti-Terrorist Financing Act of 2001, and the amendments made thereby, shall no longer have the force of law.'.

(b) EXPEDITED CONSIDERATION—Any joint resolution submitted pursuant to this section should be considered by the Congress expeditiously. In particular, it shall be considered in the Senate in accordance with the provisions of section 601(b) of the International Security Assistance and Arms Control Act of 1976.

Subtitle A—International Counter Money Laundering and Related Measures

Sec. 311. Special Measures for Jurisdictions, Financial Institutions, or International Transactions of Primary Money Laundering Concern.

(a) IN GENERAL—Subchapter II of chapter 53 of title 31, United States Code, is amended by inserting after section 5318 the following new section:

'Sec. 5318A. Special measures for jurisdictions, financial institutions, or international transactions of primary money laundering concern

'(a) INTERNATIONAL COUNTER-MONEY LAUNDERING REQUIREMENTS-

'(1) IN GENERAL—The Secretary of the Treasury may require domestic financial institutions and domestic financial agencies to take 1 or more of the special measures described in subsection (b) if the Secretary finds that reasonable grounds exist for concluding that a jurisdiction outside of the United States, 1 or more financial institutions operating outside of the United States, 1 or more classes of transactions within, or involving, a jurisdiction outside of the United States, or 1 or more types of accounts is of primary money laundering concern, in accordance with subsection (c).

'(2) FORM OF REQUIREMENT—The special measures described in—

'(A) subsection (b) may be imposed in such sequence or combination as the Secretary shall determine;

'(B) paragraphs (1) through (4) of subsection (b) may be imposed by regulation, order, or otherwise as permitted by law; and

'(C) subsection (b)(5) may be imposed only by regulation.

'(3) DURATION OF ORDERS; RULEMAKING—Any order by which a special measure described in paragraphs (1) through (4) of subsection (b) is imposed (other than an order described in section 5326)—

'(A) shall be issued together with a notice of proposed rulemaking relating to the imposition of such special measure; and

'(B) may not remain in effect for more than 120 days, except pursuant to a rule promulgated on or before the end of the 120-day period beginning on the date of issuance of such order.

'(4) PROCESS FOR SELECTING SPECIAL MEASURES—In selecting which special measure or measures to take under this subsection, the Secretary of the Treasury—

'(A) shall consult with the Chairman of the Board of Governors of the Federal Reserve System, any other appropriate Federal banking agency, as defined in section 3 of the Federal Deposit Insurance Act, the Secretary of State, the Securities and Exchange Commission, the Commodity Futures Trading Commission, the National Credit Union Administration Board, and in the sole discretion of the Secretary, such other agencies and interested parties as the Secretary may find to be appropriate; and

'(B) shall consider—

'(i) whether similar action has been or is being taken by other nations or multilateral groups;

'(ii) whether the imposition of any particular special measure would create a significant competitive disadvantage, including any undue cost or burden associated with compliance, for financial institutions organized or licensed in the United States;

'(iii) the extent to which the action or the timing of the action would have a significant adverse systemic impact on the international payment, clearance, and settlement system, or on legitimate business activities involving the particular jurisdiction, institution, or class of transactions; and

'(iv) the effect of the action on United States national security and foreign policy.

'(5) NO LIMITATION ON OTHER AUTHORITY—This section shall not be construed as superseding or otherwise restricting any other authority granted to the Secretary, or to any other agency, by this subchapter or otherwise.

'(b) SPECIAL MEASURES—The special measures referred to in subsection (a), with respect to a jurisdiction outside of the United States, financial institution operating outside of the United States, class of transaction within, or involving, a jurisdiction outside of the United States, or 1 or more types of accounts are as follows:

'(1) RECORDKEEPING AND REPORTING OF CERTAIN FINANCIAL TRANSACTIONS-

'(A) IN GENERAL—The Secretary of the Treasury may require any domestic financial institution or domestic financial agency to maintain records, file reports, or both, concerning the aggregate amount of transactions, or concerning each transaction, with respect to a jurisdiction outside of the United States, 1 or more financial institutions operating outside of the United States, 1 or more classes of transactions within, or involving, a jurisdiction outside of the United States, or 1 or more types of accounts if the Secretary finds any such jurisdiction, institution, or class of transactions to be of primary money laundering concern.

'(B) FORM OF RECORDS AND REPORTS—Such records and reports shall be made and retained at such time, in such manner, and for such period of time, as the Secretary shall determine, and shall include such information as the Secretary may determine, including—

'(i) the identity and address of the participants in a transaction or relationship, including the identity of the originator of any funds transfer;

'(ii) the legal capacity in which a participant in any transaction is acting;

'(iii) the identity of the beneficial owner of the funds involved in any transaction, in accordance with such procedures as the Secretary determines to be reasonable and practicable to obtain and retain the information; and

'(iv) a description of any transaction.

'(2) INFORMATION RELATING TO BENEFICIAL OWNERSHIP—In addition to any other requirement under any other provision of law, the Secretary may require any domestic financial institution or domestic financial agency to take such steps as the Secretary may determine to be reasonable and practicable to obtain and retain information concerning the beneficial ownership of any account opened or maintained in the United States by a foreign person (other than a foreign entity whose shares are subject to public reporting requirements or are listed and traded on a regulated exchange or trading market), or a representative of such a foreign person, that involves a jurisdiction outside of the United States, 1 or more financial institutions operating outside of the United States, 1 or more classes of transactions within, or involving, a jurisdiction outside of the United States, or 1 or more types of accounts if the Secretary finds any such jurisdiction, institution, or transaction or type of account to be of primary money laundering concern.

'(3) INFORMATION RELATING TO CERTAIN PAYABLE-THROUGH ACCOUNTS—If the Secretary finds a jurisdiction outside of the United States, 1 or more financial institutions operating outside of the United States, or 1 or more classes of transactions within, or involving, a jurisdiction outside of the United States to be of primary money laundering concern, the Secretary may require any domestic financial institution or domestic financial agency that opens or maintains a payable-through account in the United States for a foreign financial institution involving any such jurisdiction or any such financial institution operating outside of the United States, or a payable through account through which any such transaction may be conducted, as a condition of opening or maintaining such account—

'(A) to identify each customer (and representative of such customer) of such financial institution who is permitted to use, or whose transactions are routed through, such payable-through account; and

'(B) to obtain, with respect to each such customer (and each such representative), information that is substantially comparable to that which the depository institution obtains in the ordinary course of business with respect to its customers residing in the United States.

'(4) INFORMATION RELATING TO CERTAIN CORRESPONDENT ACCOUNTS—If the Secretary finds a jurisdiction outside of the United States, 1 or more financial institutions operating outside of the United States, or 1 or more classes of transactions within, or involving, a jurisdiction outside of the United States to be of primary money laundering concern, the Secretary may require any domestic financial institution or domestic financial agency that opens or maintains a correspondent account in the United States for a foreign financial institution involving any such jurisdiction or any such financial institution operating outside of the United States, or a correspondent account through which any such transaction may be conducted, as a condition of opening or maintaining such account—

'(A) to identify each customer (and representative of such customer) of any such financial institution who is permitted to use, or whose transactions are routed through, such correspondent account; and

'(B) to obtain, with respect to each such customer (and each such representative), information that is substantially comparable to that which the depository institution obtains in the ordinary course of business with respect to its customers residing in the United States.

'(5) PROHIBITIONS OR CONDITIONS ON OPENING OR MAINTAINING CERTAIN CORRESPONDENT OR PAYABLE-THROUGH ACCOUNTS—If the Secretary finds a jurisdiction outside of the United States, 1 or more financial institutions operating outside of the United States, or 1 or more classes of transactions within, or involving, a jurisdiction outside of the United States to be of primary money laundering concern, the Secretary, in consultation with the Secretary of State, the Attorney General, and the Chairman of the Board of Governors of the Federal Reserve System, may prohibit, or impose conditions upon, the opening or maintaining in the United States of a correspondent account or payable-through account by any domestic financial institution or domestic financial agency for or on behalf of a foreign banking institution, if such correspondent account or payable-through account involves any such jurisdiction or institution, or if any such transaction may be conducted through such correspondent account or payable-through account.

'(c) CONSULTATIONS AND INFORMATION TO BE CONSIDERED IN FINDING JURISDICTIONS, INSTITUTIONS, TYPES OF ACCOUNTS, OR TRANSACTIONS TO BE OF PRIMARY MONEY LAUNDERING CONCERN-

'(1) IN GENERAL—In making a finding that reasonable grounds exist for concluding that a jurisdiction outside of the United States, 1 or more financial institutions operating outside of the United States, 1 or more classes of transactions within, or involving, a jurisdiction outside of the United States, or 1 or more types of accounts is of primary money laundering concern so as to authorize the Secretary of the Treasury to take 1 or more of the special measures described in subsection (b), the Secretary shall consult with the Secretary of State and the Attorney General.

'(2) ADDITIONAL CONSIDERATIONS—In making a finding described in paragraph (1), the Secretary shall consider in addition such information as the Secretary determines to be relevant, including the following potentially relevant factors:

'(A) JURISDICTIONAL FACTORS—In the case of a particular jurisdiction—

'(i) evidence that organized criminal groups, international terrorists, or both, have transacted business in that jurisdiction;

'(ii) the extent to which that jurisdiction or financial institutions operating in that jurisdiction offer bank secrecy or special regulatory advantages to nonresidents or non-domiciliaries of that jurisdiction;

'(iii) the substance and quality of administration of the bank supervisory and counter-money laundering laws of that jurisdiction;

'(iv) the relationship between the volume of financial transactions occurring in that jurisdiction and the size of the economy of the jurisdiction;

'(v) the extent to which that jurisdiction is characterized as an offshore banking or secrecy haven by credible international organizations or multilateral expert groups;

'(vi) whether the United States has a mutual legal assistance treaty with that jurisdiction, and the experience of United States law enforcement officials and regulatory officials in obtaining information about transactions originating in or routed through or to such jurisdiction; and

'(vii) the extent to which that jurisdiction is characterized by high levels of official or institutional corruption.

'(B) INSTITUTIONAL FACTORS—In the case of a decision to apply 1 or more of the special measures described in subsection (b) only to a financial institution or institutions, or to a transaction or class of transactions, or to a type of account, or to all 3, within or involving a particular jurisdiction—

'(i) the extent to which such financial institutions, transactions, or types of accounts are used to facilitate or promote money laundering in or through the jurisdiction;

'(ii) the extent to which such institutions, transactions, or types of accounts are used for legitimate business purposes in the jurisdiction; and

'(iii) the extent to which such action is sufficient to ensure, with respect to transactions involving the jurisdiction and institutions operating in the jurisdiction, that the purposes of this subchapter continue to be fulfilled, and to guard against international money laundering and other financial crimes.

'(d) NOTIFICATION OF SPECIAL MEASURES INVOKED BY THE SECRETARY—Not later than 10 days after the date of any action taken by the Secretary of the Treasury under subsection (a)(1), the Secretary shall notify, in writing, the Committee on Financial Services of the House of Representatives and the Committee on Banking, Housing, and Urban Affairs of the Senate of any such action.

'(e) DEFINITIONS—Notwithstanding any other provision of this subchapter, for purposes of this section and subsections (i) and (j) of section 5318, the following definitions shall apply:

'(1) BANK DEFINITIONS—The following definitions shall apply with respect to a bank:

'(A) ACCOUNT—The term 'account'—

'(i) means a formal banking or business relationship established to provide regular services, dealings, and other financial transactions; and

'(ii) includes a demand deposit, savings deposit, or other transaction or asset account and a credit account or other extension of credit.

'(B) CORRESPONDENT ACCOUNT—The term 'correspondent account' means an account established to receive deposits from, make payments on behalf of a foreign financial institution, or handle other financial transactions related to such institution.

'(C) PAYABLE-THROUGH ACCOUNT—The term 'payable-through account' means an account, including a transaction account (as defined in section 19(b)(1)(C) of the Federal Reserve Act), opened at a depository institution by a foreign financial institution by means of which the foreign financial institution permits its customers to engage, either directly or through a subaccount, in banking activities usual in connection with the business of banking in the United States.

'(2) DEFINITIONS APPLICABLE TO INSTITUTIONS OTHER THAN BANKS—With respect to any financial institution other than a bank, the Secretary shall, after consultation with the appropriate Federal functional regulators (as defined in section 509 of the Gramm-Leach-Bliley Act), define by regulation the term 'account', and shall include within the meaning of that term, to the extent, if any, that the Secretary deems appropriate, arrangements similar to payable-through and correspondent accounts.

'(3) REGULATORY DEFINITION OF BENEFICIAL OWNERSHIP—The Secretary shall promulgate regulations defining beneficial ownership of an account for purposes of this section and subsections (i) and (j) of section 5318. Such regulations shall address issues related to an individual's authority to fund, direct, or manage the account (including, without limitation, the power to direct payments into or out of the account), and an individual's material interest in the income or corpus of the account, and shall ensure that the identification of individuals under this section does not extend to any individual whose beneficial interest in the income or corpus of the account is immaterial.

'(4) OTHER TERMS—The Secretary may, by regulation, further define the terms in paragraphs (1), (2), and (3), and define other terms for the purposes of this section, as the Secretary deems appropriate.'.

(b) CLERICAL AMENDMENT—The table of sections for subchapter II of chapter 53 of title 31, United States Code, is amended by inserting after the item relating to section 5318 the following new item:

'5318A. Special measures for jurisdictions, financial institutions, or international transactions of primary money laundering concern.'.

Sec. 312. Special Due Diligence for Correspondent Accounts and Private Banking Accounts.

(a) IN GENERAL—Section 5318 of title 31, United States Code, is amended by adding at the end the following:

'(i) DUE DILIGENCE FOR UNITED STATES PRIVATE BANKING AND CORRESPONDENT BANK ACCOUNTS INVOLVING FOREIGN PERSONS-

'(1) IN GENERAL—Each financial institution that establishes, maintains, administers, or manages a private banking account or a correspondent account in the United States for a non-United States person, including a foreign individual visiting the United States, or a representative of a non-United States person shall establish appropriate, specific, and, where necessary, enhanced, due diligence policies, procedures, and controls that are reasonably designed to detect and report instances of money laundering through those accounts.

'(2) ADDITIONAL STANDARDS FOR CERTAIN CORRESPONDENT ACCOUNTS-

'(A) IN GENERAL—Subparagraph (B) shall apply if a correspondent account is requested or maintained by, or on behalf of, a foreign bank operating—

'(i) under an offshore banking license; or

'(ii) under a banking license issued by a foreign country that has been designated—

'(I) as noncooperative with international anti-money laundering principles or procedures by an intergovernmental group or organization of which the United States is a member, with which designation the United States representative to the group or organization concurs; or

'(II) by the Secretary of the Treasury as warranting special measures due to money laundering concerns.

'(B) POLICIES, PROCEDURES, AND CONTROLS—The enhanced due diligence policies, procedures, and controls required under paragraph (1) shall, at a minimum, ensure that the financial institution in the United States takes reasonable steps—

'(i) to ascertain for any such foreign bank, the shares of which are not publicly traded, the identity of each of the owners of the foreign bank, and the nature and extent of the ownership interest of each such owner;

'(ii) to conduct enhanced scrutiny of such account to guard against money laundering and report any suspicious transactions under subsection (g); and

'(iii) to ascertain whether such foreign bank provides correspondent accounts to other foreign banks and, if so, the identity of those foreign banks and related due diligence information, as appropriate under paragraph (1).

'(3) MINIMUM STANDARDS FOR PRIVATE BANKING ACCOUNTS—If a private banking account is requested or maintained by, or on behalf of, a non-United States person, then the due diligence policies, procedures, and controls required under paragraph (1) shall, at a minimum, ensure that the financial institution takes reasonable steps—

'(A) to ascertain the identity of the nominal and beneficial owners of, and the source of funds deposited into, such account as needed to guard against money laundering and report any suspicious transactions under subsection (g); and

'(B) to conduct enhanced scrutiny of any such account that is requested or maintained by, or on behalf of, a senior foreign political figure, or any immediate family member or close associate of a senior foreign political figure that is reasonably designed to detect and report transactions that may involve the proceeds of foreign corruption.

'(4) DEFINITION—For purposes of this subsection, the following definitions shall apply:

'(A) OFFSHORE BANKING LICENSE—The term 'offshore banking license' means a license to conduct banking activities which, as a condition of the license, prohibits the licensed entity from conducting banking activities with the citizens of, or with the local currency of, the country which issued the license.

'(B) PRIVATE BANKING ACCOUNT—The term 'private

banking account' means an account (or any combination of accounts) that—

'(i) requires a minimum aggregate deposits of funds or other assets of not less than $1,000,000;

'(ii) is established on behalf of 1 or more individuals who have a direct or beneficial ownership interest in the account; and

'(iii) is assigned to, or is administered or managed by, in whole or in part, an officer, employee, or agent of a financial institution acting as a liaison between the financial institution and the direct or beneficial owner of the account.'.

(b) REGULATORY AUTHORITY AND EFFECTIVE DATE-

(1) REGULATORY AUTHORITY—Not later than 180 days after the date of enactment of this Act, the Secretary, in consultation with the appropriate Federal functional regulators (as defined in section 509 of the Gramm-Leach-Bliley Act) of the affected financial institutions, shall further delineate, by regulation, the due diligence policies, procedures, and controls required under section 5318(i)(1) of title 31, United States Code, as added by this section.

(2) EFFECTIVE DATE—Section 5318(i) of title 31, United States Code, as added by this section, shall take effect 270 days after the date of enactment of this Act, whether or not final regulations are issued under paragraph (1), and the failure to issue such regulations shall in no way affect the enforceability of this section or the amendments made by this section. Section 5318(i) of title 31, United States Code, as added by this section, shall apply with respect to accounts covered by that section 5318(i), that are opened before, on, or after the date of enactment of this Act.

Sec. 313. Prohibition on United States Correspondent Accounts with Foreign Shell Banks.

(a) IN GENERAL—Section 5318 of title 31, United States Code, as amended by this title, is amended by adding at the end the following:

'(j) PROHIBITION ON UNITED STATES CORRESPONDENT ACCOUNTS WITH FOREIGN SHELL BANKS-

'(1) IN GENERAL—A financial institution described in subparagraphs (A) through (G) of section 5312(a)(2) (in this subsection referred to as a 'covered financial institution') shall not establish, maintain, administer, or manage a correspondent account in the United States for, or on behalf of, a foreign bank that does not have a physical presence in any country.

'(2) PREVENTION OF INDIRECT SERVICE TO FOREIGN SHELL BANKS—A covered financial institution shall take reasonable steps to ensure that any correspondent account established, maintained, administered, or managed by that covered financial institution in the United States for a foreign bank is not being used by that foreign bank to indirectly provide banking services to another foreign bank that does not have a physical presence in any country. The Secretary of the Treasury shall, by regulation, delineate the reasonable steps necessary to comply with this paragraph.

'(3) EXCEPTION—Paragraphs (1) and (2) do not prohibit a covered financial institution from providing a correspondent account to a foreign bank, if the foreign bank—

'(A) is an affiliate of a depository institution, credit union, or foreign bank that maintains a physical presence in the United States or a foreign country, as applicable; and

'(B) is subject to supervision by a banking authority in the country regulating the affiliated depository institution, credit union, or foreign bank described in subparagraph (A), as applicable.

'(4) DEFINITIONS—For purposes of this subsection—

'(A) the term 'affiliate' means a foreign bank that is controlled by or is under common control with a depository institution, credit union, or foreign bank; and

'(B) the term 'physical presence' means a place of business that—

'(i) is maintained by a foreign bank;

'(ii) is located at a fixed address (other than solely an electronic address) in a country in which the foreign bank is authorized to conduct banking activities, at which location the foreign bank—

'(I) employs 1 or more individuals on a full-time basis; and

'(II) maintains operating records related to its banking activities; and '(iii) is subject to inspection by the banking authority which licensed the foreign bank to conduct banking activities.'.

(b) EFFECTIVE DATE—The amendment made by subsection (a) shall take effect at the end of the 60-day period beginning on the date of enactment of this Act.

Sec. 314. Cooperative Efforts to Deter Money Laundering.

(a) COOPERATION AMONG FINANCIAL INSTITUTIONS, REGULATORY AUTHORITIES, AND LAW ENFORCEMENT AUTHORITIES-

(1) REGULATIONS—The Secretary shall, within 120 days after the date of enactment of this Act, adopt regulations to encourage further cooperation among financial institutions, their regulatory authorities, and law enforcement authorities, with the specific purpose of encouraging regulatory authorities and law enforcement authorities to share with financial institutions information regarding individuals, entities, and organizations engaged in or reasonably suspected based on credible evidence of engaging in terrorist acts or money laundering activities.

(2) COOPERATION AND INFORMATION SHARING PROCEDURES—The regulations adopted under paragraph (1) may include or create procedures for cooperation and information sharing focusing on—

(A) matters specifically related to the finances of terrorist groups, the means by which terrorist groups transfer funds around the world and within the United States, including through the use of charitable organizations, nonprofit organizations, and nongovernmental organizations, and the extent to which financial institutions in the United States are unwittingly involved in such finances and the extent to which such institutions are at risk as a result;

(B) the relationship, particularly the financial relationship, between international narcotics traffickers and foreign terrorist organizations, the extent to which their memberships overlap and engage in joint activities, and the extent to which they cooperate with each other in raising and transferring funds for their respective purposes; and

(C) means of facilitating the identification of accounts and transactions involving terrorist groups and facilitating the exchange of information concerning such accounts and transactions between financial institutions and law enforcement organizations.

(3) CONTENTS—The regulations adopted pursuant to paragraph (1) may—

(A) require that each financial institution designate 1 or more persons to receive information concerning, and to monitor accounts of individuals, entities, and organizations identified, pursuant to paragraph (1); and

(B) further establish procedures for the protection of the shared information, consistent with the capacity, size, and nature of the institution to which the particular procedures apply.

(4) RULE OF CONSTRUCTION—The receipt of information by a financial institution pursuant to this section shall not relieve or otherwise modify the obligations of the financial institution with respect to any other person or account.

(5) USE OF INFORMATION—Information received by a financial institution pursuant to this section shall not be used for any purpose other than identifying and reporting on activities that may involve terrorist acts or money laundering activities.

(b) COOPERATION AMONG FINANCIAL INSTITUTIONS— Upon notice provided to the Secretary, 2 or more financial institutions and any association of financial institutions may share information with one another regarding individuals, entities, organizations, and countries suspected of possible terrorist or money laundering activities. A financial institution or association that transmits, receives, or shares such information for the purposes of identifying and reporting activities that may involve terrorist acts or money laundering activities shall not be liable to any person under any law or regulation of the United States, any constitution, law, or regulation of any State or political subdivision thereof, or under any contract or other legally enforceable agreement (including any arbitration agreement), for such disclosure or for any failure to provide notice of such disclosure to the person who is the subject of such disclosure, or any other person identified in the disclosure, except where such transmission, receipt, or sharing violates this section or regulations promulgated pursuant to this section.

(c) RULE OF CONSTRUCTION—Compliance with the provisions of this title requiring or allowing financial institutions and any association of financial institutions to disclose or share information regarding individuals, entities, and organizations engaged in or suspected of engaging in terrorist acts or money laundering activities shall not constitute a violation of the provisions of title V of the Gramm-Leach-Bliley Act (Public Law 106–102).

(d) REPORTS TO THE FINANCIAL SERVICES INDUSTRY ON SUSPICIOUS FINANCIAL ACTIVITIES—At least semiannually, the Secretary shall—

> (1) publish a report containing a detailed analysis identifying patterns of suspicious activity and other investigative insights derived from suspicious activity reports and investigations conducted by Federal, State, and local law enforcement agencies to the extent appropriate; and

> (2) distribute such report to financial institutions (as defined in section 5312 of title 31, United States Code).

Sec. 315. Inclusion of Foreign Corruption Offenses as Money Laundering Crimes.

Section 1956(c)(7) of title 18, United States Code, is amended—

> (1) in subparagraph (B)—

>> (A) in clause (ii), by striking 'or destruction of property by means of explosive or fire' and inserting 'destruction of property by means of explosive or fire, or a crime of violence (as defined in section 16)';

>> (B) in clause (iii), by striking '1978' and inserting '1978)'; and

>> (C) by adding at the end the following:

>>> '(iv) bribery of a public official, or the misappropriation, theft, or embezzlement of public funds by or for the benefit of a public official;

>>> '(v) smuggling or export control violations involving—

>>>> '(I) an item controlled on the United States Munitions List established under section 38 of the Arms Export Control Act (22 U.S.C. 2778); or

'(II)an item controlled under regulations under the Export Administration Regulations (15 C.F.R. Parts 730–774); or

'(vi) an offense with respect to which the United States would be obligated by a multilateral treaty, either to extradite the alleged offender or to submit the case for prosecution, if the offender were found within the territory of the United States;'; and

(2) in subparagraph (D)—

(A) by inserting 'section 541 (relating to goods falsely classified),' before 'section 542';

(B) by inserting 'section 922(1) (relating to the unlawful importation of firearms), section 924(n) (relating to firearms trafficking),' before 'section 956';

(C) by inserting 'section 1030 (relating to computer fraud and abuse),' before '1032'; and

(D) by inserting 'any felony violation of the Foreign Agents Registration Act of 1938,' before 'or any felony violation of the Foreign Corrupt Practices Act'.

Sec. 316. Anti-Terrorist Forfeiture Protection.

(a) RIGHT TO CONTEST—An owner of property that is confiscated under any provision of law relating to the confiscation of assets of suspected international terrorists, may contest that confiscation by filing a claim in the manner set forth in the Federal Rules of Civil Procedure (Supplemental Rules for Certain Admiralty and Maritime Claims), and asserting as an affirmative defense that—

(1) the property is not subject to confiscation under such provision of law; or

(2) the innocent owner provisions of section 983(d) of title 18, United States Code, apply to the case.

(b) EVIDENCE—In considering a claim filed under this section, a court may admit evidence that is otherwise inadmissible under the Federal Rules of Evidence, if the court determines that the evidence is reliable, and that compliance with the Federal Rules of Evidence may jeopardize the national security interests of the United States.

(c) CLARIFICATIONS-

(1) PROTECTION OF RIGHTS—The exclusion of certain provisions of Federal law from the definition of the term 'civil forfeiture statute' in section 983(i) of title 18, United States Code, shall not be construed to deny an owner of property the right to contest the confiscation of assets of suspected international terrorists under—

(A) subsection (a) of this section;

(B) the Constitution; or

(C) subchapter II of chapter 5 of title 5, United States Code (commonly known as the 'Administrative Procedure Act').

(2) SAVINGS CLAUSE—Nothing in this section shall limit or otherwise affect any other remedies that may be available to an owner of property under section 983 of title 18, United States Code, or any other provision of law.

(d) TECHNICAL CORRECTION—Section 983(i)(2)(D) of title 18, United States Code, is amended by inserting 'or the International Emergency Economic Powers Act (IEEPA) (50 U.S.C. 1701 et seq.)' before the semicolon.

Sec. 317. Long-Arm Jurisdiction Over Foreign Money Launderers.

Section 1956(b) of title 18, United States Code, is amended—

(1) by redesignating paragraphs (1) and (2) as subparagraphs (A) and (B), respectively, and moving the margins 2 ems to the right;

(2) by inserting after '(b)' the following: 'PENALTIES-
'(1) IN GENERAL—';

(3) by inserting ', or section 1957' after 'or (a)(3)'; and

(4) by adding at the end the following:

'(2) JURISDICTION OVER FOREIGN PERSONS—For purposes of adjudicating an action filed or enforcing a penalty ordered under this section, the district courts shall have jurisdiction over any foreign person, including any financial institution authorized under the laws of a foreign country, against whom the action is brought, if service of process upon the foreign person is made under the Federal Rules of Civil Procedure or the laws of the country in which the foreign person is found, and—

'(A) the foreign person commits an offense under subsection (a) involving a financial transaction that occurs in whole or in part in the United States;

'(B) the foreign person converts, to his or her own use, property in which the United States has an ownership interest by virtue of the entry of an order of forfeiture by a court of the United States; or

'(C) the foreign person is a financial institution that maintains a bank account at a financial institution in the United States.

'(3) COURT AUTHORITY OVER ASSETS—A court described in paragraph (2) may issue a pretrial restraining order or take any other action necessary to ensure that any bank account or other property held by the defendant in the United States is available to satisfy a judgment under this section.

'(4) FEDERAL RECEIVER-

'(A) IN GENERAL—A court described in paragraph (2) may appoint a Federal Receiver, in accordance with subparagraph (B) of this paragraph, to collect, marshal, and take custody, control, and possession of all assets of the defendant, wherever located, to satisfy a civil judgment under this subsection, a forfeiture judgment under section 981 or 982, or a criminal sentence under section 1957 or subsection (a) of this section, including an order of restitution to any victim of a specified unlawful activity.

'(B) APPOINTMENT AND AUTHORITY—A Federal Receiver described in subparagraph (A)—

'(i) may be appointed upon application of a Federal prosecutor or a Federal or State regulator, by the court having jurisdiction over the defendant in the case;

'(ii) shall be an officer of the court, and the powers of the Federal Receiver shall include the powers set out in section 754 of title 28, United States Code; and

'(iii) shall have standing equivalent to that of a Federal prosecutor for the purpose of submitting requests to obtain information regarding the assets of the defendant—

'(I) from the Financial Crimes Enforcement Network of the Department of the Treasury; or

'(II) from a foreign country pursuant to a mutual legal assistance treaty, multilateral agreement, or other arrangement for international law enforcement assistance, provided that such requests are in accordance with the policies and procedures of the Attorney General.'.

Sec. 318 Laundering Money Through a Foreign Bank.

Section 1956(c) of title 18, United States Code, is amended by striking paragraph (6) and inserting the following:

'(6) the term 'financial institution' includes—

'(A) any financial institution, as defined in section 5312(a)(2) of title 31, United States Code, or the regulations promulgated thereunder; and

'(B) any foreign bank, as defined in section 1 of the International Banking Act of 1978 (12 U.S.C. 3101).'.

Sec. 319. Forfeiture of Funds in United States Interbank Accounts.

(a) FORFEITURE FROM UNITED STATES INTERBANK ACCOUNT—Section 981 of title 18, United States Code, is amended by adding at the end the following:

'(k) INTERBANK ACCOUNTS-

'(1) IN GENERAL-

'(A) IN GENERAL—For the purpose of a forfeiture under this section or under the Controlled Substances Act (21 U.S.C. 801 et seq.), if funds are deposited into an account at a foreign bank, and that foreign bank has an interbank account in the United States with a covered financial institution (as defined in section 5318(j)(1) of title 31), the funds shall be deemed to have been deposited into the interbank account in the United States, and any restraining order, seizure warrant, or arrest warrant in rem regarding the funds may be served on the covered financial institution, and funds in the interbank account, up to the value of the funds deposited into the account at the foreign bank, may be restrained, seized, or arrested.

'(B) AUTHORITY TO SUSPEND—The Attorney General, in consultation with the Secretary of the Treasury, may suspend or terminate a forfeiture under this section if the Attorney

General determines that a conflict of law exists between the laws of the jurisdiction in which the foreign bank is located and the laws of the United States with respect to liabilities arising from the restraint, seizure, or arrest of such funds, and that such suspension or termination would be in the interest of justice and would not harm the national interests of the United States.

'(2) NO REQUIREMENT FOR GOVERNMENT TO TRACE FUNDS—If a forfeiture action is brought against funds that are restrained, seized, or arrested under paragraph (1), it shall not be necessary for the Government to establish that the funds are directly traceable to the funds that were deposited into the foreign bank, nor shall it be necessary for the Government to rely on the application of section 984.

'(3) CLAIMS BROUGHT BY OWNER OF THE FUNDS—If a forfeiture action is instituted against funds restrained, seized, or arrested under paragraph (1), the owner of the funds deposited into the account at the foreign bank may contest the forfeiture by filing a claim under section 983.

'(4) DEFINITIONS—For purposes of this subsection, the following definitions shall apply:

'(A) INTERBANK ACCOUNT—The term 'interbank account' has the same meaning as in section 984(c)(2)(B).

'(B) OWNER-

'(i) IN GENERAL—Except as provided in clause (ii), the term 'owner'—

'(I) means the person who was the owner, as that term is defined in section 983(d)(6), of the funds that were deposited into the foreign bank at the time such funds were deposited; and

'(II) does not include either the foreign bank or any financial institution acting as an intermediary in the transfer of the funds into the interbank account.

'(ii) EXCEPTION—The foreign bank may be considered the 'owner' of the funds (and no other person shall qualify as the owner of such funds) only if—

'(I) the basis for the forfeiture action is wrongdoing committed by the foreign bank; or

'(II) the foreign bank establishes, by a preponderance of the evidence, that prior to the restraint, seizure, or arrest of the funds, the foreign bank had discharged all or part of its obligation to the prior owner of the funds, in which case the foreign bank shall be deemed the owner of the funds to the extent of such discharged obligation.'.

(b) BANK RECORDS—Section 5318 of title 31, United States Code, as amended by this title, is amended by adding at the end the following:

'(k) BANK RECORDS RELATED TO ANTI-MONEY LAUNDERING PROGRAMS-

'(1) DEFINITIONS—For purposes of this subsection, the following definitions shall apply:

'(A) APPROPRIATE FEDERAL BANKING AGENCY—The term 'appropriate Federal banking agency' has the same meaning as in section 3 of the Federal Deposit Insurance Act (12 U.S.C. 1813).

'(B) INCORPORATED TERM—The term 'correspondent account' has the same meaning as in section 5318A(f)(1)(B).

'(2) 120-HOUR RULE—Not later than 120 hours after receiving a request by an appropriate Federal banking agency for information related to anti-money laundering compliance by a covered financial institution or a customer of such institution, a covered financial institution shall provide to the appropriate Federal banking agency, or make available at a location specified by the representative of the appropriate Federal banking agency, information and account documentation for any account opened, maintained, administered or managed in the United States by the covered financial institution.

'(3) FOREIGN BANK RECORDS-

'(A) SUMMONS OR SUBPOENA OF RECORDS-

'(i) IN GENERAL—The Secretary of the Treasury or the Attorney General may issue a summons or subpoena to any foreign bank that maintains a correspondent account in the United States and request records related to such correspondent account, including records maintained outside of the United States relating to the deposit of funds into the foreign bank.

'(ii) SERVICE OF SUMMONS OR SUBPOENA—A summons or subpoena referred to in clause (i) may be served on the foreign bank in the United States if the foreign bank has a representative in the United States, or in a foreign country pursuant to any mutual legal assistance treaty, multilateral agreement, or other request for international law enforcement assistance.

'(B) ACCEPTANCE OF SERVICE-

'(i) MAINTAINING RECORDS IN THE UNITED STATES—Any covered financial institution which maintains a correspondent account in the United States for a foreign bank shall maintain records in the United States identifying the owners of such foreign bank and the name and address of a person who resides in the United States and is authorized to accept service of legal process for records regarding the correspondent account.

'(ii) LAW ENFORCEMENT REQUEST—Upon receipt of a written request from a Federal law enforcement officer for information required to be maintained under this paragraph, the covered financial institution shall provide the information to the requesting officer not later than 7 days after receipt of the request.

'(C) TERMINATION OF CORRESPONDENT RELATIONSHIP-

'(i) TERMINATION UPON RECEIPT OF NOTICE— A covered financial institution shall terminate any correspondent relationship with a foreign bank not later than 10 business days after receipt of written notice from the Secretary or the Attorney General (in each case, after consultation with the other) that the foreign bank has failed—

'(I) to comply with a summons or subpoena issued under subparagraph (A); or

'(II) to initiate proceedings in a United States court contesting such summons or subpoena.

'(ii) LIMITATION ON LIABILITY—A covered financial institution shall not be liable to any person in any court or arbitration proceeding for terminating a correspondent relationship in accordance with this subsection.

'(iii)FAILURE TO TERMINATE RELATIONSHIP—
Failure to terminate a correspondent relationship in accordance with this subsection shall render the covered financial institution liable for a civil penalty of up to $10,000 per day until the correspondent relationship is so terminated.'.

(c) GRACE PERIOD—Financial institutions shall have 60 days from the date of enactment of this Act to comply with the provisions of section 5318(k) of title 31, United States Code, as added by this section.

(d) AUTHORITY TO ORDER CONVICTED CRIMINAL TO RETURN PROPERTY LOCATED ABROAD-

(1) FORFEITURE OF SUBSTITUTE PROPERTY—Section 413(p) of the Controlled Substances Act (21 U.S.C. 853) is amended to read as follows:

'(p) FORFEITURE OF SUBSTITUTE PROPERTY-

'(1) IN GENERAL—Paragraph (2) of this subsection shall apply, if any property described in subsection (a), as a result of any act or omission of the defendant—

'(A) cannot be located upon the exercise of due diligence;

'(B) has been transferred or sold to, or deposited with, a third party;

'(C) has been placed beyond the jurisdiction of the court;

'(D)has been substantially diminished in value; or

'(E) has been commingled with other property which cannot be divided without difficulty.

'(2) SUBSTITUTE PROPERTY—In any case described in any of subparagraphs (A) through (E) of paragraph (1), the court shall order the forfeiture of any other property of the defendant, up to the value of any property described in subparagraphs (A) through (E) of paragraph (1), as applicable.

'(3) RETURN OF PROPERTY TO JURISDICTION—In the case of property described in paragraph (1)(C), the court may, in addition to any other action authorized by this subsection, order the defendant to return the property to the jurisdiction of the court so that the property may be seized and forfeited.'.

(2) PROTECTIVE ORDERS—Section 413(e) of the Controlled Substances Act (21 U.S.C. 853(e)) is amended by adding at the end the following:

'(4) ORDER TO REPATRIATE AND DEPOSIT-

'(A) IN GENERAL—Pursuant to its authority to enter a pretrial restraining order under this section, the court may order a defendant to repatriate any property that may be seized and forfeited, and to deposit that property pending trial in the registry of the court, or with the United States Marshals Service or the Secretary of the Treasury, in an interest-bearing account, if appropriate.

'(B) FAILURE TO COMPLY—Failure to comply with an order under this subsection, or an order to repatriate property under subsection (p), shall be punishable as a civil or criminal contempt of court, and may also result in an enhancement of the sentence of the defendant under the obstruction of justice provision of the Federal Sentencing Guidelines.'.

Sec. 320. Proceeds of Foreign Crimes.

Section 981(a)(1)(B) of title 18, United States Code, is amended to read as follows:

'(B) Any property, real or personal, within the jurisdiction of the United States, constituting, derived from, or traceable to, any proceeds obtained directly or indirectly from an offense against a foreign nation, or any property used to facilitate such an offense, if the offense—

'(i) involves the manufacture, importation, sale, or distribution of a controlled substance (as that term is defined for purposes of the Controlled Substances Act), or any other conduct described in section 1956(c)(7)(B);

'(ii) would be punishable within the jurisdiction of the foreign nation by death or imprisonment for a term exceeding 1 year; and

'(iii) would be punishable under the laws of the United States by imprisonment for a term exceeding 1 year, if the act or activity constituting the offense had occurred within the jurisdiction of the United States.'.

Sec. 321. Financial Institutions Specified in Subchapter II of Chapter 53 of Title 31, United States Code.

(a) CREDIT UNIONS—Subparagraph (E) of section 5312(2) of title 31, United States Code, is amended to read as follows:

'(E) any credit union;'.

(b) FUTURES COMMISSION MERCHANT; COMMODITY TRADING ADVISOR; COMMODITY POOL OPERATOR—Section 5312 of title 31, United States Code, is amended by adding at the end the following new subsection:

'(c) ADDITIONAL DEFINITIONS—For purposes of this subchapter, the following definitions shall apply:

'(1) CERTAIN INSTITUTIONS INCLUDED IN DEFINI-TION—The term 'financial institution' (as defined in subsection (a)) includes the following:

'(A) Any futures commission merchant, commodity trading advisor, or commodity pool operator registered, or required to register, under the Commodity Exchange Act.'.

(c) CFTC INCLUDED—For purposes of this Act and any amendment made by this Act to any other provision of law, the term 'Federal functional regulator' includes the Commodity Futures Trading Commission.

Sec. 322. Corporation Represented by a Fugitive.

Section 2466 of title 18, United States Code, is amended by designating the present matter as subsection (a), and adding at the end the following:

'(b) Subsection (a) may be applied to a claim filed by a corporation if any majority shareholder, or individual filing the claim on behalf of the corporation is a person to whom subsection (a) applies.'.

Sec. 323. Enforcement of Foreign Judgments.

Section 2467 of title 28, United States Code, is amended—

(1) in subsection (d), by adding the following after paragraph (2):

'(3) PRESERVATION OF PROPERTY-

'(A) IN GENERAL—To preserve the availability of property subject to a foreign forfeiture or confiscation judgment, the

Government may apply for, and the court may issue, a restraining order pursuant to section 983(j) of title 18, at any time before or after an application is filed pursuant to subsection (c)(1) of this section.

'(B) EVIDENCE—The court, in issuing a restraining order under subparagraph (A)—

'(i) may rely on information set forth in an affidavit describing the nature of the proceeding or investigation underway in the foreign country, and setting forth a reasonable basis to believe that the property to be restrained will be named in a judgment of forfeiture at the conclusion of such proceeding; or

'(ii) may register and enforce a restraining order that has been issued by a court of competent jurisdiction in the foreign country and certified by the Attorney General pursuant to subsection (b)(2).

'(C) LIMIT ON GROUNDS FOR OBJECTION—No person may object to a restraining order under subparagraph (A) on any ground that is the subject of parallel litigation involving the same property that is pending in a foreign court.';

(2) in subsection (b)(1)(C), by striking 'establishing that the defendant received notice of the proceedings in sufficient time to enable the defendant' and inserting 'establishing that the foreign nation took steps, in accordance with the principles of due process, to give notice of the proceedings to all persons with an interest in the property in sufficient time to enable such persons';

(3) in subsection (d)(1)(D), by striking 'the defendant in the proceedings in the foreign court did not receive notice' and inserting 'the foreign nation did not take steps, in accordance with the principles of due process, to give notice of the proceedings to a person with an interest in the property'; and

(4) in subsection (a)(2)(A), by inserting ', any violation of foreign law that would constitute a violation or an offense for which property could be forfeited under Federal law if the offense were committed in the United States' after 'United Nations Convention'.

Sec. 324. Report and Recommendation.

Not later than 30 months after the date of enactment of this Act, the Secretary, in consultation with the Attorney General, the Federal banking agencies (as defined at section 3 of the Federal Deposit Insurance Act), the National Credit Union Administration Board, the Securities and Exchange Commission, and such other agencies as the Secretary may determine, at the discretion of the Secretary, shall evaluate the operations of the provisions of this subtitle and make recommendations to Congress as to any legislative action with respect to this subtitle as the Secretary may determine to be necessary or advisable.

Sec. 325. Concentration Accounts at Financial Institutions.

Section 5318(h) of title 31, United States Code, as amended by section 202 of this title, is amended by adding at the end the following:

'(3) CONCENTRATION ACCOUNTS—The Secretary may prescribe regulations under this subsection that govern maintenance of concentration accounts by financial institutions, in order to ensure that such accounts are not used to prevent association of the identity of an individual customer with the movement of funds of which the customer is the direct or beneficial owner, which regulations shall, at a minimum—

'(A) prohibit financial institutions from allowing clients to direct transactions that move their funds into, out of, or through the concentration accounts of the financial institution;

'(B) prohibit financial institutions and their employees from informing customers of the existence of, or the means of identifying, the concentration accounts of the institution; and

'(C) require each financial institution to establish written procedures governing the documentation of all transactions involving a concentration account, which procedures shall ensure that, any time a transaction involving a concentration account commingles funds belonging to 1 or more customers, the identity of, and specific amount belonging to, each customer is documented.'.

Sec. 326. Verification of Identification.

(a) IN GENERAL—Section 5318 of title 31, United States Code, as amended by this title, is amended by adding at the end the following:

'(l) IDENTIFICATION AND VERIFICATION OF ACCOUN-THOLDERS-

'(1) IN GENERAL—Subject to the requirements of this subsection, the Secretary of the Treasury shall prescribe regulations setting forth the minimum standards for financial institutions and their customers regarding the identity of the customer that shall apply in connection with the opening of an account at a financial institution.

'(2) MINIMUM REQUIREMENTS—The regulations shall, at a minimum, require financial institutions to implement, and customers (after being given adequate notice) to comply with, reasonable procedures for—

'(A) verifying the identity of any person seeking to open an account to the extent reasonable and practicable;

'(B) maintaining records of the information used to verify a person's identity, including name, address, and other identifying information; and

'(C) consulting lists of known or suspected terrorists or terrorist organizations provided to the financial institution by any government agency to determine whether a person seeking to open an account appears on any such list.

'(3) FACTORS TO BE CONSIDERED—In prescribing regulations under this subsection, the Secretary shall take into consideration the various types of accounts maintained by various types of financial institutions, the various methods of opening accounts, and the various types of identifying information available.

'(4) CERTAIN FINANCIAL INSTITUTIONS—In the case of any financial institution the business of which is engaging in financial activities described in section 4(k) of the Bank Holding Company Act of 1956 (including financial activities subject to the jurisdiction of the Commodity Futures Trading Commission), the regulations prescribed by the Secretary under paragraph (1) shall be prescribed jointly with each Federal functional regulator (as defined in section 509 of the Gramm-Leach-Bliley Act, including the Commodity Futures Trading Commission) appropriate for such financial institution.

'(5) EXEMPTIONS—The Secretary (and, in the case of any financial institution described in paragraph (4), any Federal agency described in such paragraph) may, by regulation or order, exempt any financial institution or type of account from the requirements of any regulation prescribed under this subsection in accordance with such standards and procedures as the Secretary may prescribe.

'(6) EFFECTIVE DATE—Final regulations prescribed under this subsection shall take effect before the end of the 1-year period beginning on the date of enactment of the International Money Laundering Abatement and Financial Anti-Terrorism Act of 2001.'.

(b) STUDY AND REPORT REQUIRED—Within 6 months after the date of enactment of this Act, the Secretary, in consultation with the Federal functional regulators (as defined in section 509 of the Gramm-Leach-Bliley Act) and other appropriate Government agencies, shall submit a report to the Congress containing recommendations for—

(1) determining the most timely and effective way to require foreign nationals to provide domestic financial institutions and agencies with appropriate and accurate information, comparable to that which is required of United States nationals, concerning the identity, address, and other related information about such foreign nationals necessary to enable such institutions and agencies to comply with the requirements of this section;

(2) requiring foreign nationals to apply for and obtain, before opening an account with a domestic financial institution, an identification number which would function similarly to a Social Security number or tax identification number; and

(3) establishing a system for domestic financial institutions and agencies to review information maintained by relevant Government agencies for purposes of verifying the identities of foreign nationals seeking to open accounts at those institutions and agencies.

Sec. 327. Consideration of Anti-Money Laundering Record.

(a) BANK HOLDING COMPANY ACT OF 1956-

(1) IN GENERAL—Section 3(c) of the Bank Holding Company Act of 1956 (12 U.S.C. 1842(c)) is amended by adding at the end the following new paragraph:

'(6) MONEY LAUNDERING—In every case, the Board shall take into consideration the effectiveness of the company or companies in combatting money laundering activities, including in overseas branches.'.

(2) SCOPE OF APPLICATION—The amendment made by paragraph (1) shall apply with respect to any application submitted to the Board of Governors of the Federal Reserve System under section 3 of the Bank Holding Company Act of 1956 after December 31, 2001, which has not been approved by the Board before the date of enactment of this Act.

(b) MERGERS SUBJECT TO REVIEW UNDER FEDERAL DEPOSIT INSURANCE ACT-

(1) IN GENERAL—Section 18(c) of the Federal Deposit Insurance Act (12 U.S.C. 1828(c)) is amended—

(A) by redesignating paragraph (11) as paragraph (12); and

(B) by inserting after paragraph (10), the following new paragraph:

'(11) MONEY LAUNDERING—In every case, the responsible agency, shall take into consideration the effectiveness of any insured depository institution involved in the proposed merger transaction in combatting money laundering activities, including in overseas branches.'.

(2) SCOPE OF APPLICATION—The amendment made by paragraph (1) shall apply with respect to any application submitted to the responsible agency under section 18(c) of the Federal Deposit Insurance Act after December 31, 2001, which has not been approved by all appropriate responsible agencies before the date of enactment of this Act.

Sec. 328. International Cooperation on Identification of Originators of Wire Transfers.

The Secretary shall—

(1) in consultation with the Attorney General and the Secretary of State, take all reasonable steps to encourage foreign governments to require the inclusion of the name of the originator in wire transfer instructions sent to the United States and other countries, with the information to remain with the transfer from its origination until the point of disbursement; and

(2) report annually to the Committee on Financial Services of the House of Representatives and the Committee on Banking, Housing, and Urban Affairs of the Senate on—

(A) progress toward the goal enumerated in paragraph (1), as well as impediments to implementation and an estimated compliance rate; and

(B) impediments to instituting a regime in which all appropriate identification, as defined by the Secretary, about wire transfer recipients shall be included with wire transfers from their point of origination until disbursement.

Sec. 329. Criminal Penalties.

Any person who is an official or employee of any department, agency, bureau, office, commission, or other entity of the Federal Government, and any other person who is acting for or on behalf of any such entity, who, directly or indirectly, in connection with the administration of this title, corruptly demands, seeks, receives, accepts, or agrees to receive or accept anything of value personally or for any other person or entity in return for—

(1) being influenced in the performance of any official act;

(2) being influenced to commit or aid in the committing, or to collude in, or allow, any fraud, or make opportunity for the commission of any fraud, on the United States; or

(3) being induced to do or omit to do any act in violation of the official duty of such official or person, shall be fined in an amount not more than 3 times the monetary equivalent of the thing of value, or imprisoned for not more than 15 years, or both. A violation of this section shall be subject to chapter 227 of title 18, United States Code, and the provisions of the United States Sentencing Guidelines.

Sec. 330. International Cooperation in Investigations of Money Laundering, Financial Crimes, and the Finances of Terrorist Groups.

(a) NEGOTIATIONS—It is the sense of the Congress that the President should direct the Secretary of State, the Attorney General, or the Secretary of the Treasury, as appropriate, and in consultation with the Board of Governors of the Federal Reserve System, to seek to enter into negotiations with the appropriate financial supervisory agencies and other officials of any foreign country the financial institutions of which do business with United States financial institutions or which may be utilized by any foreign terrorist organization (as designated under section 219 of the Immigration and Nationality Act), any person who is a member or representative of any such organization, or any person engaged in money laundering or financial or other crimes.

(b) PURPOSES OF NEGOTIATIONS—It is the sense of the Congress that, in carrying out any negotiations described in paragraph (1), the President should direct the Secretary of State, the Attorney General, or the Secretary of the Treasury, as appropriate, to seek to enter into and further cooperative efforts, voluntary information exchanges, the use of letters rogatory, mutual legal assistance treaties, and international agreements to—

(1) ensure that foreign banks and other financial institutions maintain adequate records of transaction and account information relating to any foreign terrorist organization (as designated under section 219 of the Immigration and Nationality Act), any person who is a member or representative of any such organization, or any person engaged in money laundering or financial or other crimes; and

(2) establish a mechanism whereby such records may be made available to United States law enforcement officials and domestic financial institution supervisors, when appropriate.

Subtitle B—Bank Secrecy Act Amendments and Related Improvements

Sec. 351. Amendments Relating to Reporting of Suspicious Activities.

(a) AMENDMENT RELATING TO CIVIL LIABILITY IMMUNITY FOR DISCLOSURES—Section 5318(g)(3) of title 31, United States Code, is amended to read as follows:

'(3) LIABILITY FOR DISCLOSURES-

'(A) IN GENERAL—Any financial institution that makes a voluntary disclosure of any possible violation of law or regulation to a government agency or makes a disclosure pursuant to this subsection or any other authority, and any director, officer, employee, or agent of such institution who makes, or requires another to make any such disclosure, shall not be liable to any person under any law or regulation of the United States, any constitution, law, or regulation of any State or political subdivision of any State, or under any contract or other legally enforceable agreement (including any arbitration agreement), for such disclosure or for any failure to provide notice of such disclosure to the person who is the subject of such disclosure or any other person identified in the disclosure.

'(B) RULE OF CONSTRUCTION—Subparagraph (A) shall not be construed as creating—

'(i) any inference that the term 'person', as used in such subparagraph, may be construed more broadly than its ordinary usage so as to include any government or agency of government; or

'(ii) any immunity against, or otherwise affecting, any civil or criminal action brought by any government or agency of government to enforce any constitution, law, or regulation of such government or agency.'.

(b) PROHIBITION ON NOTIFICATION OF DISCLOSURES—Section 5318(g)(2) of title 31, United States Code, is amended to read as follows:

'(2) NOTIFICATION PROHIBITED-

'(A) IN GENERAL—If a financial institution or any director, officer, employee, or agent of any financial institution, voluntarily or pursuant to this section or any other authority, reports a suspicious transaction to a government agency—

'(i) the financial institution, director, officer, employee, or agent may not notify any person involved in the transaction that the transaction has been reported; and

'(ii) no officer or employee of the Federal Government or of any State, local, tribal, or territorial government within the United States, who has any knowledge that such report was made may disclose to any person involved in the transaction that the transaction has been reported, other than as necessary to fulfill the official duties of such officer or employee.

'(B) DISCLOSURES IN CERTAIN EMPLOYMENT REFERENCES-

'(i) RULE OF CONSTRUCTION—Notwithstanding the application of subparagraph (A) in any other context, subparagraph (A) shall not be construed as prohibiting any financial institution, or any director, officer, employee, or agent of such institution, from including information that was included in a report to which subparagraph (A) applies—

'(I) in a written employment reference that is provided in accordance with section 18(w) of the Federal Deposit Insurance Act in response to a request from another financial institution; or

'(II) in a written termination notice or employment reference that is provided in accordance with the rules of a self-regulatory organization registered with the Securities and Exchange Commission or the Commodity Futures Trading Commission, except that such written reference or notice may not disclose that such information was also included in any such report, or that such report was made.

'(ii) INFORMATION NOT REQUIRED—Clause (i) shall not be construed, by itself, to create any affirmative duty to include any information described in clause (i) in any employment reference or termination notice referred to in clause (i).'.

Sec. 352. Anti-Money Laundering Programs.

(a) IN GENERAL—Section 5318(h) of title 31, United States Code, is amended to read as follows:

'(h) ANTI-MONEY LAUNDERING PROGRAMS-

'(1) IN GENERAL—In order to guard against money laundering through financial institutions, each financial institution shall establish anti-money laundering programs, including, at a minimum—

'(A) the development of internal policies, procedures, and controls;

'(B) the designation of a compliance officer;

'(C) an ongoing employee training program; and

'(D) an independent audit function to test programs.

'(2) REGULATIONS—The Secretary of the Treasury, after consultation with the appropriate Federal functional regulator (as defined in section 509 of the Gramm-Leach-Bliley Act), may prescribe minimum standards for programs established under paragraph (1), and may exempt from the application of those standards any financial institution that is not subject to the provisions of the rules contained in part 103 of title 31, of the Code of Federal Regulations, or any successor rule thereto, for so long as such financial institution is not subject to the provisions of such rules.'.

(b) EFFECTIVE DATE—The amendment made by subsection (a) shall take effect at the end of the 180-day period beginning on the date of enactment of this Act.

(c) DATE OF APPLICATION OF REGULATIONS; FACTORS TO BE TAKEN INTO ACCOUNT—Before the end of the 180-day period beginning on the date of enactment of this Act, the Secretary shall prescribe regulations that consider the extent to which the requirements imposed under this section are commensurate with the size, location, and activities of the financial institutions to which such regulations apply.

Sec. 353. Penalties for Violations of Geographic Targeting Orders and Certain Recordkeeping Requirements, and Lengthening Effective Period of Geographic Targeting Orders.

(a) CIVIL PENALTY FOR VIOLATION OF TARGETING ORDER —Section 5321(a)(1) of title 31, United States Code, is amended—

(1) by inserting 'or order issued' after 'subchapter or a regulation prescribed'; and

(2) by inserting ', or willfully violating a regulation prescribed under section 21 of the Federal Deposit Insurance Act or section 123 of Public Law 91–508,' after 'sections 5314 and 5315)'.

(b) CRIMINAL PENALTIES FOR VIOLATION OF TARGETING ORDER—Section 5322 of title 31, United States Code, is amended—

(1) in subsection (a)—

(A) by inserting 'or order issued' after 'willfully violating this subchapter or a regulation prescribed'; and

(B) by inserting ', or willfully violating a regulation prescribed under section 21 of the Federal Deposit Insurance Act or section 123 of Public Law 91–508,' after 'under section 5315 or 5324)'; and

(2) in subsection (b)—

(A) by inserting 'or order issued' after 'willfully violating this subchapter or a regulation prescribed'; and

(B) by inserting 'or willfully violating a regulation prescribed under section 21 of the Federal Deposit Insurance Act or section 123 of Public Law 91–508,' after 'under section 5315 or 5324),'.

(c) STRUCTURING TRANSACTIONS TO EVADE TARGETING ORDER OR CERTAIN RECORDKEEPING REQUIREMENTS— Section 5324(a) of title 31, United States Code, is amended—

(1) by inserting a comma after 'shall';

(2) by striking 'section—' and inserting 'section, the reporting or recordkeeping requirements imposed by any order issued under section 5326, or the recordkeeping requirements imposed by any regulation prescribed under section 21 of the Federal Deposit Insurance Act or section 123 of Public Law 91–508—';

(3) in paragraph (1), by inserting ', to file a report or to maintain a record required by an order issued under section 5326, or to maintain a record required pursuant to any regulation prescribed under section 21 of the Federal Deposit Insurance Act or section 123 of Public Law 91–508' after 'regulation prescribed under any such section'; and

(4) in paragraph (2), by inserting ', to file a report or to maintain a record required by any order issued under section 5326, or to maintain a record required pursuant to any regulation prescribed under section 5326, or to maintain a record required pursuant to any regulation prescribed under section 21 of the Federal Deposit Insurance Act or section 123 of Public Law 91–508,' after 'regulation prescribed under any such section'.

(d) LENGTHENING EFFECTIVE PERIOD OF GEOGRAPHIC TARGETING ORDERS—Section 5326(d) of title 31, United States Code, is amended by striking 'more than 60' and inserting 'more than 180'.

Sec. 354. Anti-Money Laundering Strategy.

Section 5341(b) of title 31, United States Code, is amended by adding at the end the following:

'(12) DATA REGARDING FUNDING OF TERRORISM—Data

concerning money laundering efforts related to the funding of acts of international terrorism, and efforts directed at the prevention, detection, and prosecution of such funding.'.

Sec. 355. Authorization to Include Suspicions of Illegal Activity in Written Employment References.

Section 18 of the Federal Deposit Insurance Act (12 U.S.C. 1828) is amended by adding at the end the following:

'(w) WRITTEN EMPLOYMENT REFERENCES MAY CONTAIN SUSPICIONS OF INVOLVEMENT IN ILLEGAL ACTIVITY-

'(1) AUTHORITY TO DISCLOSE INFORMATION—Notwithstanding any other provision of law, any insured depository institution, and any director, officer, employee, or agent of such institution, may disclose in any written employment reference relating to a current or former institution-affiliated party of such institution which is provided to another insured depository institution in response to a request from such other institution, information concerning the possible involvement of such institution-affiliated party in potentially unlawful activity.

'(2) INFORMATION NOT REQUIRED—Nothing in paragraph (1) shall be construed, by itself, to create any affirmative duty to include any information described in paragraph (1) in any employment reference referred to in paragraph (1).

'(3) MALICIOUS INTENT—Notwithstanding any other provision of this subsection, voluntary disclosure made by an insured depository institution, and any director, officer, employee, or agent of such institution under this subsection concerning potentially unlawful activity that is made with malicious intent, shall not be shielded from liability from the person identified in the disclosure.

'(4) DEFINITION—For purposes of this subsection, the term 'insured depository institution' includes any uninsured branch or agency of a foreign bank.'.

Sec. 356. Reporting of Suspicious Activities by Securities Brokers and Dealers; Investment Company Study.

(a) DEADLINE FOR SUSPICIOUS ACTIVITY REPORTING REQUIREMENTS FOR REGISTERED BROKERS AND DEALERS—

The Secretary, after consultation with the Securities and Exchange Commission and the Board of Governors of the Federal Reserve System, shall publish proposed regulations in the Federal Register before January 1, 2002, requiring brokers and dealers registered with the Securities and Exchange Commission under the Securities Exchange Act of 1934 to submit suspicious activity reports under section 5318(g) of title 31, United States Code. Such regulations shall be published in final form not later than July 1, 2002.

(b) SUSPICIOUS ACTIVITY REPORTING REQUIREMENTS FOR FUTURES COMMISSION MERCHANTS, COMMODITY TRADING ADVISORS, AND COMMODITY POOL OPERATORS—The Secretary, in consultation with the Commodity Futures Trading Commission, may prescribe regulations requiring futures commission merchants, commodity trading advisors, and commodity pool operators registered under the Commodity Exchange Act to submit suspicious activity reports under section 5318(g) of title 31, United States Code.

(c) REPORT ON INVESTMENT COMPANIES-

(1) IN GENERAL—Not later than 1 year after the date of enactment of this Act, the Secretary, the Board of Governors of the Federal Reserve System, and the Securities and Exchange Commission shall jointly submit a report to the Congress on recommendations for effective regulations to apply the requirements of subchapter II of chapter 53 of title 31, United States Code, to investment companies pursuant to section 5312(a)(2)(I) of title 31, United States Code.

(2) DEFINITION—For purposes of this subsection, the term 'investment company'—

(A) has the same meaning as in section 3 of the Investment Company Act of 1940 (15 U.S.C. 80a-3); and

(B) includes any person that, but for the exceptions provided for in paragraph (1) or (7) of section 3(c) of the Investment Company Act of 1940 (15 U.S.C. 80a-3(c)), would be an investment company.

(3) ADDITIONAL RECOMMENDATIONS—The report required by paragraph (1) may make different recommendations for different types of entities covered by this subsection.

(4) BENEFICIAL OWNERSHIP OF PERSONAL HOLDING COMPANIES—The report described in paragraph (1) shall also

include recommendations as to whether the Secretary should promulgate regulations to treat any corporation or business or other grantor trust whose assets are predominantly securities, bank certificates of deposit, or other securities or investment instruments (other than such as relate to operating subsidiaries of such corporation or trust) and that has 5 or fewer common shareholders or holders of beneficial or other equity interest, as a financial institution within the meaning of that phrase in section 5312(a)(2)(I) and whether to require such corporations or trusts to disclose their beneficial owners when opening accounts or initiating funds transfers at any domestic financial institution.

Sec. 357. Special Report on Administration of Bank Secrecy Provisions.

(a) REPORT REQUIRED—Not later than 6 months after the date of enactment of this Act, the Secretary shall submit a report to the Congress relating to the role of the Internal Revenue Service in the administration of subchapter II of chapter 53 of title 31, United States Code (commonly known as the 'Bank Secrecy Act').

(b) CONTENTS—The report required by subsection (a)—

(1) shall specifically address, and contain recommendations concerning—

(A) whether it is advisable to shift the processing of information reporting to the Department of the Treasury under the Bank Secrecy Act provisions to facilities other than those managed by the Internal Revenue Service; and

(B) whether it remains reasonable and efficient, in light of the objective of both anti-money-laundering programs and Federal tax administration, for the Internal Revenue Service to retain authority and responsibility for audit and examination of the compliance of money services businesses and gaming institutions with those Bank Secrecy Act provisions; and

(2) shall, if the Secretary determines that the information processing responsibility or the audit and examination responsibility of the Internal Revenue Service, or both, with respect to those Bank Secrecy Act provisions should be transferred to other agencies, include the specific recommendations of the Secretary regarding the

agency or agencies to which any such function should be transferred, complete with a budgetary and resources plan for expeditiously accomplishing the transfer.

Sec. 358. Bank Secrecy Provisions and Activities of United States Intelligence Agencies to Fight International Terrorism.

(a) AMENDMENT RELATING TO THE PURPOSES OF CHAPTER 53 OF TITLE 31, UNITED STATES CODE—Section 5311 of title 31, United States Code, is amended by inserting before the period at the end the following: ', or in the conduct of intelligence or counterintelligence activities, including analysis, to protect against international terrorism'.

(b) AMENDMENT RELATING TO REPORTING OF SUSPICIOUS ACTIVITIES—Section 5318(g)(4)(B) of title 31, United States Code, is amended by striking 'or supervisory agency' and inserting ', supervisory agency, or United States intelligence agency for use in the conduct of intelligence or counterintelligence activities, including analysis, to protect against international terrorism'.

(c) AMENDMENT RELATING TO AVAILABILITY OF REPORTS—Section 5319 of title 31, United States Code, is amended to read as follows:

'Sec. 5319. Availability of reports

'The Secretary of the Treasury shall make information in a report filed under this subchapter available to an agency, including any State financial institutions supervisory agency, United States intelligence agency or self-regulatory organization registered with the Securities and Exchange Commission or the Commodity Futures Trading Commission, upon request of the head of the agency or organization. The report shall be available for a purpose that is consistent with this subchapter. The Secretary may only require reports on the use of such information by any State financial institutions supervisory agency for other than supervisory purposes or by United States intelligence agencies. However, a report and records of reports are exempt from disclosure under section 552 of title 5.'.

(d) AMENDMENT RELATING TO THE PURPOSES OF THE BANK SECRECY ACT PROVISIONS—Section 21(a) of the Federal Deposit Insurance Act (12 U.S.C. 1829b(a)) is amended to read as follows:

'(a) CONGRESSIONAL FINDINGS AND DECLARATION OF PURPOSE-

'(1) FINDINGS—Congress finds that—

'(A) adequate records maintained by insured depository institutions have a high degree of usefulness in criminal, tax, and regulatory investigations or proceedings, and that, given the threat posed to the security of the Nation on and after the terrorist attacks against the United States on September 11, 2001, such records may also have a high degree of usefulness in the conduct of intelligence or counterintelligence activities, including analysis, to protect against domestic and international terrorism; and

'(B) microfilm or other reproductions and other records made by insured depository institutions of checks, as well as records kept by such institutions, of the identity of persons maintaining or authorized to act with respect to accounts therein, have been of particular value in proceedings described in subparagraph (A).

'(2) PURPOSE—It is the purpose of this section to require the maintenance of appropriate types of records by insured depository institutions in the United States where such records have a high degree of usefulness in criminal, tax, or regulatory investigations or proceedings, recognizes that, given the threat posed to the security of the Nation on and after the terrorist attacks against the United States on September 11, 2001, such records may also have a high degree of usefulness in the conduct of intelligence or counterintelligence activities, including analysis, to protect against international terrorism.'.

(e) AMENDMENT RELATING TO THE PURPOSES OF THE BANK SECRECY ACT—Section 123(a) of Public Law 91–508 (12 U.S.C. 1953(a)) is amended to read as follows:

'(a) REGULATIONS—If the Secretary determines that the maintenance of appropriate records and procedures by any uninsured bank or uninsured institution, or any person engaging in the business of carrying on in the United States any of the functions referred to in subsection (b), has a high degree of usefulness in criminal, tax, or regulatory investigations or proceedings, and that, given the threat posed to the security of the Nation on and after the terrorist attacks against the United States on September 11, 2001, such records may also have a high degree of usefulness in the conduct of intelligence or counterintelligence activities, including analysis, to protect against international terrorism, he may by regulation require such bank, institution, or person.'.

(f) AMENDMENTS TO THE RIGHT TO FINANCIAL PRIVACY ACT—The Right to Financial Privacy Act of 1978 is amended—

(1) in section 1112(a) (12 U.S.C. 3412(a)), by inserting ', or intelligence or counterintelligence activity, investigation or analysis related to international terrorism' after 'legitimate law enforcement inquiry';

(2) in section 1114(a)(1) (12 U.S.C. 3414(a)(1))—

(A) in subparagraph (A), by striking 'or' at the end;

(B) in subparagraph (B), by striking the period at the end and inserting '; or'; and

(C) by adding at the end the following:

'(C) a Government authority authorized to conduct investigations of, or intelligence or counterintelligence analyses related to, international terrorism for the purpose of conducting such investigations or analyses.'; and

(3) in section 1120(a)(2) (12 U.S.C. 3420(a)(2)), by inserting ', or for a purpose authorized by section 1112(a)' before the semicolon at the end.

(g) AMENDMENT TO THE FAIR CREDIT REPORTING ACT-

(1) IN GENERAL—The Fair Credit Reporting Act (15 U.S.C. 1681 et seq.) is amended—

(A) by redesignating the second of the 2 sections designated as section 624 (15 U.S.C. 1681u) (relating to disclosure to FBI for counterintelligence purposes) as section 625; and

(B) by adding at the end the following new section:

'Sec. 626. Disclosures to governmental agencies for counterterrorism purposes

'(a) DISCLOSURE—Notwithstanding section 604 or any other provision of this title, a consumer reporting agency shall furnish a consumer report of a consumer and all other information in a consumer's file to a government agency authorized to conduct investigations of, or intelligence or counterintelligence activities or analysis related to, international terrorism when presented with a written certification by such government agency that such information is necessary for the agency's conduct or such investigation, activity or analysis.

'(b) FORM OF CERTIFICATION—The certification described in subsection (a) shall be signed by a supervisory official designated by the head of a Federal agency or an officer of a Federal agency whose appointment to office is required to be made by the President, by and with the advice and consent of the Senate.

'(c) CONFIDENTIALITY—No consumer reporting agency, or officer, employee, or agent of such consumer reporting agency, shall disclose to any person, or specify in any consumer report, that a government agency has sought or obtained access to information under subsection (a).

'(d) RULE OF CONSTRUCTION—Nothing in section 625 shall be construed to limit the authority of the Director of the Federal Bureau of Investigation under this section.

'(e) SAFE HARBOR—Notwithstanding any other provision of this title, any consumer reporting agency or agent or employee thereof making disclosure of consumer reports or other information pursuant to this section in good-faith reliance upon a certification of a governmental agency pursuant to the provisions of this section shall not be liable to any person for such disclosure under this subchapter, the constitution of any State, or any law or regulation of any State or any political subdivision of any State.'.

(2) CLERICAL AMENDMENTS—The table of sections for the Fair Credit Reporting Act (15 U.S.C. 1681 et seq.) is amended—

(A) by redesignating the second of the 2 items designated as section 624 as section 625; and

(B) by inserting after the item relating to section 625 (as so redesignated) the following new item:

'626. Disclosures to governmental agencies for counterterrorism purposes.'.

(h) APPLICATION OF AMENDMENTS—The amendments made by this section shall apply with respect to reports filed or records maintained on, before, or after the date of enactment of this Act.

Sec. 359. Reporting of Suspicious Activities by Underground Banking Systems.

(a) DEFINITION FOR SUBCHAPTER—Section 5312(a)(2)(R) of title 31, United States Code, is amended to read as follows:

'(R) a licensed sender of money or any other person who engages as a business in the transmission of funds, including any person who engages as a business in an informal money transfer system or any network of people who engage as a business in facilitating the transfer of money domestically or internationally outside of the conventional financial institutions system;'.

(b) MONEY TRANSMITTING BUSINESS—Section 5330(d)(1)(A) of title 31, United States Code, is amended by inserting before the semicolon the following: 'or any other person who engages as a business in the transmission of funds, including any person who engages as a business in an informal money transfer system or any network of people who engage as a business in facilitating the transfer of money domestically or internationally outside of the conventional financial institutions system;'.

(c) APPLICABILITY OF RULES—Section 5318 of title 31, United States Code, as amended by this title, is amended by adding at the end the following:

'(l) APPLICABILITY OF RULES—Any rules promulgated pursuant to the authority contained in section 21 of the Federal Deposit Insurance Act (12 U.S.C. 1829b) shall apply, in addition to any other financial institution to which such rules apply, to any person that engages as a business in the transmission of funds, including any person who engages as a business in an informal money transfer system or any network of people who engage as a business in facilitating the transfer of money domestically or internationally outside of the conventional financial institutions system.'.

(d) REPORT—Not later than 1 year after the date of enactment of this Act, the Secretary of the Treasury shall report to Congress on the need for any additional legislation relating to persons who engage as a business in an informal money transfer system or any network of people who engage as a business in facilitating the transfer of money domestically or internationally outside of the conventional financial institutions system, counter money laundering and regulatory controls relating to underground money movement and banking systems, including whether the threshold for the filing of suspicious activity reports under section 5318(g) of title 31, United States Code should be lowered in the case of such systems.

Sec. 360. Use of Authority of United States Executive Directors.

(a) ACTION BY THE PRESIDENT—If the President determines that a particular foreign country has taken or has committed to take actions that contribute to efforts of the United States to respond to, deter, or prevent acts of international terrorism, the Secretary may, consistent with other applicable provisions of law, instruct the United States Executive Director of each international financial institution to use the voice and vote of the Executive Director to support any loan or other utilization of the funds of respective institutions for such country, or any public or private entity within such country.

(b) USE OF VOICE AND VOTE—The Secretary may instruct the United States Executive Director of each international financial institution to aggressively use the voice and vote of the Executive Director to require an auditing of disbursements at such institutions to ensure that no funds are paid to persons who commit, threaten to commit, or support terrorism.

(c) DEFINITION—For purposes of this section, the term 'international financial institution' means an institution described in section 1701(c)(2) of the International Financial Institutions Act (22 U.S.C. 262r(c)(2)).

Sec. 361. Financial Crimes Enforcement Network.

(a) IN GENERAL—Subchapter I of chapter 3 of title 31, United States Code, is amended—

(1) by redesignating section 310 as section 311; and

(2) by inserting after section 309 the following new section:

'Sec. 310. Financial Crimes Enforcement Network

'(a) IN GENERAL—The Financial Crimes Enforcement Network established by order of the Secretary of the Treasury (Treasury Order Numbered 105–08, in this section referred to as 'FinCEN') on April 25, 1990, shall be a bureau in the Department of the Treasury.

'(b) DIRECTOR-

'(1) APPOINTMENT—The head of FinCEN shall be the Director, who shall be appointed by the Secretary of the Treasury.

'(2) DUTIES AND POWERS—The duties and powers of the Director are as follows:

'(A) Advise and make recommendations on matters relating to financial intelligence, financial criminal activities, and other financial activities to the Under Secretary of the Treasury for Enforcement.

'(B) Maintain a government-wide data access service, with access, in accordance with applicable legal requirements, to the following:

'(i) Information collected by the Department of the Treasury, including report information filed under subchapter II of chapter 53 of this title (such as reports on cash transactions, foreign financial agency transactions and relationships, foreign currency transactions, exporting and importing monetary instruments, and suspicious activities), chapter 2 of title I of Public Law 91–508, and section 21 of the Federal Deposit Insurance Act.

'(ii) Information regarding national and international currency flows.

'(iii) Other records and data maintained by other Federal, State, local, and foreign agencies, including financial and other records developed in specific cases.

'(iv) Other privately and publicly available information.

'(C) Analyze and disseminate the available data in accordance with applicable legal requirements and policies and guidelines established by the Secretary of the Treasury and the Under Secretary of the Treasury for Enforcement to—

'(i) identify possible criminal activity to appropriate Federal, State, local, and foreign law enforcement agencies;

'(ii) support ongoing criminal financial investigations and prosecutions and related proceedings, including civil and criminal tax and forfeiture proceedings;

'(iii) identify possible instances of noncompliance with subchapter II of chapter 53 of this title, chapter 2 of title I of Public Law 91–508, and section 21 of the Federal Deposit Insurance Act to Federal agencies with statutory responsibility for enforcing compliance with such provisions and other appropriate Federal regulatory agencies;

'(iv) evaluate and recommend possible uses of special currency reporting requirements under section 5326;

'(v) determine emerging trends and methods in money laundering and other financial crimes;

'(vi) support the conduct of intelligence or counterintelligence activities, including analysis, to protect against international terrorism; and

'(vii) support government initiatives against money laundering.

'(D) Establish and maintain a financial crimes communications center to furnish law enforcement authorities with intelligence information related to emerging or ongoing investigations and undercover operations.

'(E) Furnish research, analytical, and informational services to financial institutions, appropriate Federal regulatory agencies with regard to financial institutions, and appropriate Federal, State, local, and foreign law enforcement authorities, in accordance with policies and guidelines established by the Secretary of the Treasury or the Under Secretary of the Treasury for Enforcement, in the interest of detection, prevention, and prosecution of terrorism, organized crime, money laundering, and other financial crimes.

'(F) Assist Federal, State, local, and foreign law enforcement and regulatory authorities in combatting the use of informal, nonbank networks and payment and barter system mechanisms that permit the transfer of funds or the equivalent of funds without records and without compliance with criminal and tax laws.

'(G) Provide computer and data support and data analysis to the Secretary of the Treasury for tracking and controlling foreign assets.

'(H) Coordinate with financial intelligence units in other countries on anti-terrorism and anti-money laundering initiatives, and similar efforts.

'(I) Administer the requirements of subchapter II of chapter 53 of this title, chapter 2 of title I of Public Law 91–508, and section 21 of the Federal Deposit Insurance Act, to the extent delegated such authority by the Secretary of the Treasury.

'(J) Such other duties and powers as the Secretary of the Treasury may delegate or prescribe.

'(c) REQUIREMENTS RELATING TO MAINTENANCE AND USE OF DATA BANKS—The Secretary of the Treasury shall establish and maintain operating procedures with respect to the government-wide data access service and the financial crimes communications center maintained by FinCEN which provide—

'(1) for the coordinated and efficient transmittal of information to, entry of information into, and withdrawal of information from, the data maintenance system maintained by the Network, including—

'(A) the submission of reports through the Internet or other secure network, whenever possible;

'(B) the cataloguing of information in a manner that facilitates rapid retrieval by law enforcement personnel of meaningful data; and

'(C) a procedure that provides for a prompt initial review of suspicious activity reports and other reports, or such other means as the Secretary may provide, to identify information that warrants immediate action; and

'(2) in accordance with section 552a of title 5 and the Right to Financial Privacy Act of 1978, appropriate standards and guidelines for determining—

'(A) who is to be given access to the information maintained by the Network;

'(B) what limits are to be imposed on the use of such information; and

'(C) how information about activities or relationships which involve or are closely associated with the exercise of constitutional rights is to be screened out of the data maintenance system.

'(d) AUTHORIZATION OF APPROPRIATIONS—There are authorized to be appropriated for FinCEN such sums as may be necessary for fiscal years 2002, 2003, 2004, and 2005.'.

(b) COMPLIANCE WITH REPORTING REQUIREMENTS—The Secretary of the Treasury shall study methods for improving compliance with the reporting requirements established in section 5314 of title 31, United States Code, and shall submit a report on such study to the Congress by the end of the 6-month period beginning on the date of enactment of this Act and each 1-year period thereafter. The initial report shall include historical data on compliance with such reporting requirements.

(c) CLERICAL AMENDMENT—The table of sections for subchapter I of chapter 3 of title 31, United States Code, is amended—

(1) by redesignating the item relating to section 310 as section 311; and

(2) by inserting after the item relating to section 309 the following new item:

'310. Financial Crimes Enforcement Network.'.

SEC. 362. ESTABLISHMENT OF HIGHLY SECURE NETWORK.

(a) IN GENERAL—The Secretary shall establish a highly secure network in the Financial Crimes Enforcement Network that—

(1) allows financial institutions to file reports required under subchapter II or III of chapter 53 of title 31, United States Code, chapter 2 of Public Law 91–508, or section 21 of the Federal Deposit Insurance Act through the secure network; and

(2) provides financial institutions with alerts and other information regarding suspicious activities that warrant immediate and enhanced scrutiny.

(b) EXPEDITED DEVELOPMENT—The Secretary shall take such action as may be necessary to ensure that the secure network required under subsection (a) is fully operational before the end of the 9-month period beginning on the date of enactment of this Act.

Sec. 363. Increase in Civil and Criminal Penalties for Money Laundering.

(a) CIVIL PENALTIES—Section 5321(a) of title 31, United States Code, is amended by adding at the end the following:

'(7) PENALTIES FOR INTERNATIONAL COUNTER MONEY LAUNDERING VIOLATIONS—The Secretary may impose a civil money penalty in an amount equal to not less than 2 times the amount of the transaction, but not more than $1,000,000, on any financial institution or agency that violates any provision of subsection (i) or (j) of section 5318 or any special measures imposed under section 5318A.'.

(b) CRIMINAL PENALTIES—Section 5322 of title 31, United States Code, is amended by adding at the end the following:

'(d) A financial institution or agency that violates any provision of subsection (i) or (j) of section 5318, or any special measures imposed under section 5318A, or any regulation prescribed under subsection (i) or (j) of section 5318 or section 5318A, shall be fined in an amount equal to not less than 2 times the amount of the transaction, but not more than $1,000,000.'.

Sec. 364. Uniform Protection Authority for Federal Reserve Facilities.

Section 11 of the Federal Reserve Act (12 U.S.C. 248) is amended by adding at the end the following:

'(q) UNIFORM PROTECTION AUTHORITY FOR FEDERAL RESERVE FACILITIES-

'(1) Notwithstanding any other provision of law, to authorize personnel to act as law enforcement officers to protect and safeguard the premises, grounds, property, personnel, including members of the Board, of the Board, or any Federal reserve bank, and operations conducted by or on behalf of the Board or a reserve bank.

'(2) The Board may, subject to the regulations prescribed under paragraph (5), delegate authority to a Federal reserve bank to authorize personnel to act as law enforcement officers to protect and safeguard the bank's premises, grounds, property, personnel, and operations conducted by or on behalf of the bank.

'(3) Law enforcement officers designated or authorized by the Board or a reserve bank under paragraph (1) or (2) are authorized while on duty to carry firearms and make arrests without warrants for any offense against the United States committed in their presence, or for any felony cognizable under the laws of the United States committed or being committed within the buildings and grounds of the Board or a reserve bank if they have reasonable grounds to believe that the person to be arrested has committed or is committing such a felony. Such officers shall have access to law enforcement information that may be necessary for the protection of the property or personnel of the Board or a reserve bank.

'(4) For purposes of this subsection, the term 'law enforcement officers' means personnel who have successfully completed law enforcement training and are authorized to carry firearms and make arrests pursuant to this subsection.

'(5) The law enforcement authorities provided for in this subsection may be exercised only pursuant to regulations prescribed by the Board and approved by the Attorney General.'.

Sec. 365. Reports Relating to Coins and Currency Received in Nonfinancial Trade or Business.

(a) REPORTS REQUIRED—Subchapter II of chapter 53 of title 31, United States Code, is amended by adding at the end the following new section:

'Sec. 5331. Reports relating to coins and currency received in nonfinancial trade or business

'(a) COIN AND CURRENCY RECEIPTS OF MORE THAN $10,000—Any person—

'(1) who is engaged in a trade or business; and

'(2) who, in the course of such trade or business, receives more than $10,000 in coins or currency in 1 transaction (or 2 or more related transactions), shall file a report described in subsection (b) with respect to such transaction (or related transactions) with the Financial Crimes Enforcement Network at such time and in such manner as the Secretary may, by regulation, prescribe.

'(b) FORM AND MANNER OF REPORTS—A report is described in this subsection if such report—

'(1) is in such form as the Secretary may prescribe;

'(2) contains—

'(A) the name and address, and such other identification information as the Secretary may require, of the person from whom the coins or currency was received;

'(B) the amount of coins or currency received;

'(C) the date and nature of the transaction; and

'(D) such other information, including the identification of the person filing the report, as the Secretary may prescribe.

'(c) EXCEPTIONS-

'(1) AMOUNTS RECEIVED BY FINANCIAL INSTITU-TIONS—Subsection (a) shall not apply to amounts received in a transaction reported under section 5313 and regulations prescribed under such section.

'(2) TRANSACTIONS OCCURRING OUTSIDE THE UNITED STATES—Except to the extent provided in regulations prescribed by the Secretary, subsection (a) shall not apply to any transaction if the entire transaction occurs outside the United States.

'(d) CURRENCY INCLUDES FOREIGN CURRENCY AND CERTAIN MONETARY INSTRUMENTS-

'(1) IN GENERAL—For purposes of this section, the term 'currency' includes—

'(A) foreign currency; and

'(B) to the extent provided in regulations prescribed by the Secretary, any monetary instrument (whether or not in bearer form) with a face amount of not more than $10,000.

'(2) SCOPE OF APPLICATION—Paragraph (1)(B) shall not apply to any check drawn on the account of the writer in a financial institution referred to in subparagraph (A), (B), (C), (D), (E), (F), (G), (J), (K), (R), or (S) of section 5312(a)(2).'.

(b) PROHIBITION ON STRUCTURING TRANSACTIONS-

(1) IN GENERAL—Section 5324 of title 31, United States Code, is amended—

(A) by redesignating subsections (b) and (c) as subsections (c) and (d), respectively; and

(B) by inserting after subsection (a) the following new subsection:

'(b) DOMESTIC COIN AND CURRENCY TRANSACTIONS INVOLVING NONFINANCIAL TRADES OR BUSINESSES—No person shall, for the purpose of evading the report requirements of section 5333 or any regulation prescribed under such section—

'(1) cause or attempt to cause a nonfinancial trade or business to fail to file a report required under section 5333 or any regulation prescribed under such section;

'(2) cause or attempt to cause a nonfinancial trade or business to file a report required under section 5333 or any regulation prescribed under such section that contains a material omission or misstatement of fact; or

'(3) structure or assist in structuring, or attempt to structure or assist in structuring, any transaction with 1 or more nonfinancial trades or businesses.'.

(2) TECHNICAL AND CONFORMING AMENDMENTS-

(A) The heading for subsection (a) of section 5324 of title 31, United States Code, is amended by inserting 'INVOLVING FINANCIAL INSTITUTIONS' after 'TRANSACTIONS'.

(B) Section 5317(c) of title 31, United States Code, is amended by striking '5324(b)' and inserting '5324(c)'.

(c) DEFINITION OF NONFINANCIAL TRADE OR BUSINESS-

(1) IN GENERAL—Section 5312(a) of title 31, United States Code, is amended—

(A) by redesignating paragraphs (4) and (5) as paragraphs (5) and (6), respectively; and

(B) by inserting after paragraph (3) the following new paragraph:

'(4) NONFINANCIAL TRADE OR BUSINESS—The term 'nonfinancial trade or business' means any trade or business other than a financial institution that is subject to the reporting requirements of section 5313 and regulations prescribed under such section.'.

(2) TECHNICAL AND CONFORMING AMENDMENTS-

(A) Section 5312(a)(3)(C) of title 31, United States Code, is amended by striking 'section 5316,' and inserting 'sections 5333 and 5316,'.

(B) Subsections (a) through (f) of section 5318 of title 31, United States Code, and sections 5321, 5326, and 5328 of such title are each amended—

(i) by inserting 'or nonfinancial trade or business' after 'financial institution' each place such term appears; and

(ii) by inserting 'or nonfinancial trades or businesses' after 'financial institutions' each place such term appears.

(c) CLERICAL AMENDMENT—The table of sections for chapter 53

of title 31, United States Code, is amended by inserting after the item relating to section 5332 (as added by section 112 of this title) the following new item:

'5331. Reports relating to coins and currency received in nonfinancial trade or business.'.

(f) REGULATIONS—Regulations which the Secretary determines are necessary to implement this section shall be published in final form before the end of the 6-month period beginning on the date of enactment of this Act.

Sec. 366. Efficient Use of Currency Transaction Report System.

(a) FINDINGS—The Congress finds the following:

(1) The Congress established the currency transaction reporting requirements in 1970 because the Congress found then that such reports have a high degree of usefulness in criminal, tax, and regulatory investigations and proceedings and the usefulness of such reports has only increased in the years since the requirements were established.

(2) In 1994, in response to reports and testimony that excess amounts of currency transaction reports were interfering with effective law enforcement, the Congress reformed the currency transaction report exemption requirements to provide—

(A) mandatory exemptions for certain reports that had little usefulness for law enforcement, such as cash transfers between depository institutions and cash deposits from government agencies; and

(B) discretionary authority for the Secretary of the Treasury to provide exemptions, subject to criteria and guidelines established by the Secretary, for financial institutions with regard to regular business customers that maintain accounts at an institution into which frequent cash deposits are made.

(3) Today there is evidence that some financial institutions are not utilizing the exemption system, or are filing reports even if there is an exemption in effect, with the result that the volume of currency transaction reports is once again interfering with effective law enforcement.

(b) STUDY AND REPORT-

(1) STUDY REQUIRED—The Secretary shall conduct a study of—

(A) the possible expansion of the statutory exemption system in effect under section 5313 of title 31, United States Code; and

(B) methods for improving financial institution utilization of the statutory exemption provisions as a way of reducing the submission of currency transaction reports that have little or no value for law enforcement purposes, including improvements in the systems in effect at financial institutions for regular review of the exemption procedures used at the institution and the training of personnel in its effective use.

(2) REPORT REQUIRED—The Secretary of the Treasury shall submit a report to the Congress before the end of the 1-year period beginning on the date of enactment of this Act containing the findings and conclusions of the Secretary with regard to the study required under subsection (a), and such recommendations for legislative or administrative action as the Secretary determines to be appropriate.

Subtitle C—Currency Crimes and Protection

Sec. 371. Bulk Cash Smuggling Into or Out of the United States.

(a) FINDINGS—The Congress finds the following:

(1) Effective enforcement of the currency reporting requirements of subchapter II of chapter 53 of title 31, United States Code, and the regulations prescribed under such subchapter, has forced drug dealers and other criminals engaged in cash-based businesses to avoid using traditional financial institutions.

(2) In their effort to avoid using traditional financial institutions, drug dealers and other criminals are forced to move large quantities of currency in bulk form to and through the airports, border crossings, and other ports of entry where the currency can be smuggled out of the United States and placed in a foreign financial institution or sold on the black market.

(3) The transportation and smuggling of cash in bulk form may now be the most common form of money laundering, and the movement of large sums of cash is one of the most reliable warning signs of drug trafficking, terrorism, money laundering, racketeering, tax evasion and similar crimes.

(4) The intentional transportation into or out of the United States of large amounts of currency or monetary instruments, in a manner designed to circumvent the mandatory reporting provisions of subchapter II of chapter 53 of title 31, United States Code,, is the equivalent of, and creates the same harm as, the smuggling of goods.

(5) The arrest and prosecution of bulk cash smugglers are important parts of law enforcement's effort to stop the laundering of criminal proceeds, but the couriers who attempt to smuggle the cash out of the United States are typically low-level employees of large criminal organizations, and thus are easily replaced. Accordingly, only the confiscation of the smuggled bulk cash can effectively break the cycle of criminal activity of which the laundering of the bulk cash is a critical part.

(6) The current penalties for violations of the currency reporting requirements are insufficient to provide a deterrent to the laundering of criminal proceeds. In particular, in cases where the only criminal violation under current law is a reporting offense, the law does not adequately provide for the confiscation of smuggled currency. In contrast, if the smuggling of bulk cash were itself an offense, the cash could be confiscated as the corpus delicti of the smuggling offense.

(b) PURPOSES—The purposes of this section are—

(1) to make the act of smuggling bulk cash itself a criminal offense;

(2) to authorize forfeiture of any cash or instruments of the smuggling offense; and

(3) to emphasize the seriousness of the act of bulk cash smuggling.

(c) ENACTMENT OF BULK CASH SMUGGLING OFFENSE—Subchapter II of chapter 53 of title 31, United States Code, is amended by adding at the end the following:

'Sec. 5332. Bulk cash smuggling into or out of the United States

'(a) CRIMINAL OFFENSE-

'(1) IN GENERAL—Whoever, with the intent to evade a currency reporting requirement under section 5316, knowingly conceals more than $10,000 in currency or other monetary instruments on the person of such individual or in any conveyance, article of luggage, merchandise, or other container, and transports or transfers or attempts to transport or transfer such currency or monetary instruments from a place within the United States to a place outside of the United States, or from a place outside the United States to a place within the United States, shall be guilty of a currency smuggling offense and subject to punishment pursuant to subsection (b).

'(2) CONCEALMENT ON PERSON—For purposes of this section, the concealment of currency on the person of any individual includes concealment in any article of clothing worn by the individual or in any luggage, backpack, or other container worn or carried by such individual.

'(b) PENALTY-

'(1) TERM OF IMPRISONMENT—A person convicted of a currency smuggling offense under subsection (a), or a conspiracy to commit such offense, shall be imprisoned for not more than 5 years.

'(2) FORFEITURE—In addition, the court, in imposing sentence under paragraph (1), shall order that the defendant forfeit to the United States, any property, real or personal, involved in the offense, and any property traceable to such property, subject to subsection (d) of this section.

'(3) PROCEDURE—The seizure, restraint, and forfeiture of property under this section shall be governed by section 413 of the Controlled Substances Act.

'(4) PERSONAL MONEY JUDGMENT—If the property subject to forfeiture under paragraph (2) is unavailable, and the defendant has insufficient substitute property that may be forfeited pursuant to section 413(p) of the Controlled Substances Act, the court shall enter a personal money judgment against the defendant for the amount that would be subject to forfeiture.

'(c) CIVIL FORFEITURE-

'(1) IN GENERAL—Any property involved in a violation of subsection (a), or a conspiracy to commit such violation, and any property traceable to such violation or conspiracy, may be seized and, subject to subsection (d) of this section, forfeited to the United States.

'(2) PROCEDURE—The seizure and forfeiture shall be governed

by the procedures governing civil forfeitures in money laundering cases pursuant to section 981(a)(1)(A) of title 18, United States Code.

'(3) TREATMENT OF CERTAIN PROPERTY AS INVOLVED IN THE OFFENSE—For purposes of this subsection and subsection (b), any currency or other monetary instrument that is concealed or intended to be concealed in violation of subsection (a) or a conspiracy to commit such violation, any article, container, or conveyance used, or intended to be used, to conceal or transport the currency or other monetary instrument, and any other property used, or intended to be used, to facilitate the offense, shall be considered property involved in the offense.'.

(c) CLERICAL AMENDMENT—The table of sections for subchapter II of chapter 53 of title 31, United States Code, is amended by inserting after the item relating to section 5331, as added by this Act, the following new item:

'5332. Bulk cash smuggling into or out of the United States.'.

Sec. 372. Forfeiture in Currency Reporting Cases.

(a) IN GENERAL—Subsection (c) of section 5317 of title 31, United States Code, is amended to read as follows:

'(c) FORFEITURE-

'(1) CRIMINAL FORFEITURE-

'(A) IN GENERAL—The court in imposing sentence for any violation of section 5313, 5316, or 5324 of this title, or any conspiracy to commit such violation, shall order the defendant to forfeit all property, real or personal, involved in the offense and any property traceable thereto.

'(B) PROCEDURE—Forfeitures under this paragraph shall be governed by the procedures established in section 413 of the Controlled Substances Act.

'(2) CIVIL FORFEITURE—Any property involved in a violation of section 5313, 5316, or 5324 of this title, or any conspiracy to commit any such violation, and any property traceable to any such violation or conspiracy, may be seized and forfeited to the United States in accordance with the procedures governing civil forfeitures in money laundering cases pursuant to section 981(a)(1)(A) of title

18, United States Code.'.

(b) CONFORMING AMENDMENTS-

(1) Section 981(a)(1)(A) of title 18, United States Code, is amended—

(A) by striking 'of section 5313(a) or 5324(a) of title 31, or'; and

(B) by striking 'However' and all that follows through the end of the subparagraph.

(2) Section 982(a)(1) of title 18, United States Code, is amended—

(A) by striking 'of section 5313(a), 5316, or 5324 of title 31, or'; and

(B) by striking 'However' and all that follows through the end of the paragraph.

Sec. 373. Illegal Money Transmitting Businesses.

(a) SCIENTER REQUIREMENT FOR SECTION 1960 VIOLA-TION—Section 1960 of title 18, United States Code, is amended to read as follows:

'Sec. 1960. Prohibition of unlicensed money transmitting businesses

'(a) Whoever knowingly conducts, controls, manages, supervises, directs, or owns all or part of an unlicensed money transmitting business, shall be fined in accordance with this title or imprisoned not more than 5 years, or both.

'(b) As used in this section—

'(1) the term 'unlicensed money transmitting business' means a money transmitting business which affects interstate or foreign commerce in any manner or degree and—

'(A) is operated without an appropriate money transmitting license in a State where such operation is punishable as a mis-demeanor or a felony under State law, whether or not the defen-dant knew that the operation was required to be licensed or that the operation was so punishable;

'(B) fails to comply with the money transmitting business reg-istration requirements under section 5330 of title 31, United States Code, or regulations prescribed under such section; or

'(C) otherwise involves the transportation or transmission of funds that are known to the defendant to have been derived from a criminal offense or are intended to be used to be used to promote or support unlawful activity;

'(2) the term 'money transmitting' includes transferring funds on behalf of the public by any and all means including but not limited to transfers within this country or to locations abroad by wire, check, draft, facsimile, or courier; and

'(3) the term 'State' means any State of the United States, the District of Columbia, the Northern Mariana Islands, and any commonwealth, territory, or possession of the United States.'.

(b) SEIZURE OF ILLEGALLY TRANSMITTED FUNDS—Section 981(a)(1)(A) of title 18, United States Code, is amended by striking 'or 1957' and inserting ', 1957 or 1960'.

(c) CLERICAL AMENDMENT—The table of sections for chapter 95 of title 18, United States Code, is amended in the item relating to section 1960 by striking 'illegal' and inserting 'unlicensed'.

Sec. 374. Counterfeiting Domestic Currency and Obligations.

(a) COUNTERFEIT ACTS COMMITTED OUTSIDE THE UNITED STATES—Section 470 of title 18, United States Code, is amended—

(1) in paragraph (2), by inserting 'analog, digital, or electronic image,' after 'plate, stone,'; and

(2) by striking 'shall be fined under this title, imprisoned not more than 20 years, or both' and inserting 'shall be punished as is provided for the like offense within the United States'.

(b) OBLIGATIONS OR SECURITIES OF THE UNITED STATES—Section 471 of title 18, United States Code, is amended by striking 'fifteen years' and inserting '20 years'.

(c) UTTERING COUNTERFEIT OBLIGATIONS OR SECURITIES—Section 472 of title 18, United States Code, is amended by striking 'fifteen years' and inserting '20 years'.

(d) DEALING IN COUNTERFEIT OBLIGATIONS OR SECURITIES—Section 473 of title 18, United States Code, is amended by striking 'ten years' and inserting '20 years'.

(e) PLATES, STONES, OR ANALOG, DIGITAL, OR ELECTRONIC IMAGES FOR COUNTERFEITING OBLIGATIONS OR SECURITIES-

(1) IN GENERAL—Section 474(a) of title 18, United States Code, is amended by inserting after the second paragraph the following new paragraph:

'Whoever, with intent to defraud, makes, executes, acquires, scans, captures, records, receives, transmits, reproduces, sells, or has in such person's control, custody, or possession, an analog, digital, or electronic image of any obligation or other security of the United States; or'.

(2) AMENDMENT TO DEFINITION—Section 474(b) of title 18, United States Code, is amended by striking the first sentence and inserting the following new sentence: 'For purposes of this section, the term 'analog, digital, or electronic image' includes any analog, digital, or electronic method used for the making, execution, acquisition, scanning, capturing, recording, retrieval, transmission, or reproduction of any obligation or security, unless such use is authorized by the Secretary of the Treasury.'.

(3) TECHNICAL AND CONFORMING AMENDMENT—The heading for section 474 of title 18, United States Code, is amended by striking 'or stones' and inserting ', stones, or analog, digital, or electronic images'.

(4) CLERICAL AMENDMENT—The table of sections for chapter 25 of title 18, United States Code, is amended in the item relating to section 474 by striking 'or stones' and inserting ', stones, or analog, digital, or electronic images'.

(f) TAKING IMPRESSIONS OF TOOLS USED FOR OBLIGATIONS OR SECURITIES—Section 476 of title 18, United States Code, is amended—

(1) by inserting 'analog, digital, or electronic image,' after 'impression, stamp,'; and

(2) by striking 'ten years' and inserting '25 years'.

(g) POSSESSING OR SELLING IMPRESSIONS OF TOOLS USED FOR OBLIGATIONS OR SECURITIES—Section 477 of title 18, United States Code, is amended—

(1) in the first paragraph, by inserting 'analog, digital, or electronic image,' after 'imprint, stamp,';

(2) in the second paragraph, by inserting 'analog, digital, or electronic image,' after 'imprint, stamp,'; and

(3) in the third paragraph, by striking 'ten years' and inserting '25 years'.

(h) CONNECTING PARTS OF DIFFERENT NOTES—Section 484 of title 18, United States Code, is amended by striking 'five years' and inserting '10 years'.

(i) BONDS AND OBLIGATIONS OF CERTAIN LENDING AGENCIES—The first and second paragraphs of section 493 of title 18, United States Code, are each amended by striking 'five years' and inserting '10 years'.

Sec. 375 Counterfeiting Foreign Currency and Obligations.

(a) FOREIGN OBLIGATIONS OR SECURITIES—Section 478 of title 18, United States Code, is amended by striking 'five years' and inserting '20 years'.

(b) UTTERING COUNTERFEIT FOREIGN OBLIGATIONS OR SECURITIES—Section 479 of title 18, United States Code, is amended by striking 'three years' and inserting '20 years'.

(c) POSSESSING COUNTERFEIT FOREIGN OBLIGATIONS OR SECURITIES—Section 480 of title 18, United States Code, is amended by striking 'one year' and inserting '20 years'.

(d) PLATES, STONES, OR ANALOG, DIGITAL, OR ELECTRONIC IMAGES FOR COUNTERFEITING FOREIGN OBLIGATIONS OR SECURITIES-

(1) IN GENERAL—Section 481 of title 18, United States Code, is amended by inserting after the second paragraph the following new paragraph:

'Whoever, with intent to defraud, makes, executes, acquires, scans, captures, records, receives, transmits, reproduces, sells, or has in such person's control, custody, or possession, an analog, digital, or electronic image of any bond, certificate, obligation, or other security of any foreign government, or of any treasury note, bill, or promise to pay, lawfully issued by such foreign government and intended to circulate as money; or'.

(2) INCREASED SENTENCE—The last paragraph of section 481 of title 18, United States Code, is amended by striking 'five years' and inserting '25 years'.

(3) TECHNICAL AND CONFORMING AMENDMENT—The heading for section 481 of title 18, United States Code, is amended by striking 'or stones' and inserting ', stones, or analog, digital, or electronic images'.

(4) CLERICAL AMENDMENT—The table of sections for chapter 25 of title 18, United States Code, is amended in the item relating to section 481 by striking 'or stones' and inserting ', stones, or analog, digital, or electronic images'.

(e) FOREIGN BANK NOTES—Section 482 of title 18, United States Code, is amended by striking 'two years' and inserting '20 years'.

(f) UTTERING COUNTERFEIT FOREIGN BANK NOTES— Section 483 of title 18, United States Code, is amended by striking 'one year' and inserting '20 years'.

Sec. 376. Laundering the Proceeds of Terrorism.

Section 1956(c)(7)(D) of title 18, United States Code, is amended by inserting 'or 2339B' after '2339A'.

Sec. 377. Extraterritorial Jurisdiction.

Section 1029 of title 18, United States Code, is amended by adding at the end the following:

'(h) Any person who, outside the jurisdiction of the United States, engages in any act that, if committed within the jurisdiction of the United States, would constitute an offense under subsection (a) or (b) of this section, shall be subject to the fines, penalties, imprisonment, and forfeiture provided in this title if—

'(1) the offense involves an access device issued, owned, managed, or controlled by a financial institution, account issuer, credit card system member, or other entity within the jurisdiction of the United States; and

'(2) the person transports, delivers, conveys, transfers to or through, or otherwise stores, secrets, or holds within the jurisdiction of the United States, any article used to assist in the commission of the offense or the proceeds of such offense or property derived therefrom.'.

TITLE IV—PROTECTING THE BORDER

Subtitle A—Protecting the Northern Border

Sec. 401. Ensuring Adequate Personnel on the Northern Border.

The Attorney General is authorized to waive any FTE cap on personnel assigned to the Immigration and Naturalization Service on the Northern border.

Sec. 402. Northern Border Personnel.

There are authorized to be appropriated—

(1) such sums as may be necessary to triple the number of Border Patrol personnel (from the number authorized under current law), and the necessary personnel and facilities to support such personnel, in each State along the Northern Border;

(2) such sums as may be necessary to triple the number of Customs Service personnel (from the number authorized under current law), and the necessary personnel and facilities to support such personnel, at ports of entry in each State along the Northern Border;

(3) such sums as may be necessary to triple the number of INS inspectors (from the number authorized on the date of the enactment of this Act), and the necessary personnel and facilities to support such personnel, at ports of entry in each State along the Northern Border; and

(4) an additional $50,000,000 each to the Immigration and Naturalization Service and the United States Customs Service for purposes of making improvements in technology for monitoring the Northern Border and acquiring additional equipment at the Northern Border.

Sec. 403. Access by the Department of State and the INS to Certain Identifying Information in the Criminal History Records of Visa Applicants and Applicants for Admission to the United States.

(a) AMENDMENT OF THE IMMIGRATION AND NATIONALITY ACT—Section 105 of the Immigration and Nationality Act (8 U.S.C. 1105) is amended—

(1) in the section heading, by inserting '; DATA EXCHANGE' after 'SECURITY OFFICERS';

(2) by inserting '(a)' after 'SEC. 105.';

(3) in subsection (a), by inserting 'and border' after 'internal' the second place it appears; and

(4) by adding at the end the following:

'(b)(1) The Attorney General and the Director of the Federal Bureau of Investigation shall provide the Department of State and the Service access to the criminal history record information contained in the National Crime Information Center's Interstate Identification Index (NCIC-III), Wanted Persons File, and to any other files maintained by the National Crime Information Center that may be mutually agreed upon by the Attorney General and the agency receiving the access, for the purpose of determining whether or not a visa applicant or applicant for admission has a criminal history record indexed in any such file.

'(2) Such access shall be provided by means of extracts of the records for placement in the automated visa lookout or other appropriate database, and shall be provided without any fee or charge.

'(3) The Federal Bureau of Investigation shall provide periodic updates of the extracts at intervals mutually agreed upon with the agency receiving the access. Upon receipt of such updated extracts, the receiving agency shall make corresponding updates to its database and destroy previously provided extracts.

'(4) Access to an extract does not entitle the Department of State to obtain the full content of the corresponding automated criminal history record. To obtain the full content of a criminal history record, the Department of State shall submit the applicant's fingerprints and any appropriate fingerprint processing fee authorized by law to the Criminal Justice Information Services Division of the Federal Bureau of Investigation.

'(c) The provision of the extracts described in subsection (b) may be reconsidered by the Attorney General and the receiving agency upon the development and deployment of a more cost-effective and efficient means of sharing the information.

'(d) For purposes of administering this section, the Department of State shall, prior to receiving access to NCIC data but not later than 4 months after the date of enactment of this subsection, promulgate final regulations—

'(1) to implement procedures for the taking of fingerprints; and

'(2) to establish the conditions for the use of the information received from the Federal Bureau of Investigation, in order—

'(A) to limit the redissemination of such information;

'(B) to ensure that such information is used solely to determine whether or not to issue a visa to an alien or to admit an alien to the United States;

'(C) to ensure the security, confidentiality, and destruction of such information; and

'(D) to protect any privacy rights of individuals who are subjects of such information.'.

(b) REPORTING REQUIREMENT—Not later than 2 years after the date of enactment of this Act, the Attorney General and the Secretary of State jointly shall report to Congress on the implementation of the amendments made by this section.

(c) TECHNOLOGY STANDARD TO CONFIRM IDENTITY-

(1) IN GENERAL—The Attorney General and the Secretary of State jointly, through the National Institute of Standards and Technology (NIST), and in consultation with the Secretary of the Treasury and other Federal law enforcement and intelligence agencies the Attorney General or Secretary of State deems appropriate and in consultation with Congress, shall within 2 years after the date of the enactment of this section, develop and certify a technology standard that can be used to verify the identity of persons applying for a United States visa or such persons seeking to enter the United States pursuant to a visa for the purposes of conducting background checks, confirming identity, and ensuring that a person has not received a visa under a different name or such person seeking to enter the United States pursuant to a visa.

(2) INTEGRATED—The technology standard developed pursuant to paragraph (1), shall be the technological basis for a cross-agency, cross-platform electronic system that is a cost-effective, efficient, fully integrated means to share law enforcement and intelligence information necessary to confirm the identity of such persons applying for a United States visa or such person seeking to enter the United States pursuant to a visa.

(3) ACCESSIBLE—The electronic system described in paragraph

(2), once implemented, shall be readily and easily accessible to—

(A) all consular officers responsible for the issuance of visas;

(B) all Federal inspection agents at all United States border inspection points; and

(C) all law enforcement and intelligence officers as determined by regulation to be responsible for investigation or identification of aliens admitted to the United States pursuant to a visa.

(4) REPORT—Not later than 18 months after the date of the enactment of this Act, and every 2 years thereafter, the Attorney General and the Secretary of State shall jointly, in consultation with the Secretary of Treasury, report to Congress describing the development, implementation, efficacy, and privacy implications of the technology standard and electronic database system described in this subsection.

(5) FUNDING—There is authorized to be appropriated to the Secretary of State, the Attorney General, and the Director of the National Institute of Standards and Technology such sums as may be necessary to carry out the provisions of this subsection.

(d) STATUTORY CONSTRUCTION—Nothing in this section, or in any other law, shall be construed to limit the authority of the Attorney General or the Director of the Federal Bureau of Investigation to provide access to the criminal history record information contained in the National Crime Information Center's (NCIC) Interstate Identification Index (NCIC-III), or to any other information maintained by the NCIC, to any Federal agency or officer authorized to enforce or administer the immigration laws of the United States, for the purpose of such enforcement or administration, upon terms that are consistent with the National Crime Prevention and Privacy Compact Act of 1998 (subtitle A of title II of Public Law 105–251; 42 U.S.C. 14611–16) and section 552a of title 5, United States Code.

Sec. 404. Limited Authority to Pay Overtime.

The matter under the headings 'Immigration And Naturalization Service: Salaries and Expenses, Enforcement And Border Affairs' and 'Immigration And Naturalization Service: Salaries and Expenses, Citizenship And Benefits, Immigration And Program Direction' in the Department of Justice Appropriations Act, 2001 (as enacted into law by Appendix B (H.R. 5548) of Public Law 106–553 (114 Stat. 2762A-58 to 2762A-59)) is amended by striking the following each place it occurs: '*Provided*, That none of the funds available to the Immigration and Naturalization Service shall be available to pay any employee overtime pay in an amount in excess of $30,000 during the calendar year beginning January 1, 2001:'.

Sec. 405. Report on the Integrated Automated Fingerprint Identification System for Ports of Entry and Overseas Consular Posts.

(a) IN GENERAL—The Attorney General, in consultation with the appropriate heads of other Federal agencies, including the Secretary of State, Secretary of the Treasury, and the Secretary of Transportation, shall report to Congress on the feasibility of enhancing the Integrated Automated Fingerprint Identification System (IAFIS) of the Federal Bureau of Investigation and other identification systems in order to better identify a person who holds a foreign passport or a visa and may be wanted in connection with a criminal investigation in the United States or abroad, before the issuance of a visa to that person or the entry or exit from the United States by that person.

(b) AUTHORIZATION OF APPROPRIATIONS—There is authorized to be appropriated not less than $2,000,000 to carry out this section.

Subtitle B—Enhanced Immigration Provisions

Sec. 411. Definitions Relating to Terrorism.

(a) GROUNDS OF INADMISSIBILITY—Section 212(a)(3) of the Immigration and Nationality Act (8 U.S.C. 1182(a)(3)) is amended—

    (1) in subparagraph (B)—

        (A) in clause (i)—

            (i) by amending subclause (IV) to read as follows:

            '(IV)is a representative (as defined in clause (v)) of—

                '(aa) a foreign terrorist organization, as designated by the Secretary of State under section 219, or

                '(bb) a political, social or other similar group whose public endorsement of acts of terrorist activity the Secretary of State has determined undermines United States efforts to reduce or eliminate terrorist activities,';

(ii) in subclause (V), by inserting 'or' after 'section 219,'; and

(iii) by adding at the end the following new subclauses:

'(VI) has used the alien's position of prominence within any country to endorse or espouse terrorist activity, or to persuade others to support terrorist activity or a terrorist organization, in a way that the Secretary of State has determined undermines United States efforts to reduce or eliminate terrorist activities, or

'(VII) is the spouse or child of an alien who is inadmissible under this section, if the activity causing the alien to be found inadmissible occurred within the last 5 years,';

(B) by redesignating clauses (ii), (iii), and (iv) as clauses (iii), (iv), and (v), respectively;

(C) in clause (i)(II), by striking 'clause (iii)' and inserting 'clause (iv)';

(D) by inserting after clause (i) the following:

'(ii) EXCEPTION—Subclause (VII) of clause (i) does not apply to a spouse or child—

'(I) who did not know or should not reasonably have known of the activity causing the alien to be found inadmissible under this section; or

'(II) whom the consular officer or Attorney General has reasonable grounds to believe has renounced the activity causing the alien to be found inadmissible under this section.';

(E) in clause (iii) (as redesignated by subparagraph (B))—

(i) by inserting 'it had been' before 'committed in the United States'; and

(ii) in subclause (V)(b), by striking 'or firearm' and inserting ', firearm, or other weapon or dangerous device';

(F) by amending clause (iv) (as redesignated by subparagraph

(B)) to read as follows:

'(iv) ENGAGE IN TERRORIST ACTIVITY DEFINED —As used in this chapter, the term 'engage in terrorist activity' means, in an individual capacity or as a member of an organization—

'(I) to commit or to incite to commit, under circumstances indicating an intention to cause death or serious bodily injury, a terrorist activity;

'(II) to prepare or plan a terrorist activity;

'(III) to gather information on potential targets for terrorist activity;

'(IV) to solicit funds or other things of value for—

'(aa) a terrorist activity;

'(bb) a terrorist organization described in clause (vi)(I) or (vi)(II); or

'(cc) a terrorist organization described in clause (vi)(III), unless the solicitor can demonstrate that he did not know, and should not reasonably have known, that the solicitation would further the organization's terrorist activity;

'(V) to solicit any individual—

'(aa) to engage in conduct otherwise described in this clause;

'(bb) for membership in a terrorist organization described in clause (vi)(I) or (vi)(II); or

'(cc) for membership in a terrorist organization described in clause (vi)(III), unless the solicitor can demonstrate that he did not know, and should not reasonably have known, that the solicitation would further the organization's terrorist activity; or

'(VI) to commit an act that the actor knows, or reasonably should know, affords material support, including a safe house, transportation, communications, funds, transfer of funds or other material financial benefit, false documentation or identification, weapons (including chemical, biological, or radiological weapons), explosives, or training—

'(aa) for the commission of a terrorist activity;

'(bb) to any individual who the actor knows, or reasonably should know, has committed or plans to commit a terrorist activity;

'(cc) to a terrorist organization described in clause (vi)(I) or (vi)(II); or

'(dd) to a terrorist organization described in clause (vi)(III), unless the actor can demonstrate that he did not know, and should not reasonably have known, that the act would further the organization's terrorist activity.

This clause shall not apply to any material support the alien afforded to an organization or individual that has committed terrorist activity, if the Secretary of State, after consultation with the Attorney General, or the Attorney General, after consultation with the Secretary of State, concludes in his sole unreviewable discretion, that this clause should not apply.'; and

(G) by adding at the end the following new clause:

'(vi) TERRORIST ORGANIZATION DEFINED—As used in clause (i)(VI) and clause (iv), the term 'terrorist organization' means an organization—

'(I) designated under section 219;

'(II) otherwise designated, upon publication in the Federal Register, by the Secretary of State in consultation with or upon the request of the Attorney General, as a terrorist organization, after finding that the organization engages in the activities described in subclause (I), (II), or (III) of clause (iv), or that the organization provides material support to further terrorist activity; or

'(III) that is a group of two or more individuals, whether organized or not, which engages in the activities described in subclause (I), (II), or (III) of clause (iv).'; and

(2) by adding at the end the following new subparagraph:

'(F) ASSOCIATION WITH TERRORIST ORGANIZA-TIONS—Any alien who the Secretary of State, after consultation with the Attorney General, or the Attorney General, after consultation with the Secretary of State, determines has been associated with a terrorist organization and intends while in the United States to engage solely, principally, or incidentally in activities that could endanger the welfare, safety, or security of the United States is inadmissible.'.

(b) CONFORMING AMENDMENTS-

(1) Section 237(a)(4)(B) of the Immigration and Nationality Act (8 U.S.C. 1227(a)(4)(B)) is amended by striking 'section 212(a)(3)(B)(iii)' and inserting 'section 212(a)(3)(B)(iv)'.

(2) Section 208(b)(2)(A)(v) of the Immigration and Nationality Act (8 U.S.C. 1158(b)(2)(A)(v)) is amended by striking 'or (IV)' and inserting '(IV), or (VI)'.

(c) RETROACTIVE APPLICATION OF AMENDMENTS-

(1) IN GENERAL—Except as otherwise provided in this subsection, the amendments made by this section shall take effect on the date of the enactment of this Act and shall apply to—

(A) actions taken by an alien before, on, or after such date; and

(B) all aliens, without regard to the date of entry or attempted entry into the United States—

(i) in removal proceedings on or after such date (except for proceedings in which there has been a final administrative decision before such date); or

(ii) seeking admission to the United States on or after such date.

(2) SPECIAL RULE FOR ALIENS IN EXCLUSION OR DE-PORTATION PROCEEDINGS—Notwithstanding any other provision of law, sections 212(a)(3)(B) and 237(a)(4)(B) of the Immigration and Nationality Act, as amended by this Act, shall apply to all aliens in exclusion or deportation proceedings on or after the date of the enactment of this Act (except for proceedings in which

there has been a final administrative decision before such date) as if such proceedings were removal proceedings.

(3) SPECIAL RULE FOR SECTION 219 ORGANIZATIONS AND ORGANIZATIONS DESIGNATED UNDER SECTION 212(a)(3)(B)(vi)(II)-

(A) IN GENERAL—Notwithstanding paragraphs (1) and (2), no alien shall be considered inadmissible under section 212(a)(3) of the Immigration and Nationality Act (8 U.S.C. 1182(a)(3)), or deportable under section 237(a)(4)(B) of such Act (8 U.S.C. 1227(a)(4)(B)), by reason of the amendments made by subsection (a), on the ground that the alien engaged in a terrorist activity described in subclause (IV)(bb), (V)(bb), or (VI)(cc) of section 212(a)(3)(B)(iv) of such Act (as so amended) with respect to a group at any time when the group was not a terrorist organization designated by the Secretary of State under section 219 of such Act (8 U.S.C. 1189) or otherwise designated under section 212(a)(3)(B)(vi)(II) of such Act (as so amended).

(B) STATUTORY CONSTRUCTION—Subparagraph (A) shall not be construed to prevent an alien from being considered inadmissible or deportable for having engaged in a terrorist activity—

(i) described in subclause (IV)(bb), (V)(bb), or (VI)(cc) of section 212(a)(3)(B)(iv) of such Act (as so amended) with respect to a terrorist organization at any time when such organization was designated by the Secretary of State under section 219 of such Act or otherwise designated under section 212(a)(3)(B)(vi)(II) of such Act (as so amended); or

(ii) described in subclause (IV)(cc), (V)(cc), or (VI)(dd) of section 212(a)(3)(B)(iv) of such Act (as so amended) with respect to a terrorist organization described in section 212(a)(3)(B)(vi)(III) of such Act (as so amended).

(4) EXCEPTION—The Secretary of State, in consultation with the Attorney General, may determine that the amendments made by this section shall not apply with respect to actions by an alien taken outside the United States before the date of the enactment of this Act upon the recommendation of a consular officer who has

concluded that there is not reasonable ground to believe that the alien knew or reasonably should have known that the actions would further a terrorist activity.

(c) DESIGNATION OF FOREIGN TERRORIST ORGANIZA-TIONS—Section 219(a) of the Immigration and Nationality Act (8 U.S.C. 1189(a)) is amended—

(1) in paragraph (1)(B), by inserting 'or terrorism (as defined in section 140(d)(2) of the Foreign Relations Authorization Act, Fiscal Years 1988 and 1989 (22 U.S.C. 2656f(d)(2)), or retains the capability and intent to engage in terrorist activity or terrorism' after '212(a)(3)(B)';

(2) in paragraph (1)(C), by inserting 'or terrorism' after 'terrorist activity';

(3) by amending paragraph (2)(A) to read as follows:

'(A) NOTICE-

'(i) TO CONGRESSIONAL LEADERS—Seven days before making a designation under this subsection, the Secretary shall, by classified communication, notify the Speaker and Minority Leader of the House of Representatives, the President pro tempore, Majority Leader, and Minority Leader of the Senate, and the members of the relevant committees of the House of Representatives and the Senate, in writing, of the intent to designate an organization under this subsection, together with the findings made under paragraph (1) with respect to that organization, and the factual basis therefor.

'(ii) PUBLICATION IN FEDERAL REGISTER—The Secretary shall publish the designation in the Federal Register seven days after providing the notification under clause (i).';

(4) in paragraph (2)(B)(i), by striking 'subparagraph (A)' and inserting 'subparagraph (A)(ii)';

(5) in paragraph (2)(C), by striking 'paragraph (2)' and inserting 'paragraph (2)(A)(i)';

(6) in paragraph (3)(B), by striking 'subsection (c)' and inserting 'subsection (b)';

(7) in paragraph (4)(B), by inserting after the first sentence the following: 'The Secretary also may redesignate such organization at the end of any 2-year redesignation period (but not sooner than 60 days prior to the termination of such period) for an additional 2-year period upon a finding that the relevant circumstances described in paragraph (1) still exist. Any redesignation shall be effective immediately following the end of the prior 2-year designation or redesignation period unless a different effective date is provided in such redesignation.';

(8) in paragraph (6)(A)—

(A) by inserting 'or a redesignation made under paragraph (4)(B)' after 'paragraph (1)';

(B) in clause (i)—

(i) by inserting 'or redesignation' after 'designation' the first place it appears; and

(ii) by striking 'of the designation'; and

(C) in clause (ii), by striking 'of the designation';

(9) in paragraph (6)(B)—

(A) by striking 'through (4)' and inserting 'and (3)'; and

(B) by inserting at the end the following new sentence: 'Any revocation shall take effect on the date specified in the revocation or upon publication in the Federal Register if no effective date is specified.';

(10) in paragraph (7), by inserting ', or the revocation of a redesignation under paragraph (6),' after 'paragraph (5) or (6)'; and

(11) in paragraph (8)—

(A) by striking 'paragraph (1)(B)' and inserting 'paragraph (2)(B), or if a redesignation under this subsection has become effective under paragraph (4)(B)';

(B) by inserting 'or an alien in a removal proceeding' after 'criminal action'; and

(C) by inserting 'or redesignation' before 'as a defense'.

Sec. 412. Mandatory Detention of Suspected Terrorists; Habeas Corpus; Judicial Review.

(a) IN GENERAL—The Immigration and Nationality Act (8 U.S.C. 1101 et seq.) is amended by inserting after section 236 the following:

'MANDATORY DETENTION OF SUSPECTED TERRORISTS; HABEAS CORPUS; JUDICIAL REVIEW

'SEC. 236A. (a) DETENTION OF TERRORIST ALIENS-

'(1) CUSTODY—The Attorney General shall take into custody any alien who is certified under paragraph (3).

'(2) RELEASE—Except as provided in paragraphs (5) and (6), the Attorney General shall maintain custody of such an alien until the alien is removed from the United States. Except as provided in paragraph (6), such custody shall be maintained irrespective of any relief from removal for which the alien may be eligible, or any relief from removal granted the alien, until the Attorney General determines that the alien is no longer an alien who may be certified under paragraph (3). If the alien is finally determined not to be removable, detention pursuant to this subsection shall terminate.

'(3) CERTIFICATION—The Attorney General may certify an alien under this paragraph if the Attorney General has reasonable grounds to believe that the alien—

'(A) is described in section 212(a)(3)(A)(i), 212(a)(3)(A)(iii), 212(a)(3)(B), 237(a)(4)(A)(i), 237(a)(4)(A)(iii), or 237(a)(4)(B); or

'(B) is engaged in any other activity that endangers the national security of the United States.

'(4) NONDELEGATION—The Attorney General may delegate the authority provided under paragraph (3) only to the Deputy Attorney General. The Deputy Attorney General may not delegate such authority.

'(5) COMMENCEMENT OF PROCEEDINGS—The Attorney General shall place an alien detained under paragraph (1) in removal proceedings, or shall charge the alien with a criminal offense, not later than 7 days after the commencement of such detention. If the requirement of the preceding sentence is not satisfied, the Attorney General shall release the alien.

'(6) LIMITATION ON INDEFINITE DETENTION—An alien detained solely under paragraph (1) who has not been removed under section 241(a)(1)(A), and whose removal is unlikely in the reasonably foreseeable future, may be detained for additional periods of up to six months only if the release of the alien will threaten the national security of the United States or the safety of the community or any person.

'(7) REVIEW OF CERTIFICATION—The Attorney General shall review the certification made under paragraph (3) every 6 months. If the Attorney General determines, in the Attorney General's discretion, that the certification should be revoked, the alien may be released on such conditions as the Attorney General deems appropriate, unless such release is otherwise prohibited by law. The alien may request each 6 months in writing that the Attorney General reconsider the certification and may submit documents or other evidence in support of that request.

'(b) HABEAS CORPUS AND JUDICIAL REVIEW-

'(1) IN GENERAL—Judicial review of any action or decision relating to this section (including judicial review of the merits of a determination made under subsection (a)(3) or (a)(6)) is available exclusively in habeas corpus proceedings consistent with this subsection. Except as provided in the preceding sentence, no court shall have jurisdiction to review, by habeas corpus petition or otherwise, any such action or decision.

'(2) APPLICATION-

'(A) IN GENERAL—Notwithstanding any other provision of law, including section 2241(a) of title 28, United States Code, habeas corpus proceedings described in paragraph (1) may be initiated only by an application filed with—

'(i) the Supreme Court;

'(ii) any justice of the Supreme Court;

'(iii)any circuit judge of the United States Court of Appeals for the District of Columbia Circuit; or

'(iv) any district court otherwise having jurisdiction to entertain it.

'(B) APPLICATION TRANSFER—Section 2241(b) of title 28, United States Code, shall apply to an application for a writ of habeas corpus described in subparagraph (A).

'(3) APPEALS—Notwithstanding any other provision of law, including section 2253 of title 28, in habeas corpus proceedings described in paragraph (1) before a circuit or district judge, the final order shall be subject to review, on appeal, by the United States Court of Appeals for the District of Columbia Circuit. There shall be no right of appeal in such proceedings to any other circuit court of appeals.

'(4) RULE OF DECISION—The law applied by the Supreme Court and the United States Court of Appeals for the District of Columbia Circuit shall be regarded as the rule of decision in habeas corpus proceedings described in paragraph (1).

'(c) STATUTORY CONSTRUCTION—The provisions of this section shall not be applicable to any other provision of this Act.'.

(b) CLERICAL AMENDMENT—The table of contents of the Immigration and Nationality Act is amended by inserting after the item relating to section 236 the following:

'Sec. 236A. Mandatory detention of suspected terrorist; habeas corpus; judicial review.'.

(c) REPORTS—Not later than 6 months after the date of the enactment of this Act, and every 6 months thereafter, the Attorney General shall submit a report to the Committee on the Judiciary of the House of Representatives and the Committee on the Judiciary of the Senate, with respect to the reporting period, on—

(1) the number of aliens certified under section 236A(a)(3) of the Immigration and Nationality Act, as added by subsection (a);

(2) the grounds for such certifications;

(3) the nationalities of the aliens so certified;

(4) the length of the detention for each alien so certified; and

(5) the number of aliens so certified who—

(A) were granted any form of relief from removal;

(B) were removed;

(C) the Attorney General has determined are no longer aliens who may be so certified; or

(D) were released from detention.

Sec. 413. Multilateral Cooperation Against Terrorists.

Section 222(f) of the Immigration and Nationality Act (8 U.S.C. 1202(f)) is amended—

(1) by striking 'except that in the discretion of' and inserting the following: 'except that—

'(1) in the discretion of'; and

(2) by adding at the end the following:

'(2) the Secretary of State, in the Secretary's discretion and on the basis of reciprocity, may provide to a foreign government information in the Department of State's computerized visa lookout database and, when necessary and appropriate, other records covered by this section related to information in the database—

> '(A) with regard to individual aliens, at any time on a case-by-case basis for the purpose of preventing, investigating, or punishing acts that would constitute a crime in the United States, including, but not limited to, terrorism or trafficking in controlled substances, persons, or illicit weapons; or

> '(B) with regard to any or all aliens in the database, pursuant to such conditions as the Secretary of State shall establish in an agreement with the foreign government in which that government agrees to use such information and records for the purposes described in subparagraph (A) or to deny visas to persons who would be inadmissible to the United States.'.

Sec. 414. Visa Integrity and Security.

(a) SENSE OF CONGRESS REGARDING THE NEED TO EXPEDITE IMPLEMENTATION OF INTEGRATED ENTRY AND EXIT DATA SYSTEM-

(1) SENSE OF CONGRESS—In light of the terrorist attacks perpetrated against the United States on September 11, 2001, it is the sense of the Congress that—

(A) the Attorney General, in consultation with the Secretary of State, should fully implement the integrated entry and exit data system for airports, seaports, and land border ports of entry, as specified in section 110 of the Illegal Immigration Reform and Immigrant Responsibility Act of 1996 (8 U.S.C. 1365a), with all deliberate speed and as expeditiously as practicable; and

(B) the Attorney General, in consultation with the Secretary of State, the Secretary of Commerce, the Secretary of the

Treasury, and the Office of Homeland Security, should immediately begin establishing the Integrated Entry and Exit Data System Task Force, as described in section 3 of the Immigration and Naturalization Service Data Management Improvement Act of 2000 (Public Law 106–215).

(2) AUTHORIZATION OF APPROPRIATIONS—There is authorized to be appropriated such sums as may be necessary to fully implement the system described in paragraph (1)(A).

(b) DEVELOPMENT OF THE SYSTEM—In the development of the integrated entry and exit data system under section 110 of the Illegal Immigration Reform and Immigrant Responsibility Act of 1996 (8 U.S.C. 1365a), the Attorney General and the Secretary of State shall particularly focus on—

(1) the utilization of biometric technology; and

(2) the development of tamper-resistant documents readable at ports of entry.

(c) INTERFACE WITH LAW ENFORCEMENT DATABASES—The entry and exit data system described in this section shall be able to interface with law enforcement databases for use by Federal law enforcement to identify and detain individuals who pose a threat to the national security of the United States.

(d) REPORT ON SCREENING INFORMATION—Not later than 12 months after the date of enactment of this Act, the Office of Homeland Security shall submit a report to Congress on the information that is needed from any United States agency to effectively screen visa applicants and applicants for admission to the United States to identify those affiliated with terrorist organizations or those that pose any threat to the safety or security of the United States, including the type of information currently received by United States agencies and the regularity with which such information is transmitted to the Secretary of State and the Attorney General.

Sec. 415. Participation of Office of Homeland Security on Entry-Exit Task Force.

Section 3 of the Immigration and Naturalization Service Data Management Improvement Act of 2000 (Public Law 106–215) is amended by striking 'and the Secretary of the Treasury,' and inserting 'the Secretary of the Treasury, and the Office of Homeland Security'.

Sec. 416. Foreign Student Monitoring Program.

(a) FULL IMPLEMENTATION AND EXPANSION OF FOREIGN STUDENT VISA MONITORING PROGRAM REQUIRED—The Attorney General, in consultation with the Secretary of State, shall fully implement and expand the program established by section 641(a) of the Illegal Immigration Reform and Immigrant Responsibility Act of 1996 (8 U.S.C. 1372(a)).

(b) INTEGRATION WITH PORT OF ENTRY INFORMATION— For each alien with respect to whom information is collected under section 641 of the Illegal Immigration Reform and Immigrant Responsibility Act of 1996 (8 U.S.C. 1372), the Attorney General, in consultation with the Secretary of State, shall include information on the date of entry and port of entry.

(c) EXPANSION OF SYSTEM TO INCLUDE OTHER APPROVED EDUCATIONAL INSTITUTIONS—Section 641 of the Illegal Immigration Reform and Immigrant Responsibility Act of 1996 (8 U.S.C.1372) is amended—

(1) in subsection (a)(1), subsection (c)(4)(A), and subsection (d)(1) (in the text above subparagraph (A)), by inserting ', other approved educational institutions,' after 'higher education' each place it appears;

(2) in subsections (c)(1)(C), (c)(1)(D), and (d)(1)(A), by inserting ', or other approved educational institution,' after 'higher education' each place it appears;

(3) in subsections (d)(2), (e)(1), and (e)(2), by inserting ', other approved educational institution,' after 'higher education' each place it appears; and

(4) in subsection (h), by adding at the end the following new paragraph:

'(3) OTHER APPROVED EDUCATIONAL INSTITUTION— The term 'other approved educational institution' includes any air flight school, language training school, or vocational school, approved by the Attorney General, in consultation with the Secretary of Education and the Secretary of State, under subparagraph (F), (J), or (M) of section 101(a)(15) of the Immigration and Nationality Act.'.

(d) AUTHORIZATION OF APPROPRIATIONS—There is authorized to be appropriated to the Department of Justice $36,800,000 for the period beginning on the date of enactment of this Act and ending on January 1, 2003, to fully implement and expand prior to January 1, 2003, the program established by section 641(a) of the Illegal Immigration Reform and Immigrant Responsibility Act of 1996 (8 U.S.C. 1372(a)).

Sec. 417. Machine Readable Passports.

(a) AUDITS—The Secretary of State shall, each fiscal year until September 30, 2007—

(1) perform annual audits of the implementation of section 217(c)(2)(B) of the Immigration and Nationality Act (8 U.S.C. 1187(c)(2)(B));

(2) check for the implementation of precautionary measures to prevent the counterfeiting and theft of passports; and

(3) ascertain that countries designated under the visa waiver program have established a program to develop tamper-resistant passports.

(b) PERIODIC REPORTS—Beginning one year after the date of enactment of this Act, and every year thereafter until 2007, the Secretary of State shall submit a report to Congress setting forth the findings of the most recent audit conducted under subsection (a)(1).

(c) ADVANCING DEADLINE FOR SATISFACTION OF REQUIREMENT—Section 217(a)(3) of the Immigration and Nationality Act (8 U.S.C. 1187(a)(3)) is amended by striking '2007' and inserting '2003'.

(d) WAIVER—Section 217(a)(3) of the Immigration and Nationality Act (8 U.S.C. 1187(a)(3)) is amended—

(1) by striking 'On or after' and inserting the following:

'(A) IN GENERAL—Except as provided in subparagraph (B), on or after'; and

(2) by adding at the end the following:

'(B) LIMITED WAIVER AUTHORITY—For the period beginning October 1, 2003, and ending September 30, 2007, the Secretary of State may waive the requirement of subparagraph (A) with respect to nationals of a program country (as designated under subsection (c)), if the Secretary of State finds that the program country—

'(i) is making progress toward ensuring that passports meeting the requirement of subparagraph (A) are generally available to its nationals; and

'(ii) has taken appropriate measures to protect against misuse of passports the country has issued that do not meet the requirement of subparagraph (A).'.

Sec. 418. Prevention of Consulate Shopping.

(a) REVIEW—The Secretary of State shall review how consular officers issue visas to determine if consular shopping is a problem.

(b) ACTIONS TO BE TAKEN—If the Secretary of State determines under subsection (a) that consular shopping is a problem, the Secretary shall take steps to address the problem and shall submit a report to Congress describing what action was taken.

Subtitle C—Preservation of Immigration Benefits for Victims of Terrorism

Sec. 421. Special Immigrant Status.

(a) IN GENERAL—For purposes of the Immigration and Nationality Act (8 U.S.C. 1101 et seq.), the Attorney General may provide an alien described in subsection (b) with the status of a special immigrant under section 101(a)(27) of such Act (8 U.S.C. 1101(a(27)), if the alien—

(1) files with the Attorney General a petition under section 204 of such Act (8 U.S.C. 1154) for classification under section 203(b)(4) of such Act (8 U.S.C. 1153(b)(4)); and

(2) is otherwise eligible to receive an immigrant visa and is otherwise admissible to the United States for permanent residence, except in determining such admissibility, the grounds for inadmissibility specified in section 212(a)(4) of such Act (8 U.S.C. 1182(a)(4)) shall not apply.

(b) ALIENS DESCRIBED-

(1) PRINCIPAL ALIENS—An alien is described in this subsection if—

(A) the alien was the beneficiary of—

(i) a petition that was filed with the Attorney General on or before September 11, 2001—

(I) under section 204 of the Immigration and Nationality Act (8 U.S.C. 1154) to classify the alien as a family-sponsored immigrant under section 203(a) of such Act (8 U.S.C. 1153(a)) or as an employment-based immigrant under section 203(b) of such Act (8 U.S.C. 1153(b)); or

(II) under section 214(d) (8 U.S.C. 1184(d)) of such Act to authorize the issuance of a nonimmigrant visa to the alien under section 101(a)(15)(K) of such Act (8 U.S.C. 1101(a)(15)(K)); or

(ii) an application for labor certification under section 212(a)(5)(A) of such Act (8 U.S.C. 1182(a)(5)(A)) that was filed under regulations of the Secretary of Labor on or before such date; and

(B) such petition or application was revoked or terminated (or otherwise rendered null), either before or after its approval, due to a specified terrorist activity that directly resulted in—

(i) the death or disability of the petitioner, applicant, or alien beneficiary; or

(ii) loss of employment due to physical damage to, or destruction of, the business of the petitioner or applicant.

(2) SPOUSES AND CHILDREN-

(A) IN GENERAL—An alien is described in this subsection if—

(i) the alien was, on September 10, 2001, the spouse or child of a principal alien described in paragraph (1); and

(ii) the alien—

(I) is accompanying such principal alien; or

(II) is following to join such principal alien not later than September 11, 2003.

(B) CONSTRUCTION—For purposes of construing the terms 'accompanying' and 'following to join' in subparagraph (A)(ii), any death of a principal alien that is described in paragraph (1)(B)(i) shall be disregarded.

(3) GRANDPARENTS OF ORPHANS—An alien is described in this subsection if the alien is a grandparent of a child, both of whose parents died as a direct result of a specified terrorist activity, if either of such deceased parents was, on September 10, 2001, a citizen or national of the United States or an alien lawfully admitted for permanent residence in the United States.

(c) PRIORITY DATE—Immigrant visas made available under this section shall be issued to aliens in the order in which a petition on behalf of each such alien is filed with the Attorney General under subsection (a)(1), except that if an alien was assigned a priority date with respect to a petition described in subsection (b)(1)(A)(i), the alien may maintain that priority date.

(d) NUMERICAL LIMITATIONS—For purposes of the application of sections 201 through 203 of the Immigration and Nationality Act (8 U.S.C. 1151–1153) in any fiscal year, aliens eligible to be provided status under this section shall be treated as special immigrants described in section 101(a)(27) of such Act (8 U.S.C. 1101(a)(27)) who are not described in subparagraph (A), (B), (C), or (K) of such section.

Sec. 422. Extension of Filing or Reentry Deadlines.

(a) AUTOMATIC EXTENSION OF NONIMMIGRANT STATUS-

(1) IN GENERAL—Notwithstanding section 214 of the Immigration and Nationality Act (8 U.S.C. 1184), in the case of an alien described in paragraph (2) who was lawfully present in the United States as a nonimmigrant on September 10, 2001, the alien may remain lawfully in the United States in the same nonimmigrant status until the later of—

(A) the date such lawful nonimmigrant status otherwise would have terminated if this subsection had not been enacted; or

(B) 1 year after the death or onset of disability described in paragraph (2).

(2) ALIENS DESCRIBED-

(A) PRINCIPAL ALIENS—An alien is described in this paragraph if the alien was disabled as a direct result of a specified terrorist activity.

(B) SPOUSES AND CHILDREN—An alien is described in

this paragraph if the alien was, on September 10, 2001, the spouse or child of—

    (i)   a principal alien described in subparagraph (A); or

    (ii)   an alien who died as a direct result of a specified terrorist activity.

(3) AUTHORIZED EMPLOYMENT—During the period in which a principal alien or alien spouse is in lawful nonimmigrant status under paragraph (1), the alien shall be provided an 'employment authorized' endorsement or other appropriate document signifying authorization of employment not later than 30 days after the alien requests such authorization.

(b) NEW DEADLINES FOR EXTENSION OR CHANGE OF NON-IMMIGRANT STATUS-

(1) FILING DELAYS—In the case of an alien who was lawfully present in the United States as a nonimmigrant on September 10, 2001, if the alien was prevented from filing a timely application for an extension or change of nonimmigrant status as a direct result of a specified terrorist activity, the alien's application shall be considered timely filed if it is filed not later than 60 days after it otherwise would have been due.

(2) DEPARTURE DELAYS—In the case of an alien who was lawfully present in the United States as a nonimmigrant on September 10, 2001, if the alien is unable timely to depart the United States as a direct result of a specified terrorist activity, the alien shall not be considered to have been unlawfully present in the United States during the period beginning on September 11, 2001, and ending on the date of the alien's departure, if such departure occurs on or before November 11, 2001.

(3) SPECIAL RULE FOR ALIENS UNABLE TO RETURN FROM ABROAD-

    (A) PRINCIPAL ALIENS—In the case of an alien who was in a lawful nonimmigrant status on September 10, 2001, but who was not present in the United States on such date, if the alien was prevented from returning to the United States in order to file a timely application for an extension of nonimmigrant status as a direct result of a specified terrorist activity—

        (i)   the alien's application shall be considered timely filed if it is filed not later than 60 days after it otherwise would have been due; and

(ii) the alien's lawful nonimmigrant status shall be considered to continue until the later of—

(I) the date such status otherwise would have terminated if this subparagraph had not been enacted; or

(II) the date that is 60 days after the date on which the application described in clause (i) otherwise would have been due.

(B) SPOUSES AND CHILDREN—In the case of an alien who is the spouse or child of a principal alien described in subparagraph (A), if the spouse or child was in a lawful nonimmigrant status on September 10, 2001, the spouse or child may remain lawfully in the United States in the same nonimmigrant status until the later of—

(i) the date such lawful nonimmigrant status otherwise would have terminated if this subparagraph had not been enacted; or

(ii) the date that is 60 days after the date on which the application described in subparagraph (A) otherwise would have been due.

(4) CIRCUMSTANCES PREVENTING TIMELY ACTION-

(A) FILING DELAYS—For purposes of paragraph (1), circumstances preventing an alien from timely acting are—

(i) office closures;

(ii) mail or courier service cessations or delays; and

(iii) other closures, cessations, or delays affecting case processing or travel necessary to satisfy legal requirements.

(B) DEPARTURE AND RETURN DELAYS—For purposes of paragraphs (2) and (3), circumstances preventing an alien from timely acting are—

(i) office closures;

(ii) airline flight cessations or delays; and

(iii) other closures, cessations, or delays affecting case processing or travel necessary to satisfy legal requirements.

(c) DIVERSITY IMMIGRANTS-

(1) WAIVER OF FISCAL YEAR LIMITATION—Notwithstanding section 203(e)(2) of the Immigration and Nationality Act (8 U.S.C. 1153(e)(2)), an immigrant visa number issued to an alien under section 203(c) of such Act for fiscal year 2001 may be used by the alien during the period beginning on October 1, 2001, and ending on April 1, 2002, if the alien establishes that the alien was prevented from using it during fiscal year 2001 as a direct result of a specified terrorist activity.

(2) WORLDWIDE LEVEL—In the case of an alien entering the United States as a lawful permanent resident, or adjusting to that status, under paragraph (1) or (3), the alien shall be counted as a diversity immigrant for fiscal year 2001 for purposes of section 201(e) of the Immigration and Nationality Act (8 U.S.C. 1151(e)), unless the worldwide level under such section for such year has been exceeded, in which case the alien shall be counted as a diversity immigrant for fiscal year 2002.

(3) TREATMENT OF FAMILY MEMBERS OF CERTAIN ALIENS—In the case of a principal alien issued an immigrant visa number under section 203(c) of the Immigration and Nationality Act (8 U.S.C. 1153(c)) for fiscal year 2001, if such principal alien died as a direct result of a specified terrorist activity, the aliens who were, on September 10, 2001, the spouse and children of such principal alien shall, until June 30, 2002, if not otherwise entitled to an immigrant status and the immediate issuance of a visa under subsection (a), (b), or (c) of section 203 of such Act, be entitled to the same status, and the same order of consideration, that would have been provided to such alien spouse or child under section 203(d) of such Act as if the principal alien were not deceased and as if the spouse or child's visa application had been adjudicated by September 30, 2001.

(4) CIRCUMSTANCES PREVENTING TIMELY ACTION— For purposes of paragraph (1), circumstances preventing an alien from using an immigrant visa number during fiscal year 2001 are—

(A) office closures;

(B) mail or courier service cessations or delays;

(C) airline flight cessations or delays; and

(D) other closures, cessations, or delays affecting case processing or travel necessary to satisfy legal requirements.

(d) EXTENSION OF EXPIRATION OF IMMIGRANT VISAS-

(1) IN GENERAL—Notwithstanding the limitations under section 221(c) of the Immigration and Nationality Act (8 U.S.C. 1201(c)), in the case of any immigrant visa issued to an alien that expires or expired before December 31, 2001, if the alien was unable to effect entry into the United States as a direct result of a specified terrorist activity, then the period of validity of the visa is extended until December 31, 2001, unless a longer period of validity is otherwise provided under this subtitle.

(2) CIRCUMSTANCES PREVENTING ENTRY—For purposes of this subsection, circumstances preventing an alien from effecting entry into the United States are—

(A) office closures;

(B) airline flight cessations or delays; and

(C) other closures, cessations, or delays affecting case processing or travel necessary to satisfy legal requirements.

(e) GRANTS OF PAROLE EXTENDED-

(1) IN GENERAL—In the case of any parole granted by the Attorney General under section 212(d)(5) of the Immigration and Nationality Act (8 U.S.C. 1182(d)(5)) that expires on a date on or after September 11, 2001, if the alien beneficiary of the parole was unable to return to the United States prior to the expiration date as a direct result of a specified terrorist activity, the parole is deemed extended for an additional 90 days.

(2) CIRCUMSTANCES PREVENTING RETURN—For purposes of this subsection, circumstances preventing an alien from timely returning to the United States are—

(A) office closures;

(B) airline flight cessations or delays; and

(C) other closures, cessations, or delays affecting case processing or travel necessary to satisfy legal requirements.

(f) VOLUNTARY DEPARTURE—Notwithstanding section 240B of the Immigration and Nationality Act (8 U.S.C. 1229c), if a period for voluntary departure under such section expired during the period beginning on September 11, 2001, and ending on October 11, 2001, such voluntary departure period is deemed extended for an additional 30 days.

Sec. 423. Humanitarian Relief for Certain Surviving Spouses and Children.

(a) TREATMENT AS IMMEDIATE RELATIVES-

(1) SPOUSES—Notwithstanding the second sentence of section 201(b)(2)(A)(i) of the Immigration and Nationality Act (8 U.S.C. 1151(b)(2)(A)(i)), in the case of an alien who was the spouse of a citizen of the United States at the time of the citizen's death and was not legally separated from the citizen at the time of the citizen's death, if the citizen died as a direct result of a specified terrorist activity, the alien (and each child of the alien) shall be considered, for purposes of section 201(b) of such Act, to remain an immediate relative after the date of the citizen's death, but only if the alien files a petition under section 204(a)(1)(A)(ii) of such Act within 2 years after such date and only until the date the alien remarries. For purposes of such section 204(a)(1)(A)(ii), an alien granted relief under the preceding sentence shall be considered an alien spouse described in the second sentence of section 201(b)(2)(A)(i) of such Act.

(2) CHILDREN-

(A) IN GENERAL—In the case of an alien who was the child of a citizen of the United States at the time of the citizen's death, if the citizen died as a direct result of a specified terrorist activity, the alien shall be considered, for purposes of section 201(b) of the Immigration and Nationality Act (8 U.S.C. 1151(b)), to remain an immediate relative after the date of the citizen's death (regardless of changes in age or marital status thereafter), but only if the alien files a petition under subparagraph (B) within 2 years after such date.

(B) PETITIONS—An alien described in subparagraph (A) may file a petition with the Attorney General for classification of the alien under section 201(b)(2)(A)(i) of the Immigration and Nationality Act (8 U.S.C. 1151(b)(2)(A)(i)). For purposes of such Act, such a petition shall be considered a petition filed under section 204(a)(1)(A) of such Act (8 U.S.C. 1154(a)(1)(A)).

(b) SPOUSES, CHILDREN, UNMARRIED SONS AND DAUGH-
TERS OF LAWFUL PERMANENT RESIDENT ALIENS-

(1) IN GENERAL—Any spouse, child, or unmarried son or daughter of an alien described in paragraph (3) who is included in a petition for classification as a family-sponsored immigrant under section
203(a)(2) of the Immigration and Nationality Act (8 U.S.C.
1153(a)(2)) that was filed by such alien before September 11, 2001,
shall be considered (if the spouse, child, son, or daughter has not
been admitted or approved for lawful permanent residence by such
date) a valid petitioner for preference status under such section with
the same priority date as that assigned prior to the death described
in paragraph (3)(A). No new petition shall be required to be filed.
Such spouse, child, son, or daughter may be eligible for deferred
action and work authorization.

(2) SELF-PETITIONS—Any spouse, child, or unmarried son or
daughter of an alien described in paragraph (3) who is not a beneficiary of a petition for classification as a family-sponsored immigrant under section 203(a)(2) of the Immigration and Nationality
Act may file a petition for such classification with the Attorney
General, if the spouse, child, son, or daughter was present in the
United States on September 11, 2001. Such spouse, child, son, or
daughter may be eligible for deferred action and work authorization.

(3) ALIENS DESCRIBED—An alien is described in this paragraph
if the alien—

(A) died as a direct result of a specified terrorist activity; and

(B) on the day of such death, was lawfully admitted for permanent residence in the United States.

(c) APPLICATIONS FOR ADJUSTMENT OF STATUS BY SUR-
VIVING SPOUSES AND CHILDREN OF EMPLOYMENT-BASED
IMMIGRANTS-

(1) IN GENERAL—Any alien who was, on September 10, 2001,
the spouse or child of an alien described in paragraph (2), and who
applied for adjustment of status prior to the death described in paragraph (2)(A), may have such application adjudicated as if such death
had not occurred.

(2) ALIENS DESCRIBED—An alien is described in this paragraph
if the alien—

(A) died as a direct result of a specified terrorist activity; and

(B) on the day before such death, was—

(i) an alien lawfully admitted for permanent residence in the United States by reason of having been allotted a visa under section 203(b) of the Immigration and Nationality Act (8 U.S.C. 1153(b)); or

(ii) an applicant for adjustment of status to that of an alien described in clause (i), and admissible to the United States for permanent residence.

(d) WAIVER OF PUBLIC CHARGE GROUNDS—In determining the admissibility of any alien accorded an immigration benefit under this section, the grounds for inadmissibility specified in section 212(a)(4) of the Immigration and Nationality Act (8 U.S.C. 1182(a)(4)) shall not apply.

Sec. 424. 'Age-Out' Protection for Children.

For purposes of the administration of the Immigration and Nationality Act (8 U.S.C. 1101 et seq.), in the case of an alien—

(1) whose 21st birthday occurs in September 2001, and who is the beneficiary of a petition or application filed under such Act on or before September 11, 2001, the alien shall be considered to be a child for 90 days after the alien's 21st birthday for purposes of adjudicating such petition or application; and

(2) whose 21st birthday occurs after September 2001, and who is the beneficiary of a petition or application filed under such Act on or before September 11, 2001, the alien shall be considered to be a child for 45 days after the alien's 21st birthday for purposes of adjudicating such petition or application.

Sec. 425. Temporary Administrative Relief.

The Attorney General, for humanitarian purposes or to ensure family unity, may provide temporary administrative relief to any alien who—

(1) was lawfully present in the United States on September 10, 2001;

(2) was on such date the spouse, parent, or child of an individual who died or was disabled as a direct result of a specified terrorist activity; and

(3) is not otherwise entitled to relief under any other provision of this subtitle.

Sec. 426. Evidence of Death, Disability, or Loss of Employment.

(a) IN GENERAL—The Attorney General shall establish appropriate standards for evidence demonstrating, for purposes of this subtitle, that any of the following occurred as a direct result of a specified terrorist activity:

(1) Death.

(2) Disability.

(3) Loss of employment due to physical damage to, or destruction of, a business.

(b) WAIVER OF REGULATIONS—The Attorney General shall carry out subsection (a) as expeditiously as possible. The Attorney General is not required to promulgate regulations prior to implementing this subtitle.

Sec. 427. No Benefits to Terrorists or Family Members of Terrorists.

Notwithstanding any other provision of this subtitle, nothing in this subtitle shall be construed to provide any benefit or relief to—

(1) any individual culpable for a specified terrorist activity; or

(2) any family member of any individual described in paragraph (1).

Sec. 428. Definitions.

(a) APPLICATION OF IMMIGRATION AND NATIONALITY ACT PROVISIONS—Except as otherwise specifically provided in this subtitle, the definitions used in the Immigration and Nationality Act (excluding the definitions applicable exclusively to title III of such Act) shall apply in the administration of this subtitle.

(b) SPECIFIED TERRORIST ACTIVITY—For purposes of this subtitle, the term 'specified terrorist activity' means any terrorist activity conducted against the Government or the people of the United States on September 11, 2001.

TITLE V—REMOVING OBSTACLES TO INVESTIGATING TERRORISM

Sec. 501. Attorney General's Authority to Pay Rewards to Combat Terrorism.

(a) PAYMENT OF REWARDS TO COMBAT TERRORISM—Funds available to the Attorney General may be used for the payment of rewards pursuant to public advertisements for assistance to the Department of Justice to combat terrorism and defend the Nation against terrorist acts, in accordance with procedures and regulations established or issued by the Attorney General.

(b) CONDITIONS—In making rewards under this section—

(1) no such reward of $250,000 or more may be made or offered without the personal approval of either the Attorney General or the President;

(2) the Attorney General shall give written notice to the Chairmen and ranking minority members of the Committees on Appropriations and the Judiciary of the Senate and of the House of Representatives not later than 30 days after the approval of a reward under paragraph (1);

(3) any executive agency or military department (as defined, respectively, in sections 105 and 102 of title 5, United States Code) may provide the Attorney General with funds for the payment of rewards;

(4) neither the failure of the Attorney General to authorize a payment nor the amount authorized shall be subject to judicial review; and

(5) no such reward shall be subject to any per- or aggregate reward spending limitation established by law, unless that law expressly refers to this section, and no reward paid pursuant to any such offer shall count toward any such aggregate reward spending limitation.

Sec. 502. Secretary of State's Authority to Pay Rewards.

Section 36 of the State Department Basic Authorities Act of 1956 (Public Law 885, August 1, 1956; 22 U.S.C. 2708) is amended—

(1) in subsection (b)—

(A) in paragraph (4), by striking 'or' at the end;

(B) in paragraph (5), by striking the period at the end and inserting ', including by dismantling an organization in whole or significant part; or'; and

(C) by adding at the end the following:

'(6) the identification or location of an individual who holds a key leadership position in a terrorist organization.';

(2) in subsection (d), by striking paragraphs (2) and (3) and redesignating paragraph (4) as paragraph (2); and

(3) in subsection (e)(1), by inserting ', except as personally authorized by the Secretary of State if he determines that offer or payment of an award of a larger amount is necessary to combat terrorism or defend the Nation against terrorist acts.' after '$5,000,000'.

Sec. 503. Dna Identification of Terrorists and Other Violent Offenders.

Section 3(d)(2) of the DNA Analysis Backlog Elimination Act of 2000 (42 U.S.C. 14135a(d)(2)) is amended to read as follows:

'(2) In addition to the offenses described in paragraph (1), the following offenses shall be treated for purposes of this section as qualifying Federal offenses, as determined by the Attorney General:

'(A) Any offense listed in section 2332b(g)(5)(B) of title 18, United States Code.

'(B) Any crime of violence (as defined in section 16 of title 18, United States Code).

'(C) Any attempt or conspiracy to commit any of the above offenses.'.

Sec. 504. Coordination With Law Enforcement.

(a) INFORMATION ACQUIRED FROM AN ELECTRONIC SURVEILLANCE—Section 106 of the Foreign Intelligence Surveillance Act of 1978 (50 U.S.C. 1806), is amended by adding at the end the following:

'(k)(1) Federal officers who conduct electronic surveillance to acquire foreign intelligence information under this title may consult with Federal law enforcement officers to coordinate efforts to investigate or protect against—

'(A) actual or potential attack or other grave hostile acts of a foreign power or an agent of a foreign power;

'(B) sabotage or international terrorism by a foreign power or an agent of a foreign power; or

'(C) clandestine intelligence activities by an intelligence service or network of a foreign power or by an agent of a foreign power.

'(2) Coordination authorized under paragraph (1) shall not preclude the certification required by section 104(a)(7)(B) or the entry of an order under section 105.'.

(b) INFORMATION ACQUIRED FROM A PHYSICAL SEARCH— Section 305 of the Foreign Intelligence Surveillance Act of 1978 (50 U.S.C. 1825) is amended by adding at the end the following:

'(k)(1) Federal officers who conduct physical searches to acquire foreign intelligence information under this title may consult with Federal law enforcement officers to coordinate efforts to investigate or protect against—

'(A) actual or potential attack or other grave hostile acts of a foreign power or an agent of a foreign power;

'(B) sabotage or international terrorism by a foreign power or an agent of a foreign power; or

'(C) clandestine intelligence activities by an intelligence service or network of a foreign power or by an agent of a foreign power.

'(2) Coordination authorized under paragraph (1) shall not preclude the certification required by section 303(a)(7) or the entry of an order under section 304.'.

Sec. 505. Miscellaneous National Security Authorities.

(a) TELEPHONE TOLL AND TRANSACTIONAL RECORDS— Section 2709(b) of title 18, United States Code, is amended—

(1) in the matter preceding paragraph (1), by inserting 'at Bureau headquarters or a Special Agent in Charge in a Bureau field office designated by the Director' after 'Assistant Director';

(2) in paragraph (1)—

(A) by striking 'in a position not lower than Deputy Assistant Director'; and

(B) by striking 'made that' and all that follows and inserting the following: 'made that the name, address, length of service, and toll billing records sought are relevant to an authorized investigation to protect against international terrorism or clandestine intelligence activities, provided that such an investigation of a United States person is not conducted solely on the basis of activities protected by the first amendment to the Constitution of the United States; and'; and

(3) in paragraph (2)—

(A) by striking 'in a position not lower than Deputy Assistant Director'; and

(B) by striking 'made that' and all that follows and inserting the following: 'made that the information sought is relevant to an authorized investigation to protect against international terrorism or clandestine intelligence activities, provided that such an investigation of a United States person is not conducted solely upon the basis of activities protected by the first amendment to the Constitution of the United States.'.

(b) FINANCIAL RECORDS—Section 1114(a)(5)(A) of the Right to Financial Privacy Act of 1978 (12 U.S.C. 3414(a)(5)(A)) is amended—

(1) by inserting 'in a position not lower than Deputy Assistant Director at Bureau headquarters or a Special Agent in Charge in a Bureau field office designated by the Director' after 'designee'; and

(2) by striking 'sought' and all that follows and inserting 'sought for foreign counter intelligence purposes to protect against international terrorism or clandestine intelligence activities, provided that such an investigation of a United States person is not conducted solely upon the basis of activities protected by the first amendment to the Constitution of the United States.'.

(c) CONSUMER REPORTS—Section 624 of the Fair Credit Reporting Act (15 U.S.C. 1681u) is amended—

(1) in subsection (a)—

(A) by inserting 'in a position not lower than Deputy Assistant Director at Bureau headquarters or a Special Agent in Charge of a Bureau field office designated by the Director' after 'designee' the first place it appears; and

(B) by striking 'in writing that' and all that follows through the end and inserting the following: 'in writing, that such information is sought for the conduct of an authorized investigation to protect against international terrorism or clandestine intelligence activities, provided that such an investigation of a United States person is not conducted solely upon the basis of activities protected by the first amendment to the Constitution of the United States.';

(2) in subsection (b)—

(A) by inserting 'in a position not lower than Deputy Assistant Director at Bureau headquarters or a Special Agent in Charge of a Bureau field office designated by the Director' after 'designee' the first place it appears; and

(B) by striking 'in writing that' and all that follows through the end and inserting the following: 'in writing that such information is sought for the conduct of an authorized investigation to protect against international terrorism or clandestine intelligence activities, provided that such an investigation of a United States person is not conducted solely upon the basis of activities protected by the first amendment to the Constitution of the United States.'; and

(3) in subsection (c)—

(A) by inserting 'in a position not lower than Deputy Assistant Director at Bureau headquarters or a Special Agent in Charge in a Bureau field office designated by the Director' after 'designee of the Director'; and

(B) by striking 'in camera that' and all that follows through 'States.' and inserting the following: 'in camera that the consumer report is sought for the conduct of an authorized investigation to protect against international terrorism or clandestine intelligence activities, provided that such an investigation of a United States person is not conducted solely upon the basis of activities protected by the first amendment to the Constitution of the United States.'.

Sec. 506. Extension of Secret Service Jurisdiction.

(a) Concurrent Jurisdiction Under 18 U.S.C. 1030—Section 1030(d) of title 18, United States Code, is amended to read as follows:

'(d)(1) The United States Secret Service shall, in addition to any other agency having such authority, have the authority to investigate offenses under this section.

'(2) The Federal Bureau of Investigation shall have primary authority to investigate offenses under subsection (a)(1) for any cases involving espionage, foreign counterintelligence, information protected against unauthorized disclosure for reasons of national defense or foreign relations, or Restricted Data (as that term is defined in section 11y of the Atomic Energy Act of 1954 (42 U.S.C. 2014(y)), except for offenses affecting the duties of the United States Secret Service pursuant to section 3056(a) of this title.

'(3) Such authority shall be exercised in accordance with an agreement which shall be entered into by the Secretary of the Treasury and the Attorney General.'.

(b) Reauthorization of Jurisdiction under 18 U.S.C. 1344—Section 3056(b)(3) of title 18, United States Code, is amended by striking 'credit and debit card frauds, and false identification documents or devices' and inserting 'access device frauds, false identification documents or devices, and any fraud or other criminal or unlawful activity in or against any federally insured financial institution'.

Sec. 507. Disclosure of Educational Records.

Section 444 of the General Education Provisions Act (20 U.S.C. 1232g), is amended by adding after subsection (i) a new subsection (j) to read as follows:

'(j) INVESTIGATION AND PROSECUTION OF TERRORISM-

'(1) IN GENERAL—Notwithstanding subsections (a) through (i) or any provision of State law, the Attorney General (or any Federal officer or employee, in a position not lower than an Assistant Attorney General, designated by the Attorney General) may submit a written application to a court of competent jurisdiction for an ex parte order requiring an educational agency or institution to permit the Attorney General (or his designee) to—

'(A) collect education records in the possession of the educational agency or institution that are relevant to an authorized investigation or prosecution of an offense listed in section 2332b(g)(5)(B) of title 18 United States Code, or an act of domestic or international terrorism as defined in section 2331 of that title; and

'(B) for official purposes related to the investigation or prosecution of an offense described in paragraph (1)(A), retain, disseminate, and use (including as evidence at trial or in other administrative or judicial proceedings) such records, consistent with such guidelines as the Attorney General, after consultation with the Secretary, shall issue to protect confidentiality.

'(2) APPLICATION AND APPROVAL-

'(A) IN GENERAL—An application under paragraph (1) shall certify that there are specific and articulable facts giving reason to believe that the education records are likely to contain information described in paragraph (1)(A).

'(B) The court shall issue an order described in paragraph (1) if the court finds that the application for the order includes the certification described in subparagraph (A).

'(3) PROTECTION OF EDUCATIONAL AGENCY OR INSTITUTION—An educational agency or institution that, in good faith, produces education records in accordance with an order issued under this subsection shall not be liable to any person for that production.

'(4) RECORD-KEEPING—Subsection (b)(4) does not apply to education records subject to a court order under this subsection.'.

Sec. 508. Disclosure of Information From Nces Surveys.

Section 408 of the National Education Statistics Act of 1994 (20 U.S.C. 9007), is amended by adding after subsection (b) a new subsection (c) to read as follows:

'(c) INVESTIGATION AND PROSECUTION OF TERRORISM-

'(1) IN GENERAL—Notwithstanding subsections (a) and (b), the Attorney General (or any Federal officer or employee, in a position not lower than an Assistant Attorney General, designated by the Attorney General) may submit a written application to a court of competent jurisdiction for an ex parte order requiring the Secretary to permit the Attorney General (or his designee) to—

'(A) collect reports, records, and information (including individually identifiable information) in the possession of the center that are relevant to an authorized investigation or prosecution of an offense listed in section 2332b(g)(5)(B) of title 18, United States Code, or an act of domestic or international terrorism as defined in section 2331 of that title; and

'(B) for official purposes related to the investigation or prosecution of an offense described in paragraph (1)(A), retain, disseminate, and use (including as evidence at trial or in other administrative or judicial proceedings) such information, consistent with such guidelines as the Attorney General, after consultation with the Secretary, shall issue to protect confidentiality.

'(2) APPLICATION AND APPROVAL-

'(A) IN GENERAL—An application under paragraph (1) shall certify that there are specific and articulable facts giving reason to believe that the information sought is described in paragraph (1)(A).

'(B) The court shall issue an order described in paragraph (1) if the court finds that the application for the order includes the certification described in subparagraph (A).

'(3) PROTECTION—An officer or employee of the Department who, in good faith, produces information in accordance with an order issued under this subsection does not violate subsection (b)(2) and shall not be liable to any person for that production.'.

TITLE VI—PROVIDING FOR VICTIMS OF TERRORISM, PUBLIC SAFETY OFFICERS, AND THEIR FAMILIES

Subtitle A—Aid to Families of Public Safety Officers

Sec. 611. Expedited Payment for Public Safety Officers Involved in the Prevention, Investigation, Rescue, or Recovery Efforts Related to a Terrorist Attack.

(a) IN GENERAL—Notwithstanding the limitations of subsection (b) of section 1201 or the provisions of subsections (c), (d), and (e) of such section or section 1202 of title I of the Omnibus Crime Control and Safe Streets Act of 1968 (42 U.S.C. 3796, 3796a), upon certification (containing identification of all eligible payees of benefits pursuant to section 1201 of such Act) by a public agency that a public safety officer employed by such agency was killed or suffered a catastrophic injury producing permanent and total disability as a direct and proximate result of a personal injury sustained in the line of duty as described in section 1201 of such Act in connection with prevention, investigation, rescue, or recovery efforts related to a terrorist attack, the Director of the Bureau of Justice Assistance shall authorize payment to qualified beneficiaries, said payment to be made not later than 30 days after receipt of such certification, benefits described under subpart 1 of part L of such Act (42 U.S.C. 3796 et seq.).

(b) DEFINITIONS—For purposes of this section, the terms 'catastrophic injury', 'public agency', and 'public safety officer' have the same meanings given such terms in section 1204 of title I of the Omnibus Crime Control and Safe Streets Act of 1968 (42 U.S.C. 3796b).

Sec. 612. Technical Correction With Respect to Expedited Payments for Heroic Public Safety Officers.

Section 1 of Public Law 107–37 (an Act to provide for the expedited payment of certain benefits for a public safety officer who was killed or suffered a catastrophic injury as a direct and proximate result of a personal injury sustained in the line of duty in connection with the terrorist attacks of September 11, 2001) is amended by—

(1) inserting before 'by a' the following: '(containing identification of all eligible payees of benefits pursuant to section 1201)';

(2) inserting 'producing permanent and total disability' after 'suffered a catastrophic injury'; and

(3) striking '1201(a)' and inserting '1201'.

Sec. 613. Public Safety Officers Benefit Program Payment Increase.

(a) PAYMENTS—Section 1201(a) of the Omnibus Crime Control and Safe Streets Act of 1968 (42 U.S.C. 3796) is amended by striking '$100,000' and inserting '$250,000'.

(b) APPLICABILITY—The amendment made by subsection (a) shall apply to any death or disability occurring on or after January 1, 2001.

Sec. 614. Office of Justice Programs.

Section 112 of title I of section 101(b) of division A of Public Law 105–277 and section 108(a) of appendix A of Public Law 106–113 (113 Stat. 1501A-20) are amended—

(1) after 'that Office', each place it occurs, by inserting '(including, notwithstanding any contrary provision of law (unless the same should expressly refer to this section), any organization that administers any program established in title 1 of Public Law 90-351)'; and

(2) by inserting 'functions, including any' after 'all'.

Subtitle B—Amendments to the Victims of Crime Act of 1984

Sec. 621. Crime Victims Fund.

(a) DEPOSIT OF GIFTS IN THE FUND—Section 1402(b) of the Victims of Crime Act of 1984 (42 U.S.C. 10601(b)) is amended—

(1) in paragraph (3), by striking 'and' at the end;

(2) in paragraph (4), by striking the period at the end and inserting '; and'; and

(3) by adding at the end the following:

'(5) any gifts, bequests, or donations to the Fund from private entities or individuals.'.

(b) FORMULA FOR FUND DISTRIBUTIONS—Section 1402(c) of the Victims of Crime Act of 1984 (42 U.S.C. 10601(c)) is amended to read as follows:

'(c) FUND DISTRIBUTION; RETENTION OF SUMS IN FUND; AVAILABILITY FOR EXPENDITURE WITHOUT FISCAL YEAR LIMITATION-

'(1) Subject to the availability of money in the Fund, in each fiscal year, beginning with fiscal year 2003, the Director shall distribute not less than 90 percent nor more than 110 percent of the amount distributed from the Fund in the previous fiscal year, except the Director may distribute up to 120 percent of the amount distributed in the previous fiscal year in any fiscal year that the total amount available in the Fund is more than 2 times the amount distributed in the previous fiscal year.

'(2) In each fiscal year, the Director shall distribute amounts from the Fund in accordance with subsection (d). All sums not distributed during a fiscal year shall remain in reserve in the Fund to be distributed during a subsequent fiscal year. Notwithstanding any other provision of law, all sums deposited in the Fund that are not distributed shall remain in reserve in the Fund for obligation in future fiscal years, without fiscal year limitation.'.

(c) ALLOCATION OF FUNDS FOR COSTS AND GRANTS—Section 1402(d)(4) of the Victims of Crime Act of 1984 (42 U.S.C. 10601(d)(4)) is amended—

(1) by striking 'deposited in' and inserting 'to be distributed from';

(2) in subparagraph (A), by striking '48.5' and inserting '47.5';

(3) in subparagraph (B), by striking '48.5' and inserting '47.5'; and

(4) in subparagraph (C), by striking '3' and inserting '5'.

(d) ANTITERRORISM EMERGENCY RESERVE—Section 1402(d)(5) of the Victims of Crime Act of 1984 (42 U.S.C. 10601(d)(5)) is amended to read as follows:

'(5)(A)   In addition to the amounts distributed under paragraphs (2), (3), and (4), the Director may set aside up to $50,000,000 from the amounts transferred to the Fund in response to the airplane hijackings and terrorist acts that occurred on September 11, 2001, as an antiterrorism emergency reserve. The Director may replenish any amounts expended from such reserve in subsequent fiscal years by setting aside up to 5 percent of the amounts remaining in the Fund in any fiscal year after distributing amounts under paragraphs (2), (3) and (4). Such reserve shall not exceed $50,000,000.

'(B) The antiterrorism emergency reserve referred to in subparagraph (A) may be used for supplemental grants under section 1404B and to provide compensation to victims of international terrorism under section 1404C.

'(C) Amounts in the antiterrorism emergency reserve established pursuant to subparagraph (A) may be carried over from fiscal year to fiscal year. Notwithstanding subsection (c) and section 619 of the Departments of Commerce, Justice, and State, the Judiciary, and Related Agencies Appropriations Act, 2001 (and any similar limitation on Fund obligations in any future Act, unless the same should expressly refer to this section), any such amounts carried over shall not be subject to any limitation on obligations from amounts deposited to or available in the Fund.'.

(e) VICTIMS OF SEPTEMBER 11, 2001—Amounts transferred to the Crime Victims Fund for use in responding to the airplane hijackings and terrorist acts (including any related search, rescue, relief, assistance, or other similar activities) that occurred on September 11, 2001, shall not be subject to any limitation on obligations from amounts deposited to or available in the Fund, notwithstanding—

(1) section 619 of the Departments of Commerce, Justice, and State, the Judiciary, and Related Agencies Appropriations Act, 2001, and any similar limitation on Fund obligations in such Act for Fiscal Year 2002; and

(2) subsections (c) and (d) of section 1402 of the Victims of Crime Act of 1984 (42 U.S.C. 10601).

Sec. 622. Crime Victim Compensation.

(a) ALLOCATION OF FUNDS FOR COMPENSATION AND ASSISTANCE—Paragraphs (1) and (2) of section 1403(a) of the Victims of Crime Act of 1984 (42 U.S.C. 10602(a)) are amended by inserting 'in fiscal year 2002 and of 60 percent in subsequent fiscal years' after '40 percent'.

(b) LOCATION OF COMPENSABLE CRIME—Section 1403(b)(6)(B) of the Victims of Crime Act of 1984 (42 U.S.C. 10602(b)(6)(B)) is amended by striking 'are outside the United States (if the compensable crime is terrorism, as defined in section 2331 of title 18), or'.

(c) RELATIONSHIP OF CRIME VICTIM COMPENSATION TO MEANS-TESTED FEDERAL BENEFIT PROGRAMS—Section 1403 of the Victims of Crime Act of 1984 (42 U.S.C. 10602) is amended by striking subsection (c) and inserting the following:

'(c) EXCLUSION FROM INCOME, RESOURCES, AND ASSETS FOR PURPOSES OF MEANS TESTS—Notwithstanding any other law (other than title IV of Public Law 107–42), for the purpose of any maximum allowed income, resource, or asset eligibility requirement in any Federal, State, or local government program using Federal funds that provides medical or other assistance (or payment or reimbursement of the cost of such assistance), any amount of crime victim compensation that the applicant receives through a crime victim compensation program under this section shall not be included in the income, resources, or assets of the applicant, nor shall that amount reduce the amount of the assistance available to the applicant from Federal, State, or local government programs using Federal funds, unless the total amount of assistance that the applicant receives from all such programs is sufficient to fully compensate the applicant for losses suffered as a result of the crime.'.

(d) DEFINITIONS OF 'COMPENSABLE CRIME' AND 'STATE'— Section 1403(d) of the Victims of Crime Act of 1984 (42 U.S.C. 10602(d)) is amended—

(1) in paragraph (3), by striking 'crimes involving terrorism,'; and

(2) in paragraph (4), by inserting 'the United States Virgin Islands,' after 'the Commonwealth of Puerto Rico,'.

(e) RELATIONSHIP OF ELIGIBLE CRIME VICTIM COMPEN-SATION PROGRAMS TO THE SEPTEMBER 11TH VICTIM COM-PENSATION FUND-

(1) IN GENERAL—Section 1403(e) of the Victims of Crime Act of 1984 (42 U.S.C. 10602(e)) is amended by inserting 'including the program established under title IV of Public Law 107–42,' after 'Federal program,'.

(2) COMPENSATION—With respect to any compensation payable under title IV of Public Law 107–42, the failure of a crime victim compensation program, after the effective date of final regulations issued pursuant to section 407 of Public Law 107–42, to provide compensation otherwise required pursuant to section 1403 of the Victims of Crime Act of 1984 (42 U.S.C. 10602) shall not render that program ineligible for future grants under the Victims of Crime Act of 1984.

Sec. 623. Crime Victim Assistance.

(a) ASSISTANCE FOR VICTIMS IN THE DISTRICT OF COLUM-BIA, PUERTO RICO, AND OTHER TERRITORIES AND POS-SESSIONS—Section 1404(a) of the Victims of Crime Act of 1984 (42 U.S.C. 10603(a)) is amended by adding at the end the following:

'(6) An agency of the Federal Government performing local law enforcement functions in and on behalf of the District of Columbia, the Commonwealth of Puerto Rico, the United States Virgin Islands, or any other territory or possession of the United States may qual-ify as an eligible crime victim assistance program for the purpose of grants under this subsection, or for the purpose of grants under sub-section (c)(1).'.

(b) PROHIBITION ON DISCRIMINATION AGAINST CERTAIN VICTIMS—Section 1404(b)(1) of the Victims of Crime Act of 1984 (42 U.S.C. 10603(b)(1)) is amended—

(1) in subparagraph (D), by striking 'and' at the end;

(2) in subparagraph (E), by striking the period at the end and inserting '; and'; and

(3) by adding at the end the following:

'(F) does not discriminate against victims because they disagree with the way the State is prosecuting the criminal case.'.

(c) GRANTS FOR PROGRAM EVALUATION AND COMPLIANCE EFFORTS—Section 1404(c)(1)(A) of the Victims of Crime Act of 1984 (42 U.S.C. 10603(c)(1)(A)) is amended by inserting ', program evaluation, compliance efforts,' after 'demonstration projects'.

(d) ALLOCATION OF DISCRETIONARY GRANTS—Section 1404(c)(2) of the Victims of Crime Act of 1984 (42 U.S.C. 10603(c)(2)) is amended—

(1) in subparagraph (A), by striking 'not more than' and inserting 'not less than'; and

(2) in subparagraph (B), by striking 'not less than' and inserting 'not more than'.

(e) FELLOWSHIPS AND CLINICAL INTERNSHIPS—Section 1404(c)(3) of the Victims of Crime Act of 1984 (42 U.S.C. 10603(c)(3)) is amended—

(1) in subparagraph (C), by striking 'and' at the end;

(2) in subparagraph (D), by striking the period at the end and inserting '; and'; and

(3) by adding at the end the following:

'(E) use funds made available to the Director under this subsection—

'(i) for fellowships and clinical internships; and

'(ii) to carry out programs of training and special workshops for the presentation and dissemination of information resulting from demonstrations, surveys, and special projects.'.

Sec. 624. Victims of Terrorism.

(a) COMPENSATION AND ASSISTANCE TO VICTIMS OF DOMESTIC TERRORISM—Section 1404B(b) of the Victims of Crime Act of 1984 (42 U.S.C. 10603b(b)) is amended to read as follows:

'(b) VICTIMS OF TERRORISM WITHIN THE UNITED STATES— The Director may make supplemental grants as provided in section 1402(d)(5) to States for eligible crime victim compensation and assistance programs, and to victim service organizations, public agencies (including Federal, State, or local governments) and nongovernmental organizations that provide assistance to victims of crime, which shall be used to provide emergency relief, including crisis response efforts, assistance, compensation, training and technical assistance, and ongoing assistance, including during any investigation or prosecution, to victims of terrorist acts or mass violence occurring within the United States.'.

(b) ASSISTANCE TO VICTIMS OF INTERNATIONAL TERRORISM—Section 1404B(a)(1) of the Victims of Crime Act of 1984 (42 U.S.C. 10603b(a)(1)) is amended by striking 'who are not persons eligible for compensation under title VIII of the Omnibus Diplomatic Security and Antiterrorism Act of 1986'.

(c) COMPENSATION TO VICTIMS OF INTERNATIONAL TERRORISM—Section 1404C(b) of the Victims of Crime of 1984 (42 U.S.C. 10603c(b)) is amended by adding at the end the following: 'The amount of compensation awarded to a victim under this subsection shall be reduced by any amount that the victim received in connection with the same act of international terrorism under title VIII of the Omnibus Diplomatic Security and Antiterrorism Act of 1986.'.

TITLE VII—INCREASED INFORMATION SHARING FOR CRITICAL INFRASTRUCTURE PROTECTION

Sec. 701. Expansion of Regional Information Sharing System to Facilitate Federal-State-Local Law Enforcement Response Related to Terrorist Attacks.

Section 1301 of title I of the Omnibus Crime Control and Safe Streets Act of 1968 (42 U.S.C. 3796h) is amended—

(1) in subsection (a), by inserting 'and terrorist conspiracies and activities' after 'activities';

(2) in subsection (b)—

(A) in paragraph (3), by striking 'and' after the semicolon;

(B) by redesignating paragraph (4) as paragraph (5); and

(C) by inserting after paragraph (3) the following:

'(4) establishing and operating secure information sharing systems to enhance the investigation and prosecution abilities of participating enforcement agencies in addressing multi-jurisdictional terrorist conspiracies and activities; and (5)'; and

(3) by inserting at the end the following:

'(d) AUTHORIZATION OF APPROPRIATION TO THE BUREAU OF JUSTICE ASSISTANCE—There are authorized to be appropriated to the Bureau of Justice Assistance to carry out this section $50,000,000 for fiscal year 2002 and $100,000,000 for fiscal year 2003.'.

TITLE VIII—STRENGTHENING THE CRIMINAL LAWS AGAINST TERRORISM

Sec. 801. Terrorist Attacks and Other Acts of Violence Against Mass Transportation Systems.

Chapter 97 of title 18, United States Code, is amended by adding at the end the following:

'Sec. 1993. Terrorist attacks and other acts of violence against mass transportation systems

'(a) GENERAL PROHIBITIONS—Whoever willfully—

'(1) wrecks, derails, sets fire to, or disables a mass transportation vehicle or ferry;

'(2) places or causes to be placed any biological agent or toxin for use as a weapon, destructive substance, or destructive device in, upon, or near a mass transportation vehicle or ferry, without previously obtaining the permission of the mass transportation provider, and with intent to endanger the safety of any passenger or employee of the mass transportation provider, or with a reckless disregard for the safety of human life;

'(3) sets fire to, or places any biological agent or toxin for use as a weapon, destructive substance, or destructive device in, upon, or near any garage, terminal, structure, supply, or facility used in the operation of, or in support of the operation of, a mass transportation vehicle or ferry, without previously obtaining the permission of the mass transportation provider, and knowing or having reason to know such activity would likely derail, disable, or wreck a mass transportation vehicle or ferry used, operated, or employed by the mass transportation provider;

'(4) removes appurtenances from, damages, or otherwise impairs the operation of a mass transportation signal system, including a train control system, centralized dispatching system, or rail grade crossing warning signal without authorization from the mass transportation provider;

'(5) interferes with, disables, or incapacitates any dispatcher, driver, captain, or person while they are employed in dispatching, operating, or maintaining a mass transportation vehicle or ferry, with intent to endanger the safety of any passenger or employee of the mass transportation provider, or with a reckless disregard for the safety of human life;

'(6) commits an act, including the use of a dangerous weapon, with the intent to cause death or serious bodily injury to an employee or passenger of a mass transportation provider or any other person while any of the foregoing are on the property of a mass transportation provider;

'(7) conveys or causes to be conveyed false information, knowing the information to be false, concerning an attempt or alleged attempt being made or to be made, to do any act which would be a crime prohibited by this subsection; or

'(8) attempts, threatens, or conspires to do any of the aforesaid acts, shall be fined under this title or imprisoned not more than twenty years, or both, if such act is committed, or in the case of a threat or conspiracy such act would be committed, on, against, or affecting a mass transportation provider engaged in or affecting interstate or foreign commerce, or if in the course of committing such act, that person travels or communicates across a State line in order to commit such act, or transports materials across a State line in aid of the commission of such act.

'(b) AGGRAVATED OFFENSE—Whoever commits an offense under subsection (a) in a circumstance in which—

'(1) the mass transportation vehicle or ferry was carrying a passenger at the time of the offense; or

'(2) the offense has resulted in the death of any person, shall be guilty of an aggravated form of the offense and shall be fined under this title or imprisoned for a term of years or for life, or both.

'(c) DEFINITIONS—In this section—

'(1) the term 'biological agent' has the meaning given to that term in section 178(1) of this title;

'(2) the term 'dangerous weapon' has the meaning given to that term in section 930 of this title;

'(3) the term 'destructive device' has the meaning given to that term in section 921(a)(4) of this title;

'(4) the term 'destructive substance' has the meaning given to that term in section 31 of this title;

'(5) the term 'mass transportation' has the meaning given to that term in section 5302(a)(7) of title 49, United States Code, except that the term shall include schoolbus, charter, and sightseeing transportation;

'(6) the term 'serious bodily injury' has the meaning given to that term in section 1365 of this title;

'(7) the term 'State' has the meaning given to that term in section 2266 of this title; and

'(8) the term 'toxin' has the meaning given to that term in section 178(2) of this title.'.

(f) CONFORMING AMENDMENT—The analysis of chapter 97 of title 18, United States Code, is amended by adding at the end:

'1993. Terrorist attacks and other acts of violence against mass transportation systems.'.

Sec. 802. Definition of Domestic Terrorism.

(a) DOMESTIC TERRORISM DEFINED—Section 2331 of title 18, United States Code, is amended—

(1) in paragraph (1)(B)(iii), by striking 'by assassination or kidnapping' and inserting 'by mass destruction, assassination, or kidnapping';

(2) in paragraph (3), by striking 'and';

(3) in paragraph (4), by striking the period at the end and inserting '; and'; and

(4) by adding at the end the following:

'(5) the term 'domestic terrorism' means activities that—

'(A) involve acts dangerous to human life that are a violation of the criminal laws of the United States or of any State;

'(B) appear to be intended—

'(i) to intimidate or coerce a civilian population;

'(ii) to influence the policy of a government by intimidation or coercion; or

'(iii) to affect the conduct of a government by mass destruction, assassination, or kidnapping; and

'(C) occur primarily within the territorial jurisdiction of the United States.'.

(b) CONFORMING AMENDMENT—Section 3077(1) of title 18, United States Code, is amended to read as follows:

'(1) 'act of terrorism' means an act of domestic or international terrorism as defined in section 2331;'.

Sec. 803. Prohibition Against Harboring Terrorists.

(a) IN GENERAL—Chapter 113B of title 18, United States Code, is amended by adding after section 2338 the following new section:

'Sec. 2339. Harboring or concealing terrorists

'(a) Whoever harbors or conceals any person who he knows, or has reasonable grounds to believe, has committed, or is about to commit, an offense under section 32 (relating to destruction of aircraft or aircraft facilities), section 175 (relating to biological weapons), section 229 (relating to chemical weapons), section 831 (relating to nuclear materials), paragraph (2) or (3) of section 844(f) (relating to arson and bombing of government property risking or causing injury or death), section 1366(a) (relating to the destruction of an energy facility), section 2280 (relating to violence against maritime navigation), section 2332a (relating to weapons of mass destruction), or section 2332b (relating to acts of terrorism transcending national boundaries) of this title, section 236(a) (relating to sabotage of nuclear facilities or fuel) of the Atomic Energy

Act of 1954 (42 U.S.C. 2284(a)), or section 46502 (relating to aircraft piracy) of title 49, shall be fined under this title or imprisoned not more than ten years, or both.'.

'(b) A violation of this section may be prosecuted in any Federal judicial district in which the underlying offense was committed, or in any other Federal judicial district as provided by law.'.

(b) TECHNICAL AMENDMENT—The chapter analysis for chapter 113B of title 18, United States Code, is amended by inserting after the item for section 2338 the following:

'2339. Harboring or concealing terrorists.'.

Sec. 804. Jurisdiction Over Crimes Committed at U.S. Facilities Abroad.

Section 7 of title 18, United States Code, is amended by adding at the end the following:

'(9) With respect to offenses committed by or against a national of the United States as that term is used in section 101 of the Immigration and Nationality Act—

'(A) the premises of United States diplomatic, consular, military or other United States Government missions or entities in foreign States, including the buildings, parts of buildings, and land appurtenant or ancillary thereto or used for purposes of those missions or entities, irrespective of ownership; and

'(B) residences in foreign States and the land appurtenant or ancillary thereto, irrespective of ownership, used for purposes of those missions or entities or used by United States personnel assigned to those missions or entities.

Nothing in this paragraph shall be deemed to supersede any treaty or international agreement with which this paragraph conflicts. This paragraph does not apply with respect to an offense committed by a person described in section 3261(a) of this title.'.

Sec. 805. Material Support for Terrorism.

(a) IN GENERAL—Section 2339A of title 18, United States Code, is amended—

(1) in subsection (a)—

(A) by striking ', within the United States,';

(B) by inserting '229,' after '175,';

(C) by inserting '1993,' after '1992,';

(D) by inserting ', section 236 of the Atomic Energy Act of 1954 (42 U.S.C. 2284),' after 'of this title';

(E) by inserting 'or 60123(b)' after '46502'; and

(F) by inserting at the end the following: 'A violation of this section may be prosecuted in any Federal judicial district in which the underlying offense was committed, or in any other Federal judicial district as provided by law.'; and

(2) in subsection (b)—

(A) by striking 'or other financial securities' and inserting 'or monetary instruments or financial securities'; and

(B) by inserting 'expert advice or assistance,' after 'training,'.

(b) TECHNICAL AMENDMENT—Section 1956(c)(7)(D) of title 18, United States Code, is amended by inserting 'or 2339B' after '2339A'.

Sec. 806. Assets of Terrorist Organizations.

Section 981(a)(1) of title 18, United States Code, is amended by inserting at the end the following:

'(G) All assets, foreign or domestic—

'(i) of any individual, entity, or organization engaged in planning or perpetrating any act of domestic or international terrorism (as defined in section 2331) against the United States, citizens or residents of the United States, or their property, and all assets, foreign or domestic, affording any person a source of influence over any such entity or organization;

'(ii) acquired or maintained by any person with the intent and for the purpose of supporting, planning, conducting, or concealing an act of domestic or international terrorism (as defined in section 2331) against the United States, citizens or residents of the United States, or their property; or

'(iii) derived from, involved in, or used or intended to be used to commit any act of domestic or international terrorism (as defined in section 2331) against the United States, citizens or residents of the United States, or their property.'.

Sec. 807. Technical Clarification Relating to Provision of Material Support to Terrorism.

No provision of the Trade Sanctions Reform and Export Enhancement Act of 2000 (title IX of Public Law 106–387) shall be construed to limit or otherwise affect section 2339A or 2339B of title 18, United States Code.

Sec. 808. Definition of Federal Crime of Terrorism.

Section 2332b of title 18, United States Code, is amended—

(1) in subsection (f), by inserting 'and any violation of section 351(e), 844(e), 844(f)(1), 956(b), 1361, 1366(b), 1366(c), 1751(e), 2152, or 2156 of this title,' before 'and the Secretary'; and

(2) in subsection (g)(5)(B), by striking clauses (i) through (iii) and inserting the following:

'(i) section 32 (relating to destruction of aircraft or aircraft facilities), 37 (relating to violence at international airports), 81 (relating to arson within special maritime and territorial jurisdiction), 175 or 175b (relating to biological weapons), 229 (relating to chemical weapons), subsection (a), (b), (c), or (d) of section 351 (relating to congressional, cabinet, and Supreme Court assassination and kidnaping), 831 (relating to nuclear materials), 842(m) or (n) (relating to plastic explosives), 844(f)(2) or (3) (relating to arson and bombing of Government property risking or causing death), 844(i) (relating to arson and bombing of property used in interstate commerce), 930(c) (relating to killing or attempted killing during an attack on a Federal facility with a dangerous weapon), 956(a)(1) (relating to conspiracy to murder, kidnap, or maim persons abroad), 1030(a)(1) (relating to protection of computers), 1030(a)(5)(A)(i) resulting in damage as defined in 1030(a)(5)(B)(ii) through (v) (relating to protection of computers), 1114 (relating to killing or attempted killing of officers and employees of the United States), 1116 (relating to murder or manslaughter of foreign officials, official guests, or internationally protected persons), 1203 (relating to hostage taking), 1362 (relating to destruction of communication lines, stations, or systems), 1363 (relating to injury to buildings or property within special maritime and territorial jurisdiction of the United States), 1366(a) (relating to destruction of an energy facility), 1751(a), (b), (c), or (d) (relating to Presidential and Presidential staff assassination and kidnaping), 1992 (relating to wrecking trains), 1993 (relating to terrorist attacks and other acts of violence against mass transportation systems), 2155 (relating to destruction of national defense materials, premises, or utilities), 2280 (relating to violence against maritime navigation), 2281 (relating to violence against maritime fixed platforms), 2332 (relating to certain homicides and other violence against United States nationals occurring outside of the United States), 2332a (relating to use of weapons of mass destruction), 2332b (relating to acts of terrorism transcending national boundaries), 2339 (relating to harboring terrorists), 2339A (relating to providing material support to terrorists), 2339B (relating to providing material support to terrorist organizations), or 2340A (relating to torture) of this title;

'(ii) section 236 (relating to sabotage of nuclear facilities or fuel) of the Atomic Energy Act of 1954 (42 U.S.C. 2284); or

'(iii) section 46502 (relating to aircraft piracy), the second sentence of section 46504 (relating to assault on a flight crew with a dangerous weapon), section 46505(b)(3) or (c) (relating to explosive or incendiary devices, or endangerment of human life by means of weapons, on aircraft), section 46506 if homicide or attempted homicide is involved (relating to application of certain criminal laws to acts on aircraft), or section 60123(b) (relating to destruction of interstate gas or hazardous liquid pipeline facility) of title 49.'.

Sec. 809. No Statute of Limitation for Certain Terrorism Offenses.

(a) IN GENERAL—Section 3286 of title 18, United States Code, is amended to read as follows:

'Sec. 3286. Extension of statute of limitation for certain terrorism offenses

'(a) EIGHT-YEAR LIMITATION—Notwithstanding section 3282, no person shall be prosecuted, tried, or punished for any noncapital offense involving a violation of any provision listed in section 2332b(g)(5)(B), or a violation of section 112, 351(e), 1361, or 1751(e) of this title, or section 46504, 46505, or 46506 of title 49, unless the indictment is found or the information is instituted within 8 years after the offense was committed. Notwithstanding the preceding sentence, offenses listed in section 3295 are subject to the statute of limitations set forth in that section.

'(b) NO LIMITATION—Notwithstanding any other law, an indictment may be found or an information instituted at any time without limitation for any offense listed in section 2332b(g)(5)(B), if the commission of such offense resulted in, or created a forseeable risk of, death or serious bodily injury to another person.'.

(b) APPLICATION—The amendments made by this section shall apply to the prosecution of any offense committed before, on, or after the date of the enactment of this section.

Sec. 810. Alternate Maximum Penalties for Terrorism Offenses.

(a) ARSON—Section 81 of title 18, United States Code, is amended in the second undesignated paragraph by striking 'not more than twenty years' and inserting 'for any term of years or for life'.

(b) DESTRUCTION OF AN ENERGY FACILITY—Section 1366 of title 18, United States Code, is amended—

(1) in subsection (a), by striking 'ten' and inserting '20'; and

(2) by adding at the end the following:

'(d) Whoever is convicted of a violation of subsection (a) or (b) that has resulted in the death of any person shall be subject to imprisonment for any term of years or life.'.

(c) MATERIAL SUPPORT TO TERRORISTS—Section 2339A(a) of title 18, United States Code, is amended—

(1) by striking '10' and inserting '15'; and

(2) by striking the period and inserting ', and, if the death of any person results, shall be imprisoned for any term of years or for life.'.

(d) MATERIAL SUPPORT TO DESIGNATED FOREIGN TERRORIST ORGANIZATIONS—Section 2339B(a)(1) of title 18, United States Code, is amended—

(1) by striking '10' and inserting '15'; and

(2) by striking the period after 'or both' and inserting ', and, if the death of any person results, shall be imprisoned for any term of years or for life.'.

(e) DESTRUCTION OF NATIONAL-DEFENSE MATERIALS—Section 2155(a) of title 18, United States Code, is amended—

(1) by striking 'ten' and inserting '20'; and

(2) by striking the period at the end and inserting ', and, if death results to any person, shall be imprisoned for any term of years or for life.'.

(f) SABOTAGE OF NUCLEAR FACILITIES OR FUEL—Section 236 of the Atomic Energy Act of 1954 (42 U.S.C. 2284), is amended—

(1) by striking 'ten' each place it appears and inserting '20';

(2) in subsection (a), by striking the period at the end and inserting ', and, if death results to any person, shall be imprisoned for any term of years or for life.'; and

(3) in subsection (b), by striking the period at the end and inserting ', and, if death results to any person, shall be imprisoned for any term of years or for life.'.

(g) SPECIAL AIRCRAFT JURISDICTION OF THE UNITED STATES—Section 46505(c) of title 49, United States Code, is amended—

(1) by striking '15' and inserting '20'; and

(2) by striking the period at the end and inserting ', and, if death results to any person, shall be imprisoned for any term of years or for life.'.

(h) DAMAGING OR DESTROYING AN INTERSTATE GAS OR HAZARDOUS LIQUID PIPELINE FACILITY—Section 60123(b) of title 49, United States Code, is amended—

(1) by striking '15' and inserting '20'; and

(2) by striking the period at the end and inserting ', and, if death results to any person, shall be imprisoned for any term of years or for life.'.

Sec. 811. Penalties for Terrorist Conspiracies.

(a) ARSON—Section 81 of title 18, United States Code, is amended in the first undesignated paragraph—

(1) by striking ', or attempts to set fire to or burn'; and

(2) by inserting 'or attempts or conspires to do such an act,' before 'shall be imprisoned'.

(b) KILLINGS IN FEDERAL FACILITIES—Section 930(c) of title 18, United States Code, is amended—

(1) by striking 'or attempts to kill';

(2) by inserting 'or attempts or conspires to do such an act,' before 'shall be punished'; and

(3) by striking 'and 1113' and inserting '1113, and 1117'.

(c) COMMUNICATIONS LINES, STATIONS, OR SYSTEMS— Section 1362 of title 18, United States Code, is amended in the first undesignated paragraph—

(1) by striking 'or attempts willfully or maliciously to injure or destroy'; and

(2) by inserting 'or attempts or conspires to do such an act,' before 'shall be fined'.

(d) BUILDINGS OR PROPERTY WITHIN SPECIAL MARITIME AND TERRITORIAL JURISDICTION—Section 1363 of title 18, United States Code, is amended—

(1) by striking 'or attempts to destroy or injure'; and

(2) by inserting 'or attempts or conspires to do such an act,' before 'shall be fined' the first place it appears.

(e) WRECKING TRAINS—Section 1992 of title 18, United States Code, is amended by adding at the end the following:

'(c) A person who conspires to commit any offense defined in this section shall be subject to the same penalties (other than the penalty of death) as the penalties prescribed for the offense, the commission of which was the object of the conspiracy.'.

(f) MATERIAL SUPPORT TO TERRORISTS—Section 2339A of title 18, United States Code, is amended by inserting 'or attempts or conspires to do such an act,' before 'shall be fined'.

(g) TORTURE—Section 2340A of title 18, United States Code, is amended by adding at the end the following:

'(c) CONSPIRACY—A person who conspires to commit an offense under this section shall be subject to the same penalties (other than the penalty of death) as the penalties prescribed for the offense, the commission of which was the object of the conspiracy.'.

(h) SABOTAGE OF NUCLEAR FACILITIES OR FUEL—Section 236 of the Atomic Energy Act of 1954 (42 U.S.C. 2284), is amended—

   (1) in subsection (a)—

      (A) by striking ', or who intentionally and willfully attempts to destroy or cause physical damage to';

      (B) in paragraph (4), by striking the period at the end and inserting a comma; and

      (C) by inserting 'or attempts or conspires to do such an act,' before 'shall be fined'; and

   (2) in subsection (b)—

      (A) by striking 'or attempts to cause'; and

      (B) by inserting 'or attempts or conspires to do such an act,' before 'shall be fined'.

(i) INTERFERENCE WITH FLIGHT CREW MEMBERS AND ATTENDANTS—Section 46504 of title 49, United States Code, is amended by inserting 'or attempts or conspires to do such an act,' before 'shall be fined'.

(j) SPECIAL AIRCRAFT JURISDICTION OF THE UNITED STATES—Section 46505 of title 49, United States Code, is amended by adding at the end the following:

'(e) CONSPIRACY—If two or more persons conspire to violate subsection (b) or (c), and one or more of such persons do any act to effect the object of the conspiracy, each of the parties to such conspiracy shall be punished as provided in such subsection.'.

(k) DAMAGING OR DESTROYING AN INTERSTATE GAS OR HAZARDOUS LIQUID PIPELINE FACILITY—Section 60123(b) of title 49, United States Code, is amended—

   (1) by striking ', or attempting to damage or destroy,'; and

   (2) by inserting ', or attempting or conspiring to do such an act,' before 'shall be fined'.

Sec. 812. Post-Release Supervision of Terrorists.

Section 3583 of title 18, United States Code, is amended by adding at the end the following:

'(j) SUPERVISED RELEASE TERMS FOR TERRORISM PREDI-CATES—Notwithstanding subsection (b), the authorized term of supervised release for any offense listed in section 2332b(g)(5)(B), the commission of which resulted in, or created a foreseeable risk of, death or serious bodily injury to another person, is any term of years or life.'.

Sec. 813. Inclusion of Acts of Terrorism as Racketeering Activity.

Section 1961(1) of title 18, United States Code, is amended—

(1) by striking 'or (F)' and inserting '(F)'; and

(2) by inserting before the semicolon at the end the following: ', or (G) any act that is indictable under any provision listed in section 2332b(g)(5)(B)'.

Sec. 814. Deterrence and Prevention of Cyberterrorism.

(a) CLARIFICATION OF PROTECTION OF PROTECTED COMPUTERS—Section 1030(a)(5) of title 18, United States Code, is amended—

(1) by inserting '(i)' after '(A)';

(2) by redesignating subparagraphs (B) and (C) as clauses (ii) and (iii), respectively;

(3) by adding 'and' at the end of clause (iii), as so redesignated; and

(4) by adding at the end the following:

'(B) by conduct described in clause (i), (ii), or (iii) of subparagraph (A), caused (or, in the case of an attempted offense, would, if completed, have caused)—

'(i) loss to 1 or more persons during any 1-year period (and, for purposes of an investigation, prosecution, or other proceeding brought by the United States only, loss resulting from a related course of conduct affecting 1 or more other protected computers) aggregating at least $5,000 in value;

'(ii) the modification or impairment, or potential modification or impairment, of the medical examination, diagnosis, treatment, or care of 1 or more individuals;

'(iii) physical injury to any person;

'(iv) a threat to public health or safety; or

'(v) damage affecting a computer system used by or for a government entity in furtherance of the administration of justice, national defense, or national security;'.

(b) PROTECTION FROM EXTORTION—Section 1030(a)(7) of title 18, United States Code, is amended by striking ', firm, association, educational institution, financial institution, government entity, or other legal entity,'.

(c) PENALTIES—Section 1030(c) of title 18, United States Code, is amended—

(1) in paragraph (2)—

(A) in subparagraph (A)—

(i) by inserting 'except as provided in subparagraph (B),' before 'a fine';

(ii) by striking '(a)(5)(C)' and inserting '(a)(5)(A)(iii)'; and

(iii) by striking 'and' at the end;

(B) in subparagraph (B), by inserting 'or an attempt to commit an offense punishable under this subparagraph,' after 'subsection (a)(2),' in the matter preceding clause (i); and

(C) in subparagraph (C), by striking 'and' at the end;

(2) in paragraph (3)—

(A) by striking ', (a)(5)(A), (a)(5)(B),' both places it appears; and

(B) by striking '(a)(5)(C)' and inserting '(a)(5)(A)(iii)'; and

(3) by adding at the end the following:

'(4)(A) a fine under this title, imprisonment for not more than 10 years, or both, in the case of an offense under subsection (a)(5)(A)(i), or an attempt to commit an offense punishable under that subsection;

'(B) a fine under this title, imprisonment for not more than 5 years, or both, in the case of an offense under subsection (a)(5)(A)(ii), or an attempt to commit an offense punishable under that subsection;

'(C) a fine under this title, imprisonment for not more than 20 years, or both, in the case of an offense under subsection (a)(5)(A)(i) or (a)(5)(A)(ii), or an attempt to commit an offense punishable under either subsection, that occurs after a conviction for another offense under this section.'.

(d) DEFINITIONS—Section 1030(e) of title 18, United States Code is amended—

(1) in paragraph (2)(B), by inserting ', including a computer located outside the United States that is used in a manner that affects interstate or foreign commerce or communication of the United States' before the semicolon;

(2) in paragraph (7), by striking 'and' at the end;

(3) by striking paragraph (8) and inserting the following:

'(8) the term 'damage' means any impairment to the integrity or availability of data, a program, a system, or information;';

(4) in paragraph (9), by striking the period at the end and inserting a semicolon; and

(5) by adding at the end the following:

'(10) the term 'conviction' shall include a conviction under the law of any State for a crime punishable by imprisonment for more than 1 year, an element of which is unauthorized access, or exceeding authorized access, to a computer;

'(11) the term 'loss' means any reasonable cost to any victim, including the cost of responding to an offense, conducting a damage assessment, and restoring the data, program, system, or information to its condition prior to the offense, and any revenue lost, cost incurred, or other consequential damages incurred because of interruption of service; and

'(12) the term 'person' means any individual, firm, corporation, educational institution, financial institution, governmental entity, or legal or other entity.'.

(e) DAMAGES IN CIVIL ACTIONS—Section 1030(g) of title 18, United States Code is amended—

(1) by striking the second sentence and inserting the following: 'A civil action for a violation of this section may be brought only if the conduct involves 1 of the factors set forth in clause (i), (ii), (iii), (iv), or (v) of subsection (a)(5)(B). Damages for a violation involving only conduct described in subsection (a)(5)(B)(i) are limited to economic damages.'; and

(2) by adding at the end the following: 'No action may be brought under this subsection for the negligent design or manufacture of computer hardware, computer software, or firmware.'.

(f) AMENDMENT OF SENTENCING GUIDELINES RELATING TO CERTAIN COMPUTER FRAUD AND ABUSE—Pursuant to its authority under section 994(p) of title 28, United States Code, the United States Sentencing Commission shall amend the Federal sentencing guidelines to ensure that any individual convicted of a violation of section 1030 of title 18, United States Code, can be subjected to appropriate penalties, without regard to any mandatory minimum term of imprisonment.

Sec. 815. Additional Defense to Civil Actions Relating to Preserving Records in Response to Government Requests.

Section 2707(e)(1) of title 18, United States Code, is amended by inserting after 'or statutory authorization' the following: '(including a request of a governmental entity under section 2703(f) of this title)'.

Sec. 816. Development and Support of Cybersecurity Forensic Capabilities.

(a) IN GENERAL—The Attorney General shall establish such regional computer forensic laboratories as the Attorney General considers appropriate, and provide support to existing computer forensic laboratories, in order that all such computer forensic laboratories have the capability—

(1) to provide forensic examinations with respect to seized or intercepted computer evidence relating to criminal activity (including cyberterrorism);

(2) to provide training and education for Federal, State, and local law enforcement personnel and prosecutors regarding investigations, forensic analyses, and prosecutions of computer-related crime (including cyberterrorism);

(3) to assist Federal, State, and local law enforcement in enforcing Federal, State, and local criminal laws relating to computer-related crime;

(4) to facilitate and promote the sharing of Federal law enforcement expertise and information about the investigation, analysis, and prosecution of computer-related crime with State and local law

enforcement personnel and prosecutors, including the use of multijurisdictional task forces; and

(5) to carry out such other activities as the Attorney General considers appropriate.

(b) AUTHORIZATION OF APPROPRIATIONS-

(1) AUTHORIZATION—There is hereby authorized to be appropriated in each fiscal year $50,000,000 for purposes of carrying out this section.

(2) AVAILABILITY—Amounts appropriated pursuant to the authorization of appropriations in paragraph (1) shall remain available until expended.

Sec. 817. Expansion of the Biological Weapons Statute.

Chapter 10 of title 18, United States Code, is amended—

(1) in section 175—

(A) in subsection (b)—

(i) by striking 'does not include' and inserting 'includes';

(ii) by inserting 'other than' after 'system for'; and

(iii) by inserting 'bona fide research' after 'protective';

(B) by redesignating subsection (b) as subsection (c); and

(C) by inserting after subsection (a) the following:

'(b) ADDITIONAL OFFENSE—Whoever knowingly possesses any biological agent, toxin, or delivery system of a type or in a quantity that, under the circumstances, is not reasonably justified by a prophylactic, protective, bona fide research, or other peaceful purpose, shall be fined under this title, imprisoned not more than 10 years, or both. In this subsection, the terms 'biological agent' and 'toxin' do not encompass any biological agent or toxin that is in its naturally occurring environment, if the biological agent or toxin has not been cultivated, collected, or otherwise extracted from its natural source.';

(2) by inserting after section 175a the following:

'Sec. 175b. Possession By Restricted Persons.

'(a) No restricted person described in subsection (b) shall ship or transport interstate or foreign commerce, or possess in or affecting commerce, any biological agent or toxin, or receive any biological agent or toxin that has been shipped or transported in interstate or foreign commerce, if the biological agent or toxin is listed as a select agent in subsection (j) of section 72.6 of title 42, Code of Federal Regulations, pursuant to section 511(d)(l) of the Antiterrorism and Effective Death Penalty Act of 1996 (Public Law 104–132), and is not exempted under subsection (h) of such section 72.6, or appendix A of part 72 of the Code of Regulations.

'(b) In this section:

'(1) The term 'select agent' does not include any such biological agent or toxin that is in its naturally-occurring environment, if the biological agent or toxin has not been cultivated, collected, or otherwise extracted from its natural source.

'(2) The term 'restricted person' means an individual who—

'(A) is under indictment for a crime punishable by imprisonment for a term exceeding 1 year;

'(B) has been convicted in any court of a crime punishable by imprisonment for a term exceeding 1 year;

'(C) is a fugitive from justice;

'(D) is an unlawful user of any controlled substance (as defined in section 102 of the Controlled Substances Act (21 U.S.C. 802));

'(E) is an alien illegally or unlawfully in the United States;

'(F) has been adjudicated as a mental defective or has been committed to any mental institution;

'(G) is an alien (other than an alien lawfully admitted for permanent residence) who is a national of a country as to which the Secretary of State, pursuant to section 6(j) of the Export Administration Act of 1979 (50 U.S.C. App. 2405(j)), section 620A of chapter 1 of part M of the Foreign Assistance Act of 1961 (22 U.S.C. 2371), or section 40(d) of chapter 3 of the Arms Export Control Act (22 U.S.C. 2780(d)), has made a determination (that remains in effect) that such country has repeatedly provided support for acts of international terrorism; or

'(H) has been discharged from the Armed Services of the United States under dishonorable conditions.

'(3) The term 'alien' has the same meaning as in section 1010(a)(3) of the Immigration and Nationality Act (8 U.S.C. 1101(a)(3)).

'(4) The term 'lawfully admitted for permanent residence' has the same meaning as in section 101(a)(20) of the Immigration and Nationality Act (8 U.S.C. 1101(a)(20)).

'(c) Whoever knowingly violates this section shall be fined as provided in this title, imprisoned not more than 10 years, or both, but the prohibition contained in this section shall not apply with respect to any duly authorized United States governmental activity.'; and

(3) in the chapter analysis, by inserting after the item relating to section 175a the following:

'175b. Possession by restricted persons.'.

TITLE IX—IMPROVED INTELLIGENCE

Sec. 901. Responsibilities of Director of Central Intelligence Regarding Foreign Intelligence Collected Under Foreign Intelligence Surveillance Act of 1978.

Section 103(c) of the National Security Act of 1947 (50 U.S.C. 403–3(c)) is amended—

(1) by redesignating paragraphs (6) and (7) as paragraphs (7) and (8), respectively; and

(2) by inserting after paragraph (5) the following new paragraph (6):

'(6) establish requirements and priorities for foreign intelligence information to be collected under the Foreign Intelligence Surveillance Act of 1978 (50 U.S.C. 1801 et seq.), and provide assistance to the Attorney General to ensure that information derived from electronic surveillance or physical searches under that Act is disseminated so it may be used efficiently and effectively for foreign intelligence purposes, except that the Director shall have no authority to direct, manage, or undertake electronic surveillance or physical search operations pursuant to that Act unless otherwise authorized by statute or Executive order;'.

Sec. 902. Inclusion of International Terrorist Activities Within Scope of Foreign Intelligence Under National Security Act of 1947.

Section 3 of the National Security Act of 1947 (50 U.S.C. 401a) is amended—

(1) in paragraph (2), by inserting before the period the following: ', or international terrorist activities'; and

(2) in paragraph (3), by striking 'and activities conducted' and inserting ', and activities conducted,'.

Sec. 903. Sense of Congress on the Establishment And Maintenance of Intelligence Relationships to Acquire Information on Terrorists and Terrorist Organizations.

It is the sense of Congress that officers and employees of the intelligence community of the Federal Government, acting within the course of their official duties, should be encouraged, and should make every effort, to establish and maintain intelligence relationships with any person, entity, or group for the purpose of engaging in lawful intelligence activities, including the acquisition of information on the identity, location, finances, affiliations, capabilities, plans, or intentions of a terrorist or terrorist organization, or information on any other person, entity, or group (including a foreign government) engaged in harboring, comforting, financing, aiding, or assisting a terrorist or terrorist organization.

Sec. 904. Temporary Authority to Defer Submittal to Congress of Reports on Intelligence and Intelligence-Related Matters.

(a) AUTHORITY TO DEFER—The Secretary of Defense, Attorney General, and Director of Central Intelligence each may, during the effective period of this section, defer the date of submittal to Congress of any covered intelligence report under the jurisdiction of such official until February 1, 2002.

(b) COVERED INTELLIGENCE REPORT—Except as provided in subsection (c), for purposes of subsection (a), a covered intelligence report is as follows:

(1) Any report on intelligence or intelligence-related activities of the United States Government that is required to be submitted to Congress by an element of the intelligence community during the effective period of this section.

(2) Any report or other matter that is required to be submitted to the Select Committee on Intelligence of the Senate and Permanent Select Committee on Intelligence of the House of Representatives by the Department of Defense or the Department of Justice during the effective period of this section.

(c) EXCEPTION FOR CERTAIN REPORTS—For purposes of subsection (a), any report required by section 502 or 503 of the National Security Act of 1947 (50 U.S.C. 413a, 413b) is not a covered intelligence report.

(d) NOTICE TO CONGRESS—Upon deferring the date of submittal to Congress of a covered intelligence report under subsection (a), the official deferring the date of submittal of the covered intelligence report shall submit to Congress notice of the deferral. Notice of deferral of a report shall specify the provision of law, if any, under which the report would otherwise be submitted to Congress.

(e) EXTENSION OF DEFERRAL—(1) Each official specified in subsection (a) may defer the date of submittal to Congress of a covered intelligence report under the jurisdiction of such official to a date after February 1, 2002, if such official submits to the committees of Congress specified in subsection (b)(2) before February 1, 2002, a certification that preparation and submittal of the covered intelligence report on February 1, 2002, will impede the work of officers or employees who are engaged in counterterrorism activities.

(2) A certification under paragraph (1) with respect to a covered intelligence report shall specify the date on which the covered intelligence report will be submitted to Congress.

(f) EFFECTIVE PERIOD—The effective period of this section is the period beginning on the date of the enactment of this Act and ending on February 1, 2002.

(g) ELEMENT OF THE INTELLIGENCE COMMUNITY DEFINED —In this section, the term 'element of the intelligence community' means any element of the intelligence community specified or designated under section 3(4) of the National Security Act of 1947 (50 U.S.C. 401a(4)).

Sec. 905. Disclosure to Director of Central Intelligence of Foreign Intelligence-Related Information With Respect to Criminal Investigations.

(a) IN GENERAL—Title I of the National Security Act of 1947 (50 U.S.C. 402 et seq.) is amended—

(1) by redesignating subsection 105B as section 105C; and

(2) by inserting after section 105A the following new section 105B:

'DISCLOSURE OF FOREIGN INTELLIGENCE ACQUIRED

IN CRIMINAL INVESTIGATIONS; NOTICE OF CRIMINAL INVESTIGATIONS OF FOREIGN INTELLIGENCE SOURCES 'SEC. 105B. (a) DISCLOSURE OF FOREIGN INTELLIGENCE —(1) Except as otherwise provided by law and subject to paragraph (2), the Attorney General, or the head of any other department or agency of the Federal Government with law enforcement responsibilities, shall expeditiously disclose to the Director of Central Intelligence, pursuant to guidelines developed by the Attorney General in consultation with the Director, foreign intelligence acquired by an element of the Department of Justice or an element of such department or agency, as the case may be, in the course of a criminal investigation.

'(2) The Attorney General by regulation and in consultation with the Director of Central Intelligence may provide for exceptions to the applicability of paragraph (1) for one or more classes of foreign intelligence, or foreign intelligence with respect to one or more targets or matters, if the Attorney General determines that disclosure of such foreign intelligence under that paragraph would jeopardize an ongoing law enforcement investigation or impair other significant law enforcement interests.

'(b) PROCEDURES FOR NOTICE OF CRIMINAL INVESTIGATIONS—Not later than 180 days after the date of enactment of this section, the Attorney General, in consultation with the Director of Central Intelligence, shall develop guidelines to ensure that after receipt of a report from an element of the intelligence community of activity of a foreign intelligence source or potential foreign intelligence source that may warrant investigation as criminal activity, the Attorney General provides notice to the Director of Central Intelligence, within a reasonable period of time, of his intention to commence, or decline to commence, a criminal investigation of such activity.

'(c) PROCEDURES—The Attorney General shall develop procedures for the administration of this section, including the disclosure of foreign intelligence by elements of the Department of Justice, and elements of other departments and agencies of the Federal Government, under subsection (a) and the provision of notice with respect to criminal investigations under subsection (b).'.

(b) CLERICAL AMENDMENT—The table of contents in the first section of that Act is amended by striking the item relating to section 105B and inserting the following new items:

'Sec. 105B. Disclosure of foreign intelligence acquired in criminal investigations; notice of criminal investigations of foreign intelligence sources.
'Sec. 105C. Protection of the operational files of the National Imagery and Mapping Agency.'.

Sec. 906. Foreign Terrorist Asset Tracking Center.

(a) REPORT ON RECONFIGURATION—Not later than February 1, 2002, the Attorney General, the Director of Central Intelligence, and the Secretary of the Treasury shall jointly submit to Congress a report on the feasibility and desirability of reconfiguring the Foreign Terrorist Asset Tracking Center and the Office of Foreign Assets Control of the Department of the Treasury in order to establish a capability to provide for the effective and efficient analysis and dissemination of foreign intelligence relating to the financial capabilities and resources of international terrorist organizations.

(b) REPORT REQUIREMENTS—(1) In preparing the report under subsection (a), the Attorney General, the Secretary, and the Director shall consider whether, and to what extent, the capacities and resources of the Financial Crimes Enforcement Center of the Department of the Treasury may be integrated into the capability contemplated by the report.

(2) If the Attorney General, Secretary, and the Director determine that it is feasible and desirable to undertake the reconfiguration described in subsection (a) in order to establish the capability described in that subsection, the Attorney General, the Secretary, and the Director shall include with the report under that subsection a detailed proposal for legislation to achieve the reconfiguration.

Sec. 907. National Virtual Translation Center.

(a) REPORT ON ESTABLISHMENT—(1) Not later than February 1, 2002, the Director of Central Intelligence shall, in consultation with the Director of the Federal Bureau of Investigation, submit to the appropriate committees of Congress a report on the establishment and maintenance within the intelligence community of an element for purposes of providing timely and accurate translations of foreign intelligence for all other elements of the intelligence community. In the report, the element shall be referred to as the 'National Virtual Translation Center'.

(2) The report on the element described in paragraph (1) shall discuss the use of state-of-the-art communications technology, the inte-

gration of existing translation capabilities in the intelligence community, and the utilization of remote-connection capacities so as to minimize the need for a central physical facility for the element.

(b) RESOURCES—The report on the element required by subsection (a) shall address the following:

(1) The assignment to the element of a staff of individuals possessing a broad range of linguistic and translation skills appropriate for the purposes of the element.

(2) The provision to the element of communications capabilities and systems that are commensurate with the most current and sophisticated communications capabilities and systems available to other elements of intelligence community.

(3) The assurance, to the maximum extent practicable, that the communications capabilities and systems provided to the element will be compatible with communications capabilities and systems utilized by the Federal Bureau of Investigation in securing timely and accurate translations of foreign language materials for law enforcement investigations.

(4) The development of a communications infrastructure to ensure the efficient and secure use of the translation capabilities of the element.

(c) SECURE COMMUNICATIONS—The report shall include a discussion of the creation of secure electronic communications between the element described by subsection (a) and the other elements of the intelligence community.

(d) DEFINITIONS—In this section:

(1) FOREIGN INTELLIGENCE—The term 'foreign intelligence' has the meaning given that term in section 3(2) of the National Security Act of 1947 (50 U.S.C. 401a(2)).

(2) ELEMENT OF THE INTELLIGENCE COMMUNITY—The term 'element of the intelligence community' means any element of the intelligence community specified or designated under section 3(4) of the National Security Act of 1947 (50 U.S.C. 401a(4)).

Sec. 908. Training of Government Officials Regarding Identification and Use of Foreign Intelligence.

(a) PROGRAM REQUIRED—The Attorney General shall, in consultation with the Director of Central Intelligence, carry out a program to provide appropriate training to officials described in subsection (b) in order to assist such officials in—

(1) identifying foreign intelligence information in the course of their duties; and

(2) utilizing foreign intelligence information in the course of their duties, to the extent that the utilization of such information is appropriate for such duties.

(b) OFFICIALS—The officials provided training under subsection (a) are, at the discretion of the Attorney General and the Director, the following:

(1) Officials of the Federal Government who are not ordinarily engaged in the collection, dissemination, and use of foreign intelligence in the performance of their duties.

(2) Officials of State and local governments who encounter, or may encounter in the course of a terrorist event, foreign intelligence in the performance of their duties.

(c) AUTHORIZATION OF APPROPRIATIONS—There is hereby authorized to be appropriated for the Department of Justice such sums as may be necessary for purposes of carrying out the program required by subsection (a).

TITLE X—MISCELLANEOUS

Sec. 1001. Review of the Department of Justice.

The Inspector General of the Department of Justice shall designate one official who shall—

(1) review information and receive complaints alleging abuses of civil rights and civil liberties by employees and officials of the Department of Justice;

(2) make public through the Internet, radio, television, and newspaper advertisements information on the responsibilities and functions of, and how to contact, the official; and

(3) submit to the Committee on the Judiciary of the House of Representatives and the Committee on the Judiciary of the Senate on a semi-annual basis a report on the implementation of this subsection and detailing any abuses described in paragraph (1), including a description of the use of funds appropriations used to carry out this subsection.

Sec. 1002. Sense of Congress.

(a) FINDINGS—Congress finds that—

(1) all Americans are united in condemning, in the strongest possible terms, the terrorists who planned and carried out the attacks against the United States on September 11, 2001, and in pursuing all those responsible for those attacks and their sponsors until they are brought to justice;

(2) Sikh-Americans form a vibrant, peaceful, and law-abiding part of America's people;

(3) approximately 500,000 Sikhs reside in the United States and are a vital part of the Nation;

(4) Sikh-Americans stand resolutely in support of the commitment of our Government to bring the terrorists and those that harbor them to justice;

(5) the Sikh faith is a distinct religion with a distinct religious and ethnic identity that has its own places of worship and a distinct holy text and religious tenets;

(6) many Sikh-Americans, who are easily recognizable by their turbans and beards, which are required articles of their faith, have suffered both verbal and physical assaults as a result of misguided anger toward Arab-Americans and Muslim-Americans in the wake of the September 11, 2001 terrorist attack;

(7) Sikh-Americans, as do all Americans, condemn acts of prejudice against any American; and

(8) Congress is seriously concerned by the number of crimes against Sikh-Americans and other Americans all across the Nation that have been reported in the wake of the tragic events that unfolded on September 11, 2001.

(b) SENSE OF CONGRESS—Congress—

(1) declares that, in the quest to identify, locate, and bring to justice the perpetrators and sponsors of the terrorist attacks on the United States on September 11, 2001, the civil rights and civil liberties of all Americans, including Sikh-Americans, should be protected;

(2) condemns bigotry and any acts of violence or discrimination against any Americans, including Sikh-Americans;

(3) calls upon local and Federal law enforcement authorities to work to prevent crimes against all Americans, including Sikh-Americans; and

(4) calls upon local and Federal law enforcement authorities to prosecute to the fullest extent of the law all those who commit crimes.

Sec. 1003. Definition of 'Electronic Surveillance'.

Section 101(f)(2) of the Foreign Intelligence Surveillance Act (50 U.S.C. 1801(f)(2)) is amended by adding at the end before the semicolon the following: ', but does not include the acquisition of those communications of computer trespassers that would be permissible under section 2511(2)(i) of title 18, United States Code'.

Sec. 1004. Venue in Money Laundering Cases.

Section 1956 of title 18, United States Code, is amended by adding at the end the following:

'(i) VENUE—(1) Except as provided in paragraph (2), a prosecution for an offense under this section or section 1957 may be brought in—

'(A) any district in which the financial or monetary transaction is conducted; or

'(B) any district where a prosecution for the underlying specified unlawful activity could be brought, if the defendant participated in the transfer of the proceeds of the specified unlawful activity from that district to the district where the financial or monetary transaction is conducted.

'(2) A prosecution for an attempt or conspiracy offense under this section or section 1957 may be brought in the district where venue would lie for the completed offense under paragraph (1), or in any other district where an act in furtherance of the attempt or conspiracy took place.

'(3) For purposes of this section, a transfer of funds from 1 place to another, by wire or any other means, shall constitute a single, continuing transaction. Any person who conducts (as that term is defined in subsection (c)(2)) any portion of the transaction may be charged in any district in which the transaction takes place.'.

Sec. 1005. First Responders Assistance Act.

(a) GRANT AUTHORIZATION—The Attorney General shall make grants described in subsections (b) and (c) to States and units of local government to improve the ability of State and local law enforcement, fire department and first responders to respond to and prevent acts of terrorism.

(b) TERRORISM PREVENTION GRANTS—Terrorism prevention grants under this subsection may be used for programs, projects, and other activities to—

(1) hire additional law enforcement personnel dedicated to intelligence gathering and analysis functions, including the formation of full-time intelligence and analysis units;

(2) purchase technology and equipment for intelligence gathering and analysis functions, including wire-tap, pen links, cameras, and computer hardware and software;

(3) purchase equipment for responding to a critical incident, including protective equipment for patrol officers such as quick masks;

(4) purchase equipment for managing a critical incident, such as communications equipment for improved interoperability among surrounding jurisdictions and mobile command posts for overall scene management; and

(5) fund technical assistance programs that emphasize coordination among neighboring law enforcement agencies for sharing resources, and resources coordination among law enforcement agencies for combining intelligence gathering and analysis functions, and the development of policy, procedures, memorandums of understanding, and other best practices.

(c) ANTITERRORISM TRAINING GRANTS—Antiterrorism training grants under this subsection may be used for programs, projects, and other activities to address—

(1) intelligence gathering and analysis techniques;

(2) community engagement and outreach;

(3) critical incident management for all forms of terrorist attack;

(4) threat assessment capabilities;

(5) conducting followup investigations; and

(6) stabilizing a community after a terrorist incident.

(d) APPLICATION-

(1) IN GENERAL—Each eligible entity that desires to receive a grant under this section shall submit an application to the Attorney General, at such time, in such manner, and accompanied by such addi-

tional information as the Attorney General may reasonably require.

(2) CONTENTS—Each application submitted pursuant to paragraph (1) shall—

(A) describe the activities for which assistance under this section is sought; and

(B) provide such additional assurances as the Attorney General determines to be essential to ensure compliance with the requirements of this section.

(e) MINIMUM AMOUNT—If all applications submitted by a State or units of local government within that State have not been funded under this section in any fiscal year, that State, if it qualifies, and the units of local government within that State, shall receive in that fiscal year not less than 0.5 percent of the total amount appropriated in that fiscal year for grants under this section.

(f) AUTHORIZATION OF APPROPRIATIONS—There are authorized to be appropriated $25,000,000 for each of the fiscal years 2003 through 2007.

Sec. 1006. Inadmissibility of Aliens Engaged in Money Laundering.

(a) AMENDMENT TO IMMIGRATION AND NATIONALITY ACT—Section 212(a)(2) of the Immigration and Nationality Act (8 U.S.C. 1182(a)(2)) is amended by adding at the end the following:

'(I) MONEY LAUNDERING—Any alien—

'(i) who a consular officer or the Attorney General knows, or has reason to believe, has engaged, is engaging, or seeks to enter the United States to engage, in an offense which is described in section 1956 or 1957 of title 18, United States Code (relating to laundering of monetary instruments); or

'(ii) who a consular officer or the Attorney General knows is, or has been, a knowing aider, abettor, assister, conspirator, or colluder with others in an offense which is described in such section; is inadmissible.'.

(b) MONEY LAUNDERING WATCHLIST—Not later than 90 days after the date of the enactment of this Act, the Secretary of State shall develop, implement, and certify to the Congress that there has been established a money laundering watchlist, which identifies individuals worldwide who are known or suspected of money laundering, which is readily accessible to, and shall be checked by, a consular or other Federal official prior to the issuance of a visa or admission to the United States. The Secretary of State shall develop and continually update the watchlist in cooperation with the Attorney General, the Secretary of the Treasury, and the Director of Central Intelligence.

Sec. 1007. Authorization of Funds for Dea Police Training in South and Central Asia.

In addition to amounts otherwise available to carry out section 481 of the Foreign Assistance Act of 1961 (22 U.S.C. 2291), there is authorized to be appropriated to the President not less than $5,000,000 for fiscal year 2002 for regional antidrug training in the Republic of Turkey by the Drug Enforcement Administration for police, as well as increased precursor chemical control efforts in the South and Central Asia region.

Sec. 1008. Feasibility Study on Use of Biometric Identifier Scanning System With Access to the FBI Integrated Automated Fingerprint Identification System at Overseas Consular Posts and Points of Entry to the United States.

(a) IN GENERAL—The Attorney General, in consultation with the Secretary of State and the Secretary of Transportation, shall conduct a study on the feasibility of utilizing a biometric identifier (fingerprint) scanning system, with access to the database of the Federal Bureau of Investigation Integrated Automated Fingerprint Identification System, at consular offices abroad and at points of entry into the United States to enhance the ability of State Department and immigration officials to identify aliens who may be wanted in connection with criminal or terrorist investigations in the United States or abroad prior to the issuance of visas or entry into the United States.

(b) REPORT TO CONGRESS—Not later than 90 days after the date of the enactment of this Act, the Attorney General shall submit a report summarizing the findings of the study authorized under subsection (a) to the Committee on International Relations and the Committee on the Judiciary of the House of Representatives and the Committee on Foreign Relations and the Committee on the Judiciary of the Senate.

Sec. 1009. Study of Access.

(a) IN GENERAL—Not later than 120 days after enactment of this Act, the Federal Bureau of Investigation shall study and report to Congress on the feasibility of providing to airlines access via computer to the names of passengers who are suspected of terrorist activity by Federal officials.

(b) AUTHORIZATION—There are authorized to be appropriated not more than $250,000 to carry out subsection (a).

Sec. 1010. Temporary Authority to Contract With Local and State Governments for Performance of Security Functions at United States Military Installations.

(a) IN GENERAL—Notwithstanding section 2465 of title 10, United States Code, during the period of time that United States armed forces are engaged in Operation Enduring Freedom, and for the period of 180 days thereafter, funds appropriated to the Department of Defense may be obligated and expended for the purpose of entering into contracts or other agreements for the performance of security functions at any military installation or facility in the United States with a proximately located local or State government, or combination of such governments, whether or not any such government is obligated to provide such services to the general public without compensation.

(b) TRAINING—Any contract or agreement entered into under this section shall prescribe standards for the training and other qualifications of local government law enforcement personnel who perform security functions under this section in accordance with criteria established by the Secretary of the service concerned.

(c) REPORT—One year after the date of enactment of this section, the Secretary of Defense shall submit a report to the Committees on Armed Services of the Senate and the House of Representatives describing the use of the authority granted under this section and the use by the Department of Defense of other means to improve the performance of security functions on military installations and facilities located within the United States.

Sec. 1011. Crimes Against Charitable Americans.

(a) SHORT TITLE—This section may be cited as the 'Crimes Against Charitable Americans Act of 2001'.

(b) TELEMARKETING AND CONSUMER FRAUD ABUSE—The Telemarketing and Consumer Fraud and Abuse Prevention Act (15 U.S.C. 6101 et seq.) is amended—

(1) in section 3(a)(2), by inserting after 'practices' the second place it appears the following: 'which shall include fraudulent charitable solicitations, and';

(2) in section 3(a)(3)—

(A) in subparagraph (B), by striking 'and' at the end;

(B) in subparagraph (C), by striking the period at the end and inserting '; and'; and

(C) by adding at the end the following:

'(D)a requirement that any person engaged in telemarketing for the solicitation of charitable contributions, donations, or gifts of money or any other thing of value, shall promptly and clearly disclose to the person receiving the call that the purpose of the call is to solicit charitable contributions, donations, or gifts, and make such other disclosures as the Commission considers appropriate, including the name and mailing address of the charitable organization on behalf of which the solicitation is made.'; and

(3) in section 7(4), by inserting ', or a charitable contribution, donation, or gift of money or any other thing of value,' after 'services'.

(c) RED CROSS MEMBERS OR AGENTS—Section 917 of title 18, United States Code, is amended by striking 'one year' and inserting '5 years'.

(d) TELEMARKETING FRAUD—Section 2325(1) of title 18, United States Code, is amended—

(1) in subparagraph (A), by striking 'or' at the end;

(2) in subparagraph (B), by striking the comma at the end and inserting '; or';

(3) by inserting after subparagraph (B) the following:

'(C)a charitable contribution, donation, or gift of money or any other thing of value,'; and

(4) in the flush language, by inserting 'or charitable contributor, or donor' after 'participant'.

Sec. 1012. Limitation on Issuance of Hazmat Licenses.

(a) LIMITATION-

(1) IN GENERAL—Chapter 51 of title 49, United States Code, is amended by inserting after section 5103 the following new section:

'Sec. 5103a. Limitation on issuance of hazmat licenses

'(a) LIMITATION-

'(1) ISSUANCE OF LICENSES—A State may not issue to any individual a license to operate a motor vehicle transporting in commerce a hazardous material unless the Secretary of Transportation has first determined, upon receipt of a notification under subsection (c)(1)(B), that the individual does not pose a security risk warranting denial of the license.

'(2) RENEWALS INCLUDED—For the purposes of this section, the term 'issue', with respect to a license, includes renewal of the license.

'(b) HAZARDOUS MATERIALS DESCRIBED—The limitation in subsection (a) shall apply with respect to—

'(1) any material defined as a hazardous material by the Secretary of Transportation; and

'(2) any chemical or biological material or agent determined by the Secretary of Health and Human Services or the Attorney General as being a threat to the national security of the United States.

'(c) BACKGROUND RECORDS CHECK-

'(1) IN GENERAL—Upon the request of a State regarding issuance of a license described in subsection (a)(1) to an individual, the Attorney General—

'(A) shall carry out a background records check regarding the individual; and

'(B) upon completing the background records check, shall notify the Secretary of Transportation of the completion and results of the background records check.

'(2) SCOPE—A background records check regarding an individual under this subsection shall consist of the following:

'(A) A check of the relevant criminal history data bases.

'(B) In the case of an alien, a check of the relevant data bases to determine the status of the alien under the immigration laws of the United States.

'(C) As appropriate, a check of the relevant international data bases through Interpol-U.S. National Central Bureau or other appropriate means.

'(d) REPORTING REQUIREMENT—Each State shall submit to the Secretary of Transportation, at such time and in such manner as the Secretary may prescribe, the name, address, and such other information as the Secretary may require, concerning—

'(1) each alien to whom the State issues a license described in subsection (a); and

'(2) each other individual to whom such a license is issued, as the Secretary may require.

'(e) ALIEN DEFINED—In this section, the term 'alien' has the meaning given the term in section 101(a)(3) of the Immigration and Nationality Act.'.

(2) CLERICAL AMENDMENT—The table of sections at the beginning of such chapter is amended by inserting after the item relating to section 5103 the following new item:

'5103a. Limitation on issuance of hazmat licenses.'.

(b) REGULATION OF DRIVER FITNESS—Section 31305(a)(5) of title 49, United States Code, is amended—

(1) by striking 'and' at the end of subparagraph (A);

(2) by inserting 'and' at the end of subparagraph (B); and

(3) by adding at the end the following new subparagraph:

'(C) is licensed by a State to operate the vehicle after having first been determined under section 5103a of this title as not posing a security risk warranting denial of the license.'.

(c) AUTHORIZATION OF APPROPRIATIONS—There is authorized to be appropriated for the Department of Transportation and the Department of Justice such amounts as may be necessary to carry out section 5103a of title 49, United States Code, as added by subsection (a).

Sec. 1013. Expressing the Sense of the Senate Concerning the Provision of Funding for Bioterrorism Preparedness and Response.

(a) FINDINGS—The Senate finds the following:

(1) Additional steps must be taken to better prepare the United States to respond to potential bioterrorism attacks.

(2) The threat of a bioterrorist attack is still remote, but is increasing for a variety of reasons, including—

(A) public pronouncements by Osama bin Laden that it is his religious duty to acquire weapons of mass destruction, including chemical and biological weapons;

(B) the callous disregard for innocent human life as demonstrated by the terrorists' attacks of September 11, 2001;

(C) the resources and motivation of known terrorists and their sponsors and supporters to use biological warfare;

(D) recent scientific and technological advances in agent delivery technology such as aerosolization that have made weaponization of certain germs much easier; and

(E) the increasing access to the technologies and expertise necessary to construct and deploy chemical and biological weapons of mass destruction.

(3) Coordination of Federal, State, and local terrorism research, preparedness, and response programs must be improved.

(4) States, local areas, and public health officials must have enhanced resources and expertise in order to respond to a potential bioterrorist attack.

(5) National, State, and local communication capacities must be enhanced to combat the spread of chemical and biological illness.

(6) Greater resources must be provided to increase the capacity of hospitals and local health care workers to respond to public health threats.

(7) Health care professionals must be better trained to recognize, diagnose, and treat illnesses arising from biochemical attacks.

(8) Additional supplies may be essential to increase the readiness of the United States to respond to a bio-attack.

(9) Improvements must be made in assuring the safety of the food supply.

(10) New vaccines and treatments are needed to assure that we have an adequate response to a biochemical attack.

(11) Government research, preparedness, and response programs need to utilize private sector expertise and resources.

(12) Now is the time to strengthen our public health system and ensure that the United States is adequately prepared to respond to

potential bioterrorist attacks, natural infectious disease outbreaks, and other challenges and potential threats to the public health.

(b) SENSE OF THE SENATE—It is the sense of the Senate that the United States should make a substantial new investment this year toward the following:

(1) Improving State and local preparedness capabilities by upgrading State and local surveillance epidemiology, assisting in the development of response plans, assuring adequate staffing and training of health professionals to diagnose and care for victims of bioterrorism, extending the electronics communications networks and training personnel, and improving public health laboratories.

(2) Improving hospital response capabilities by assisting hospitals in developing plans for a bioterrorist attack and improving the surge capacity of hospitals.

(3) Upgrading the bioterrorism capabilities of the Centers for Disease Control and Prevention through improving rapid identification and health early warning systems.

(4) Improving disaster response medical systems, such as the National Disaster Medical System and the Metropolitan Medical Response System and Epidemic Intelligence Service.

(5) Targeting research to assist with the development of appropriate therapeutics and vaccines for likely bioterrorist agents and assisting with expedited drug and device review through the Food and Drug Administration.

(6) Improving the National Pharmaceutical Stockpile program by increasing the amount of necessary therapies (including smallpox vaccines and other post-exposure vaccines) and ensuring the appropriate deployment of stockpiles.

(7) Targeting activities to increase food safety at the Food and Drug Administration.

(8) Increasing international cooperation to secure dangerous biological agents, increase surveillance, and retrain biological warfare specialists.

Sec. 1014. Grant Program for State and Local Domestic Preparedness Support.

(a) IN GENERAL—The Office for State and Local Domestic Preparedness Support of the Office of Justice Programs shall make a grant to each State, which shall be used by the State, in conjunction with units of local government, to enhance the capability of State and local jurisdictions to prepare for and respond to terrorist acts including events of terrorism involving weapons of mass destruction and biological, nuclear, radiological, incendiary, chemical, and explosive devices.

(b) USE OF GRANT AMOUNTS—Grants under this section may be used to purchase needed equipment and to provide training and technical assistance to State and local first responders.

(c) AUTHORIZATION OF APPROPRIATIONS-

(1) IN GENERAL—There is authorized to be appropriated to carry out this section such sums as necessary for each of fiscal years 2002 through 2007.

(2) LIMITATIONS—Of the amount made available to carry out this section in any fiscal year not more than 3 percent may be used by the Attorney General for salaries and administrative expenses.

(3) MINIMUM AMOUNT—Each State shall be allocated in each fiscal year under this section not less than 0.75 percent of the total amount appropriated in the fiscal year for grants pursuant to this section, except that the United States Virgin Islands, America Samoa, Guam, and the Northern Mariana Islands each shall be allocated 0.25 percent.

Sec. 1015. Expansion and Reauthorization of the Crime Identification Technology Act for Antiterrorism Grants to States and Localities.

Section 102 of the Crime Identification Technology Act of 1998 (42 U.S.C. 14601) is amended—

(1) in subsection (b)—

(A) in paragraph (16), by striking 'and' at the end;

(B) in paragraph (17), by striking the period and inserting '; and'; and

(C) by adding at the end the following:

'(18) notwithstanding subsection (c), antiterrorism purposes as they relate to any other uses under this section or for other antiterrorism programs.'; and

(2) in subsection (e)(1), by striking 'this section' and all that follows and inserting 'this section $250,000,000 for each of fiscal years 2002 through 2007.'.

Sec. 1016. Critical Infrastructures Protection.

(a) SHORT TITLE—This section may be cited as the 'Critical Infrastructures Protection Act of 2001'.

(b) FINDINGS—Congress makes the following findings:

(1) The information revolution has transformed the conduct of business and the operations of government as well as the infrastructure relied upon for the defense and national security of the United States.

(2) Private business, government, and the national security apparatus increasingly depend on an interdependent network of critical physical and information infrastructures, including telecommunications, energy, financial services, water, and transportation sectors.

(3) A continuous national effort is required to ensure the reliable provision of cyber and physical infrastructure services critical to maintaining the national defense, continuity of government, economic prosperity, and quality of life in the United States.

(4) This national effort requires extensive modeling and analytic capabilities for purposes of evaluating appropriate mechanisms to ensure the stability of these complex and interdependent systems, and to underpin policy recommendations, so as to achieve the continuous viability and adequate protection of the critical infrastructure of the Nation.

(c) POLICY OF THE UNITED STATES—It is the policy of the United States—

(1) that any physical or virtual disruption of the operation of the critical infrastructures of the United States be rare, brief, geographically limited in effect, manageable, and minimally detrimental to the economy, human and government services, and national security of the United States;

(2) that actions necessary to achieve the policy stated in paragraph (1) be carried out in a public-private partnership involving corporate and non-governmental organizations; and

(3) to have in place a comprehensive and effective program to ensure the continuity of essential Federal Government functions under all circumstances.

(d) ESTABLISHMENT OF NATIONAL COMPETENCE FOR CRITICAL INFRASTRUCTURE PROTECTION-

(1) SUPPORT OF CRITICAL INFRASTRUCTURE PROTECTION AND CONTINUITY BY NATIONAL INFRASTRUCTURE SIMULATION AND ANALYSIS CENTER—There shall be established the National Infrastructure Simulation and Analysis Center (NISAC) to serve as a source of national competence to address critical infrastructure protection and continuity through support for activities related to counterterrorism, threat assessment, and risk mitigation.

(2) PARTICULAR SUPPORT—The support provided under paragraph (1) shall include the following:

(A) Modeling, simulation, and analysis of the systems comprising critical infrastructures, including cyber infrastructure, telecommunications infrastructure, and physical infrastructure, in order to enhance understanding of the large-scale complexity of such systems and to facilitate modification of such systems to mitigate the threats to such systems and to critical infrastructures generally.

(B) Acquisition from State and local governments and the private sector of data necessary to create and maintain models of such systems and of critical infrastructures generally.

(C) Utilization of modeling, simulation, and analysis under subparagraph (A) to provide education and training to policymakers on matters relating to—

(i) the analysis conducted under that subparagraph;

(ii) the implications of unintended or unintentional disturbances to critical infrastructures; and

(iii) responses to incidents or crises involving critical infrastructures, including the continuity of government and private sector activities through and after such incidents or crises.

(D) Utilization of modeling, simulation, and analysis under subparagraph (A) to provide recommendations to policymakers, and to departments and agencies of the Federal Government and private sector persons and entities upon request, regarding means of enhancing the stability of, and preserving, critical infrastructures.

(3) RECIPIENT OF CERTAIN SUPPORT—Modeling, simulation, and analysis provided under this subsection shall be provided, in particular, to relevant Federal, State, and local entities responsible for critical infrastructure protection and policy.

(e) CRITICAL INFRASTRUCTURE DEFINED—In this section, the term 'critical infrastructure' means systems and assets, whether physical or virtual, so vital to the United States that the incapacity or destruction of such systems and assets would have a debilitating impact on security, national economic security, national public health or safety, or any combination of those matters.

(f) AUTHORIZATION OF APPROPRIATIONS—There is hereby authorized for the Department of Defense for fiscal year 2002, $20,000,000 for the Defense Threat Reduction Agency for activities of the National Infrastructure Simulation and Analysis Center under this section in that fiscal year.

Speaker of the House of Representatives.

Vice President of the United States and

President of the Senate.

END